The Philokalia

VOLUME II

THE PHILOKALIA

THE COMPLETE TEXT
compiled by
ST NIKODIMOS OF THE HOLY MOUNTAIN
and
ST MAKARIOS OF CORINTH

translated from the Greek
and edited by
G. E. H. PALMER
PHILIP SHERRARD
KALLISTOS WARE

with the assistance of
THE HOLY TRANSFIGURATION MONASTERY
(BROOKLINE)
CONSTANTINE CAVARNOS
BASIL OSBORNE
NORMAN RUSSELL

VOLUME II

faber and faber
LONDON·BOSTON

First published in the UK in 1981
by Faber and Faber Limited

First paperback edition published in the USA in 1986
by Faber and Faber, Inc.
50 Cross Street
Winchester, MA 01890

© *The Eling Trust 1981*

Library of Congress Cataloging in Publication Data

The Philokalia.

☐Translation of: Philokalia.
☐Includes bibliographical references and indexes.
☐1. Spiritual life—Orthodox Eastern authors.
2. Asceticism—Early works to 1800. I. Nikodemos, ho
Hagioreites, 1749-1809. II. Makarios, Saint, Metropoli-
tan of Corinth, 1731-1805. III. Palmer, G.E.H.
(Gerald Eustace Howell), 1904-1984. IV. Sherrard,
Philip. V. Ware, Kallistos, 1934-
BX382.P413 1979 248.4'819 82-202671
ISBN 0-571-12548-4

CONTENTS

INTRODUCTORY NOTE

As in the first volume, we have rewritten the notes which St Nikodimos placed before each text or series of texts by a single author.

We are likewise responsible for the footnotes unless otherwise indicated.

The Glossary in this volume is largely a reproduction of that in volume i. Apart from minor alterations, there are changes in the sections on Age, Appetitive Aspect of the Soul, and Thought.

We would like, once again, to thank Mrs Ian Busby for her invaluable work.

Finally, the Eling Trust and the Editorial Committee would like to express their gratitude to the Leverhulme Trust Fund for a research award made to Dr Sherrard in support of his work on this translation.

G. E. H. Palmer
Philip Sherrard
Archimandrite Kallistos Ware

NOTE ON BIBLICAL QUOTATIONS
AND REFERENCES

All Biblical passages have been translated directly from the Greek as given in the original *Philokalia*. This means that quotations from the Old Testament are normally based on the Greek Septuagint text. Where this differs significantly from the Hebrew, we have indicated the fact by adding the Roman numeral LXX after the reference.

Even though we follow the Septuagint text, in giving references we use the numbering and titles of the Hebrew, as reproduced in the Authorized Version (King James Bible), since this is more widely familiar in the Western world. In particular the following differences between the Hebrew and the Septuagint should be noted:

NUMBERING OF PSALMS

Hebrew (*Authorized Version*)	Greek (*Septuagint*)
1–8	1–8
9 and 10	9
11–113	Subtract one from the number of each Psalm in the Hebrew
114 and 115	113
116: 1–9	114
116: 10–16	115
117–146	Subtract one from the number of each Psalm in the Hebrew
147: 1–11	146
147: 12–20	147
148–150	148–150

TITLES OF BOOKS

Hebrew (*Authorized Version*)	Greek (*Septuagint*)
1 Samuel	1 Kingdoms
2 Samuel	2 Kingdoms
1 Kings	3 Kingdoms
2 Kings	4 Kingdoms

Where authors in the *Philokalia* merely refer to a passage or paraphrase it, but do not quote it exactly, 'cf.' is added before the reference.

ST THEODOROS
THE GREAT ASCETIC

Introductory Note

The two works that follow, *A Century of Spiritual Texts* and *Theo-retikon*,[1] are ascribed in the Greek *Philokalia* to St Theodoros the Great Ascetic, a monk of the monastery of St Sabas near Jerusalem, who subsequently became bishop of Edessa in Syria (commemorated in the church calendar on 19 July). Historically he remains a shadowy figure, since his *Life*, written by Basil of Emesa, is often untrustworthy. Whereas St Nikodimos dates him to the seventh century, probably he should be placed two centuries later.

The *Century* may be the work of St Theodoros, but the *Theoretikon* almost certainly is not. Largely a free paraphrase of Evagrios, the *Century* is not earlier than the seventh century, since it draws on St Maximos the Confessor's teaching concerning self-love, and not later than the beginning of the eleventh century, since it is found in a manuscript of 1023; a ninth-century date is therefore possible. The *Theoretikon*, a valuable summary of the spiritual life, is hard to fix chronologically, but it is undoubtedly much later than the *Century*. Its style and outlook suggest perhaps a fourteenth-century date, but it may even be as recent as the seventeenth century, which would make it one of the latest texts in the *Philokalia*. It is apparently incomplete, lacking both opening and conclusion.

[1] See J. Gouillard, 'Supercheries et méprises littéraires. L'oeuvre de saint Théodore d'Edesse', *Revue des études byzantines* v (1947), pp. 137–57.

A Century of Spiritual Texts

1. Since by God's grace we have renounced Satan and his works and have sworn allegiance to Christ, both at our baptism and now again through our profession as monks, let us keep His commandments. Not only does our double profession demand this of us, but it is also our natural duty, for since we were originally created by God as 'very good' (Gen. 1 : 31), we owe it to God to be such. Although sin entered us through our negligence and introduced into us what is contrary to nature, we have been reclaimed through God's great mercy, and renewed by the passion of Him who is dispassionate. We have been 'bought with a price' (1 Cor. 6 : 20), namely by the blood of Christ, and liberated from the ancient ancestral sin. If, then, we become righteous, this is nothing great; but to fall from righteousness is pitiable and deserves condemnation.

2. Just as a good act performed without genuine faith is quite dead and ineffective, so too faith alone without works of righteousness does not save us from eternal fire; for 'he who loves Me', says the Lord, 'will keep My commandments' (cf. John 14 : 15, 23). If, then, we love the Lord and believe in Him, we shall exert ourselves to fulfil His commandments, so as to be granted eternal life. But how can we call ourselves faithful if we neglect to keep His ordinances, which all creation obeys, and if, although we have been honoured above all creation, we are the only creatures who disobey the Creator and show ourselves ungrateful to our Benefactor?

3. When we keep Christ's commandments we do not benefit Him in any way, since He is in need of nothing and is the bestower of every blessing. It is ourselves that we benefit, since we win for ourselves eternal life and the enjoyment of ineffable blessings.

4. If anyone whatsoever opposes us in the fulfilment of God's commandments, even if it is our father or mother, we ought to re-

gard him with hatred and loathing, lest we be told: 'He who loves father or mother or anyone else whatsoever more than Me is not worthy of Me' (cf. Matt. 10 : 37).

5. Let us bind ourselves with all our strength to fulfil the Lord's commandments, lest we ourselves should be held by the unbreak-able cords of our evil desires and soul-corrupting pleasures (cf. Prov. 5 : 22), and lest the sentence passed on the barren fig tree should be passed on us as well: 'Cut it down, so that it does not clutter up the ground' (Luke 13 : 7). For, as Christ says, whatever 'does not produce good fruit is hewn down, and cast into the fire' (Matt. 3 : 10).

6. He who gives himself to desires and sensual pleasures and lives according to the world's way will quickly be caught in the nets of sin. And sin, when once committed, is like fire put to straw, a stone rolling downhill or a torrent eating away its banks. Such pleasures, then, bring complete perdition on him who embraces them.

7. So long as the soul is in a state contrary to nature, running wild with the weeds and thorns of sensual pleasures, it is a dwelling-place of grotesque beasts. Isaiah's words apply to it: ass-centaurs shall rest there, and hedgehogs make their lair in it, and there demons will consort with ass-centaurs (cf. Isa. 34 : 11, 14. LXX) – for all these animals signify the various shameful passions. But the soul, so long as it is joined to the flesh, can recall itself to its natural state at any time it wishes; and whenever it does so and disciplines itself with diligent effort, living in accordance with God's law, the wild beasts that were lurking inside it will take to flight, while the angels who guard our life will come to its aid, making the soul's return a day of rejoicing (cf. Luke 15 : 7). And the grace of the Holy Spirit will be present in it, teaching it spiritual knowledge, so that it may be strengthened in what is good and rise to higher levels.

8. The Fathers define prayer as a spiritual weapon. Unless we are armed with it we cannot engage in warfare, but are carried off as prisoners to the enemy's country. Nor can we acquire pure prayer unless we cleave to God with an upright heart. For it is God who gives prayer to him who prays and who teaches man spiritual knowledge.

9. It does not lie within our power to decide whether or not the passions are going to harass and attack the soul. But it does lie within

our power to prevent impassioned thoughts from lingering within us and arousing the passions to action. The first of these conditions is not sinful, inasmuch as it is outside our control; where the second is concerned, if we fight against the passions and overcome them we are rewarded, but we shall be punished if because of laziness and cowardice we let them overcome us.

10. There are three principal passions, through which all the rest arise: love of sensual pleasure, love of riches, and love of praise. Close in their wake follow five other evil spirits, and from these five arise a great swarm of passions and all manner of evil. Thus he who defeats the three leaders and rulers simultaneously overcomes the other five and so subdues all the passions.

11. Memories of all the impassioned actions we have performed exert an impassioned tyranny over the soul. But when impassioned thoughts have been completely erased from our heart, so that they no longer affect it even as provocations, this is a sign that our former sinful acts have been forgiven. For so long as the heart is stimulated by passion, sin clearly reigns there.

12. Bodily passions or passions concerned with material things are reduced and withered through bodily hardship, while the unseen passions of the soul are destroyed through humility, gentleness and love.

13. Self-control together with humility withers passionate desire, love calms inflamed anger, and intense prayer together with mindfulness of God concentrates distracted thoughts. Thus the tripartite soul is purified. It was to this end that the apostle said: 'Pursue peace with all men and the holiness without which no one will see the Lord' (Heb. 12 : 14).

14. Many people wonder whether thought stimulates the passions or the passions stimulate thought. Some say the first and some the second. My own view is that thoughts are stimulated by the passions. For unless passions were in the soul, thoughts about them would not disturb it.

15. The demons, who are always waging war against us, try to prevent us from performing actions that are within our power and that would help us to acquire the virtues, while at the same time they suggest ways of accomplishing things that in fact are impossible or else out of place. They compel those progressing in obedience to follow the hesychasts' way of life; and they implant in hesychasts

and hermits a desire for the coenobitic rule. They use a similar
method with respect to every virtue. So let us be mindful of their
designs, knowing that all things are good in their proper time and
measure, while things lacking measure and out of place are noxious.

16. With those who live in the world and are associated with the
material things that feed the passions, the demons wage war
through practical activities; while with those who dwell in the
wilderness, where material things are rare, they fight by troubling
them with evil thoughts. This second mode of warfare is far more
difficult to cope with; for warfare through things requires a specific
time and place, and a fit occasion, whereas warfare of the intellect
is mercurial and hard to control. But as our trusty weapon in this
incorporeal fight we have been given pure prayer: that is why we are
told to pray without ceasing (cf. 1 Thess. 5 : 17). Prayer strengthens the intellect in the struggle, since it can be practised even without the body taking part.

17. With reference to the perfect mortification of the passions
St Paul says: 'They that are Christ's have crucified the flesh together
with the passions and desires' (Gal. 5 : 24). For when we mortify
the passions, utterly destroy desires, and subjugate the will of the
flesh to the Spirit, we take up the cross and follow Christ (cf. Matt.
16 : 24). For withdrawal from the world is nothing else but the
mortification of the passions and the manifestation of the life that is
hidden in Christ (cf. Col. 3 : 3–4).

18. Those who have given up their hour-by-hour warfare, because of their distress at the rebelliousness of 'the body of this death'
(Rom. 7 : 24), should blame not the flesh, but themselves. For if
they had not given it the strength, providing for it so it could gratify
its desires (cf. Rom. 13 : 14), they would not have been so greatly
distressed by it. Do they not see how those who have crucified themselves together with their passions and desires, and who proclaim
the death of Jesus in their mortal flesh (cf. 2 Cor. 4 : 10), have
made the flesh tractable and obedient to the law of God, so that it
proves an ally rather than an adversary in their aspirations towards
the divine? Let them do likewise and they will enjoy the same peace.

19. Every assent in thought to some forbidden desire, that is,
every submission to self-indulgence, is a sin for a monk. For first
the thought begins to darken the intellect through the passible
aspect of the soul, and then the soul submits to the pleasure, not

holding out in the fight. This is what is called assent, which – as has
been said – is a sin. When assent persists it stimulates the passion in
question. Then little by little it leads to the actual committing of the
sin. This is why the prophet calls blessed those who dash the children of Babylon against the stones (cf. Ps. 137 : 9). People with
understanding and discretion will know what is meant.

20. Being servants of love and peace, the angels rejoice over our
repentance (cf. Luke 15 : 7) and our progress in holiness. Hence
they try to develop spiritual contemplation within us and they co-
operate with us in the achieving of every form of blessing. The
demons, on the contrary, being producers of anger and of evil, rejoice when holiness diminishes in us, and they attempt to seduce our
souls with shameful fantasies.

21. Faith is a quality inherent in our nature. It begets in us the
fear of God; and fear of God instils that keeping of the commandments which constitutes the practice of the virtues. From such
practice grows the precious flower of dispassion. The offspring of
dispassion is love, which is the fulfilment of all the commandments
(cf. Rom. 13 : 10), binding and holding them in unity.

22. When the body's perception is sound one is aware of what
sickness afflicts it, while if one is not aware one is a victim of obtuse-
ness. Similarly, the intellect, as long as it preserves its own proper
energy, is conscious of its powers and knows from where the tyran-
nizing passions enter it; and it makes a determined stand against
them. But it is terrible to pass one's days in a state of oblivion, like
one who fights by night, not being able to see the evil thoughts
against which one is battling.

23. When our intelligence unyieldingly devotes itself to the contemplation of the virtues, and our desire is focused solely on this
and on Christ who bestows it, while our soul's incensive power
arms itself against the demons, then our faculties are acting according to nature.

24. Every deiform soul is tripartite, according to Gregory the
Theologian.[1] Virtue, when established in the intelligence, he calls
discretion, understanding and wisdom; when in the incensive
power, he calls it courage and patience; and when in the faculty of
desire, he calls it love, self-restraint and self-control. Justice or

[1] See St Gregory of Nazianzos, Poems II, i, 47 (P.G. xxxvii, 1381A–1384A).

right judgment penetrates all three aspects of the soul, enabling them to function in harmony. Through discretion the soul fights against the hostile powers and defends the virtues. Through self-restraint it views things dispassionately. Through love it urges a man to love all men as himself. Through self-control it eliminates every sensual pleasure. Finally, through courage and patience it arms itself against its invisible enemies. This is the harmony of the melodious organ of the soul.

25. Let him who cultivates self-restraint and longs for blessed purity – which could rightly be called dispassion – discipline the flesh and bring it into subjection, with humble thoughts invoking divine grace, and he will achieve the aim he desires. But he who feeds the body intemperately will be tormented by the demon of unchastity. Just as much water puts out a flame, so hunger or self-control combined with humility of soul extinguishes the fever of the flesh and of shameful fantasies.

26. If you love Christ you must keep the passion of rancour far from your soul. You should on no account yield to feelings of hostility: rancour lurking in the heart is like fire hidden in stalks of dry flax. Rather you should pray fervently for anyone who has grieved you, and you should help him, if you have the means. By this action your soul will be delivered from death (cf. Tobit 4 : 10) and nothing will hinder your communion with God when you pray.

27. The Lord dwells in the souls of the humble; but shameful passions fill the hearts of the proud. Nothing so strengthens these passions against us as arrogant thoughts, and nothing uproots the evil herbs of the soul so effectively as blessed humility. Hence humility is rightly called the executioner of passions.

28. Let your soul be free of evil fantasies and illumined with thoughts of what is truly noble. Constantly remember the saying, 'A self-indulgent heart becomes a prison and a chain for the soul when it leaves this life; whereas an assiduous heart is an open door.'[1] Truly, when pure souls leave the body they are guided by angels who lead them to the life of blessedness. But unclean and unrepentant souls will be taken in charge by the demons.

29. Beautiful is a head adorned with a precious diadem, set with Indian stones and lustrous pearls. But incomparably more beautiful

---

[1] St Mark the Ascetic, *On the Spiritual Law*, §20 (*The Philokalia*, vol. i, p. 111).

is a soul rich in the knowledge of God, illumined by the most lucid contemplation and having the Holy Spirit dwelling within it. Who can adequately describe the beauty of that blessed soul?

30. Do not let anger and wrath make their home in you; for 'an angry man is not dignified' (Prov. 11 : 25. LXX), whereas wisdom dwells in the hearts of the gentle. If the passion of anger dominates your soul, those who live in the world will prove to be better than you, and you will be put to shame as unworthy of monastic solitude.

31. In every trial and in all warfare use prayer as your invincible weapon, and by the grace of Christ you will be victorious. Let your prayer be pure, as our wise teacher counsels. For he says: 'I would have men pray everywhere, lifting up holy hands, without anger and without quarrelling' (1 Tim. 2 : 8). But the person who neglects such prayer will be delivered over to trials and passions.

32. 'Wine makes glad the heart of man' (Ps. 104 : 15). But you who have professed sorrow and grief should turn away from such gladness and rejoice in spiritual gifts. If you rejoice in wine, you will live with shameful thoughts and distress will overwhelm you.

33. Do not plan to spend feast-days in drinking wine, but in regenerating your intellect and purifying your soul. If you eat gluttonously and drink wine you will provoke anger in the person whom the feast is honouring.

34. We have been instructed to keep vigil – with prayers, readings, and the recitation of the Psalter – at all times, and especially at feasts. A monk who keeps vigil refines his mind for contemplation, whereas much sleep coarsens the intellect. But take care that during vigils you do not pass the time in empty gossip or evil thoughts. It is better to be asleep than to keep vigil with vain words and thoughts.

35. He who keeps a serpent in his breast and he who keeps an evil thought in his heart will both be killed, the one by being bitten in the body by venomous fangs and the other by injecting a lethal poison into his soul. Let us, then, speedily slay the 'offspring of vipers' (Matt. 3 : 7), and let us not bring forth evil thoughts from our heart, lest we suffer bitter pangs.

36. A pure soul can truly be called a 'chosen vessel' (Acts 9 : 15), 'an enclosed garden', 'a sealed fountain' (Song of Solomon 4 : 12), and 'a throne of perceptiveness' (Prov. 12 : 23. LXX). But a soul polluted with filthy impurities stinks like a sewer.

37. I have heard from elders experienced in the practice of the virtues that evil thoughts are engendered in the soul by showy clothes, the belly's repletion and bad company.

38. Desire for material wealth must not lodge in the souls of those pursuing the spiritual way. For a monk with many possessions is an over-laden ship, driven by the storm of cares and sinking in the deep waters of distress. Love of riches begets many passions, and has aptly been called 'the root of all evil' (1 Tim. 6 : 10).

39. A condition of total poverty, combined with silence, is a treasure hidden in the field of the monastic life (cf. Matt. 13 : 44). So 'go and sell all you have and give to the poor' (Matt. 19 : 21), and acquire this field. And when you have dug up the treasure, keep it inviolate, so that you may become rich with a wealth that is inexhaustible.

40. When you have taken up your dwelling with a spiritual father and find that he helps you, let no one separate you from his love and from living with him. Do not judge him in any respect, do not revile him even though he censures or strikes you, do not listen to someone who slanders him to you, do not side with anyone who criticizes him, lest the Lord should be angered with you and blot you out of the book of the living (cf. Exod. 32 : 33).

41. The struggle to achieve obedience is won by means of renunciation, as we have learned. He who seeks to be obedient must arm himself with three weapons: faith, hope, and divine and holy love (cf. 1 Cor. 13 : 13). Thus defended, he will 'fight the good fight' and receive 'a crown of righteousness' (2 Tim. 4 : 7–8).

42. Do not judge the actions of your spiritual father, but obey his commands. For the demons are in the habit of showing you his defects, so that your ears may be deaf to what he tells you. They aim either to drive you from the arena as a feeble and cowardly fighter, or simply to terrify you with thoughts that undermine your faith, and so to make you sluggish about every form of virtue.

43. A monk who disobeys the commands of his spiritual father transgresses the special vows of his profession. But he who has embraced obedience and slain his own will with the sword of humility has indeed fulfilled the promise that he made to Christ in the presence of many witnesses.

44. From our own observations we have clearly perceived that the enemies of our life, the demons, are exceedingly jealous of those

pursuing the ascetic way under obedience to a spiritual father. Gnashing their teeth at them and devising all sorts of schemes, they do and suggest everything possible so as to separate a monk from his spiritual father's care. They propose plausible excuses, they contrive irritations, they arouse hatred against the father, they represent his admonitions as rebukes, they make his words of correction seem like sharpened arrows. Why, they ask, since you are free, have you become a slave – a slave to a merciless master? How long will you wear yourself out under the yoke of servitude and not see the light of freedom? Then they make suggestions about giving hospitality, visiting the sick and caring for the poor. Next they extol above measure the rewards of extreme stillness and solitude, and sow all sorts of evil weeds in the heart of the devout warrior, simply to cast him out of the fold of his spiritual father; and having unmoored him from that untroubled haven they drive him out to sea, into the fierce and soul-destroying tempest. Finally, when they have enslaved him to their own authority, they use him according to their own evil desires.

45. You who are under obedience to a spiritual father must be alert to the cunning of your enemies and adversaries. Do not forget your profession and promise to God; do not be defeated by insults; do not be afraid of reproof, mockery or sneering; do not give way to the proliferation of evil thoughts; do not evade your father's strictures; do not dishonour the blessed yoke of humility by daring to be self-satisfied and presumptuous. Instead, rooting in your heart the Lord's words, 'He who endures to the end will be saved' (Matt. 10 : 22), patiently run the race that is set before you, 'looking to Jesus, the author and perfecter of our faith' (Heb. 12 : 1–2).

46. The goldsmith purifies gold by smelting it in a furnace. And a novice must surrender himself to the struggle for obedience and to the fiery ordeals of a holy life, learning with toil and much patience the practice of obedience. And once his old manners and habits have been melted down and he learns true humility, he becomes radiant, fit for heavenly treasures, for a life of immortality and a blessed repose whence 'pain and sorrow have fled away' (Isa. 35 : 10. LXX), and where gladness and continual joy flourish.

47. True inward faith begets fear of God. Fear of God teaches us to keep the commandments. For where there is fear, it is said, there the commandments are kept. The keeping of the commandments

establishes practical virtue, the precursor of contemplative virtue. Of these the fruit is dispassion. Through dispassion, love is born in us. Concerning love the beloved disciple said, 'God is love, and he who dwells in love dwells in God, and God in him' (1 John 4 : 16).

48. The monk's way of life is truly full of beauty and excellence, provided it accords with the rules and laws laid down by its founders and directors, taught as they were by the Holy Spirit. The warrior of Christ must be above material things and detached from all worldly thoughts and deeds; for, as St Paul says: 'In order to please the leader who has chosen him, the soldier going to war does not entangle himself in the affairs of this life' (2 Tim. 2 : 4).

49. The monk, therefore, must be detached from material things, must be dispassionate, free from all evil desires, not given to soft living, not a tippler, not slothful, not indolent, not a lover of wealth, pleasure or praise. Unless he raises himself above all these things, he will fail to achieve the angelic way of life. For those who do achieve it, the yoke is easy and the burden is light (cf. Matt. 11 : 30), divine hope sustaining them in all things. This life and its activities are full of delight, and the lot of the soul that has attained it is blessed and 'cannot be taken away' (Luke 10 : 42).

50. If you have renounced worldly cares and undertaken the ascetic struggle you should not desire to have wealth for distribution to the poor. For this is another trick of the devil who arouses self-esteem in you so as to fill your intellect with worry and restlessness. Even if you have only bread or water, with these you can still meet the dues of hospitality. Even if you do not have these, but simply make the stranger welcome and offer him a word of encouragement, you will not be failing in hospitality. Think of the widow mentioned in the Gospel by our Lord: with two mites she surpassed the generous gifts of the wealthy (cf. Mark 12 : 42–44).

51. These things apply to monks pursuing the life of stillness. But those under obedience to a spiritual father should have only one thought in mind – to depart in nothing from his commands. For if they achieve this, they achieve everything. But if they depart from such strict obedience they will fail completely in the spiritual life and in every form of virtue.

52. Since you are a friend of Christ, let me give you this further piece of advice. You must aspire to live in exile, free from the conditions and ways of your own country. Do not be caught up by

anxiety for your parents or by ties of affection to your relatives. Do not stay in a town but persevere in the wilderness, saying like the prophet: 'Lo, then would I wander far off, and remain in the wilderness' (Ps. 55 : 7. LXX).

53. Seek out places which are secluded and far from the world. And even if there is a scarcity of essentials in the place you choose, do not be afraid. If your enemies should encircle you like bees (cf. Ps. 118 : 12) or pernicious drones, assaulting you and disturbing you with all kinds of thoughts, do not be scared, do not listen to them, do not withdraw from the struggle. Rather, endure patiently, always saying to yourself: 'I waited patiently for the Lord; and He heard me, and listened to my supplication' (Ps. 40 : 1. LXX). And then you will see the great things God does, His help, His care and all His forethought for your salvation.

54. If you are a friend of Christ you should have as friends persons who are of benefit to you and contribute to your way of life. Let your friends be men of peace, spiritual brethren, holy fathers. It is of such that our Lord was speaking when He said: 'My mother and brethren are those who do the will of My Father who is in heaven' (cf. Matt. 12 : 49–50).

55. Do not hanker after varied and costly foods or lethal pleasures. For 'she that indulges in pleasure', it is said, 'is dead while still alive' (1 Tim. 5 : 6). Even with ordinary foods, avoid satiety as far as possible. For it is written: 'Do not be deceived by the filling of the belly' (Prov. 24 : 15. LXX).

56. You must avoid continually wasting time outside your cell, if you have indeed chosen to practise stillness. For it is most harmful, depriving you of grace, darkening your mind and sapping your aspiration. This is why it is said: 'Restlessness of desire perverts the guileless intellect' (Wisd. 4 : 12). So restrict your relationships with other people, lest your intellect should become distracted and your life of stillness disrupted.

57. When sitting in your cell, do not act in a mindless and lazy manner. 'To journey without direction', it is said, 'is wasted effort.'[1] Instead, work purposefully, concentrate your intellect and always keep before your eyes the last hour before your death. Recall the vanity of the world, how deceptive it is, how sickly and worth-

---

[1] St Mark the Ascetic, *On the Spiritual Law*, §54 (*The Philokalia*, vol. i, p. 114).

less; reflect on the dreadful reckoning that is to come, how the harsh keepers of the toll houses will bring before us one by one the actions, words and thoughts which they suggested but which we accepted and made our own. Recall the chastisements in hell, and the state of the souls imprisoned there. Recall, too, that great and fearful day, the day of the general resurrection, when we are brought before God, and the final sentence of the infallible Judge. Bring to mind the punishment that befalls sinners, the reproach, the reprobation of the conscience, how they will be rejected by God and cast into the age-long fire, to the worm that does not die, to the impenetrable darkness where there is weeping and gnashing of teeth (cf. Mark 9 : 44, Matt. 8 : 12). Meditate on all the other chastisements, and let your tears continually drench your cheeks, your clothes, the place where you are sitting. I have known many men in whom such thoughts have produced an abundance of tears, and who in this way have wonderfully cleansed all the powers of their soul.

58. But think also of the blessings which await the righteous: how they will stand at Christ's right hand, the gracious voice of the Master, the inheritance of the heavenly kingdom, the gift which is beyond the intellect's grasp, that sweet light, the endless joy, never interrupted by grief, those heavenly mansions, life with the angels, and all the other promises made to those who fear the Lord.

59. Let these thoughts dwell with you, sleep with you, arise with you. See that you never forget them but, wherever you are, keep them in mind, so that evil thoughts may depart and you may be filled with divine solace. Unless a soul is strengthened with these thoughts it cannot achieve stillness. For a spring which has no water does not deserve its name.

60. This is the way of life ordained for those who live in stillness: fasting to the limit of one's strength, vigils, sleeping on the ground, and every other form of hardship for the sake of future repose. For, says St Paul, 'the sufferings of this present time are not worthy to be compared with the glory which shall be revealed in us' (Rom. 8 : 18). Especially important is pure prayer – prayer which is unceasing and uninterrupted. Such prayer is a safe fortress, a sheltered harbour, a protector of virtues, a destroyer of passions. It brings vigour to the soul, purifies the intellect, gives rest to those who suffer, consoles those who mourn. Prayer is converse with God, contemplation of the invisible, the angelic mode of life, a stimulus

towards the divine, the assurance of things longed for, 'making real
th : things for which we hope' (Heb. 11 : 1). As an ascetic you must
en brace this queen of the virtues with all your strength. Pray day
and night. Pray at times of dejection and at times of exhilaration.
Pray with fear and trembling, with a watchful and vigilant mind, so
that your prayer may be accepted by the Lord. For, as the psalmist
says: 'The eyes of the Lord are on the righteous, and His ears are
open to their prayer' (Ps. 34 : 15).

61. It has been said aptly and appositely by one of the ancients[1]
that, among the demons opposing us, there are three groups that
fight in the front line: those entrusted with the appetites of gluttony, those that suggest avaricious thoughts, and those that incite us
to self-esteem. All the other demons follow behind and in their turn
attack those already wounded by the first three groups.

62. Indeed, we have come to know from our own observations
that it is not possible for a man to fall into sin or be subject to a particular passion unless he has previously been wounded by one of
these three. That is why the devil attacked our Saviour with these
three thoughts (cf. Matt. 4 : 1–10). But our Lord, having shown
Himself superior to them, commanded the devil to depart, in His
goodness and compassion bequeathing to us the victory He had
achieved. He assumed a body in all respects like ours, but without
sin (cf. Heb. 4 : 15), and showed us the unerring path of sinless-
ness, by following which we form in ourselves the new man, who is
'formed again . . . according to the image of his Creator' (Col.
3 : 10).

63. David teaches us to hate the demons 'with perfect hatred'
(Ps. 139 : 22), inasmuch as they are the enemies of our salvation.
This hatred is most necessary for the task of acquiring holiness. But
who is the man who hates his enemies with perfect hatred? He who
no longer sins either in act or in thought. Yet so long as the instruments of our friendship with them – that is to say, the things that
provoke the passions – are still present in us, how shall we achieve
such hatred against them? For a self-indulgent heart cannot nurture
this hatred within itself.

64. Dispassion is the wedding garment of the deiform soul that is
separated from worldly pleasures, has renounced misdirected de-

---

[1] cf. Evagrios, *Texts on Discrimination*, §1 (*The Philokalia*. vol. i, p. 38).

sires, and is occupied with devout thoughts and the practice of contemplation in its purest form. But through intercourse with shameful passions the soul discards its robe of self-restraint and debases itself by wearing filthy rags and tatters. The man in the Gospels who was bound hand and foot and cast into outer darkness was clothed in a garment woven out of such thoughts and acts; and so the Logos declared him to be unworthy of the divine and immortal wedding-feast (cf. Matt. 22 : 11-13).

65. From self-love, which causes hatred for all men, everything evil in men is derived, as a wise man has told us.[1] For this terrible enemy, self-love, is the foremost of all evil dispositions, and is like some tyrant with the help of which the three principal passions and the five that come in their wake overwhelm the intellect.[2]

66. I wonder if a man who sates himself with food is able to acquire dispassion. By dispassion I do not mean abstinence from actual sin – for this is called self-control. I mean the abstinence that uproots passionate thoughts from the mind and is also called purity of heart.

67. It is less difficult to cleanse an impure soul than to restore to health a soul which was once cleansed but has been wounded anew. For it is less difficult for those who have recently renounced the confusion of the world to attain dispassion, whatever faults they may previously have committed, than it is for those who have tasted the blessed words of God and walked in the path of salvation and then gone back to sin. This is due partly to the influence of bad habit and partly to the fact that the demon of dejection is always dangling the image of sin before them. But, with the co-operation of divine grace, a diligent and assiduous soul may readily achieve even this difficult feat of regaining its dispassion; for, long-suffering and compassionate, grace invites us to repentance, and with inexpressible mercy accepts those who return, as we have been taught in the Gospels through the parable of the prodigal son (cf. Luke 15 : 11-32).

68. No one among us can prevail by his own unaided strength

---

[1] Probably once more a reference to Evagrios: see J. Muyldermans, in *Muséon* xliv (1931), p. 55, §41. But the reference may also be to St Maximos: cf., for example, *Various Texts* i,31-33 (see below, pp. 171-2); or to St Thalassios, *On Love* iii, 86-90 (see below, p. 324).

[2] On 'the three' and 'the five', see above, §10.

over the devices and wiles of the evil one; he can prevail only through the invincible power of Christ. Vainly, therefore, do conceited people wander about claiming that they have abolished sin through their ascetic accomplishments and their free will. Sin is abolished only through the grace of God, for it was made dead through the mystery of the Cross. This is why that luminary of the Church, St John Chrysostom, says: 'A man's readiness and commitment are not enough if he does not enjoy help from above as well; equally help from above is no benefit to us unless there is also commitment and readiness on our part. These two facts are proved by Judas and Peter. For although Judas enjoyed much help, it was of no benefit to him, since he had no desire for it and contributed nothing from himself. But Peter, although willing and ready, fell because he enjoyed no help from above. So holiness is woven of these two strands. Thus I entreat you neither to entrust everything to God and then fall asleep, nor to think, when you are striving diligently, that you will achieve everything by your own efforts.

69. 'God does not want us to be lying idly on our backs; therefore He does not effect everything Himself. Nor does He want us to be boastful; therefore He did not give us everything. But having taken away from each of the two alternatives what is harmful, He has left us what is for our good.'[1] Truly does the psalmist say: 'Unless the Lord builds the house, they labour in vain that build it; unless the Lord guards the city, the watchman keeps awake in vain' (Ps. 127 : 1). For it is impossible to 'tread on the asp and basilisk and trample on the lion and dragon' (Ps. 91 : 13. LXX), unless you have first cleansed yourself as far as you can, and have been strengthened by Him who said to the apostles: 'See, I have given you authority to tread on serpents and scorpions, and on all the enemy's power' (Luke 10 : 19). It is on this account that we have been commanded to entreat the Master not to 'lead us into temptation, but to deliver us from the evil one' (Matt. 6 : 13). For if we are not delivered from 'the fiery arrows of the evil one' (Eph. 6 : 16) through the power and help of Christ, and found worthy of attaining dispassion, we are labouring in vain, thinking that through our own powers or efforts we shall accomplish something. Therefore, he who wishes 'to stand against the wiles of the devil' (Eph. 6 : 11) and render

---

[1] St John Chrysostom, *Homily 82 on Matthew*, §4 (*P.G.* lviii, 742–3).

them ineffectual, and to share in the divine glory, ought day and night to seek God's help and divine succour with tears and sighs, with insatiable longing and fire in his soul. He who wishes to share in this glory purges his soul of all worldly pleasures and of hostile passions and desires. It is of such souls that God speaks when He says: 'I will dwell in them and walk in them' (2 Cor. 6 : 16). And the Lord said to His disciples: 'If a man loves Me, he will keep My commandments; and My Father will love him, and We will come to him, and take up Our abode with him' (John 14 : 23).

70. One of the ancients spoke wisely and simply about thoughts.[1] Judge thoughts, he said, before the judgment seat of the heart, to discern whether they are ours or those of our enemy. Place those which are good and properly our own in the inmost shrine of the soul, keeping them in this inviolable treasury. But chastise hostile thoughts with the whip of the intelligence and banish them, giving them no place, no abode within the bounds of your soul. Or, to speak more fittingly, slay them completely with the sword of prayer and divine meditation, so that when the robbers have been destroyed, their chief may take fright. For, so he says, a man who examines his thoughts strictly is one who also truly loves the commandments.

71. He who is battling to repulse what harasses and wars against him must enlist the help of other allies – I mean humility of soul, bodily toil and every other kind of ascetic hardship, together with prayer that springs from an afflicted heart and is accompanied by many tears. He must be like David who says: 'Look on my humility and my toil, and forgive all my sins' (Ps. 25 : 18); 'Do not pass my tears over in silence' (Ps. 39 : 12); 'My tears have been my bread day and night' (Ps. 42 : 3); and 'I mingled my drink with weeping' (Ps. 102 : 9).

72. The adversary of our life, the devil, employs many devices to make our sins seem small to us. Often he cloaks them with forgetfulness, so that, after suffering a little on their account, we no longer trouble to lament over them. But, my brethren, let us not forget our offences, even if we wrongly think that they have been forgiven through repentance; let us always remember our sinful acts and never cease to mourn over them, so that we may acquire humility as

---

[1] cf. Neilos (? Evagrios), *To the Monk Evlogios*, §12 (*P.G.* lxxix, 1108D).

our constant companion, and thus escape the snares of self-esteem and pride.

73. Let no one think that he endures suffering and achieves holiness through his own powers. For God is the cause of all the good that comes to us, just as the demon that deceives our souls is the cause of all the evils. Therefore, give thanks to their Cause for whatever good acts you perform; and attribute to their instigator the evils that trouble you.

74. He who yokes the practice of the virtues to spiritual knowledge is a skilful farmer, watering the fields of his soul from two pure springs. For the spring of spiritual knowledge raises the immature soul to the contemplation of higher realities; while the spring of ascetic practice mortifies our earthly members: 'unchastity, uncleanness, passion, evil desire' (Col. 3 : 5). Once these are dead, the virtues come into flower and bear the fruits of the Spirit: 'love, joy, peace, long-suffering, kindness, goodness, faith, gentleness, self-control' (Gal. 5 : 22–23). And then this prudent farmer, having 'crucified the flesh together with the passions and desires' (Gal. 5 : 24), will say together with St Paul: 'I no longer live, but Christ lives in me; and the life I now live . . . I live through faith in the Son of God, who loved me and gave Himself for me' (Gal. 2 : 20).

75. Take note, too, you who are a good friend of Christ, that if one passion finds a place in you and takes root there, it will introduce other passions also into the same shrine. For even though the passions, as well as their instigators the demons, are opposed to each other, yet they are all at one in seeking our perdition.

76. A man who through ascetic effort withers the flower of the flesh, and cuts off all its desires, bears in his mortal flesh the marks of the Lord (cf. Gal. 6 : 17).

77. The hardships of the ascetic life end in the repose of dispassion, while soft ways of living breed shameful passions.

78. Do not place reliance on your many years of monastic life and do not fall victim to pride because of the harshness of your ascetic struggles and the way you have endured the wilderness; but keep in mind the saying of the Lord that you are a 'useless servant' (Luke 17 : 10) and have not yet fulfilled the commandment. Indeed, so long as we are in this life, we have not yet been recalled from exile, but are still sitting by the river of Babylon; we still slave at making bricks in Egypt, having not yet seen the promised land. Since we

have not yet 'put off . . . the old man, who is corrupt because of his deceitful desires' (Eph. 4 : 22), we have not yet put on 'the image of Him who is from heaven', for we still bear 'the image of him who is from earth' (1 Cor. 15 : 49). Accordingly, we have no cause to boast, but ought to weep, calling in prayer to Him who can save us from the burdensome slavery of the harshest of Pharaohs, and can deliver us from this terrible tyranny and bring us to the blessings of the promised land, there to find rest in the holy place of God and to be established at the right hand of the Most High. For these blessed realities, which are above thought, are not to be attained through our own works, however righteous we may think them, but depend on the immeasurable mercy of God. So let us not cease from weeping day and night, following the example of him who says: 'I make myself weary with my sighing; every night I bathe my bed with tears, I water my couch with them' (Ps. 6 : 6); for 'they that sow in tears shall reap in joy' (Ps. 126 : 5).

79. Expel from yourself the spirit of talkativeness. For in it lurk the most dreadful passions: lying, loose speech, absurd chatter, buffoonery, obscenity. To put the matter succinctly, 'through talkativeness you will not escape sin' (Prov. 10 : 19. LXX), whereas a silent man 'is a throne of perceptiveness' (Prov. 12 : 23. LXX). Moreover, the Lord has said that we shall have to give an account of every idle word (cf. Matt. 12 : 36). Thus silence is most necessary and profitable.

80. We have been commanded not to revile or abuse in return those who revile and insult us, but rather to speak well of them and to bless them (cf. Matt. 5 : 44). For in so far as we are at peace with men we fight against the demons; but when we feel rancour towards our brothers and fight against them, we are at peace with the demons, whom we have been taught to hate 'with perfect hatred' (Ps. 139 : 22), fighting against them without mercy.

81. Do not try to trip your neighbour up with deceitful words, lest you yourself be tripped up by the destroyer. For, as the prophet affirms, 'The Lord will abhor the bloody and deceitful man' (Ps. 5 : 6); 'The Lord will destroy all deceitful lips, and the tongue that speaks proud words' (Ps. 12 : 3). Similarly, do not revile your brother for his faults, lest you lapse from kindness and love. For the person who does not show kindness and love towards his brother 'does not know God, for God is love' (1 John 4 : 8), as John the

son of thunder and beloved disciple of Christ proclaims; and he adds
that if Christ, the Saviour of all, 'laid down His soul for us, then we
ought to lay down our souls for our brethren' (1 John 3 : 16).

82. Love has fittingly been called the citadel of the virtues, the
sum of the Law and the prophets (cf. Matt. 22 : 40; Rom. 13 : 10).
So let us make every effort until we attain it. Through love we shall
shake off the tyranny of the passions and rise to heaven, lifted up on
the wings of the virtues; and we shall see God, so far as this is possible for human nature.

83. If God is love, he who has love has God within himself. If
love is absent, nothing is of the least profit to us (cf. 1 Cor. 13 : 3);
and unless we love others we cannot say that we love God. For,
writes St John, 'If a man says, I love God, and hates his brother, he is
a liar' (1 John 4 : 20). And again he states: 'No man has ever seen
God. If we love one another, God dwells in us, and His love is perfected in us' (1 John 4 : 12). From this it is clear that love is the
most comprehensive and the highest of all the divine blessings
spoken of in the Holy Scriptures. And there is no form of virtue
through which a man may become akin to God and united with Him
that is not dependent upon love and encompassed by it; for love
unites and protects the virtues in an indescribable manner.

84. When we receive visits from our brethren, we should not
consider this an irksome interruption of our stillness, lest we cut
ourselves off from the law of love. Nor should we receive them as if
we were doing them a favour, but rather as if it is we ourselves who
are receiving a favour; and because we are indebted to them, we
should beg them cheerfully to enjoy our hospitality, as the patriarch
Abraham has shown us. This is why St John, too, says: 'My children,
let us love not in word or tongue, but in action and truth. And by
this we know that we belong to the truth' (1 John 3 : 18–19).

85. Accepting the task of hospitality, the patriarch used to sit at
the entrance to his tent (cf. Gen. 18 : 1), inviting all who passed by,
and his table was laden for all comers including the impious and barbarians, without distinction. Hence he was found worthy of that
wonderful banquet when he received angels and the Master of all as
his guests. We too, then, should actively and eagerly cultivate hospitality, so that we may receive not only angels, but also God Himself. For 'inasmuch', says the Lord, 'as you have done it to one of the
least of these My brethren you have done it to Me' (Matt. 25 : 40).

It is good to be generous to all, especially to those who cannot repay you.

86. If a man's heart does not condemn him (cf. 1 John 3 : 21) for having rejected a commandment of God, or for negligence, or for accepting a hostile thought, then he is pure in heart and worthy to hear Christ say to him: 'Blessed are the pure in heart, for they shall see God' (Matt. 5 : 8).

87. Let us try to use our intelligence in training our senses, especially the eyes, the ears and the tongue, not allowing them to see, hear and speak in an impassioned way, but only to our profit. For nothing can more easily slip into sin than these organs, when they are not trained by the intelligence. Again, there is nothing more apt for keeping them safe than the intelligence, which guides and regulates them and leads them towards what is necessary and what it wishes. For when they are rebellious, the sense of smell becomes effeminate, the sense of touch becomes indiscriminate, and innumerable passions come swarming in. But when they are subordinate to the intelligence, there is deep peace and settled calm in the whole person.

88. The fragrance of a costly aromatic oil, even though kept in a vessel, pervades the atmosphere of the whole house, and gives pleasure not only to those near it but also to others in the vicinity; similarly the fragrance of a holy soul, beloved of God, when given out through all the senses of the body, conveys to those who perceive it the holiness that lies within. When in the presence of one whose tongue utters nothing harsh and discordant, but only what is a blessing and benefit for those who listen, whose eyes are humble, whose ears do not listen to improper songs or words, who moves discreetly and whose face is not dissolute with laughter but rather disposed to tears and mourning, which of us will not feel that such a soul is filled with the fragrance of holiness? Thus the Saviour says: 'Let your light so shine before men, that they may see your good works, and glorify your Father who is in heaven' (Matt. 5 : 16).

89. What Christ our God called the 'narrow way' (Matt. 7 : 14), He also called an 'easy yoke' and 'light burden' (Matt. 11 : 30). How could He equate these things when they seem to be contraries? For our nature, certainly, this path is harsh and steep, but those who pursue it wholeheartedly and with good hope, and who aspire after holiness, find it attractive and full of delight, for it brings them

pleasure, not affliction. Hence they eagerly follow the narrow and painful way, greatly preferring it to that which is broad and spacious. Listen to St Luke, who tells us how the apostles, after being beaten, departed from the presence of the council rejoicing (cf. Acts 5 : 41), even though this is not the natural effect of a beating. For scourges normally cause, not pleasure and joy, but pain and suffering. Yet if, because of Christ, they resulted in joy, what wonder is it if other forms of bodily hardship and ill-treatment have, because of Him, the same effect?

90. While we are oppressed and imprisoned by the passions, we are often at a loss to know why we suffer from them. We must, therefore, realize that it is because we allow ourselves to be diverted from the contemplation of God that we are taken captive in this way. But if a man fixes his intellect without distraction on our Master and God, then the Saviour of all can Himself be trusted to deliver such a soul from its impassioned servitude. It is of this that the prophet speaks when he says: 'I have set the Lord always before me; for He is at my right hand, so that I shall not be moved' (Ps. 16 : 8). What is sweeter or safer than always to have the Lord at our right hand, protecting and guarding us and not letting us be moved? And to attain this is within our power.

91. There is no gainsaying what the fathers have so well affirmed, that a man does not find rest except by acquiring inwardly the thought that God and he alone exist;[1] and so he does not let his intellect wander at all towards anything whatsoever, but longs only for Him, cleaving to Him alone. Such a man will find true rest and freedom from the tyranny of the passions. 'My soul', as David says, 'is bound to Thee; Thy right hand has upheld me' (Ps. 63 : 8. LXX).

92. Self-love, love of pleasure and love of praise banish remembrance of God from the soul. Self-love begets unimaginable evils. And when remembrance of God is absent, there is a tumult of the passions within us.

93. He who has completely uprooted self-love from his heart will, with God's help, easily conquer all the other passions. For a man dominated by self-love is under the power of other passions as well, since from it arise anger, irritation, rancour, love of pleasure,

[1] See *Apophthegmata*, alphabetical collection, Alonios 1: trans. Sister Benedicta Ward, *The Sayings of the Desert Fathers* (London, 1975), p. 30.

licentiousness. By self-love we mean an impassioned disposition towards and love for the body, and the fulfilment of carnal desires.

94. Whatever a man loves, he desires at all costs to be near to
continuously and uninterruptedly, and he turns himself away from
everything that hinders him from being in contact and dwelling with
the object of his love. It is clear therefore that he who loves God
also desires always to be with Him and to converse with Him. This
comes to pass in us through pure prayer. Accordingly, let us apply
ourselves to prayer with all our power; for it enables us to become
akin to God. Such a man was he who said: 'O God, my God, I cry
to Thee at dawn; my soul has thirsted for Thee' (Ps. 63 : 1. LXX).
For the man who cries to God at dawn has withdrawn his intellect
from every vice and clearly is wounded by divine love.

95. We have been taught that dispassion is born from self-control
and humility, while spiritual knowledge is born from faith. Through
these the soul makes progress in discrimination and love. And once
she has embraced divine love, she never ceases to rise towards its
height on the wings of pure prayer, until she comes 'to the knowledge of the Son of God', as St Paul says, 'to a perfect man, to the
measure of the stature of the fulness of Christ' (Eph. 4 : 13).

96. Through active virtue desire is brought under control and
anger is bridled. Through spiritual knowledge and contemplation
the intellect makes its spiritual ascent and, being raised above
material things, departs towards God, attaining true blessedness.

97. Our first struggle is this: to reduce the passions and to conquer them entirely. Our second task is to acquire the virtues, and
not allow our soul to be empty and idle. The third stage of the
spiritual journey is watchfully to preserve the fruits of our virtues
and our labours. For we have been commanded not only to work
diligently, but also to preserve vigilantly (cf. Gen. 2 : 15).

98. 'Let your loins be girded, and your lamps burning', says the
Lord (Luke 12 : 35). A good girdle for our loins – one which enables us to be nimble and unhampered – is self-control combined
with humility of heart. By self-control I mean abstinence from all
the passions. Our spiritual lamp is lit by pure prayer and perfect
love. Those who have prepared themselves in this way are indeed
like men who wait expectantly for their Lord. When He comes and
knocks, they open at once; and when He has entered – together
with the Father and the Holy Spirit – He will take up His abode with

them (cf. John 14 : 23). Blessed are those servants whom the Lord when He comes will find acting in this manner (cf. Luke 12 : 37).

99. A monk, as a son, must love God with all his heart and all his mind (cf. Deut. 6 : 5; Mark 12 : 30), and, as a servant, he must reverence and obey Him, and fulfil His commandments with 'fear and trembling' (Phil. 2 : 12). He must be 'fervent in spirit' (Rom. 12 : 11), and wear 'the whole armour' of the Holy Spirit (cf. Eph. 6 : 11). He must strive for the enjoyment of eternal life and do all that is prescribed. He must be in a state of inner wakefulness, guard his heart from evil thoughts, and through good thoughts must continually practise divine meditation. He must examine himself daily concerning his evil thoughts and acts, and must correct any defects. He must not become proud because of his achievements, but must call himself a 'useless servant' (Luke 17 : 10), altogether in arrears over fulfilling his duties. He must give thanks to God and ascribe to Him the grace of his achievements, and do nothing at all from self-esteem or love of popularity, but do everything in secret and seek praise only from God (cf. Rom. 2 : 29). Above all and in all things he must completely fortify his soul with the Orthodox faith, according to the dogmas of the Holy Catholic Church as taught by the divine message-bearers, the apostles, and by the holy fathers. Great is the reward for those who live in such a manner. They receive everlasting life and an indestructible abode with the Father, the Son and the Holy Spirit, the coessential Divinity in three Persons.

100. 'Let us hear the conclusion of the whole matter: fear God, and keep His commandments, for this is the whole man' (Eccles. 12 : 13. LXX). Here the Preacher says to us: I show you in summary form the best way to salvation: fear God and keep His commandments. By fear he means not the initial fear of punishments, but the perfect and perfecting fear, which we ought to have out of love for Him who has given the commandments. For if we refrain from sin merely out of fear of punishment, it is quite clear that, unless punishment had awaited us, we should have done things deserving punishment, since our propensity is for sinning. But if we abstain from evil actions not through threat of punishment, but because we hate such actions, then it is from love of the Master that we practise the virtues, fearful lest we should fall away from Him. For when we fear that we may neglect something that has been en-

joined, the fear is clean (cf. Ps. 19 : 9), arising for the sake of the good itself. This fear purifies our souls, being equal in power to perfect love. He who has this fear and keeps the commandments is the 'whole man', in other words, the perfect and complete man.

Knowing these things, let us fear God and keep His commandments, so that we may be perfect and entire in the virtues. And having a humbled spirit and a contrite heart, let us repeat unceasingly to the Lord the prayer of the great and divine Arsenios: 'My God, do not abandon me. I have done nothing good before Thee, but grant me, in Thy compassion, the power to make a start.'[1] For the whole of our salvation lies in God's mercy and compassion. To Him be glory, might and worship: to the Father, the Son and the Holy Spirit, now and for ever and through all the ages. Amen.

[1] Desert Father of Sketis in Egypt (early 5th century). For this saying, see *Apophthegmata*, alphabetical collection, Arsenios 3: trans. Ward, *op. cit.*, p. 8.

Theoretikon

What an immense struggle it is to break the fetter binding us so strongly to material things, to stop worshipping these things, and to acquire instead a state of holiness. Indeed, unless our soul is truly noble and courageous it cannot embark on such a task. For our goal is not merely the purification of the passions: this by itself is not real virtue, but preparation for virtue. To purification from vicious habits must be added the acquisition of the virtues.

With respect to its intelligent aspect, to purify the soul is to eradicate and completely expunge from it all degrading and distorted features, all 'worldly cares', as the Divine Liturgy puts it, all turbulence, evil tendencies and senseless prepossessions. With respect to its desiring aspect, it is to purge away every impulse towards what is material, to cease from viewing things according to the senses, and to be obedient to the intelligence. And with respect to the soul's incensive power, purification consists in never being perturbed by anything that happens.

In the wake of this purification, and the mortification or correction of ugly features, there should follow spiritual ascent and deification. For after abandoning what is evil, one must practise what is good. One must first deny oneself and then, taking up the cross, must follow the Master towards the supreme state of deification.

What are ascent and deification? For the intellect, they are perfect knowledge of created things, and of Him who is above created things, so far as such knowledge is accessible to human nature. For the will, they are total and continuous striving towards primal goodness. And for the incensive power, they are energetic and effective impulsion towards the object of aspiration, persistent, relentless, and unarrested by any practical difficulties, pressing forward impetuously and undeviatingly.

The soul's impulsion towards beauty should surpass its impulsion towards what is base to the same degree as intelligible beauty surpasses sensible beauty. One should provide the body only with what is needed to keep it functioning properly. To intend to do this is easy, but to achieve it is more difficult, for without great effort one cannot uproot the soul's well-entrenched habits.

Nor indeed is knowledge to be acquired without effort. Certainly, to keep one's vision intently fixed on divine things until the will acquires the habit of doing this requires considerable labour over a long period of time. The intellect has to exert itself to oppose the downward drag of the senses; and this contest and battle against the body continues until death, even if it seems to diminish as anger and desire wither away, and as the senses are subjugated to the transcendent knowledge of the intellect.

It should be remarked, however, that an unillumined[1] soul, since it has no help from God, can neither be genuinely purified, nor ascend to the divine light. What was said above refers to those who are baptized.

Moreover, a distinction should be made between different kinds of knowledge. Knowledge here on earth is of two kinds: natural and supranatural. The second can be understood by reference to the first. Natural knowledge is that which the soul can acquire through the use of its natural faculties and powers when investigating creation and the cause of creation – in so far, of course, as this is possible for a soul bound to matter. For, when speaking of the senses, the imagination and the intellect, it has to be said that the energy of the intellect is blunted by being joined and mingled with the body. As a result, it cannot have direct contact with intelligible forms, but requires, in order to apprehend them, the imagination, which by nature uses images, and shares in material extension and density. Accordingly, the intellect while in the flesh needs to use material images in order to apprehend intelligible forms. We call natural knowledge, then, whatever knowledge the intellect in such a state acquires by its own natural means.

Supranatural knowledge, on the other hand, is that which enters the intellect in a manner transcending its own means and power; that is to say, the intelligible objects that constitute such knowledge

---

[1] This refers to the illumination of baptism.

surpass the capacity of an intellect joined to a body, so that a knowledge of them pertains naturally only to an intellect which is free from the body. Such knowledge is infused by God alone when He finds an intellect purified of all material attachment and inspired by divine love.

Not only knowledge but virtue as well is divided in this way. One kind of virtue does not transcend nature, and this can fittingly be called natural virtue. The other, which is energized only by the primal source of beauty, is above our natural capacity and state; and this kind of virtue should be called supranatural.

Knowledge and virtue, then, are divided in this way. An unillumined person may possess natural knowledge and virtue, but never those which are supranatural. How could he, since he does not participate in their energizing cause? But the illumined man can possess both. Moreover, although he cannot acquire supranatural virtue at all unless he has first acquired natural virtue, he can participate in supranatural knowledge without first acquiring natural knowledge. In addition, just as sense and imagination are far superior and more noble in man than they are in animals, so natural virtue and knowledge are far superior and more noble in the person who is illumined than in the person who is unillumined, although both may possess them.

Further, that aspect of natural knowledge concerned with the virtues and with the habits opposing them also seems to be of two kinds. One kind is theoretical knowledge, when a man speculates about these matters but lacks experience of them, and is sometimes unsure about what he says. The other is practical and, so to speak, alive, since the knowledge in question is confirmed by experience, and so is clear and trustworthy, and in no way uncertain or doubtful.

In view of all this, there appear to be four obstacles which hinder the intellect in the acquisition of virtue. First, there is prepossession, that is, the ingrained influence of habits running counter to virtue; and this, operative over a long period, exerts a pressure which drags the intellect down towards earthly things. Secondly, there is the action of the senses, stimulated by sensible beauty and drawing the intellect after it. Thirdly, there is the dulling of noetic energy due to the intellect's connection with the body. The intellect of an embodied soul is not related to an intelligible object in the same way as sight is to a visible object or, in general, the senses are to sensory objects. Immaterial intellects apprehend intelligible objects more effectively than sight apprehends visible objects. But just as faulty sight visualizes its images of natural objects somewhat indistinctly and unclearly, so does our intellect, when embodied, apprehend intelligible objects. And since it cannot now clearly discern intelligible beauties, it cannot aspire after them either. For one has a longing for something only to the degree that one possesses knowledge of it. Hence the intellect – since it cannot help being drawn towards what appears to be beautiful, whether or not it really is so – is drawn down to sensible beauty, for this now makes a clearer impression on it.

The fourth of the obstacles impeding the intellect in its acquisition of virtue is the pernicious influence of unclean and hostile demons. It is impossible to speak of all the various snares they set on the spiritual path, making use of the senses, the reason, the intellect – in fact, of everything that exists. If He who carries the lost sheep on His shoulders (cf. Luke 15 : 5) did not in His infinite care protect those who turn to Him, not a single soul would escape.

Three things are needed in order to overcome these obstacles. The first and most important thing is to look to God with our whole soul, to ask for help from His hand, and to put all our trust in Him, knowing full well that without His assistance we shall inevitably be dragged away from Him. The second – which I regard as an overture to the first – is constantly to nourish the intellect with knowledge. By knowledge I mean that of all created things, sensible and intelligible, both as they are in themselves and with reference to the primal Source, since they derive from it and are related to it; and in addition to this, the contemplation, as far as is possible, of the Cause of all created things, through the qualities that appertain to Him. To be concerned with the nature of created things has a very purifying effect. It frees us from passionate attachment to them and from delusion about them; and it is the surest of means for raising our soul to the Source of all. For all beauty, miracle, magnificence reflects what is supremely beautiful, miraculous and magnificent – reflects, rather, the Source that is above beauty, miracle and magnificence.

If the mind is always occupied with these things, how can it not long for supernal goodness itself? If it can be drawn to what is alien to it, how will it not be far more strongly drawn to what is cognate?

When the soul cleaves to what is kindred to it, how can it turn away from what it loves to anything inferior? It will even resent its incarnate life, finding it a hindrance to the attaining of the beautiful. For though the intellect, while living in matter, beholds intelligible beauty but dimly, yet intelligible blessings are such that even a slight emanation from that overflowing beauty, or a faint vision of it, can impel the intellect to soar beyond all that is outside the intelligible realm, and to aspire to that alone, never letting itself lapse from the delight it offers, come what distress there may.

The third way by which we can overcome the obstacles already mentioned is to mortify our partner, the body; for otherwise we cannot attain a clear and distinct vision of the intelligible world. The flesh is mortified or, rather, crucified with Christ, through fasting, vigils, sleeping on the ground, wearing coarse clothing and only what is essential, through suffering and toil. In this fashion it is refined and purified, made light and subtle, readily and unresistingly following the guidance of the intellect and rising upwards with it. Without such mortification all our efforts are vain.

When these three holy ways are established in mutual harmony, they beget in the soul the choir of blessed virtues; for those whom they adorn are free from all trace of sin and blessed with every virtue. Yet the rejection of material wealth, or of fame, may distress the intelligence; for the soul, still bound to such things, is pierced by many passions. None the less I firmly maintain that a soul attached to wealth and praise cannot mount upwards. Equally I say that a soul loses all attachment to these things once it has practised this triad of ways sufficiently for it to have become habitual. For if the soul is persuaded that only the beauty which is beyond everything is to be regarded as truly beautiful, while of other things the most beautiful is that which is most like the supreme beauty, and so on down the scale, how can it relish silver, gold or fame, or any other degrading thing?

Even what most holds us back – I mean our cares and concerns – is no exception to the rule. For what cares will a man have, if he is not attached to anything worldly or involved with it? The cloud of cares comes from the fumes, so to speak, of the main passions – self-indulgence, avarice, love of praise. Once you are free of these you will also have cast off your cares.

Sound moral judgment has the same effect as wisdom, and is a most powerful factor drawing us upwards. Hence it too has its part to play. For the knowledge of the virtues involves the most scrupulous discrimination between good and evil; and this requires sound moral judgment. Experience and the struggle with the body teach us how to use such judgment in our warfare.

Fear also comes into the argument. For the greater our longing for God the greater grows our fear; and the more we hope to attain God, the more we fear Him. If we are wounded by divine love, the sting of fear exceeds that of a thousand threats of punishment. For as nothing is more blessed than to attain God, so nothing is more terrible than this great fear of losing Him.

To come to another point: everything may be understood in terms of its purpose. It is this that determines the division of everything into its constituent parts, as well as the mutual relationship of those parts. Now the purpose of our life is blessedness or, what is the same thing, the kingdom of heaven or of God. This is not only to behold the Trinity, supreme in Kingship, but also to receive an influx of the divine and, as it were, to suffer deification; for by this influx what is lacking and imperfect in us is supplied and perfected. And the provision by such divine influx of what is needed is the food of spiritual beings. There is a kind of eternal circle, which ends where it begins. For the greater our noetic perception, the more we long to perceive; and the greater our longing, the greater our enjoyment; and the greater our enjoyment, the more our perception is deepened, and so the motionless movement, or the motionless immobility, begins again. Such then is our purpose, in so far as we can understand it. We must now see how we can attain it.

To intelligent souls, which as intellective beings are only a little lower than angelic intellects, life in this world is a struggle and incarnate life an open contest. The prize of victory is the state we have described, a gift worthy both of God's goodness and of His justice: of His justice, because these blessings are attained not without our own sweat; of His goodness, because His boundless generosity surpasses all our toil – especially as the very capacity for doing good and the actual doing of it are themselves gifts of God.

What, then, is the nature of our contest in this world? The intelligent soul is conjoined with an animal-like body, which has its being from the earth and gravitates downwards. It is so mixed with the body that though they are total opposites they form a single being. Without change or confusion in either of them, and with each acting in accordance with its nature, they compose a single person, or hypostasis, with two complete natures. In this composite two-natured being, man, each of his natures functions in accordance with its own particular powers. It is characteristic of the body to desire what is akin to it. This longing for what is akin to them is natural to created beings, since indeed their existence depends on the inter-course of like with like, and on their enjoyment of material things through the senses. Then, being heavy, the body welcomes relaxa-tion. These things are proper and desirable for our animal-like nature. But to the intelligent soul, as an intellective entity, what is natural and desirable is the realm of intelligible realities and its enjoyment of them in the manner characteristic of it. Before and above all what is characteristic of the intellect is an intense longing for God. It desires to enjoy Him and other intelligible realities, though it cannot do this without encountering obstacles.

The first man could indeed, without any hindrance, apprehend and enjoy sensory things by means of the senses and intelligible things with the intellect. But he should have given his attention to the higher rather than to the lower, for he was as able to commune with intelligible things through the intellect, as he was with sensory things through the senses. I do not say that Adam ought not to have used the senses, for it was not for nothing that he was invested with a body. But he should not have indulged in sensory things. When perceiving the beauty of creatures, he should have referred it to its source and as a consequence have found his enjoyment and his wonder fulfilled in that, thus giving himself a twofold reason for marvelling at the Creator. He should not have attached himself, as he did, to sensory things and have lost himself in wonder at them, neglecting the Creator of intelligible beauty.

Thus Adam used the senses wrongly and was spellbound by sensory beauty; and because the fruit appeared to him to be beauti-ful and good to eat (Gen. 3 : 6), he tasted it and forsook the enjoy-ment of intelligible things. So it was that the just Judge judged him unworthy of what he had rejected – the contemplation of God and of created beings – and, making darkness His secret place (cf. 2 Sam. 22 : 12; Ps. 18 : 11), deprived him of Himself and of im-material realities. For holy things must not be made available to the impure. What he fell in love with, God permitted him to enjoy, allowing him to live according to the senses, with but faint vestiges of intellectual perception.

Henceforward our struggle against the things of this world became harder, because it is now no longer in our power to enjoy intelligible realities in a way corresponding to that in which we enjoy sensory realities with the senses, even though we are greatly assisted by baptism, which purifies and exalts us. Yet, in so far as we can, we must give our attention to the intelligible and not to the sensible world. We must reverence it and aspire to it; but we must not reverence any sensory object in and for itself, or try to enjoy it in that way; for in truth what is sensory cannot compare with what is intelligible. Just as the essence of the one far excels that of the other, so does its beauty. To aspire to what is ugly rather than to what is beautiful, to what is ignoble rather than to what is noble, is sheer lunacy. And if that is the case where both sensible and intelligible creations are involved, how much more so is it when we prefer matter, formless and ugly, to God Himself.

This, then, is our contest and struggle: strictly to watch ourselves, so that we always strive to enjoy intelligible realities, directing intellect and appetite to that end, and never allowing them secretly to be beguiled by the senses into revering sensory things for their own sake. And if we have to use the senses, we should use them in order to grasp the Creator through His creation, seeing Him reflected in created things as the sun is reflected in water, since in their inner beings they are in varying degrees images of the primal cause of all.

Such, then, is our aim. How can we achieve it? As we said, the body desires to enjoy through the senses what is akin to it; and the stronger it is, the stronger its desire. But this conflicts with the soul's purpose. So the soul must make every effort to curb the senses, so that we do not indulge in sensible realities in the way described. But since the stronger the body, the stronger its desire, and the stronger its desire the harder it is to check, the soul must mortify the body through fasting, vigils, standing, sleeping on the ground, going unwashed, and through every other kind of hardship, thus reducing its strength and making it tractable and obedient to the soul's noetic activities. This is the aim. Yet it is easy to wish, hard to achieve; and failures greatly outnumber the successes, because even if we are most attentive, the senses often beguile us. So a third remedy has been devised: prayer and tears. Prayer gives thanks for blessings received and asks for failures to be forgiven and for power to strengthen us for the future; for without God's help the soul can indeed do nothing. None the less, to persuade the will to have the strongest possible desire for union with and enjoyment of Him, for whom it longs, and to direct itself totally towards Him, is the major part of the achievement of our aim. And tears too have great power. They gain God's mercy for our faults, purify us of the defilements produced through sensual pleasures, and spur our desire upwards.

Thus, our aim is the contemplation of intelligible realities and total aspiration towards them. The mortification of the flesh, together with the fasting, self-restraint and other things that contribute to it, are all practised as a means to this end. And in their company is prayer. Each has many aspects; some contribute to one thing, some to another.

Love of praise and love of material wealth must not be regarded as pertaining to the body. Only the love of sensual pleasure pertains to the body. The fitting remedy for this is bodily hardship. Love of praise and love of material wealth are the progeny of ignorance. Having no experience of true blessings and no knowledge of noetic realities, the soul has adopted such bastard offspring, thinking that riches can supply its needs. Also it plunges after material wealth in order to satisfy its love for pleasure and praise, and even for its own sake, as if such wealth were a blessing in itself. All this results from ignorance of true blessings. Love of praise does not derive from any lack on the part of the body, for it satisfies no physical need. Inexperience and ignorance of primal goodness and true glory give rise to it. Indeed, ignorance is the root of all evils. For no one who has once grasped as he should the true nature of things – from where each thing comes and how it is perverted – can then totally disregard his own purpose and be dragged down to worldly things. The soul does not want a good that is only apparent. And if it is under the sway of some habit, it is also quite able to overcome this habit. Yet even before the habit was formed it had been deceived by ignorance. Hence one should above all strive after a true knowledge of created beings, and then spur one's will towards primal goodness, scorning all worldly things and aware of their great vanity. For what do they contribute to our own true purpose?

To sum up briefly. An intelligent soul, while in the body, has but

one task: to realize its own purpose. But since the will's energy remains unstimulated unless there is intellection, we begin by trying
to energize noetically. Noetic activity is either for the sake of willing or, more commonly, for its own sake as well as for the sake of
willing. Blessedness – of which any significant life on earth is not
only an overture but also a prefigurement – is characterized by both
energies: by both intellection and willing, that is, by both love and
spiritual pleasure. Whether both these energies are supreme, or one
is superior to the other, is open to discussion. For the moment we
shall regard both of them as supreme. One we call contemplative
and the other practical. Where these supreme energies are concerned, the one cannot be found without the other. In the case of
the lower energies, sequent to these two, each may be found singly.
Whatever hinders these two energies, or opposes them, we call
vice. Whatever fosters them, or frees them from obstacles, we call
virtue. Energies that spring from the virtues are good; those that
spring from their opposites are distorted and sinful. The supreme
goal, whose energy, as we know, is compound of intellection and
willing, endows each particular energy with a specific form, which
may be used for either good or evil.

ST MAXIMOS THE CONFESSOR

Introductory Note

The extreme importance of St Maximos the Confessor (580–662) for the Orthodox spiritual tradition is indicated by the fact that no other writer is assigned so much space in the *Philokalia*. A member of the aristocracy, after receiving an elaborate education St Maximos served at first in the civil service, perhaps as secretary to the Emperor Heraklios. Around 614 he became a monk at the monastery of Philippikos in Chrysopolis (Scutari), close to Constantinople, subsequently moving to another monastery not far distant at Cyzikos (Erdek). In 626, at the time of the Persian invasion, he fled to Crete and eventually to Africa, where he remained for some years. From 633–4 onwards he played a leading part in opposing the heresies of Monoenergism and Monotheletism, and because of this he was arrested in 653 by the imperial authorities, brought to Constantinople for trial, and sent into exile. Further trials and condemnations followed, the last being at Constantinople in 662, after which he was flogged, his tongue was plucked out and his right hand cut off. He died soon afterwards as an exile in the Caucasus. His memorial is observed in the Orthodox Church on 21 January, and also on the day of his death, 13 August.

In his numerous writings St Maximos discusses almost all aspects of Christian truth, including the interpretation of Scripture, the doctrine of the incarnation, ascetic practice, and the Divine Liturgy. He insists upon the close link between dogma and prayer. When he opposed Monotheletism, this was not because of some technicality, but because such a view subverted the understanding of the full reality of man's salvation and deification in Christ. The Monotheletes wished to reconcile the supporters of the Council of Chalcedon (451), who ascribed two natures to the incarnate Christ, with the Monophysites, who believed that He has only one nature; and so they proposed as a compromise the theory that Christ has two natures, the one divine and the other human, but only a single will. Against this St Maximos maintained that human nature without a human will is an unreal abstraction: if Christ does not have a human will as well as a divine will, He is not truly man; and if He is not truly man, the Christian message of salvation is rendered void. What we see in Christ our Saviour is precisely a human will, genuinely free yet held in unwavering obedience to His divine will; and it is by virtue of this voluntary co-operation of manhood with divinity in Christ, which restored the integrity of human nature, that we are enabled to make our own wills freely obedient to the will of God and so to attain salvation. St Maximos' teaching was confirmed after his death by the Sixth Ecumenical Council, meeting at Constantinople in 680–1.

The *Philokalia* contains four works under the name of St Maximos:

(1) *Four Hundred Texts on Love*. This is the most immediately attractive of all his works and also one of the easiest to understand. It is among his earlier writings, probably composed by 626, while he was at Cyzikos.[1]

(2) *Two Hundred Texts on Theology and the Incarnate Dispensation of the Son of God*. This seems to have been written in Africa between 630 and 634, and is far more complex in its argument. With remarkable subtlety St Maximos has adapted and drawn into a single synthesis ideas taken from Origen (c. 185–c. 254), Evagrios (345/6–399) and St Dionysios the Areopagite (c. 500).[2] Although doubts have sometimes been expressed, there seems no good reason to question the attribution to St Maximos.

(3) *Various Texts on Theology, the Divine Economy, and Virtue and Vice* (500 in number). In the Greek edition of the *Philokalia* this is treated as a continuation of the preceding treatise, *Two Hundred Texts*; but in fact the two works are altogether distinct, and are treated as such in this translation. The *Various Texts*, in their present form, are not an authentic work of St Maximos himself but rather a

[1] There is an earlier English translation, with valuable introduction and notes, by Dom Polycarp Sherwood, *St. Maximus the Confessor: The Ascetic Life, The Four Centuries on Charity (Ancient Christian Writers* 21: Westminster, Maryland, 1955).

[2] On St Maximos' use of his sources, see Hans Urs von Balthasar, *Die 'Gnostischen Centurien' des Maximus Confessor (Freiburger Theologische Studien* 61: Freiburg im Breisgau, 1941); incorporated, in revised form, in *Kosmische Liturgie. Das Weltbild Maximus' des Bekenners* (2nd ed., Einsiedeln, 1961), pp. 482–643. For a French translation of the first century of the *Two Hundred Texts*, see A. Riou, *Le monde et l'Eglise selon Maxime le Confesseur (Théologie Historique* 22: Paris, 1973), pp. 240–61.

'Maximian anthology', a collection of extracts from his writings made by a later compiler, probably not before the eleventh or twelfth century. The sources of this anthology are as follows:

Various Texts i, 1–25 cannot be traced in the known writings of St Maximos. The manuscript evidence strongly suggests that sections 1–15 are his genuine work; in the case of sections 16–25 Maximian authorship is less certain, but is not to be excluded.

i, 26–47 are extracted from his *Letters*.

i, 48–v, 61 are taken from the treatise *To Thalassios: On Various Questions relating to Holy Scripture*, which was probably written in Africa during 630–4. Together with extracts from St Maximos, the compiler has also included many passages from the *scholia* or commentaries on the work *To Thalassios: On Various Questions*; there is general agreement that these *scholia* are not by St Maximos himself and they probably date for the most part from the tenth century.

v, 62–100 are taken from the *Ambigua*, a discussion of disputed texts in the works of St Gregory of Nazianzos, which St Maximos wrote in Africa during 628–34. The compiler has inserted here some extracts from St Dionysios the Areopagite.

In an appendix we have briefly indicated which of the *Various Texts* are from St Maximos, and which from the scholiast or St Dionysios.[1] As can be seen from marginal notes in the Greek *Philokalia*, St Nikodimos and St Makarios realized that parts of the *Various Texts* came not from St Maximos himself but from the scholiast. Why, in that case, did they choose to include this later compilation, and not the original text of *To Thalassios: On Various Questions*? A possible answer is that the original text is very lengthy and at times highly obscure; the compiler, while sometimes increasing the obscurity by omitting vital passages, has on the whole selected the sections more immediately relevant to the spiritual life. Perhaps, then, by choosing the later anthology and not the original work, the editors hoped to render these writings accessible to a wider readership.

[1] For fuller details, with exact references, see W. Soppa, *Die Diversa Capita unter den Schriften des hl. Maximus Confessor in deutscher Bearbeitung und quellenkritischer Beleuchtung* (Dresden, 1922); M.-Th. Disdier, 'Une oeuvre douteuse de saint Maxime le Confesseur: Les cinq Centuries théologiques', *Echos d'Orient* xxx (1931), pp. 160–78; P. Sherwood, *An Annotated Date-List of the Works of Maximus the Confessor* (*Studia Anselmiana* 30: Rome, 1952), pp. 35–36.

(4) *On the Lord's Prayer*. This is generally accepted as an authentic work of St Maximos, perhaps written about 628–30.[1]

For the *Four Hundred Texts on Love* we have used the critical edition of the Greek text by A. Ceresa-Gastaldo (*Verba Seniorum*, N.S. 3: Rome, 1963). For the other three works we have compared the Greek text in the *Philokalia* with that of Combefis and Oehler in Migne, *P.G.* xc–xci, which is on the whole more reliable.

[1] French translation in Riou, *op. cit.*, pp. 214–39.

Four Hundred Texts on Love

FOREWORD TO ELPIDIOS THE PRESBYTER

In addition to my treatise on the ascetic life I am also sending you, Father Elpidios, this treatise on love divided, on the analogy of the four Gospels, into four centuries of chapters. It may not fulfil your expectations, but it is the best that I can do. Moreover, you should know, Father, that these chapters are not the products of my own mind. On the contrary, I have gone through the writings of the holy fathers and collected from them passages relevant to my subject, condensing much material into short paragraphs and in this way making it easy to remember and to assimilate.

In sending these chapters to you I beg you to read them with sympathy and to seek out only what is profitable in them, overlooking the inelegant language. I also ask you to pray for my unworthy self, bereft as I am of all spiritual blessing. I have this request too: do not be annoyed by what I have written, for I have merely carried out what I was commanded to do. I say this because we who plague people with words are many nowadays, while those who teach or are taught by actions are very few.

Please give careful attention to each chapter. For I suspect that not all the chapters are easy for everyone to understand. Many of them will need to be studied closely by most readers even if what they say seems to be very simple. If anything in these chapters should prove useful to the soul, it will be revealed to the reader by the grace of God, provided that he reads, not out of curiosity, but in the fear and love of God. If a man reads this or any other work not to gain spiritual benefit but to track down matter with which to abuse the author, so that in his conceit he can show himself to be the more learned, nothing profitable will ever be revealed to him in anything.

First Century

1. Love is a holy state of the soul, disposing it to value knowledge of God above all created things. We cannot attain lasting possession of such love while we are still attached to anything worldly.

2. Dispassion engenders love, hope in God engenders dispassion, and patience and forbearance engender hope in God; these in turn are the product of complete self-control, which itself springs from fear of God. Fear of God is the result of faith in God.

3. If you have faith in the Lord you will fear punishment, and this fear will lead you to control the passions. Once you control the passions you will accept affliction patiently, and through such acceptance you will acquire hope in God. Hope in God separates the intellect from every worldly attachment, and when the intellect is detached in this way it will acquire love for God.

4. The person who loves God values knowledge of God more than anything created by God, and pursues such knowledge ardently and ceaselessly.

5. If everything that exists was made by God and for God, and God is superior to the things made by Him, he who abandons what is superior and devotes himself to what is inferior shows that he values things made by God more than God Himself.

6. When your intellect is concentrated on the love of God you will pay little attention to visible things and will regard even your own body as something alien.

7. Since the soul is more noble than the body and God incomparably more noble than the world created by Him, he who values the body more than the soul and the world created by God more than the Creator Himself is simply a worshipper of idols.

8. If you distract your intellect from its love for God and

concentrate it, not on God, but on some sensible object, you thereby show that you value the body more than the soul and the things made by God more than God Himself.

9. Since the light of spiritual knowledge is the intellect's life, and since this light is engendered by love for God, it is rightly said that nothing is greater than divine love (cf. 1 Cor. 13 : 13).

10. When in the intensity of its love for God the intellect goes out of itself, then it has no sense of itself or of any created thing. For when it is illumined by the infinite light of God, it becomes insensible to everything made by Him, just as the eye becomes insensible to the stars when the sun rises.

11. All the virtues co-operate with the intellect to produce this intense longing for God, pure prayer above all. For by soaring towards God through this prayer the intellect rises above the realm of created beings.

12. When the intellect is ravished through love by divine knowledge and stands outside the realm of created beings, it becomes aware of God's infinity. It is then, according to Isaiah, that a sense of amazement makes it conscious of its own lowliness and in all sincerity it repeats the prophet's words: 'How abject I am, for I am pierced to the heart; because I am a man of unclean lips, and I dwell among a people of unclean lips; and my eyes have seen the King, the Lord of hosts' (Isa. 6 : 5).

13. The person who loves God cannot help loving every man as himself, even though he is grieved by the passions of those who are not yet purified. But when they amend their lives, his delight is indescribable and knows no bounds.

14. A soul filled with thoughts of sensual desire and hatred is unpurified.

15. If we detect any trace of hatred in our hearts against any man whatsoever for committing any fault, we are utterly estranged from love for God, since love for God absolutely precludes us from hating any man.

16. He who loves Me, says the Lord, will keep My commandments (cf. John 14 : 15, 23); and 'this is My commandment, that you love one another' (John 15 : 12). Thus he who does not love his neighbour fails to keep the commandment, and so cannot love the Lord.

17. Blessed is he who can love all men equally.

18. Blessed is he who is not attached to anything transitory or corruptible.

19. Blessed is the intellect that transcends all sensible objects and ceaselessly delights in divine beauty.

20. If you make provision for the desires of the flesh (cf. Rom. 13 : 14) and bear a grudge against your neighbour on account of something transitory, you worship the creature instead of the Creator.

21. If you keep your body free from disease and sensual pleasure it will help you to serve what is more noble.

22. He who forsakes all worldly desires sets himself above all worldly distress.

23. He who loves God will certainly love his neighbour as well. Such a person cannot hoard money, but distributes it in a way befitting God, being generous to everyone in need.

24. He who gives alms in imitation of God does not discriminate between the wicked and the virtuous, the just and the unjust, when providing for men's bodily needs. He gives equally to all according to their need, even though he prefers the virtuous man to the bad man because of the probity of his intention.

25. God, who is by nature good and dispassionate, loves all men equally as His handiwork. But He glorifies the virtuous man because in his will he is united to God. At the same time, in His goodness He is merciful to the sinner and by chastising him in this life brings him back to the path of virtue. Similarly, a man of good and dispassionate judgment also loves all men equally. He loves the virtuous man because of his nature and the probity of his intention; and he loves the sinner, too, because of his nature and because in his compassion he pities him for foolishly stumbling in darkness.

26. The state of love may be recognized in the giving of money, and still more in the giving of spiritual counsel and in looking after people in their physical needs.

27. He who has genuinely renounced worldly things, and lovingly and sincerely serves his neighbour, is soon set free from every passion and made a partaker of God's love and knowledge.

28. He who has realized love for God in his heart is tireless, as Jeremiah says (cf. Jer. 17 : 16. LXX), in his pursuit of the Lord his God, and bears every hardship, reproach and insult nobly, never thinking the least evil of anyone.

29. When you are insulted by someone or humiliated, guard against angry thoughts, lest they arouse a feeling of irritation, and so cut you off from love and place you in the realm of hatred.

30. You should know that you have been greatly benefited when you have suffered deeply because of some insult or indignity; for by means of the indignity self-esteem has been driven out of you.

31. Just as the thought of fire does not warm the body, so faith without love does not actualize the light of spiritual knowledge in the soul.

32. Just as the light of the sun attracts a healthy eye, so through love knowledge of God naturally draws to itself the pure intellect.

33. A pure intellect is one divorced from ignorance and illumined by divine light.

34. A pure soul is one freed from passions and constantly delighted by divine love.

35. A culpable passion is an impulse of the soul that is contrary to nature.

36. Dispassion is a peaceful condition of the soul in which the soul is not easily moved to evil.

37. A man who has been assiduous in acquiring the fruits of love will not cease loving even if he suffers a thousand calamities. Let Stephen, the disciple of Christ, and others like him persuade you of the truth of this (cf. Acts 7 : 60). Our Lord Himself prayed for His murderers and asked the Father to forgive them because they did not know what they were doing (cf. Luke 23 : 34).

38. If love is long-suffering and kind (cf. 1 Cor. 13 : 4), a man who is contentious and malicious clearly alienates himself from love. And he who is alienated from love is alienated from God, for God is love.

39. Do not say that you are the temple of the Lord, writes Jeremiah (cf. Jer. 7 : 4); nor should you say that faith alone in our Lord Jesus Christ can save you, for this is impossible unless you also acquire love for Him through your works. As for faith by itself, 'the devils also believe, and tremble' (Jas. 2 : 19).

40. We actively manifest love in forbearance and patience towards our neighbour, in genuinely desiring his good, and in the right use of material things.

41. He who loves God neither distresses nor is distressed with anyone on account of transitory things. There is only one kind of

distress which he both suffers and inflicts on others: that salutary
distress which the blessed Paul suffered and which he inflicted on
the Corinthians (cf. 2 Cor. 7 : 8–11).

42. He who loves God lives the angelic life on earth, fasting and
keeping vigils, praying and singing psalms and always thinking good
of every man.

43. If a man desires something, he makes every effort to attain
it. But of all things which are good and desirable the divine is incomparably the best and the most desirable. How assiduous, then,
we should be in order to attain what is of its very nature good and
desirable.

44. Stop defiling your flesh with shameful deeds and polluting
your soul with wicked thoughts; then the peace of God will descend upon you and bring you love.

45. Afflict your flesh with hunger and vigils and apply yourself
tirelessly to psalmody and prayer; then the sanctifying gift of self-
restraint will descend upon you and bring you love.

46. He who has been granted divine knowledge and has through
love acquired its illumination will never be swept hither and thither
by the demon of self-esteem. But he who has not yet been granted
such knowledge will readily succumb to this demon. However, if in
all that he does he keeps his gaze fixed on God, doing everything for
His sake, he will with God's help soon escape.

47. He who has not yet attained divine knowledge energized by
love is proud of his spiritual progress. But he who has been granted
such knowledge repeats with deep conviction the words uttered by
the patriarch Abraham when he was granted the manifestation of
God: 'I am dust and ashes' (Gen. 18 : 27).

48. The person who fears the Lord has humility as his constant
companion and, through the thoughts which humility inspires,
reaches a state of divine love and thankfulness. For he recalls his
former worldly way of life, the various sins he has committed and
the temptations which have befallen him since his youth; and he recalls, too, how the Lord delivered him from all this, and how He
led him away from a passion-dominated life to a life ruled by God.
Then, together with fear, he also receives love, and in deep
humility continually gives thanks to the Benefactor and Helmsman of
our lives.

49. Do not befoul your intellect by clinging to thoughts filled

with anger and sensual desire. Otherwise you will lose your capacity for pure prayer and fall victim to the demon of listlessness.

50. When the intellect associates with evil and sordid thoughts it loses its intimate communion with God.

51. The foolish man under attack from the passions, when stirred to anger, is senselessly impelled to leave his brethren. But when heated by desire he quickly changes his mind and seeks their company. An intelligent person behaves differently in both cases. When anger flares up he cuts off the source of disturbance and so frees himself from his feeling of irritation against his brethren. When desire is uppermost he checks every unruly impulse and chance conversation.

52. In time of trial do not leave your monastery but stand up courageously against the thoughts that surge over you, especially those of irritation and listlessness. For when you have been tested by afflictions in this way, according to divine providence, your hope in God will become firm and secure. But if you leave, you will show yourself to be worthless, unmanly and fickle.

53. If you wish not to fall away from the love of God, do not let your brother go to bed feeling irritated with you, and do not go to bed yourself feeling irritated with him. Reconcile yourself with your brother, and then come to Christ with a clear conscience and offer Him your gift of love in earnest prayer (cf. Matt. 5 : 24).

54. St Paul says that, if we have all the gifts of the Spirit but do not have love, we are no further forward (cf. 1 Cor. 13 : 2). How assiduous, then, we ought to be in our efforts to acquire this love.

55. If 'love prevents us from harming our neighbour' (Rom. 13 : 10), he who is jealous of his brother or irritated by his reputation, and damages his good name with cheap jibes or in any way spitefully plots against him, is surely alienating himself from love and is guilty in the face of eternal judgment.

56. If 'love is the fulfilling of the law' (Rom. 13 : 10), he who is full of rancour towards his neighbour and lays traps for him and curses him, exulting in his fall, must surely be a transgressor deserving eternal punishment.

57. If 'he who speaks evil of his brother, and judges his brother, speaks evil of the law, and judges the law' (Jas. 4 : 11), and the law of Christ is love, surely he who speaks evil of Christ's love falls away from it and is the cause of his own perdition.

58. Do not listen gleefully to gossip at your neighbour's expense or chatter to a person who likes finding fault. Otherwise you will fall away from divine love and find yourself cut off from eternal life.

59. Do not permit any abuse of your spiritual father or encourage anyone who dishonours him. Otherwise the Lord will be angry with your conduct and will obliterate you from the land of the living (cf. Deut. 6 : 15).

60. Silence the man who utters slander in your hearing. Otherwise you sin twice over: first, you accustom yourself to this deadly passion and, second you fail to prevent him from gossiping against his neighbour.

61. 'But I say to you,' says the Lord, 'love your enemies . . . do good to those who hate you, and pray for those who mistreat you' (Matt. 5 : 44). Why did He command this? To free you from hatred, irritation, anger and rancour, and to make you worthy of the supreme gift of perfect love. And you cannot attain such love if you do not imitate God and love all men equally. For God loves all men equally and wishes them 'to be saved and to come to the knowledge of the truth' (1 Tim. 2 : 4).

62. 'But I say to you, do not resist evil; but if someone hits you on the right cheek, turn to him the other cheek as well. And if anyone sues you in the courts, and takes away your coat, let him have your cloak also. And if anyone forces you to go a mile, go with him for two miles' (Matt. 5 : 39–41). Why did He say this? Both to keep you free from anger and irritation, and to correct the other person by means of your forbearance, so that like a good Father He might bring the two of you under the yoke of love.

63. We carry about with us impassioned images of the things we have experienced. If we can overcome these images we shall be indifferent to the things which they represent. For fighting against the thoughts of things is much harder than fighting against the things themselves, just as to sin in the mind is easier than to sin through outward action.

64. Some passions pertain to the body, others to the soul. The first are occasioned by the body, the second by external objects. Love and self-control overcome both kinds, the first curbing the passions of the soul and the second those of the body.

65. Some passions pertain to the soul's incensive power, and

others to its desiring aspect. Both kinds are aroused through the senses. They are aroused when the soul lacks love and self-control.

66. The passions of the soul's incensive power are more difficult to combat than those of its desiring aspect. Consequently our Lord has given a stronger remedy against them: the commandment of love.

67. While passions such as forgetfulness and ignorance affect but one of the soul's three aspects – the incensive, the desiring or the intelligent – listlessness alone seizes control of all the soul's powers and rouses almost all the passions together. That is why this passion is more serious than all the others. Hence our Lord has given us an excellent remedy against it, saying: 'You will gain possession of your souls through your patient endurance' (Luke 21 : 19).

68. Never strike any of the brethren, especially without reason, in case he is unable to bear the affliction and leaves the monastery. For then you would never escape the reproach of your conscience. It would always bring you distress in the time of prayer and divert your intellect from intimate communion with God.

69. Shun all suspicions and all persons that cause you to take offence. If you are offended by anything, whether intended or unintended, you do not know the way of peace, which through love brings the lovers of divine knowledge to the knowledge of God.

70. You have not yet acquired perfect love if your regard for people is still swayed by their characters – for example, if, for some particular reason, you love one person and hate another, or if for the same reason you sometimes love and sometimes hate the same person.

71. Perfect love does not split up the single human nature, common to all, according to the diverse characteristics of individuals; but, fixing attention always on this single nature, it loves all men equally. It loves the good as friends and the bad as enemies, helping them, exercising forbearance, patiently accepting whatever they do, not taking the evil into account at all but even suffering on their behalf if the opportunity offers, so that, if possible, they too become friends. If it cannot achieve this, it does not change its own attitude; it continues to show the fruits of love to all men alike. It was on account of this that our Lord and God Jesus Christ, showing His love for us, suffered for the whole of mankind and gave to all men an equal hope of resurrection, although each man determines his own fitness for glory or punishment.

72. If you are not indifferent to both fame and dishonour, riches and poverty, pleasure and distress, you have not yet acquired perfect love. For perfect love is indifferent not only to these but even to this fleeting life and to death.

73. Listen to the words of those who have been granted perfect love: 'What can separate us from the love of Christ? Can affliction, or distress, or persecution, or famine, or nakedness, or peril, or the sword? As it is written, "For Thy sake we are put to death all the day long; we are regarded as sheep for slaughtering" (Ps. 44 : 22). But in all these things we are more than conquerors through Him that loved us. For I am convinced that neither death, nor life, nor angels, nor principalities, nor powers, nor things present, nor things to come, nor height, nor depth, nor any other created thing, can separate us from the love of God that is in Christ Jesus our Lord' (Rom. 8 : 35–39). Those who speak and act thus with regard to divine love are all saints.

74. Listen now to what they say about love for our neighbour: 'I speak the truth in Christ, I do not lie, my conscience also bears me witness in the Holy Spirit: I have great distress and continual sorrow in my heart. For I could wish that I myself were severed from Christ for the sake of my brethren, my kinsmen according to the flesh, who are Israelites' (Rom. 9 : 1–3). Moses and the other saints speak in a similar manner.

75. He who is not indifferent to fame and pleasure, as well as to the love of riches that exists because of them and increases them, cannot cut off occasions for anger. And he who does not cut these off cannot attain perfect love.

76. Humility and ascetic hardship free a man from all sin, for the one cuts out the passions of the soul, the other those of the body. This is what the blessed David indicates when he prays to God, saying, 'Look on my humility and my toil, and forgive all my sins' (Ps. 25 : 18).

77. It is through our fulfilling of the commandments that the Lord makes us dispassionate; and it is through His divine teachings that He gives us the light of spiritual knowledge.

78. All such teachings are concerned either with God, or with things visible and invisible, or else with the providence and judgment relating to them.

79. Almsgiving heals the soul's incensive power; fasting withers

sensual desire; prayer purifies the intellect and prepares it for the contemplation of created beings. For the Lord has given us commandments which correspond to the powers of the soul.

80. 'Learn from Me', He said, 'for I am gentle and humble in heart' (Matt. 11 : 29). Gentleness keeps the soul's incensive power in a calm state; humility frees the intellect from conceit and self-esteem.

81. Fear of God is of two kinds. The first is generated in us by the threat of punishment. It is through such fear that we develop in due order self-control, patience, hope in God and dispassion; and it is from dispassion that love comes. The second kind of fear is linked with love and constantly produces reverence in the soul, so that it does not grow indifferent to God because of the intimate communion of its love.

82. The first kind of fear is expelled by perfect love when the soul has acquired this and is no longer afraid of punishment (cf. 1 John 4 : 18). The second kind, as we have already said, is always found united with perfect love. The first kind of fear is referred to in the following two verses: 'Out of fear of the Lord men shun evil' (Prov. 16 : 6), and 'Fear of the Lord is the beginning of wisdom' (Ps. 111 : 10). The second kind is mentioned in the following verses: 'Fear of the Lord is pure, and endures for ever' (Ps. 19 : 9. LXX), and 'Those who fear the Lord will not want for anything' (Ps. 34 : 10. LXX).

83. 'Put to death therefore whatever is earthly in you: unchastity, uncleanness, passion, evil desire and greed' (Col. 3 : 5). Earth is the name St Paul gives to the will of the flesh. Unchastity is his word for the actual committing of sin. Uncleanness is how he designates assent to sin. Passion is his term for impassioned thoughts. By evil desire he means the simple act of accepting the thought and the desire. And greed is his name for what generates and promotes passion. All these St Paul ordered us to mortify as 'aspects' expressing the will of the flesh.

84. First the memory brings some passion-free thought into the intellect. By its lingering there, passion is aroused. When the passion is not eradicated, it persuades the intellect to assent to it. Once this assent is given, the actual sin is then committed. Therefore, when writing to converts from paganism, St Paul in his wisdom orders them first to eliminate the actual sin and then systematically to work back to the cause. The cause, as we have already said, is

greed, which generates and promotes passion. I think that greed in this case means gluttony, because this is the mother and nurse of unchastity. For greed is a sin not only with regard to possessions but also with regard to food, just as self-control likewise relates to both food and possessions.

85. When a sparrow tied by the leg tries to fly, it is held back by the string and pulled down to the earth. Similarly, when the intellect that has not yet attained dispassion flies up towards heavenly knowledge, it is held back by the passions and pulled down to the earth.

86. The intellect, once totally free from passions, proceeds undistracted to the contemplation of created beings, making its way towards knowledge of the Holy Trinity.

87. When in a pure state, the intellect, on receiving the conceptual images of things, is moved to contemplate these things spiritually. But when it is sullied through indolence, while its conceptual images may in general be free from passion, those concerned with people produce in it thoughts that are shameful or wicked.

88. When during prayer no conceptual image of anything worldly disturbs your intellect, then know that you are within the realm of dispassion.

89. Once the soul starts to feel its own good health, the images in its dreams are also calm and free from passion.

90. Just as the physical eye is attracted to the beauty of things visible, so the purified intellect is attracted to the knowledge of things invisible. By things invisible, I mean things incorporeal.

91. It is already much not to be roused to any passion by material things. It is even more to remain dispassionate when presented with mental images of such things. For the war which the demons wage against us by means of thoughts is more severe than the war they wage by means of material things.

92. He who has succeeded in attaining the virtues and is enriched with spiritual knowledge sees things clearly in their true nature. Consequently, he both acts and speaks with regard to all things in a manner which is fitting, and he is never deluded. For according to whether we use things rightly or wrongly we become either good or bad.

93. If the conceptual images that continually rise up in the heart are free from passion whether the body is awake or asleep, then we may know that we have attained the highest state of dispassion.

94. Through fulfilling the commandments the intellect strips itself of the passions. Through spiritual contemplation of things visible it casts off impassioned conceptions of such things. Through knowledge of things invisible it discards the contemplation of things visible. Finally it denudes itself even of this through knowledge of the Holy Trinity.

95. When the sun rises and casts its light on the world, it reveals both itself and the things it illumines. Similarly, when the Sun of righteousness rises in the pure intellect, He reveals both Himself and the inner principles of all that has been and will be brought into existence by Him.

96. We do not know God from His essence. We know Him rather from the grandeur of His creation and from His providential care for all creatures. For through these, as though they were mirrors, we may attain insight into His infinite goodness, wisdom and power.

97. The pure intellect is occupied either with passion-free conceptual images of human affairs, or with the natural contemplation of things visible or invisible, or with the light of the Holy Trinity.

98. When the intellect is engaged in the contemplation of things visible, it searches out either the natural principles of these things or the spiritual principles which they reflect, or else it seeks their original cause.

99. When the intellect is absorbed in the contemplation of things invisible, it seeks their natural principles, the cause of their generation and whatever follows from this, as well as the providential order and judgment which relates to them.

100. When the intellect is established in God, it at first ardently longs to discover the principles of His essence. But God's inmost nature does not admit of such investigation, which is indeed beyond the capacity of everything created. The qualities that appertain to His nature, however, are accessible to the intellect's longing: I mean the qualities of eternity, infinity, indeterminateness, goodness, wisdom, and the power of creating, preserving and judging creatures. Yet of these, only infinity may be grasped fully; and the very fact of knowing nothing is knowledge surpassing the intellect, as the theologians Gregory of Nazianzos and Dionysios have said.[1]

---

[1] See Gregory of Nazianzos, *Orations* 38, 7 and 45, 3 (*P.G.* xxxvi, 317BC, 628A); and Dionysios the Areopagite, *Mystical Theology* i, 3 (*P.G.* iii, 1001).

Second Century

1. He who truly loves God prays entirely without distraction, and he who prays entirely without distraction loves God truly. But he whose intellect is fixed on any worldly thing does not pray without distraction, and consequently he does not love God.

2. The intellect that dallies with some sensible thing clearly is attached to it by some passion, such as desire, irritation, anger or rancour; and unless it becomes detached from that thing it will not be able to free itself from the passion affecting it.

3. When passions dominate the intellect, they separate it from God, binding it to material things and preoccupying it with them. But when love of God dominates the intellect, it frees it from its bonds, persuading it to rise above not only sensible things but even this transitory life.

4. The effect of observing the commandments is to free from passion our conceptual images of things. The effect of spiritual reading and contemplation is to detach the intellect from form and matter. It is this which gives rise to undistracted prayer.

5. Unless various successive spiritual contemplations also occupy the intellect, the practice of virtues by itself cannot free it so entirely from passions that it is able to pray undistractedly. Practice of the virtues frees the intellect only from dissipation and hatred; spiritual contemplation releases it also from forgetfulness and ignorance. In this way the intellect can pray as it should.

6. Two states of pure prayer are exalted above all others. One is to be found in those who have not advanced beyond the practice of the virtues, the other in those leading the contemplative life. The first is engendered in the soul by fear of God and a firm hope in Him, the second by an intense longing for God and by total purification. The sign of the first is that the intellect, abandoning all conceptual

images of the world, concentrates itself and prays without distraction or disturbance as if God Himself were present, as indeed He is. The sign of the second is that at the very onset of prayer the intellect is so ravished by the divine and infinite light that it is aware neither of itself nor of any other created thing, but only of Him who through love has activated such radiance in it. It is then that, being made aware of God's qualities, it receives clear and distinct reflections of Him.

7. Whatever a man loves he inevitably clings to, and in order not to lose it he rejects everything that keeps him from it. So he who loves God cultivates pure prayer, driving out every passion that keeps him from it.

8. He who drives out self-love, the mother of the passions, will with God's help easily rid himself of the rest, such as anger, irritation, rancour and so on. But he who is dominated by self-love is overpowered by the other passions, even against his will. Self-love is the passion of attachment to the body.

9. Men love one another, commendably or reprehensibly, for the following five reasons: either for the sake of God, as the virtuous man loves everyone and as the man not yet virtuous loves the virtuous; or by nature, as parents love their children and children their parents; or because of self-esteem, as he who is praised loves the man who praises him; or because of avarice, as with one who loves a rich man for what he can get out of him; or because of self-indulgence, as with the man who serves his belly and his genitals. The first of these is commendable, the second is of an intermediate kind, the rest are dominated by passion.

10. If there are some men you hate and some you neither love nor hate, and others you love strongly and others again you love but moderately, recognize from this inequality that you are far from perfect love. For perfect love presupposes that you love all men equally.

11. 'Shun evil and do good' (Ps. 34 : 14), that is to say, fight the enemy in order to diminish the passions, and then be vigilant lest they increase once more. Again, fight to acquire the virtues and then be vigilant in order to keep them. This is the meaning of 'cultivating' and 'keeping' (cf. Gen. 2 : 15).

12. Those permitted by God to test us either inflame the desiring aspect of the soul, or stir up its incensive power, or darken its in-

telligence, or envelop its body in pain, or deprive us of bodily necessities.

13. The demons either tempt us themselves or arm against us those who have no fear of the Lord. They tempt us themselves when we withdraw from human society, as they tempted our Lord in the desert. They tempt us through other people when we spend our time in the company of others, as they tempted our Lord through the Pharisees. But whichever line of attack they choose, let us repel them by keeping our gaze fixed on the Lord's example.

14. When the intellect begins to advance in love for God, the demon of blasphemy starts to tempt it, suggesting thoughts such as no man but only the devil, their father, could invent. He does this out of envy, so that the man of God, in his despair at thinking such thoughts, no longer dares to soar up to God in his accustomed prayer. But the demon does not further his own ends by this means. On the contrary, he makes us more steadfast. For through his attacks and our retaliation we grow more experienced and genuine in our love for God. May his sword enter into his own heart and may his bows be broken (cf. Ps. 37 : 15).

15. When the intellect turns its attention to the visible world, it perceives things through the medium of the senses in a way that accords with nature. And the intellect is not evil, nor is its natural capacity to form conceptual images of things, nor are the things themselves, nor are the senses, for all are the work of God. What, then, is evil? Clearly it is the passion that enters into the conceptual images formed in accordance with nature by the intellect; and this need not happen if the intellect keeps watch.

16. Passion is an impulse of the soul contrary to nature, as in the case of mindless love or mindless hatred for someone or for some sensible thing. In the case of love, it may be for needless food, or for a woman, or for money, or for transient glory, or for other sensible objects or on their account. In the case of hatred, it may be for any of the things mentioned, or for someone on account of these things.

17. Again, vice is the wrong use of our conceptual images of things, which leads us to misuse the things themselves. In relation to women, for example, sexual intercourse, rightly used, has as its purpose the begetting of children. He, therefore, who seeks in it only sensual pleasure uses it wrongly, for he reckons as good what is

not good. When such a man has intercourse with a woman, he mis-
uses her. And the same is true with regard to other things and our
conceptual images of them.

18. When the demons expel self-restraint from your intellect
and besiege you with thoughts of unchastity, turn to the Lord with
tears and say, 'Now they have driven me out and encircled me' (Ps.
17 : 11. LXX); 'Thou art my supreme joy: deliver me from those
who encircle me' (Ps. 32 : 7. LXX). Then you will be safe.

19. The demon of unchastity is powerful and violently attacks
those who struggle against passion, particularly if they are lax about
matters of diet and often meet women. With the lubricity of sensual
pleasure he imperceptibly steals into the intellect and thereafter
persecutes the hesychast by means of the memory, setting his body
on fire and presenting various forms to his intellect. In this way he
evokes his assent to sin. If you do not want these forms to linger in
you, turn again to fasting, labour, vigils and blessed stillness with
intense prayer.

20. Those who are always trying to lay hold of our soul do so by
means of impassioned thoughts, so that they may drive it to sin
either in the mind or in action. Consequently, when they find the
intellect unreceptive, they will be disgraced and put to shame; and
when they find the intellect occupied with spiritual contemplation,
they will 'be turned back and suddenly ashamed' (Ps. 6 : 10).

21. He who anoints his intellect for spiritual contest and drives
all impassioned thoughts out of it has the quality of a deacon. He
who illuminates his intellect with the knowledge of created beings
and utterly destroys false knowledge has the quality of a priest. And
he who perfects his intellect with the holy myrrh of the knowledge
and worship of the Holy Trinity has the quality of a bishop.

22. The demons are weakened when the passions in us decrease
through our keeping the commandments; and they are defeated
totally when they are routed by dispassion, for then they no longer
find anything through which they can enter the soul and fight
against it. This is what is meant by 'they will be weakened and defeated before Thy face' (Ps. 9 : 3).

23. Some men abstain from the passions because of human fear,
others because of self-esteem, and others through self-control.
Some, however, are delivered from the passions by divine providence.

24. All the discourses of our Lord contain these four elements: commandments, doctrines, threats and promises. With the help of these we patiently accept every kind of hardship, such as fasting, vigils, sleeping on the ground, toil and labour in acts of service, insults, dishonour, torture, death and so on. 'Helped by the words of Thy lips,' says the psalmist, 'I have kept to difficult paths' (Ps. 17 : 4. LXX).

25. The reward of self-control is dispassion, and the reward of faith is spiritual knowledge. Dispassion engenders discrimination, and spiritual knowledge engenders love for God.

26. When the intellect practises the virtues correctly, it advances in moral understanding. When it practises contemplation, it advances in spiritual knowledge. The first leads the spiritual contestant to discriminate between virtue and vice; the second leads the participant to the inner qualities of incorporeal and corporeal things. Finally, the intellect is granted the grace of theology when, carried on wings of love beyond these two former stages, it is taken up into God and with the help of the Holy Spirit discerns – as far as this is possible for the human intellect – the qualities of God.

27. If you are about to enter the realm of theology, do not seek to descry God's inmost nature, for neither the human intellect nor that of any other being under God can experience this; but try to discern, as far as possible, the qualities that appertain to His nature – qualities of eternity, infinity, indeterminateness, goodness, wisdom, and the power of creating, preserving and judging creatures, and so on. For he who discovers these qualities, to however small an extent, is a great theologian.

28. He who combines the practice of the virtues with spiritual knowledge is a man of power. For with the first he withers his desire and tames his incensiveness, and with the second he gives wings to his intellect and goes out of himself to God.

29. When our Lord says, 'I and My Father are one' (John 10 : 30), He indicates their identity of essence. Again, when He says, 'I am in the Father, and the Father in Me' (John 14 : 11), He shows that the Persons cannot be divided. The tritheists,[1] therefore, who divide the Son from the Father, find themselves in a dilemma. Either they say that the Son is coeternal with the Father, but nevertheless

---

[1] Here St Maximos is attacking the theories of John Philoponos (6th century).

divide Him from the Father, and so they are forced to say that He is not begotten from the Father; thus they fall into the error of claiming that there are three Gods and three first principles. Or else they say that the Son is begotten from the Father but nevertheless divide Him from the Father, and so they are forced to say that He is not coeternal with the Father; thus they make the Lord of time subject to time. For, as St Gregory of Nazianzos says,[1] it is necessary both to maintain the one God and to confess the three Persons, each in His own individuality. According to St Gregory, the Divinity is divided but without division and is united but with distinctions. Because of this both the division and the union are paradoxical. For what paradox would there be if the Son were united to the Father and divided from Him only in the same manner as one human being is united to and divided from another, and nothing more?

30. For him who is perfect in love and has reached the summit of dispassion there is no difference between his own or another's, or between Christians and unbelievers, or between slave and free, or even between male and female. But because he has risen above the tyranny of the passions and has fixed his attention on the single nature of man, he looks on all in the same way and shows the same disposition to all. For in him there is neither Greek nor Jew, male nor female, bond nor free, but Christ who 'is all, and in all' (Col. 3 : 11; cf. Gal. 3 : 28).

31. The passions lying hidden in the soul provide the demons with the means of arousing impassioned thoughts in us. Then, fighting the intellect through these thoughts, they force it to give its assent to sin. When it has been overcome, they lead it to sin in the mind; and when this has been done they induce it, captive as it is, to commit the sin in action. Having thus desolated the soul by means of these thoughts, the demons then retreat, taking the thoughts with them, and only the spectre or idol of sin remains in the intellect. Referring to this our Lord says, 'When you see the abominable idol of desolation standing in the holy place (let him who reads understand) . . .' (Matt. 24 : 15). For man's intellect is a holy place and a temple of God in which the demons, having desolated the soul by means of impassioned thoughts, set up the idol of sin. That these things have already taken place in history no one, I think,

[1] *Orations* 20, 6 (*P.G.* xxxv, 1072D); 25, 17 (1221C); 28, 1 (*P.G.* xxxvi, 28A); 31, 14 (149A).

who has read Josephus[1] will doubt; though some say that they will also come to pass in the time of the Antichrist.

32. There are three things that impel us towards what is holy: natural instincts, angelic powers and probity of intention. Natural instincts impel us when, for example, we do to others what we would wish them to do to us (cf. Luke 6 : 31), or when we see someone suffering deprivation or in need and naturally feel compassion. Angelic powers impel us when, being ourselves impelled to something worthwhile, we find we are providentially helped and guided. We are impelled by probity of intention when, discriminating between good and evil, we choose the good.

33. There are also three things that impel us towards evil: passions, demons and sinfulness of intention. Passions impel us when, for example, we desire something beyond what is reasonable, such as food which is unnecessary or untimely, or a woman who is not our wife or for a purpose other than procreation, or else when we are excessively angered or irritated by, for instance, someone who has dishonoured or injured us. Demons impel us when, for example, they catch us off our guard and suddenly launch a violent attack upon us, stirring up the passions already mentioned and others of a similar nature. We are impelled by sinfulness of intention when, knowing the good, we choose evil instead.

34. The rewards for the toils of virtue are dispassion and spiritual knowledge. For these are mediators of the kingdom of heaven, just as passions and ignorance are mediators of eternal punishment. It is because of this that he who seeks these rewards for the sake of human glory and not for their intrinsic goodness is rebuked by the words of Scripture, 'You ask, and do not receive, because you ask wrongly' (Jas. 4 : 3).

35. Many human activities, good in themselves, are not good because of the motive for which they are done. For example, fasting and vigils, prayer and psalmody, acts of charity and hospitality are by nature good, but when performed for the sake of self-esteem they are not good.

36. In everything that we do God searches out our purpose to see whether we do it for Him or for some other motive.

37. When you hear the words of Scripture, 'Thou shalt render to

[1] Jewish historian of the first century AD; see especially his *Jewish War* VI, iv, 3–5; VII, i, 3.

every man according to his work' (Ps. 62 : 12. LXX), do not think
that God bestows blessings when something is done for the wrong
purpose, even though it seems to be good. Quite clearly He bestows
blessings only when something is done for the right purpose. For God's
judgment looks not at the actions but at the purpose behind them.

38. The malice of the demon of pride takes two forms. Either he
persuades the monk to ascribe his achievements to himself and not
to God, the Giver of all goodness and helper in every achievement;
or, if this fails, he suggests that he should belittle those of his
brethren who are as yet less perfect than himself. Influenced in this
way, he does not realize that the demon is persuading him to deny
God's help. For if he belittles his brethren for their lack of achievement, he clearly infers that he has achieved something through his
own powers. But this is impossible, since, as our Lord has said,
'Without Me you can do nothing' (John 15 : 5). For even when
impelled towards what is good, our weakness cannot bring anything
to fruition without the Giver of all goodness.

39. The person who has come to know the weakness of human
nature has gained experience of divine power. Such a man, having
achieved some things and eager to achieve others through this divine
power, never belittles anyone. For he knows that just as God has
helped him and freed him from many passions and difficulties, so,
when God wishes, He is able to help all men, especially those pursuing the spiritual way for His sake. And if in His providence He
does not deliver all men together from their passions, yet like a good
and loving physician He heals with individual treatment each of those
who are trying to make progress.

40. We grow proud when the passions cease to be active in us,
and this whether they are inactive because their causes have been
eradicated or because the demons have deliberately withdrawn in
order to deceive us.

41. Almost every sin is committed for the sake of sensual
pleasure; and sensual pleasure is overcome by hardship and distress
arising either voluntarily from repentance, or else involuntarily as a
result of some salutary and providential reversal. 'For if we would
judge ourselves, we should not be judged; but when we are judged,
we are chastened by the Lord, so that we should not be condemned
with the world' (1 Cor. 11 : 31–32).

42. When a trial comes upon you unexpectedly, do not blame

the person through whom it came but try to discover the reason why it came, and then you will find a way of dealing with it. For whether through this person or through someone else you had in any case to drink the wormwood of God's judgments.

43. As long as you have bad habits do not reject hardship, so that through it you may be humbled and eject your pride.

44. Sometimes men are tested by pleasure, sometimes by distress or by physical suffering. By means of His prescriptions the Physician of souls administers the remedy according to the cause of the passions lying hidden in the soul.

45. Trials are sent to some so as to take away past sins, to others so as to eradicate sins now being committed, and to yet others so as to forestall sins which may be committed in the future. These are distinct from the trials that arise in order to test men in the way that Job was tested.

46. The sensible man, taking into account the remedial effect of the divine prescriptions, gladly bears the sufferings which they bring upon him, since he is aware that they have no cause other than his own sin. But when the fool, ignorant of the supreme wisdom of God's providence, sins and is corrected, he regards either God or men as responsible for the hardships he suffers.

47. Certain things stop the movement of the passions and do not allow them to grow; others subdue them and make them diminish. For instance, where desire is concerned, fasting, labour and vigils do not allow it to grow, while withdrawal, contemplation, prayer and intense longing for God subdue it and make it disappear. The same is true with regard to anger. Forbearance, freedom from rancour, gentleness, for example, all arrest it and prevent it from growing, while love, acts of charity, kindness and compassion make it diminish.

48. When a man's intellect is constantly with God, his desire grows beyond all measure into an intense longing for God and his incensiveness is completely transformed into divine love. For by continual participation in the divine radiance his intellect becomes totally filled with light; and when it has reintegrated its passible aspect, it redirects this aspect towards God, as we have said, filling it with an incomprehensible and intense longing for Him and with unceasing love, thus drawing it entirely away from worldly things to the divine.

49. If a man is not envious or angry, and does not bear a grudge against someone who has offended him, that does not necessarily mean that he loves him. For, while still lacking love, he may be capable of not repaying evil with evil, in accordance with the commandment (cf. Rom. 12 : 17), and yet by no means be capable of rendering good for evil without forcing himself. To be spontaneously disposed to 'do good to those who you hate you' (Matt. 5 : 44) belongs to perfect spiritual love alone.

50. If a man does not love someone, it does not necessarily mean that he hates him; and conversely, if he does not hate him, it does not necessarily mean that he loves him, since he can be neutral towards him, that is, neither love him nor hate him. For the disposition to love is created only in the five ways listed in the ninth text of this Century, one commendable, one of an intermediate kind, and three reprehensible.

51. When you find your intellect occupied pleasurably with material things and becoming fondly attached to its conceptual images of them, you may be sure that you love these things more than God. 'For where your treasure is, there will your heart be also' (Matt. 6 : 21).

52. The intellect joined to God for long periods through prayer and love becomes wise, good, powerful, compassionate, merciful and long-suffering; in short, it includes within itself almost all the divine qualities. But when the intellect withdraws from God and attaches itself to material things, either it becomes self-indulgent like some domestic animal, or like a wild beast it fights with men for the sake of these things.

53. Scripture calls material things 'the world'; and worldly men are those who occupy their intellect with these things. It is such men that Scripture rebukes when it says: 'Do not love the world or the things that are in the world . . . The desire of the flesh, and the desire of the eyes, and pride in one's possessions, are not of God but of the world' (cf. 1 John 2 : 15–16).

54. A monk is a man who has freed his intellect from attachment to material things and by means of self-control, love, psalmody and prayer cleaves to God.

55. The herdsman signifies the man practising the virtues, for moral achievements may be represented by cattle. That is why Jacob said, 'Your servants are herdsmen' (Gen. 46 : 34). The

shepherd signifies the gnostic, for sheep represent thoughts pastured by the intellect on the mountains of contemplation. That is why 'every shepherd is an abomination to the Egyptians' (Gen. 46 : 34), that is, to the demonic powers.

56. When the body is urged by the senses to indulge its own desires and pleasures, the corrupted intellect readily succumbs and assents to its impassioned fantasies and impulses. But the regenerated intellect exercises self-control and withholds itself from them. Moreover, as a true philosopher it studies how to rectify such impulses.

57. There are virtues of the body and virtues of the soul. Those of the body include fasting, vigils, sleeping on the ground, ministering to people's needs, working with one's hands so as not to be a burden or in order to give to others (cf. 1 Thess. 2 : 9, Ephes. 4 : 28). Those of the soul include love, long-suffering, gentleness, self-control and prayer (cf. Gal. 5 : 22). If as a result of some constraint or bodily condition, such as illness or the like, we find we cannot practise the bodily virtues mentioned above, we are forgiven by the Lord because He knows the reasons. But if we fail to practise the virtues of the soul, we shall not have a single excuse, for it is always within our power to practise them.

58. Love for God leads him who shares in it to be indifferent to every transient pleasure and every labour and distress. Let all the saints, who have suffered joyfully so much for Christ, convince you of this.

59. Guard yourself from that mother of vices, self-love, which is mindless love for the body. For it gives birth with specious justification to the three first and most general of the impassioned thoughts. I mean those of gluttony, avarice and self-esteem, which take as their pretext some so-called need of the body. All further vices are generated by these three. You must therefore be on your guard, as we have already said, and fight against self-love with great vigilance. For when this vice is eradicated, all the others are eradicated too.

60. The passion of self-love suggests to the monk that he should have pity on his body and in the name of its proper care and governance should take food more often than is fitting; for in this way self-love will lead him on step by step to fall into the pit of self-indulgence. On the other hand, self-love prompts those who are not monks to fulfil the body's desires at once.

61. It is said that the highest state of prayer is reached when the intellect goes beyond the flesh and the world, and while praying is utterly free from matter and form. He who maintains this state has truly attained unceasing prayer.

62. When the body dies, it is wholly separated from the things of this world. Similarly, when the intellect dies while in that supreme state of prayer, it is separated from all conceptual images of this world. If it does not die such a death, it cannot be with God and live with Him.

63. Let no one deceive you, monk, with the notion that you can be saved while a slave to sensual pleasure and self-esteem.

64. When the body sins through material things, it has the bodily virtues to teach it self-restraint. Similarly, when the intellect sins through impassioned conceptual images, it has the virtues of the soul to instruct it, so that by seeing things in a pure and dispassionate way, it too may learn self-restraint.

65. Just as night follows day and winter summer, so distress and pain follow self-esteem and sensual pleasure, either in this life or after death.

66. No sinner can escape future judgment without experiencing in this life either voluntary hardships or afflictions he has not chosen.

67. There are said to be five reasons why God allows us to be assailed by demons. The first is so that, by attacking and counter-attacking, we should learn to discriminate between virtue and vice. The second is so that, having acquired virtue through conflict and toil, we should keep it secure and immutable. The third is so that, when making progress in virtue, we should not become haughty but learn humility. The fourth is so that, having gained some experience of evil, we should 'hate it with perfect hatred' (cf. Ps. 139 : 22). The fifth and most important is so that, having achieved dispassion, we should forget neither our own weakness nor the power of Him who has helped us.

68. Just as the intellect of a hungry man imagines bread and that of a thirsty man water, so the intellect of a glutton imagines a profusion of foods, that of a sensualist the forms of women, that of a vain man worldly honour, that of an avaricious man financial gain, that of a rancorous man revenge on whoever has offended him, that of an envious man how to harm the object of his envy, and so on with all the other passions. For an intellect agitated by passions is beset by

impassioned conceptual images whether the body is awake or asleep.

69. When desire grows strong, the intellect in sleep imagines things that give sensual pleasure; and when the incensive power grows strong, it imagines things that cause fear. For the impure demons, finding an ally in our negligence, strengthen and excite the passions. But holy angels, by inducing us to perform works of virtue, make them weaker.

70. When the desiring aspect of the soul is frequently excited, it implants in the soul a habit of self-indulgence which is difficult to break. When the soul's incensive power is constantly stimulated, it becomes in the end cowardly and unmanly. The first of these failings is cured by long exercise in fasting, vigils and prayer; the second by kindness, compassion, love and mercy.

71. The demons fight against us either through things themselves or through our impassioned conceptual images of these things. They fight through things against those who are occupied with things and through conceptual images against those who are not attached to things.

72. Just as it is easier to sin in the mind than in action, so warfare through our impassioned conceptual images of things is harder than warfare through the things themselves.

73. Things are outside the intellect, but the conceptual images of these things are formed within it. It is consequently in the intellect's power to make good or bad use of these conceptual images. Their wrong use is followed by the misuse of the things themselves.

74. The intellect receives impassioned conceptual images in three ways: through the senses, through the body's condition and through the memory. It receives them through the senses when the senses themselves receive impressions from things in relation to which we have acquired passion, and when these things stir up impassioned thoughts in the intellect; through the body's condition when, as a result either of an undisciplined way of life, or of the activity of demons, or of some illness, the balance of elements in the body is disturbed and again the intellect is stirred to impassioned thoughts or to thoughts contrary to providence; through the memory when the memory recalls the conceptual images of things in relation to which we were once made passionate, and so stirs up impassioned thoughts in a similar way.

75. Some of the things given to us by God for our use are in the soul, others are in the body and others relate to the body. In the soul are its powers; in the body are the sense organs and other members; relating to the body are food, money, possessions and so on. Our good or bad use of these things given us by God, or of what is contingent upon them, reveals whether we are virtuous or evil.

76. Of the things contingent upon those given us by God, some are in the soul, some are in the body, and some relate to the body. Those in the soul are spiritual knowledge and ignorance, forgetfulness and memory, love and hate, fear and courage, distress and joy, and so on. Those in the body are pleasure and pain, sensation and numbness, health and disease, life and death, and so on. Those relating to the body are having children and not having children, wealth and poverty, fame and obscurity, and so on. Some of these are regarded as good and others as evil. Not one of them is evil in itself. According to how they are used they may rightly be called good or evil.

77. Both spiritual knowledge and health are good by nature, yet their contraries have been of more benefit to many people. For such knowledge may serve no good purpose where the wicked are concerned, even though, as we have said, it is good in itself. The same is true with regard to health, riches and joy, for they are not used advantageously by such people. But certainly their contraries do benefit them. Therefore not one of them is evil in itself, even though it may appear to be evil.

78. Do not misuse your conceptual images of things, lest you are forced to make a wrong use of the things themselves. For if a man does not first sin in his mind, he will never sin in action.

79. The principal vices – stupidity, cowardice, licentiousness, injustice – are the 'image' of the 'earthy' man. The principal virtues – intelligence, courage, self-restraint, justice – are the 'image' of the 'heavenly' man. As we have borne the image of the earthy, let us also bear the image of the heavenly (cf. 1 Cor. 15 : 49).

80. If you wish to find the way that leads to life, look for it in the Way who says, 'I am the way, the door, the truth and the life' (John 10 : 7; 14 : 6), and there you will find it. Only let your search be diligent and painstaking, for 'few there are that find it' (Matt. 7 : 14) and if you are not among the few you will find yourself with the many.

81. Five things make a soul cut itself off from sin: fear of men, fear of judgment, hope of future reward, love of God and, lastly, the prompting of conscience.

82. Some say that there would be no evil in the created world unless there were some power outside this world dragging us towards evil. But this so-called power is in fact our neglect of the natural energies of the intellect. For those who nurture these energies always do good, never evil. If this, then, is what you too wish to do, get rid of negligence and you will also drive out evil, which is the wrong use of our conceptual images of things, followed by the wrong use of the things themselves.

83. In its natural state, the human intelligence is subject to the divine intelligence and itself rules over the non-intelligent element in us. Let this order be maintained in all things, and there will be no evil among creatures nor anything which draws us towards evil.

84. Some thoughts are simple, others are composite. Thoughts which are not impassioned are simple. Passion-charged thoughts are composite, consisting as they do of a conceptual image combined with passion. This being so, when composite thoughts begin to provoke a sinful idea in the mind, many simple thoughts may be seen to follow them. For instance, an impassioned thought about gold rises in someone's mind. He has the urge mentally to steal the gold and commits the sin in his intellect. Then thoughts of the purse, the chest, the room and so on follow hard on the thought of the gold. The thought of the gold was composite – for it was combined with passion – but those of the purse, the chest and so on were simple; for the intellect had no passion in relation to these things. And the same is true for every thought – thoughts of self-esteem, women and so on. For not all thoughts which follow impassioned thought are themselves impassioned, as our example has shown. From this, then, we may know which conceptual images are impassioned and which are not.

85. Some say that the demons first touch the genitals during sleep and so arouse the passion of unchastity. Once aroused, the passion, by means of the memory, brings the form of a woman into the intellect. But others say that the demons appear first to the intellect in the guise of a woman and then excite the appetite by touching the genitals and so fantasies arise. Yet others say that the passion dominant in the approaching demon stirs the corresponding

passion in us, and thus the soul is incited to sinful thoughts and brings these female forms into the intellect by means of the memory. The same is true with regard to other impassioned fantasies. Some say they happen in one way, others in another. However, if love and self-control are present in the soul, the demons have no power to arouse any passion at all in any of the ways described, whether the body is awake or asleep.

86. Some commandments of the Mosaic Law must be kept both physically and spiritually, others only spiritually. For example, 'You shall not commit adultery, you shall not kill, you shall not steal' (Exod. 20 : 13–15) and so on must be kept both physically and spiritually (the spiritual observance is threefold, as explained below). To be circumcised (cf. Lev. 12 : 3), to keep the sabbath (cf. Exod. 31 : 13), and to slaughter the lamb and eat unleavened bread with bitter herbs (cf. Exod. 12 : 8; 23 : 15) and similar injunctions are to be kept only spiritually.

87. There are three main inner states characterizing the life of the monk. The first consists in not sinning in actions; the second in not allowing the soul to dally with impassioned thoughts; the third in being able to contemplate dispassionately in the mind the forms of women and of those who have given one offence.

88. A man who is truly without possessions is one who has renounced all his worldly goods and has absolutely nothing on earth except his body; and who, breaking his attachment to the body, has entrusted himself to the care of God and of the devout.

89. Some people with possessions possess them dispassionately, and so when deprived of them they are not dismayed but are like those who accepted the seizure of their goods with joy (cf. Heb. 10 : 34). Others possess with passion, so that when they are in danger of being dispossessed they become utterly dejected, like the rich man in the Gospel who went away full of sorrow (cf. Matt. 19 : 22); and if they actually are dispossessed, they remain dejected until they die. Dispossession, then, reveals whether a man's inner state is dispassionate or dominated by passion.

90. The demons attack the person who has attained the summits of prayer in order to prevent his conceptual images of sensible things from being free from passion; they attack the gnostic so that he will dally with impassioned thoughts; and they attack the person who has not advanced beyond the practice of the virtues so as to persuade

him to sin through his actions. They contend with all men by every possible means in order to separate them from God.

91. Those whom divine providence is leading towards holiness in this life are tested by the following three tests: by the gift of agreeable things, such as health, beauty, fine children, money, fame and so on; by afflictions causing distress, such as the loss of children, money and fame; and by bodily sufferings, such as disease, torture and so on. To those in the first category the Lord says, 'If a person does not forsake all that he has, he cannot be My disciple' (Luke 14 : 33); and to those in the second and third He says, 'You will gain possession of your souls through your patient endurance' (Luke 21 : 19).

92. The following four things are said to change the body's temperament and through it to produce either impassioned or dispassionate thoughts in the intellect: angels, demons, the winds and diet. It is said that angels change it by thought, demons by touch, the winds by varying, and diet by the quality of our food and drink and by whether we eat too much or too little. There are also changes brought about by means of memory, hearing and sight – namely when the soul is affected by joyful or distressing experiences as a result of one of these three means, and then changes the body's temperament. Thus changed, this temperament in its turn induces corresponding thoughts in the intellect.

93. Death in the true sense is separation from God, and 'the sting of death is sin' (1 Cor. 15 : 56). Adam, who received the sting, became at the same time an exile from the tree of life, from paradise and from God (cf. Gen. 3); and this was necessarily followed by the body's death. Life, in the true sense, is He who said, 'I am the life' (John 11 : 25), and who, having entered into death, led back to life him who had died.

94. A man writes either to assist his memory, or to help others, or for both reasons; or else he writes in order to injure certain people, or to show off, or out of necessity.

95. In Psalm 23, 'green pasture' represents the practice of the virtues; 'water of refreshment', spiritual knowledge of created things.

96. 'The shadow of death' is human life. Therefore if a man is with God and God is with him, clearly he is able to say, 'Though I walk through the midst of the shadow of death, I will fear no evil, for Thou art with me'.

97. A pure intellect sees things correctly. A trained intelligence puts them in order. A keen hearing takes in what is said. He who is lacking in these three qualities insults the person who has spoken.

98. He who knows the Holy Trinity, the Trinity's creation, and providence, and who has brought his soul's passible aspect into a state of dispassion, is with God.

99. Again in Psalm 23 'the rod' is said to signify God's judgment and 'the staff' His providence. So he who has received spiritual knowledge of these things is able to say, 'Thy rod and Thy staff have comforted me.'

100. When the intellect is stripped of passions and illuminated with the contemplation of created beings, then it can enter into God and pray as it should.

Third Century

1. An intelligent use of conceptual images and their corresponding physical objects produces self-restraint, love and spiritual knowledge; an unintelligent use produces licentiousness, hatred and ignorance.

2. 'You have prepared a table before me . . .' (Ps. 23 : 5). In this passage, 'table' stands for the practice of the virtues, for this has been prepared for us by Christ to use 'against those who afflict' us. The 'oil' anointing the intellect is the contemplation of created things. The 'cup' of God is the knowledge of God. His 'mercy' is His divine Logos. For through His incarnation the Logos pursues us 'all the days' until He overtakes all those who are to be saved, as He did in the case of Paul (cf. Phil. 3 : 12). The 'house' is the kingdom in which all the saints will dwell. 'Length of days' means eternal life.

3. When we misuse the soul's powers their evil aspects dominate us. For instance, misuse of our power of intelligence results in ignorance and stupidity; misuse of our incensive power and of our desire produces hatred and licentiousness. The proper use of these powers produces spiritual knowledge, moral judgment, love and self-restraint. This being so, nothing created and given existence by God is evil.

4. It is not food that is evil but gluttony, not the begetting of children but unchastity, not material things but avarice, not esteem but self-esteem. This being so, it is only the misuse of things that is evil, and such misuse occurs when the intellect fails to cultivate its natural powers.

5. Among the demons, says the blessed Dionysios,[1] evil takes the form of mindless anger, desire uncontrolled by the intellect, and

---

[1] Dionysios the Areopagite, *On the Divine Names* iv, 23 (*P.G.* iii, 725B).

impetuous imagination. But mindlessness, lack of intellectual control and impetuosity in intelligent beings are privations of intelligence, intellect and circumspection. But a privation is posterior to the possession of something. There was a time, then, when the demons possessed intelligence, intellect and devout circumspection. This being the case, not even the demons are evil by nature, but they have become evil through the misuse of their natural powers.

6. Some of the passions produce licentiousness, some hatred, while others produce both dissipation and hatred.

7. Overeating and gluttony cause licentiousness. Avarice and self-esteem cause one to hate one's neighbour. Self-love, the mother of vices, is the cause of all these things.

8. Self-love is an impassioned, mindless love for one's body. Its opposite is love and self-control. A man dominated by self-love is dominated by all the passions.

9. 'No man has ever hated his own flesh', says the Apostle (Eph. 5 : 29), but he disciplines it and makes it his servant (cf. 1 Cor. 9 : 27), allowing it nothing but food and clothing (cf. 1 Tim. 6 : 8), and then only what is necessary for life. In this way a man loves his flesh dispassionately and nourishes it and cares for it as a servant of divine things, supplying it only with what meets its basic needs.

10. If a man loves someone, he naturally makes every effort to be of service to that person. If, then, a man loves God, he naturally strives to conform to His will. But if he loves the flesh, he panders to the flesh.

11. Love, self-restraint, contemplation and prayer accord with God's will, while gluttony, licentiousness and things that increase them pander to the flesh. That is why 'they that are in the flesh cannot conform to God's will' (Rom. 8 : 8). But 'they that are Christ's have crucified the flesh together with the passions and desires' (Gal. 5 : 24).

12. If the intellect inclines to God, it treats the body as its servant and provides it with no more than it needs to sustain life. But if it inclines to the flesh, it becomes the servant of the passions and is always thinking about how to fulfil its desires.

13. If you wish to master your thoughts, concentrate on the passions and you will easily drive the thoughts arising from them out of your intellect. With regard to unchastity, for instance, fast and keep vigils, labour and avoid meeting people. With regard to anger

and resentment, be indifferent to fame, dishonour and material things. With regard to rancour, pray for him who has offended you and you will be delivered.

14. Do not compare yourself with weaker men but rather apply yourself to fulfilling the commandment of love. For by comparing yourself with the weak you will fall into the pit of conceit, but by applying yourself to the commandment of love you will reach the height of humility.

15. If you totally fulfil the command to love your neighbour, you will feel no bitterness or resentment against him whatever he does. If this is not the case, then the reason why you fight against your brother is clearly because you seek after transitory things and prefer them to the commandment of love.

16. It is not so much because of need that gold has become an object of desire among men, as because of the power it gives most people to indulge in sensual pleasure.

17. There are three things which produce love of material wealth: self-indulgence, self-esteem and lack of faith. Lack of faith is more dangerous than the other two.

18. The self-indulgent person loves wealth because it enables him to live comfortably; the person full of self-esteem loves it because through it he can gain the esteem of others; the person who lacks faith loves it because, fearful of starvation, old age, disease, or exile, he can save it and hoard it. He puts his trust in wealth rather than in God, the Creator who provides for all creation, down to the least of living things.

19. There are four kinds of men who hoard wealth: the three already mentioned and the treasurer or bursar. Clearly, it is only the last who conserves it for a good purpose – namely, so as always to have the means of supplying each person's basic needs.

20. All impassioned thoughts either stimulate the soul's desiring power, or disturb its incensive power, or darken its intelligence. It is in this way that the intellect's capacity for spiritual contemplation and for the ecstasy of prayer is dulled. And for this reason a monk, especially the hesychast, must pay close attention to such thoughts, searching out and eliminating their causes. For example, the soul's power of desire is stimulated by impassioned thoughts of women. Such thoughts are caused by intemperance in eating and drinking, and by frequent and senseless talk with the women in question; and

they are cut off by hunger, thirst, vigils and withdrawal from human society. Again, the incensive power is disturbed by impassioned thoughts about those who have offended us. This is caused by self-indulgence, self-esteem and love of material things. For it is on account of such vices that the passion-dominated man feels resentment, being frustrated or otherwise failing to attain what he wants. These thoughts are cut off when the vices provoking them are rejected and nullified through the love of God.

21. God knows Himself and He knows the things He has created. The angelic powers, too, know God and know the things He has created. But they do not know God and the things He has created in the same way that God knows Himself and the things He has created.

22. God knows Himself through knowing His blessed essence. And the things created by Him He knows through knowing His wisdom, by means of which and in which He made all things. But the angelic powers know God by participation, though God Himself transcends such participation; and the things He has created they know by apprehending that which may be spiritually contemplated in them.

23. Although the intellect apprehends its vision of created things within itself, they are actually outside it. This is not the case with respect to God's knowledge of created things, for He is eternal, infinite and undetermined, and has bestowed on everything that exists its being, well-being and eternal being.

24. Natures endowed with intelligence and intellect participate in God through their very being, through their capacity for well-being, that is for goodness and wisdom, and through the grace that gives them eternal being. This, then, is how they know God. They know God's creation, as we have said, by apprehending the harmonious wisdom to be contemplated in it. This wisdom is apprehended by the intellect in a non-material way, and has no independent existence of its own.

25. When God brought into being natures endowed with intelligence and intellect He communicated to them, in His supreme goodness, four of the divine attributes by which He sustains, protects and preserves created things. These attributes are being, eternal being, goodness and wisdom. Of the four He granted the first two, being and eternal being, to their essence, and the second two, goodness and wisdom, to their volitive faculty, so that what He is in

His essence the creature may become by participation. This is why man is said to have been created in the image and likeness of God (cf. Gen. 1 : 26). He is made in the image of God, since his being is in the image of God's being, and his eternal being is in the image of God's eternal being (in the sense that, though not without origin, it is nevertheless without end). He is also made in the likeness of God, since he is good in the likeness of God's goodness, and wise in the likeness of God's wisdom, God being good and wise by nature, and man by grace. Every intelligent nature is in the image of God, but only the good and the wise attain His likeness.

26. All beings endowed with intelligence and intellect are either angelic or human. All angelic beings may be subdivided further into two general moral categories or classes, the holy and the accursed – that is, the holy powers and the impure demons. All human beings may also be divided into two moral categories only, the godly and the ungodly.

27. Since God is absolute existence, absolute goodness and absolute wisdom, or rather, to put it more exactly, since God is beyond all such things, there is nothing whatsoever that is opposite to Him. Creatures, on the other hand, all exist through participation and grace, while those endowed with intelligence and intellect also have a capacity for goodness and wisdom. Hence they do have opposites. As the opposite to existence they have non-existence, and as the opposite to the capacity for goodness and wisdom they have evil and ignorance. Whether or not they are to exist eternally lies within the power of their Maker. But whether or not intelligent creatures are to participate in His goodness and wisdom depends on their own will.

28. The ancient Greek philosophers say that the being of created things has coexisted with God from all eternity and that God has only given it its qualities. They say that this being itself has no opposite, and that opposition lies only in the qualities. But we maintain that only the divine essence has no opposite, since it is eternal and infinite and bestows eternity on other things. The being of created things, on the other hand, has non-being as its opposite. Whether or not it exists eternally depends on the power of Him who alone exists in a substantive sense. But since 'the gifts of God are irrevocable' (Rom. 11 : 29), the being of created things always is and always will be sustained by His almighty power, even though it

has, as we said, an opposite; for it has been brought into being from non-being, and whether or not it exists depends on the will of God.

29. Just as evil is a privation of good, and ignorance a privation of knowledge, so non-being is a privation of being – not of being in a substantive sense, for that does not have any opposite, but of being that exists by participation in substantive being. The first two privations mentioned depend on the will of creatures; the third lies in the will of the Maker, who in His goodness wills beings always to exist and always to receive His blessings.

30. All creatures are either endowed with intelligence and intellect, and thus possess a capacity for opposites such as virtue and vice, knowledge and ignorance; or else they are physical bodies of various kinds made up of opposites, that is, of earth, air, fire and water. The former are altogether incorporeal and immaterial, although some of them are joined to bodies; the latter are composed of matter and form.

31. By nature all bodies lack a capacity for motion; they are given motion by the soul, either by one that is intelligent, or by one without intelligence, or by one that is insensate, as the case may be.

32. The soul has three powers: first, the power of nourishment and growth; second, that of imagination and instinct; third, that of intelligence and intellect. Plants share only in the first of these powers; animals share in the first and second; men share in all three. The first two powers are perishable; the third is clearly imperishable and immortal.

33. In communicating illumination to each other, the angelic powers also communicate either their virtue or their knowledge to human nature. As regards their virtue, they communicate a goodness which imitates the goodness of God, and through this goodness they confer blessings on themselves, on one another and on their inferiors, thus making them like God. As regards their knowledge, they communicate either a more sublime knowledge about God – for, as Scripture says, 'Thou, Lord, art most high for evermore' (Ps. 92 : 8) – or a more profound knowledge about embodied beings, or one that is more exact about incorporeal beings, or more distinct about divine providence, or more precise about divine judgment.

34. Impurity of intellect consists first in having false knowledge; secondly in being ignorant of any of the universals (I refer to the human intellect, for it is a property of the angelic intellect not to be

ignorant even of particulars); thirdly in having impassioned thoughts; and fourthly in assenting to sin.

35. Impurity of soul lies in its not functioning in accordance with nature. It is because of this that impassioned thoughts are produced in the intellect. The soul functions in accordance with nature when its passible aspects – that is, its incensive power and its desire – remain dispassionate in the face of provocations both from things and from the conceptual images of these things.

36. Impurity of body consists in the actual committing of sin.

37. He who is not attracted by worldly things cherishes stillness. He who loves nothing merely human loves all men. And he who takes no offence at anyone either on account of their faults, or on account of his own suspicious thoughts, has knowledge of God and of things divine.

38. It is a great achievement not to be attracted by things. But it is a far greater achievement to remain dispassionate in the face both of things and of the conceptual images we derive from them.

39. Love and self-control keep the intellect dispassionate in the face both of things and of the conceptual images we form of them.

40. The intellect of a man who enjoys the love of God does not fight against things or against conceptual images of them. It battles against the passions which are linked with these images. It does not, for example, fight against a woman, or against a man who has offended it, or even against the images it forms of them; but it fights against the passions which are linked with the images.

41. The whole purpose of the monk's warfare against the demons is to separate the passions from conceptual images. Otherwise he will not be able to look on things dispassionately.

42. A thing, a conceptual image and a passion are all quite different one from the other. For example, a man, a woman, gold and so forth are things; a conceptual image is a passion-free thought of one of these things; a passion is mindless affection or indiscriminate hatred for one of these same things. The monk's battle is therefore against passion.

43. An impassioned conceptual image is a thought compounded of passion and a conceptual image. If we separate the passion from the conceptual image, what remains is the passion-free thought. We can make this separation by means of spiritual love and self-control, if only we have the will.

44. The virtues separate the intellect from the passions; spiritual contemplation separates it from its passion-free conceptual images of things; pure prayer brings it into the presence of God Himself.

45. The virtues exist for the sake of the knowledge of creatures; knowledge for the sake of the knower; the knower, for the sake of Him who is known through unknowing and who knows beyond all knowledge.

46. God, full beyond all fulness, brought creatures into being not because He had need of anything, but so that they might participate in Him in proportion to their capacity and that He Himself might rejoice in His works (cf. Ps. 104 : 31), through seeing them joyful and ever filled to overflowing with His inexhaustible gifts.

47. There are many people in the world who are poor in spirit, but not in the way that they should be; there are many who mourn, but for some financial loss or the death of their children; many are gentle, but towards unclean passions; many hunger and thirst, but only to seize what does not belong to them and to profit from injustice; many are merciful, but towards their bodies and the things that serve the body; many are pure in heart, but for the sake of self-esteem; many are peace-makers, but by making the soul submit to the flesh; many are persecuted, but as wrongdoers; many are reviled, but for shameful sins. Only those are blessed who do or suffer these things for the sake of Christ and after His example. Why? Because theirs is the kingdom of heaven, and they shall see God (cf. Matt. 5 : 3–12). It is not because they do or suffer these things that they are blessed, for those of whom we have spoken above do the same; it is because they do them and suffer them for the sake of Christ and after His example.

48. As has been said many times, in everything we do God examines our motive, to see whether we are doing it for His sake or for some other purpose. Thus when we desire to do something good, we should not do it for the sake of popularity; we should have God as our goal, so that, with our gaze always fixed on Him, we may do everything for His sake. Otherwise we shall undergo all the trouble of performing the act and yet lose the reward.

49. In time of prayer clear your intellect of both the passion-free conceptual images of human things and the contemplation of creatures. Otherwise in imagining lesser things you may fall away from Him who is incomparably greater than all created beings.

50. Through genuine love for God we can drive out the passions. Love for God is this: to choose Him rather than the world, and the soul rather than the flesh, by despising the things of this world and by devoting ourselves constantly to Him through self-control, love, prayer, psalmody and so on.

51. If we persistently devote ourselves to God and keep a careful watch on the soul's passible aspect, we are no longer driven headlong by the provocations of our thoughts. On the contrary, as we acquire a more exact understanding of their causes and cut them off, we become more discerning. In this way the following words come to apply to us: 'My eye also sees my enemies, and my ear shall hear the wicked that rise up against me' (Ps. 92 : 11. LXX).

52. When you see that your intellect reflects upon its conceptual images of the world with reverence and justice, you may be sure that your body, too, continues to be pure and sinless. But when you see that your intellect is occupied with thoughts of sin, and you do not check it, you may be sure that before very long your body, too, will fall into those sins.

53. As the world of the body consists of things, so the world of the intellect consists of conceptual images. And as the body fornicates with the body of a woman, so the intellect, forming a picture of its own body, fornicates with the conceptual image of a woman. For in the mind it sees the form of its own body having intercourse with the form of a woman. Similarly, through the form of its own body, it mentally attacks the form of someone who has given it offence. The same is true with respect to other sins. For what the body acts out in the world of things, the intellect also acts out in the world of conceptual images.

54. One should not be startled or astonished because God the Father judges no one but has given all judgment to the Son (cf. John 5 : 22). The Son teaches us, 'Do not judge, so that you may not be judged' (Matt. 7 : 1); 'Do not condemn, so that you may not be condemned' (Luke 6 : 37). St Paul likewise says, 'Judge nothing before the time, until the Lord comes' (1 Cor. 4 : 5); and 'By judging another you condemn yourself' (Rom. 2 : 1). But men have given up weeping for their own sins and have taken judgment away from the Son. They themselves judge and condemn one another as if they were sinless. 'Heaven was amazed at this' (Jer. 2 : 12. LXX) and earth shuddered, but men in their obduracy are not ashamed.

55. He who busies himself with the sins of others, or judges his brother on suspicion, has not yet even begun to repent or to examine himself so as to discover his own sins, which are truly heavier than a great lump of lead; nor does he know why a man becomes heavy-hearted when he loves vanity and chases after falsehood (cf. Ps. 4 : 2). That is why, like a fool who walks in darkness, he no longer attends to his own sins but lets his imagination dwell on the sins of others, whether these sins are real or merely the products of his own suspicious mind.

56. Self-love, as has often been said, is the cause of all impassioned thoughts. For from it are produced the three principal thoughts of desire: those of gluttony, avarice and self-esteem. From gluttony is born the thought of unchastity; from avarice, the thought of greed; from self-esteem, the thought of pride. All the rest – the thoughts of anger, resentment, rancour, listlessness, envy, backbiting and so on – are consequent upon one or other of these three. These passions, then, tie the intellect to material things and drag it down to earth, pressing on it like a massive stone, although by nature it is lighter and swifter than fire.

57. The origin of all the passions is self-love; their consummation is pride. Self-love is a mindless love for the body. He who cuts this off cuts off at the same time all the passions that come from it.

58. Just as parents have a special affection for the children who are the fruit of their own bodies, so the intellect naturally clings to its own thoughts. And just as to passionately fond parents their own children seem the most capable and most beautiful of all – though they may be quite the most ridiculous in every way – so to a foolish intellect its own thoughts appear the most intelligent of all, though they may be utterly degraded. The wise man does not regard his own thoughts in this way. It is precisely when he feels convinced that they are true and good that he most distrusts his own judgment. He makes other wise men the judges of his thoughts and arguments – lest he should run, or may have run, in vain (cf. Gal. 2 : 2) – and from them receives assurance.

59. When you overcome one of the grosser passions, such as gluttony, unchastity, anger or greed, the thought of self-esteem at once assails you. If you defeat this thought, the thought of pride succeeds it.

60. All the gross passions that dominate the soul drive from it the thought of self-esteem. But when all these passions have been defeated, they leave self-esteem free to take control.

61. Self-esteem, whether it is eradicated or whether it remains, begets pride. When it is eradicated, it generates self-conceit; when it remains, it produces boastfulness.

62. Self-esteem is eradicated by the hidden practice of the virtues, pride, by ascribing our achievements to God.

63. He who has been granted knowledge of God, and fully enjoys the pleasure that comes from it, despises all the pleasures produced by the soul's desiring power.

64. He who desires earthly things desires either food, or things which satisfy his sexual appetite, or human fame, or wealth, or some other thing consequent upon these. Unless the intellect finds something more noble to which it may transfer its desire, it will not be persuaded to scorn these things completely. The knowledge of God and of divine things is incomparably more noble than these earthly things.

65. Those who scorn sensual pleasures do so either from fear, or from hope, or from knowledge and love for God.

66. Passion-free knowledge of divine things does not persuade the intellect to scorn material things completely; it is like the passion-free thought of a sensible thing. It is therefore possible to find many men who have much knowledge and yet wallow in the passions of the flesh like pigs in the mire. Through their diligence they temporarily cleanse themselves and attain knowledge, but then they grow negligent. In this they resemble Saul: for Saul was granted the kingdom, but conducted himself unworthily and was driven out with terrible wrath (cf. 1 Sam. 10–15).

67. Just as passion-free thought of human things does not compel the intellect to scorn divine things, so passion-free knowledge of divine things does not fully persuade it to scorn human things. For in this world truth exists in shadows and conjectures. That is why there is need for the blessed passion of holy love, which binds the intellect to spiritual contemplation and persuades it to prefer what is immaterial to what is material, and what is intelligible and divine to what is apprehended by the senses.

68. If a man has cut off the passions and so has freed his thoughts from passion, it does not necessarily mean that his thoughts are

already orientated towards the divine. It may be that he feels no passionate attraction either for human or for divine things. This occurs in the case of those simply living the life of ascetic practice without yet having been granted spiritual knowledge. Such men keep the passions at bay either by fear of punishment or by hope of the kingdom.

69. 'We walk by faith, not by sight' (2 Cor. 5 : 7); and we gain spiritual knowledge through symbols, indistinctly as in a mirror (cf. 1 Cor. 13 : 12). Thus we must devote much time to this kind of knowledge, so that by long study and constant application we may achieve a persistent state of contemplation.

70. If we cut off the causes of the passions for only a short while, and occupy ourselves with spiritual contemplation without making it our sole and constant concern, we easily revert to the passions of the flesh, gaining nothing from our labour but theoretical knowledge coupled with conceit. The result is a gradual darkening of this knowledge itself and a complete turning of the intellect towards material things.

71. The passion of love, when reprehensible, occupies the intellect with material things, but when rightly directed unites it with the divine. For the intellect tends to develop its powers among those things to which it devotes its attention; and where it develops its powers, there it will direct its desire and love. It will direct them, that is to say, either to what is divine, intelligible and proper to its nature, or to the passions and things of the flesh.

72. God created both the invisible and the visible worlds, and so He obviously also made both the soul and the body. If the visible world is so beautiful, what must the invisible world be like? And if the invisible world is superior to the visible world, how much superior to both is God their Creator? If, then, the Creator of everything that is beautiful is superior to all His creation, on what grounds does the intellect abandon what is superior to all and engross itself in what is worst of all – I mean the passions of the flesh? Clearly this happens because the intellect has lived with these passions and grown accustomed to them since birth, whereas it has not yet had perfect experience of Him who is superior to all and beyond all things. Thus, if we gradually wean the intellect away from this relationship by long practice of controlling our indulgence in pleasure and by persistent meditation on divine realities, the intel-

lect will gradually devote itself more and more to these realities, will recognize its own dignity, and finally transfer all its desire to the divine.

73. He who speaks dispassionately of his brother's sins does so either to correct him or to benefit another. If he speaks for any other reason, either to the brother himself or to another person, he speaks to abuse him or ridicule him. In this case he will not escape being abandoned by God. On the contrary, he will fall into the same sin or other sins and, censured and reproached by other men, will be put to shame.

74. It is not always for the same reason that sinners commit the same sin. The reasons vary. For example, it is one thing to sin through force of habit and another to sin through being carried away by a sudden impulse. In the latter case the man did not deliberately choose the sin either before committing it, or afterwards; on the contrary, he is deeply distressed that the sin has occurred. It is quite different with the man who sins through force of habit. Prior to the act itself he was already sinning in thought, and after it he is still in the same state of mind.

75. He who cultivates the virtues for the sake of self-esteem also seeks after spiritual knowledge for the same reason. Such a man plainly does not do anything or discuss anything for the edification of others. On the contrary, he always seeks the praise of those who see him or hear him. His passion is brought to light when some of these people censure his actions or words. This distresses him greatly, not because he has failed to edify them – for that was not his aim – but because he has been humiliated.

76. The presence of the passion of avarice reveals itself when a person enjoys receiving but resents having to give. Such a person is not fit to fulfil the office of treasurer or bursar.

77. A man endures suffering either for the love of God, or for hope of reward, or for fear of punishment, or for fear of men, or because of his nature, or for pleasure, or for gain, or out of self-esteem, or from necessity.

78. It is one thing to be delivered from sinful thoughts and another to be free from passions. Frequently a man is delivered from such thoughts when the things which rouse his passions are not present. But the passions lie hidden in the soul and are brought to light when the things themselves are present. Hence one must

watch over the intellect in the presence of things and must discern for which of them it manifests a passion.

79. A true friend is one who in times of trial calmly and imperturbably suffers with his neighbour the ensuing afflictions, privations and disasters as if they were his own.

80. Do not treat your conscience with contempt, for it always advises you to do what is best. It sets before you the will of God and the angels; it frees you from the secret defilements of the heart; and when you depart this life it grants you the gift of intimacy with God.

81. If you wish to be a person of understanding and moderation, and not to be a slave to the passion of conceit, continually search among created things for what is hidden from your knowledge. When you find that there are vast numbers of different things that escape your notice, you will wonder at your ignorance and abase your presumption. And when you have come to know yourself, you will understand many great and wonderful things; for to think that one knows prevents one from advancing in knowledge.

82. The person who truly wishes to be healed is he who does not refuse treatment. This treatment consists of the pain and distress brought on by various misfortunes. He who refuses them does not realize what they accomplish in this world or what he will gain from them when he departs this life.

83. Self-esteem and avarice produce each other. Those who are full of self-esteem acquire riches and those who are rich become full of self-esteem. That is what happens to people living in the world. In the case of a monk, if he has renounced possessions, he becomes still more full of self-esteem; but if he has money he is ashamed and hides it as something unworthy of one who wears the habit.

84. The mark of monastic self-esteem is to be puffed up about one's virtue and its consequences. The mark of monastic pride is to be conceited about one's own achievements, to ascribe these achievements to oneself and not to God, and to hold others in contempt. The mark of worldly self-esteem and pride is to be puffed up and conceited about one's beauty, wealth, power and moral judgment.

85. The achievements of the worldly man constitute the failings of the monk, and the achievements of the monk constitute the failings of the worldly man. For example, the achievements of the worldly man are wealth, fame, power, luxury, comfort, children

and what is consequent upon all these things. But the monk is destroyed if he obtains any of them. His achievements are the total shedding of possessions, the rejection of esteem and power, self-control, hardship, and all that is consequent upon them. If a lover of the world obtains these against his will, he considers it a great calamity and is often in danger even of killing himself; some people have actually done this.

86. Food was created for nourishment and healing. Those who eat food for purposes other than these two are therefore to be condemned as self-indulgent, because they misuse the gifts God has given us for our use. In all things misuse is a sin.

87. Humility consists in constant prayer combined with tears and suffering. For this ceaseless calling upon God for help prevents us from foolishly growing confident in our own strength and wisdom, and from putting ourselves above others. These are dangerous diseases of the passion of pride.

88. It is one thing to fight against a passion-free thought so that it will not stimulate a passion; it is another to fight against an impassioned thought so that there will be no assent to it. Both these two forms of counter-attack prevent the thoughts themselves from persisting.

89. Resentment is linked with rancour. When the intellect forms the image of a brother's face with a feeling of resentment, it is clear that it harbours rancour against him. 'The way of the rancorous leads to death' (Prov. 12 : 28. LXX), because 'whoever harbours rancour is a transgressor' (Prov. 21 : 24. LXX).

90. If you harbour rancour against anybody, pray for him and you will prevent the passion from being aroused; for by means of prayer you will separate your resentment from the thought of the wrong he has done you. When you have become loving and compassionate towards him, you will wipe the passion completely from your soul. If somebody regards you with rancour, be pleasant to him, be humble and agreeable in his company, and you will deliver him from his passion.

91. You will find it hard to check the resentment of an envious person, for what he envies in you he considers his own misfortune. You cannot check his envy except by hiding from him the thing that arouses his passion. If this thing benefits many but fills him with resentment, which side will you take? You have to help the majority

but without, as far as possible, disregarding him, and without being seduced by the cunning of the passion itself, for you are defending not the passion but the sufferer. You must in humility consider him superior to yourself, and always, everywhere and in every matter put his interest above yours. As for your own envy, you will be able to check it if you rejoice with the man whom you envy whenever he rejoices, and grieve whenever he grieves, thus fulfilling St Paul's words, 'Rejoice with those who rejoice, and weep with those who weep' (Rom. 12 : 15).

92. Our intellect lies between angel and demon, each of which works for its own ends, the one encouraging virtue and the other vice. The intellect has both the authority and the power to follow or resist whichever it wishes to.

93. The angelic powers urge us towards what is holy. Our natural instincts and our probity of intention assist us. But the passions and sinfulness of intention reinforce the provocations of the demons.

94. When the intellect is pure, sometimes God Himself approaches and teaches it; and sometimes the angelic powers, or the nature of the created things that it contemplates, suggest holy things to it.

95. An intellect which has been granted spiritual knowledge must keep its conceptual images free from passion, its contemplation unfaltering, and its state of prayer untroubled. But it cannot always guard these from intrusions by the flesh, because it is obscured by the ploys of demons.

96. The things that distress us are not always the same as those that make us angry, the things that distress us being far more numerous than those which make us angry. For example, the fact that something has been broken, or lost, or that a certain person has died, may only distress us. But other things may both distress us and make us angry, if we lack the spirit of divine philosophy.

97. When the intellect gives attention to conceptual images of physical objects, it is assimilated to the configuration of each image. If it contemplates these objects spiritually, it is transformed in various ways according to which of them it contemplates. But once it is established in God, it loses form and configuration altogether, for by contemplating Him who is simple it becomes simple itself and wholly filled with spiritual radiance.

98. A soul is perfect if its passible aspect is totally orientated towards God.

99. A perfect intellect is one which by true faith and in a manner beyond all unknowing supremely knows the supremely Unknowable; and which, in surveying the entirety of God's creation, has received from God an all-embracing knowledge of the providence and judgment which governs it — in so far, of course, as all this is possible to man.

100. Time has three divisions. Faith is coextensive with all three, hope with one, and love with the remaining two. Moreover, faith and hope will last to a certain point; but love, united beyond union with Him who is more than infinite, will remain for all eternity, always increasing beyond all measure. That is why 'the greatest of them is love' (1 Cor. 13 : 13).

Fourth Century

1. First the intellect marvels when it reflects on the absolute infinity of God, that boundless sea for which it longs so much. Then it is amazed at how God has brought things into existence out of nothing. But just as 'His magnificence is without limit' (Ps. 145 : 3. LXX), so 'there is no penetrating His purposes' (Isa. 40 : 28).

2. How can the intellect not marvel when it contemplates that immense and more than astonishing sea of goodness? Or how is it not astounded when it reflects on how and from what source there have come into being both nature endowed with intelligence and intellect, and the four elements which compose physical bodies, although no matter existed before their generation? What kind of potentiality was it which, once actualized, brought these things into being? But all this is not accepted by those who follow the pagan Greek philosophers, ignorant as they are of that all-powerful goodness and its effective wisdom and knowledge, transcending the human intellect.

3. God is the Creator from all eternity, and He creates when He wills, in His infinite goodness, through His coessential Logos and Spirit. Do not raise the objection : 'Why did He create at a particular moment since He is good from all eternity?' For I reply that the unsearchable wisdom of the infinite essence does not come within the compass of human knowledge.

4. When the Creator willed, He gave being to and manifested that knowledge of created things which already existed in Him from all eternity. For in the case of almighty God it is ridiculous to doubt that He can give being to anything when He so wills.

5. Try to learn why God created; for that is true knowledge. But do not try to learn how He created or why He did so comparatively recently; for that does not come within the compass of your intel-

lect. Of divine realities some may be apprehended by men and others may not. Unbridled speculation, as one of the saints has said, can drive one headlong over the precipice.

6. Some say that the created order has coexisted with God from eternity; but this is impossible. For how can things which are limited in every way coexist from eternity with Him who is altogether infinite? Or how are they really creations if they are coeternal with the Creator? This notion is drawn from the pagan Greek philosophers, who claim that God is in no way the creator of being but only of qualities. We, however, who know almighty God, say that He is the creator not only of qualities but also of the being of created things. If this is so, created things have not coexisted with God from eternity.

7. Divinity and divine realities are in some respects knowable and in some respects unknowable. They are knowable in the contemplation of what appertains to God's essence and unknowable as regards that essence itself.

8. Do not look for conditions and properties in the simple and infinite essence of the Holy Trinity; otherwise you will make It composite like created beings – a ridiculous and blasphemous thing to do in the case of God.

9. Only the infinite Being, all-powerful and creative of all things, is simple, unique, unqualified, peaceful and stable. Every creature, consisting as it does of being and accident, is composite and always in need of divine providence, for it is not free from change.

10. Both intelligible and sensible nature, on being brought into existence by God, received powers to apprehend created beings. Intelligible nature received powers of intellection, and sensible nature powers of sense-perception.

11. God is only participated in. Creation both participates and communicates: it participates in being and in well-being, but communicates only well-being. But corporeal nature communicates this in one way and incorporeal nature in another.

12. Incorporeal nature communicates well-being by speaking, by acting, and by being contemplated; corporeal nature only by being contemplated.

13. Whether or not a nature endowed with intelligence and intellect is to exist eternally depends on the will of the Creator whose

every creation is good; but whether such a nature is good or bad depends on its own will.

14. Evil is not to be imputed to the essence of created beings, but to their erroneous and mindless motivation.

15. A soul's motivation is rightly ordered when its desiring power is subordinated to self-control, when its incensive power rejects hatred and cleaves to love, and when its power of intelligence, through prayer and spiritual contemplation, advances towards God.

16. If in time of trial a man does not patiently endure his afflictions, but cuts himself off from the love of his spiritual brethren, he does not yet possess perfect love or a deep knowledge of divine providence.

17. The aim of divine providence is to unite by means of true faith and spiritual love those separated in various ways by vice. Indeed, the Saviour endured His sufferings so that 'He should gather together into one the scattered children of God' (John 11 : 52). Thus, he who does not resolutely bear trouble, endure affliction, and patiently sustain hardship, has strayed from the path of divine love and from the purpose of providence.

18. If 'love is long-suffering and kind' (1 Cor. 13 : 4), a man who is fainthearted in the face of his afflictions and who therefore behaves wickedly towards those who have offended him, and stops loving them, surely lapses from the purpose of divine providence.

19. Watch yourself, lest the vice which separates you from your brother lies not in him but in yourself. Be reconciled with him without delay, so that you do not lapse from the commandment of love.

20. Do not hold the commandment of love in contempt, for through it you will become a son of God. But if you transgress it, you will become a son of Gehenna.

21. What separates us from the love of friends is envying or being envied, causing or receiving harm, insulting or being insulted, and suspicious thoughts. Would that you had never done or experienced anything of this sort and in this way separated yourself from the love of a friend.

22. Has a brother been the occasion of some trial for you and has your resentment led you to hatred? Do not let yourself be overcome by this hatred, but conquer it with love. You will succeed in this by praying to God sincerely for your brother and by accepting his

apology; or else by conciliating him with an apology yourself, by regarding yourself as responsible for the trial and by patiently waiting until the cloud has passed.

23. A long-suffering man is one who waits patiently for his trial to end and hopes that his perseverance will be rewarded.

24. 'The long-suffering man abounds in understanding' (Prov. 14 : 29), because he endures everything to the end and, while awaiting that end, patiently bears his distress. The end, as St Paul says, is everlasting life (cf. Rom. 6 : 22). 'And this is life eternal, that they might know Thee the only true God, and Jesus Christ whom Thou has sent' (John 17 : 3).

25. Do not lightly discard spiritual love: for men there is no other road to salvation.

26. Because today an assault of the devil has aroused some hatred in you, do not judge as base and wicked a brother whom yesterday you regarded as spiritual and virtuous; but with long-suffering love dwell on the goodness you perceived yesterday and expel today's hatred from your soul.

27. Do not condemn today as base and wicked the man whom yesterday you praised as good and commended as virtuous, changing from love to hatred, because he has criticized you; but even though you are still full of resentment, commend him as before, and you will soon recover the same saving love.

28. When talking with other brethren, do not adulterate your usual praise of a brother by surreptitiously introducing censure into the conversation because you still harbour some hidden resentment against him. On the contrary, in the company of others give unmixed praise and pray for him sincerely as if you were praying for yourself; then you will soon be delivered from this destructive hatred.

29. Do not say, 'I do not hate my brother', when you simply efface the thought of him from your mind. Listen to Moses, who said, 'Do not hate your brother in your mind; but reprove him and you will not incur sin through him' (Lev. 19 : 17. LXX).

30. If a brother happens to be tempted and persists in insulting you, do not be driven out of your state of love, even though the same evil demon troubles your mind. You will not be driven out of that state if, when abused, you bless; when slandered, you praise; and when tricked, you maintain your affection. This is the way of

Christ's philosophy: if you do not follow it you do not share His company.

31. Do not think that those who bring you reports which fill you with resentment and make you hate your brother are affectionately disposed towards you, even if they seem to speak the truth. On the contrary, turn away from them as if they were poisonous snakes, so that you may both prevent them from uttering slanders and deliver your own soul from wickedness.

32. Do not irritate your brother by speaking to him equivocally; otherwise you may receive the same treatment from him and so drive out both your love and his. Rather, rebuke him frankly and affectionately, thus removing the grounds for resentment and freeing both him and yourself from your irritation and distress.

33. Examine your conscience scrupulously, in case it is your fault that your brother is still hostile. Do not cheat your conscience, for it knows your secrets, and at the hour of your death it will accuse you and in time of prayer it will be a stumbling-block to you.

34. In times of peaceful relationships do not recall what was said by a brother when there was bad feeling between you, even if offensive things were said to your face, or to another person about you and you subsequently heard of them. Otherwise you will harbour thoughts of rancour and revert to your destructive hatred of your brother.

35. The deiform soul cannot nurse hatred against a man and yet be at peace with God, the giver of the commandments. 'For', He says, 'if you do not forgive men their faults, neither will your heavenly Father forgive you your faults' (cf. Matt. 6 : 14–15). If your brother does not wish to live peaceably with you, nevertheless guard yourself against hatred, praying for him sincerely and not abusing him to anybody.

36. The perfect peace of the holy angels lies in their love for God and their love for one another. This is also the case with all the saints from the beginning of time. Most truly therefore is it said that 'on these two commandments hang all the law and the prophets' (Matt. 22 : 40).

37. Stop pleasing yourself and you will not hate your brother; stop loving yourself and you will love God.

38. Once you have decided to share your life with spiritual brethren, renounce your own wishes from the start. Unless you do

this you will not be able to live peaceably either with God or with your brethren.

39. He who has attained perfect love, and has ordered his whole life in accordance with it, is the person who says 'Lord Jesus' in the Holy Spirit (cf. 1 Cor. 12 : 3).

40. Love for God always aspires to give wings to the intellect in its communion with God; love for one's neighbour makes one always think good thoughts about him.

41. The man who still loves empty fame, or is attached to some material object, is naturally vexed with people on account of transitory things, or harbours rancour or hatred against them, or is a slave to shameful thoughts. Such things are quite foreign to the soul that loves God.

42. If you have no thought of any shameful word or action in your mind, harbour no rancour against someone who has injured or slandered you, and, while praying, always keep your intellect free from matter and form, you may be sure that you have attained the full measure of dispassion and perfect love.

43. It is no small struggle to be freed from self-esteem. Such freedom is to be attained by the inner practice of the virtues and by more frequent prayer; and the sign that you have attained it is that you no longer harbour rancour against anybody who abuses or has abused you.

44. If you want to be a just person, assign to each aspect of yourself – to your soul and your body – what accords with it. To the intelligent aspect of the soul assign spiritual reading, contemplation and prayer; to the incensive aspect, spiritual love, the opposite of hatred; to the desiring aspect, moderation and self-control; to the fleshly part, food and clothing, for these alone are necessary (cf. 1 Tim. 6 : 8).

45. The intellect functions in accordance with nature when it keeps the passions under control, contemplates the inner essences of created beings, and abides with God.

46. As health and disease are to the body of a living thing, and light and darkness to the eye, so virtue and vice are to the soul, and knowledge and ignorance to the intellect.

47. The commandments, the doctrines, the faith: these are the three objects of the Christian's philosophy. The commandments separate the intellect from the passions; the doctrines lead it to the

spiritual knowledge of created beings; and faith to the contemplation of the Holy Trinity.

48. Some of those pursuing the spiritual way only repel impassioned thoughts; others cut off the passions themselves. Such thoughts are repelled by psalmody, or by prayer, or by raising one's mind to God, or by occupying one's attention in some similar way. The passions are cut off through appropriate detachment from those things by which they are roused.

49. The passions are roused in us by, for example, women, wealth, fame and so on. We can achieve detachment with regard to women when, after withdrawing from the world, we wither the body, as we should, through self-control. We can achieve detachment where wealth is concerned when we make up our mind to be frugal in all things. We can become indifferent to fame by practising the virtues inwardly, in a way visible only to God. And we can act in a similar fashion with respect to other things. A person who has achieved such detachment as this will never hate anybody.

50. He who has renounced such things as marriage, possessions and other worldly pursuits is outwardly a monk, but may not yet be a monk inwardly. Only he who has renounced the impassioned conceptual images of these things has made a monk of the inner self, the intellect. It is easy to be a monk in one's outer self if one wants to be; but no small struggle is required to be a monk in one's inner self.

51. Who in this generation is completely freed from impassioned conceptual images, and has been granted uninterrupted, pure and spiritual prayer? Yet this is the mark of the inner monk.

52. Many passions are hidden in our souls; they can be brought to light only when the objects that rouse them are present.

53. A man can enjoy partial dispassion and not be disturbed by passions when the objects which rouse them are absent. But once those objects are present, the passions quickly distract his intellect.

54. Do not imagine that you enjoy perfect dispassion when the object arousing your passion is not present. If when it is present you remain unmoved by both the object and the subsequent thought of it, you may be sure that you have entered the realm of dispassion. But even so do not be over-confident; for virtue when habitual kills the passions, but when it is neglected they come to life again.

55. He who loves Christ is bound to imitate Him to the best of his ability. Christ, for example, was always conferring blessings on people; He was long-suffering when they were ungrateful and blasphemed Him; and when they beat Him and put Him to death, He endured it, imputing no evil at all to anyone. These are the three acts which manifest love for one's neighbour. If he is incapable of them, the person who says that he loves Christ or has attained the kingdom deceives himself. For 'not everyone who says to Me: "Lord, Lord" shall enter into the kingdom of heaven; but he that does the will of My Father' (Matt. 7 : 21); and again, 'He who loves Me will keep My commandments' (cf. John 14 : 15, 23).

56. The whole purpose of the Saviour's commandments is to free the intellect from dissipation and hatred, and to lead it to the love of Him and one's neighbour. From this love springs the light of active holy knowledge.

57. When God has granted you a degree of spiritual knowledge, do not neglect love and self-control; for it is these which, once they have purified the soul's passible aspect, always keep open for you the way to such knowledge.

58. Dispassion and humility lead to spiritual knowledge. Without them no one will see the Lord.

59. Since 'knowledge puffs up, but love edifies' (1 Cor. 8 : 1), unite love with knowledge and you will free yourself from arrogance and be a spiritual builder, edifying both yourself and all who draw near you.

60. Love edifies because it does not envy, or feel any bitterness towards those who are envious, or ostentatiously display what provokes envy; it does not reckon that its purpose has yet been attained (cf. Phil. 3 : 13), and it unhesitatingly confesses its ignorance of what it does not know. Hence it frees the intellect from arrogance and always equips it to advance in knowledge.

61. It is natural for spiritual knowledge to produce conceit and envy, especially in the early stages. Conceit comes only from within, but envy comes both from within and from without — from within when we feel envious of those who have knowledge, from without when those who love knowledge feel envious of us. Love destroys all three of these failings: conceit, because love is not puffed up; envy from within, because love is not jealous; and envy from without, because love is 'long-suffering and kind' (1 Cor. 13 : 4). A

person with spiritual knowledge must, then, also acquire love, so that he may always keep his intellect in a healthy state.

62. He who has been granted the grace of spiritual knowledge and yet harbours resentment, rancour or hatred for anybody, is like someone who lacerates his eyes with thorns and thistles. Hence knowledge must be accompanied by love.

63. Do not devote all your time to your body but apply to it a measure of asceticism appropriate to its strength, and then turn all your intellect to what is within. 'Bodily asceticism has only a limited use, but true devotion is useful in all things' (1 Tim. 4 : 8).

64. He who always concentrates on the inner life becomes restrained, long-suffering, kind and humble. He will also be able to contemplate, theologize and pray. That is what St Paul meant when he said: 'Walk in the Spirit' (Gal. 5 : 16).

65. One ignorant of the spiritual path is not on his guard against impassioned conceptual images, but devotes himself entirely to the flesh. He is either a glutton, or licentious, or full of resentment, anger and rancour. As a result he darkens his intellect, or he practises excessive asceticism and so confuses his mind.

66. Scripture does not forbid anything which God has given us for our use; but it condemns immoderation and thoughtless behaviour. For instance, it does not forbid us to eat, or to beget children, or to possess material things and to administer them properly. But it does forbid us to be gluttonous, to fornicate and so on. It does not forbid us to think of these things – they were made to be thought of – but it forbids us to think of them with passion.

67. Some of the things which we do for the sake of God are done in obedience to the commandments; others are done not in obedience to the commandments but, so to speak, as a voluntary offering. For example, we are required by the commandments to love God and our neighbour, to love our enemies, not to commit adultery or murder and so on. And when we transgress these commandments, we are condemned. But we are not commanded to live as virgins, to abstain from marriage, to renounce possessions, to withdraw into solitude and so forth. These are of the nature of gifts, so that if through weakness we are unable to fulfil some of the commandments, we may by these free gifts propitiate our blessed Master.

68. He who honours celibacy and virginity must keep his loins girded and his lamp burning (cf. Luke 12 : 35). He keeps his loins

girded through self-control, and his lamp burning through prayer, contemplation and spiritual love.

69. Some of the brethren think that they are excluded from the Holy Spirit's gifts of grace. Because they neglect to practise the commandments they do not know that he who has an unadulterated faith in Christ has within him the sum total of all the divine gifts. Since through our laziness we are far from having an active love for Him – a love which shows us the divine treasures within us – we naturally think that we are excluded from these gifts.

70. If, as St Paul says, Christ dwells in our hearts through faith (cf. Eph. 3 : 17), and all the treasures of wisdom and spiritual knowledge are hidden in Him (cf. Col. 2 : 3), then all the treasures of wisdom and spiritual knowledge are hidden in our hearts. They are revealed to the heart in proportion to our purification by means of the commandments.

71. This is the treasure hidden in the field of your heart (cf. Matt. 13 : 44), which you have not yet found because of your laziness. Had you found it, you would have sold everything and bought that field. But now you have abandoned that field and give all your attention to the land nearby, where there is nothing but thorns and thistles.

72. It is for this reason that the Saviour says, 'Blessed are the pure in heart, for they shall see God' (Matt. 5 : 8): for He is hidden in the hearts of those who believe in Him. They shall see Him and the riches that are in Him when they have purified themselves through love and self-control; and the greater their purity, the more they will see.

73. And that is why He also says, 'Sell what you possess and give alms' (Luke 12 : 33), 'and you will find that all things are clean for you' (Luke 11 : 41). This applies to those who no longer spend their time on things to do with the body, but strive to cleanse the intellect (which the Lord calls 'heart') from hatred and dissipation. For these defile the intellect and do not allow it to see Christ, who dwells in it by the grace of holy baptism.

74. In Scripture the virtues are called 'ways'. The greatest of all the virtues is love. That is why St Paul said, 'Now I will show you the best way of all' (1 Cor. 12 : 31), one that persuades us to scorn material things and value nothing transitory more than what is eternal.

75. Love of God is opposed to desire, for it persuades the intellect to control itself with regard to sensual pleasures. Love for our neighbour is opposed to anger, for it makes us scorn fame and riches. These are the two pence which our Saviour gave to the innkeeper (cf. Luke 10 : 35), so that he should take care of you. But do not be thoughtless and associate with robbers; otherwise you will be beaten again and left not merely unconscious but dead.

76. Cleanse your intellect from anger, rancour and shameful thoughts, and you will be able to perceive the indwelling of Christ.

77. Who enlightened you with faith in the holy, coessential and adorable Trinity? Or who made known to you the incarnate dispensation of one of the Holy Trinity? Who taught you about the inner essences of incorporeal beings, or about the origin and consummation of the visible world, or about the resurrection from the dead and eternal life, or about the glory of the kingdom of heaven and the dreadful judgment? Was it not the grace of Christ dwelling in you, which is the pledge of the Holy Spirit? What is greater than this grace? What is more noble than this wisdom and knowledge? What is more lofty than these promises? But if we are lazy and negligent, and if we do not cleanse ourselves from the passions which defile us, blinding our intellect and so preventing us from seeing the inner nature of these realities more clearly than the sun, let us blame ourselves and not deny the indwelling of grace.

78. God, who has promised you eternal blessings (cf. Tit. 1 : 2) and has given you the pledge of the Spirit in your hearts (cf. 2 Cor. 1 : 22), has commanded you to pay attention to how you live, so that the inner man may be freed from the passions and begin here and now to enjoy these blessings.

79. When you have been granted the higher forms of the contemplation of divine realities, give your utmost attention to love and self-control, so that you may keep your soul's passible aspect undisturbed and preserve the light of your soul in undiminished splendour.

80. Bridle your soul's incensive power with love, quench its desire with self-control, give wings to its intelligence with prayer, and the light of your intellect will never be darkened.

81. Disgrace, injury, slander either against one's faith or one's manner of life, beatings, blows and so on — these are the things which dissolve love, whether they happen to oneself or to any of

one's relatives or friends. He who loses his love because of these things has not yet understood the purpose of Christ's commandments.

82. Strive as hard as you can to love every man. If you cannot yet do this, at least do not hate anybody. But even this is beyond your power unless you scorn worldly things.

83. Has someone vilified you? Do not hate him; hate the vilification and the demon which induced him to utter it. If you hate the vilifier, you have hated a man and so broken the commandment. What he has done in word you do in action. To keep the commandment, show the qualities of love and help him in any way you can, so that you may deliver him from evil.

84. Christ does not want you to feel the least hatred, resentment, anger or rancour towards anyone in any way or on account of any transitory thing whatsoever. This is proclaimed throughout the four Gospels.

85. Many of us are talkers, few are doers. But no one should distort the word of God through his own negligence. He must confess his weakness and not hide God's truth. Otherwise he will be guilty not only of breaking the commandments but also of falsifying the word of God.

86. Love and self-control free the soul from passions; spiritual reading and contemplation deliver the intellect from ignorance; and the state of prayer brings it into the presence of God Himself.

87. When the demons see that we scorn the things of this world in order not to hate men on account of such things, and so to fall away from love, then they incite slanders against us. In this way they hope that, unable to contain our resentment, we will be provoked into hating those who slander us.

88. Nothing pains the soul more than slander, whether directed against one's faith or one's manner of life. No one can be indifferent to it except those who like Susanna have their eyes firmly fixed on God (cf. Sus. verse 35). For only God has the power to rescue from peril, as He rescued her, to convince men of the truth, as He did in her case, and to encourage the soul with hope.

89. To the extent that you pray with all your soul for the person who slanders you, God will make the truth known to those who have been scandalized by the slander.

90. Only God is good by nature (cf. Matt. 19 : 17), and only he

who imitates God is good in will and purpose. For it is the intention of such a person to unite the wicked to Him who is good by nature, so that they too may become good. That is why, though reviled by them, he blesses; persecuted, he endures; vilified, he supplicates (cf. 1 Cor. 4 : 12–13); put to death, he prays for them. He does everything so as not to lapse from the purpose of love, which is God Himself.

91. The Lord's commandments teach us to use neutral things intelligently. Such use purifies the soul's state. A state of purity begets discrimination; discrimination begets dispassion; and it is from dispassion that perfect love is born.

92. If when some trial occurs you cannot overlook a friend's fault, whether real or apparent, you have not yet attained dispassion. For when the passions which lie deep in the soul are disturbed, they blind the mind, preventing it from perceiving the light of truth and from discriminating between good and evil. If you are in such a state you have likewise not yet attained perfect love, the love which expels the fear of judgment (cf. 1 John 4 : 18).

93. 'A faithful friend is beyond price' (Ecclus. 6 : 15), since he regards his friend's misfortunes as his own and suffers with him, sharing his trials until death.

94. Friends are many, but in times of prosperity (cf. Prov. 19 : 4). In times of adversity you will have difficulty in finding even one.

95. One should love every man from the soul, but one should place one's hope only in God and serve Him with all one's strength. For so long as He protects us against harm, all our friends treat us with respect and all our enemies are powerless to injure us. But once He abandons us, all our friends turn away from us while all our enemies prevail against us.

96. There are four principal ways in which God abandons us. The first is the way of the divine dispensation, so that through our apparent abandonment others who are abandoned may be saved. Our Lord is an example of this (cf. Matt. 27 : 46). The second is the way of trial and testing, as in the case of Job and Joseph; for it made Job a pillar of courage and Joseph a pillar of self-restraint (cf. Gen. 39 : 8). The third is the way of fatherly correction, as in the case of St Paul, so that by being humble he might preserve the superabundance of grace (cf. 2 Cor. 12 : 7). The fourth is the way of rejection,

as in the case of the Jews, so that by being punished they might be brought to repentance. These are all ways of salvation, full of divine blessing and wisdom.

97. Only those who scrupulously keep the commandments, and are true initiates into divine judgments, do not abandon their friends when God permits these friends to be put to the test. Those who scorn the commandments and who are ignorant about divine judgments rejoice with their friend in the times of his prosperity; but when in times of trial he suffers hardships, they abandon him and sometimes even side with those who attack him.

98. The friends of Christ love all truly but are not themselves loved by all; the friends of the world neither love all nor are loved by all. The friends of Christ persevere in love to the end; the friends of the world persevere only until they fall out with each other over some worldly thing.

99. 'A faithful friend is a strong defence' (Ecclus. 6 : 14); for when things are going well with you, he is a good counsellor and a sympathetic collaborator, while when things are going badly, he is the truest of helpers and a most compassionate supporter.

100. Many have said much about love, but you will find love itself only if you seek it among the disciples of Christ. For only they have true Love as love's teacher. 'Though I have the gift of prophecy', says St Paul, 'and know all mysteries and all knowledge . . . and have no love, it profits me nothing' (1 Cor. 13 : 2–3). He who possesses love possesses God Himself, for 'God is love' (1 John 4 : 8). To Him be glory throughout the ages. Amen.

Two Hundred Texts on Theology and the Incarnate Dispensation of the Son of God
WRITTEN FOR THALASSIOS

First Century

1. God is one, unoriginate, incomprehensible, possessing completely the total potentiality of being, altogether excluding notions of when and how, inaccessible to all, and not to be known through natural image by any creature.

2. So far as we are able to understand, for Himself God does not constitute either an origin, or an intermediary state, or a consummation, or anything else at all which can be seen to qualify naturally things that are sequent to Him. For He is undetermined, unchanging and infinite, since He is infinitely beyond all being, potentiality and actualization.

3. Every being whose self-limitation is intrinsic to it is by nature the origin of the activity perceived as potentially present within it. Every natural activity in the process of actualization – and such activity is, on the conceptual level, sequent to the being itself but prior to its own actualization – is an intermediary state, since by nature it lies between the being in which it is present potentially and its own actualization. Every actualization, limited as it naturally is by its own inner principle, is the consummation of that activity which has its origin in the being and which, conceptually speaking, precedes the actualization.

4. God is not a being either in the general or in any specific sense of the word, and so He cannot be an origin. Nor is He a potentiality either in the general or in any specific sense, and so He is not an intermediary state. Nor is He an actualization in the

general or in any specific sense, and so He cannot be the consummation of that activity which proceeds from a being in which it is perceived to pre-exist as a potentiality. On the contrary, He is the author of being and simultaneously an entity transcending being; He is the author of potentiality and simultaneously the ground transcending potentiality; and He is the active and inexhaustible state of all actualization. In short, He is the author of all being, potentiality and actualization, and of every origin, intermediary state and consummation.

5. Origin, the intermediary state and consummation characterize things divided by time, as indeed they characterize things existing in the aeon. For time, by which change is measured, is defined numerically; while the aeon, whose existence presupposes a 'when', possesses dimensionality, since its existence has an origin. And if time and the aeon have an origin, how much more so will those things that exist within them.

6. God by nature is always one and alone, substantively and absolutely, containing in Himself all-inclusively the totality of substantive being, since He transcends even substantiveness itself. If this is so, there is nothing whatsoever among all the things to which we ascribe being that possess substantive being. Thus nothing whatsoever different in essence from God can be envisaged as coexisting with Him from eternity – neither the aeon, nor time, nor anything which exists within them. For substantive being and being which is not substantive never coincide.

7. No origin, intermediary state or consummation can ever be altogether free from the category of relationship. God, being infinitely beyond every kind of relationship, is by nature neither an origin, nor an intermediary state, nor a consummation, nor any of those things to which it is possible to apply the category of relationship.

8. Created beings are termed intelligible because each of them has an origin that can be known rationally. But God cannot be termed intelligible, while from our apprehension of intelligible beings we can do no more than believe that He exists. On this account no intelligible being is in any way to be compared with Him.

9. Created beings can be known rationally by means of the inner principles which are by nature intrinsic to such beings and by which

they are naturally defined. But from our apprehension of these principles inherent in created beings we can do no more than believe that God exists. To the devout believer God gives something more sure than any proof: the recognition and the faith that He sub-stantively is. Faith is true knowledge, the principles of which are beyond rational demonstration; for faith makes real for us things beyond intellect and reason (cf. Heb. 11 :1).

10. God is the origin, intermediary state and consummation of all created things, but as acting upon things not as acted upon, which is also the case where everything else we call Him is concerned. He is origin as Creator, intermediary state as provident ruler, and con-summation as final end. For, as Scripture says, 'All things are from Him and through Him, and have Him as their goal' (Rom. 11 : 36).

11. No deiform soul is in its essence of greater value than any other deiform soul. For when God in His supernal goodness creates each soul in His own image, He brings it into being endowed with self-determination. By exercising this freedom of choice each soul either reaffirms its true nobility or through its actions deliberately embraces what is ignoble.

12. God, it is said, is the Sun of righteousness (cf. Mal. 4 : 2), and the rays of His supernal goodness shine down on all men alike. The soul is wax if it cleaves to God, but clay if it cleaves to matter. Which it does depends upon its own will and purpose. Clay hardens in the sun, while wax grows soft. Similarly, every soul that, despite God's admonitions, deliberately cleaves to the material world, hardens like clay and drives itself to destruction, just as Pharaoh did (cf. Exod. 7 : 13). But every soul that cleaves to God is softened like wax and, receiving the impress and stamp of divine realities, it becomes 'in spirit the dwelling-place of God' (Eph. 2 : 22).

13. If a person's intellect is illumined with intellections of the divine, if his speech is unceasingly devoted to singing the praises of the Creator, and if his senses are hallowed by unsullied images – he has enhanced that sanctity which is his by nature, as created in the image of God, by adding to it the sanctity of the divine likeness that is attained through the exercise of his own free will.

14. A man keeps his soul undefiled before God if he compels his mind to meditate only on God and His supreme goodness, makes his thought a true interpreter and exponent of this goodness, and teaches his senses to form holy images of the visible world and all

the things in it, and to convey to the soul the magnificence of the inner principles lying within all things.

15. God has freed us from bitter slavery to tyrannical demons and has given us humility as a compassionate yoke of devoutness. It is humility which tames every demonic power, produces in those who accept it every kind of sanctity, and keeps that sanctity inviolate.

16. He who believes fears; he who fears is humble; he who is humble becomes gentle and renders inactive those impulses of incensiveness and desire which are contrary to nature. A person who is gentle keeps the commandments; he who keeps the commandments is purified; he who is purified is illumined; he who is illumined is made a consort of the divine Bridegroom and Logos in the shrine of the mysteries.

17. Sometimes when a farmer is looking for a suitable spot to which to transplant a tree, he unexpectedly comes across a treasure. Something similar may happen to the seeker after God. If he is humble and unaffected, and if his soul, after the example of the blessed Jacob (cf. Gen. 27 : 11), is sleek, and not hirsute with materiality, then God may grant him the contemplation of divine wisdom even though he has not laboured for it. But if the Father then asks him how he came by this knowledge, saying to him 'What is this you have found so quickly, My son?' he should reply, as Jacob did, 'It is what the Lord God has granted to me' (Gen. 27 : 20. LXX). We should realize in such a case that what he has found is a spiritual treasure; for the devoted seeker after God is a spiritual farmer who transplants, as if it were a tree, his contemplation of visible and sensory things to the field of noetic realities; and in so doing he find a treasure – the revelation by grace of the wisdom in created things.

18. Although in his humility he has not expected it, the seeker after God may suddenly receive spiritual knowledge of divine contemplation. But this may so devastate the mind of someone else who is unsuccessfully toiling to acquire such knowledge for the sake of self-display that, mad with jealousy, he plots to murder his brother and grows sick with resentment because he does not experience the elation that comes from being praised.

19. Those who seek spiritual knowledge with much labour, but do not succeed in finding it, fail either through lack of faith or perhaps because in their stupidity and jealousy they have it in mind to

attack those who possess knowledge, just as the people of old once attacked Moses. We can rightly apply to them the passage in Scripture which says that when some men tried to force their way up the mountain, the Amorites dwelling in that mountain came out and wounded them (cf. Deut. 1 : 43–44). For inevitably those who put on a show of holiness for the sake of self-display not only fail to achieve anything through their false piety, but also are wounded by their conscience.

20. He who pursues spiritual knowledge for the sake of display and fails to attain it should not envy his neighbour or be cast down. On the contrary, as commanded, let him observe the preparation for the sabbath in some nearby place: through the practice of the virtues, by working hard with his body, he will prepare his soul for that knowledge.

21. Those who truly and devoutly aspire to an understanding of created beings, and have no thoughts of self-display, will find that they are granted lucid insight into such beings and that through this insight they attain the knowledge they seek in a most precise fashion. To such people the Law says, 'You will come and inherit fine large cities, and houses which you did not build, full of good things, and deep wells which you did not dig, and vines and olive trees which you did not plant' (cf. Deut. 6 : 10–11). For he who lives not for himself but for God (cf. 2 Cor. 5 : 15) is filled with all the gifts of grace, which were not previously apparent in him because of the disturbance produced by the passions.

22. There are said to be two forms of sense-perception. The first is a habitual state and persists even when we are asleep. It does not grasp any particular object and it serves no purpose because it is not directed towards an action. The second is the active sense-perception through which we apprehend sensible objects. Similarly, there are two forms of knowledge. First, there is academic knowledge, which is theoretical information, gathered merely from habit, about the inner principles of created beings, and which serves no purpose because it is not directed towards the practical execution of the commandments. Secondly, there is actively effective knowledge, which confers a true experiential apprehension of created beings.

23. A hypocrite, hunting after the glory that comes from an apparent righteousness, is untroubled so long as he thinks that he

escapes notice. But when he is detected, he utters streams of impre-
cation, imagining that by abusing others he can hide his own de-
formity. Because of his craftiness Scripture has compared him to the
offspring of vipers and has commanded him to bring forth appropriate fruits of repentance (cf. Matt. 3 : 7–8), that is, to refashion the
hidden state of his heart so that it conforms to his outward behaviour.

24. Some say that every living creature inhabiting air, earth or
sea which the Law does not judge to be clean (cf. Lev. 11 : 1–43)
is wild, even if it seems from its behaviour to be tame. By the same
principle, every man subject to some passion is also wild, whatever
his outward behaviour.

25. He who puts on a show of friendship in order to do his
neighbour some injury is a wolf hiding his wickedness under sheep's
clothing. Whenever he finds a custom or saying which is genuinely
Christian, although somewhat naive, he seizes on it and attacks it;
in numberless ways he finds fault with these sayings or customs,
prying into the liberty which the brethren have in Christ (cf. Gal.
2 : 4).

26. He who hypocritically keeps silent for some evil purpose prepares a trap for his neighbour; and if his plan fails, he slinks off,
having brought distress on himself because of his own passion. But
he who is silent for a good end nourishes friendship and goes on his
way rejoicing, for he has received the enlightenment which dispels
darkness.

27. If a man impetuously interrupts a speech at a public meeting,
he clearly reveals his lust for self-glory. Overpowered by this
passion, he tries to obstruct the course of the discussion with endless complicated proposals.

28. A wise man, whether teaching or learning, only wishes to
learn or teach those things which are useful. He who merely has the
appearance of wisdom, whether asking or answering questions, only
deals with relatively trivial things.

29. A person who through the grace of God partakes of divine
blessings is under an obligation to share them ungrudgingly with
others. For Scripture says, 'Freely you have received, freely give'
(Matt. 10 : 8). He who hides the gift in the earth accuses the Lord
of being hard-hearted and mean (cf. Matt. 25 : 24), and in order to
spare the flesh he pretends to know nothing about holiness; while

he who sells the truth to enemies, and is then revealed as avid for self-glory, hangs himself, unable to bear the disgrace (cf. Matt. 26 : 15; 27 : 5).

30. Those who still fear the war against the passions and dread the assaults of invisible enemies must keep silent; in their struggle for virtue they must not enter into disputes with their enemies but through prayer must entrust all anxiety about themselves to God. To them apply the words of Exodus: 'The Lord will fight for you, and you must be silent' (Exod. 14 : 14). Those, secondly, who have been released from the enemy's attacks and who genuinely seek instruction in the ways of acquiring the virtues, need only to keep the ear of their mind open. To them Scripture says, 'Hear O Israel' (Deut. 6 : 4). Thirdly, those who as a result of their purification ardently long for divine knowledge may commune with God freely. To them it will be said, 'What is it that you are calling to Me?' (Exod. 14 : 15. LXX). Thus, he who is commanded to keep silent because of his fear should seek refuge in God; he who is commanded to listen should be ready to obey the commandments; and he who pursues spiritual knowledge should call ceaselessly to God, beseeching Him for deliverance from evil and thanking Him for communion in His blessings.

31. A soul can never attain the knowledge of God unless God Himself in His condescension takes hold of it and raises it up to Himself. For the human intellect lacks the power to ascend and to participate in divine illumination, unless God Himself draws it up – in so far as this is possible for the human intellect – and illumines it with rays of divine light.

32. He who imitates the disciples of the Lord does not refuse, out of fear for the Pharisees, to walk through the cornfields on the sabbath and pluck ears of corn (cf. Matt. 12 : 1–2). On the contrary, when after practising the virtues he attains the state of dispassion, he culls the inner principles of created beings and devoutly nourishes himself with the divine knowledge they contain.

33. According to the Gospel, the person who is simply a man of faith can remove the mountain of his sin through the practice of the virtues (cf. Matt. 17 : 20), thus freeing himself from his former attachment to the restless gyration of sensible things. If he has the capacity to be a disciple he receives fragments of the loaves of spiritual knowledge from the hands of the Logos and feeds thousands

of people (cf. Matt. 14 : 19–20), demonstrating by his action how the power of the Logos is increased and multiplied by the practice of the virtues. If he also has the strength to be an apostle he cures every disease and infirmity: he casts out demons (cf. Matt. 10 : 8; Luke 10 : 17), that is, he banishes the activity of the passions; he heals the sick, through hope restoring a state of devotion to those who have lost it, and through his teaching about judgment stiffening the resolve of those who have been softened by sloth. For, since he has been commanded 'to tread on serpents and scorpions' (Luke 10 : 19), he destroys the beginning and end of sin.

34. An apostle is necessarily also a disciple and a man of faith. A disciple is not necessarily also an apostle but he is certainly a man of faith. A person who is simply a man of faith is neither a disciple nor an apostle. However, through his manner of life and through contemplation he can be raised to the rank and dignity of a disciple, and a disciple can be raised to the rank and dignity of an apostle.

35. When what has been created in time according to the temporal order has reached maturity, it ceases from natural growth. But when what has been brought about by the knowledge of God through the practice of the virtues has reached maturity, it starts to grow anew. For the end of one stage constitutes the starting-point of the next. He who has put an end to the root of corruption in himself by practising the virtues is initiated into other more divine experiences. There is never an end, as there is never a beginning, to the good which God does: just as the property of light is to illuminate, so the property of God is to do good. Thus in the Law, which is concerned with the structure of temporal things subject to generation and decay, the sabbath is honoured by rest from work (cf. Exod. 31 : 14), whereas in the Gospel, which initiates us into the realm of spiritual realities, lustre is shed on the sabbath by good actions (cf. Luke 6 : 9; John 5 : 16–17). This is so in spite of the indignation of those who do not yet understand that 'the sabbath was made for man and not man for the sabbath', and that 'the Son of Man is Lord also of the sabbath' (Mark 2 : 27–28).

36. In the Law and the prophets reference is made to the sabbath (cf. Isa. 66 : 23), sabbaths (cf. Exod. 31 : 13) and sabbaths of sabbaths (cf. Lev. 16 : 31. LXX); and to circumcision and circumcision of circumcision (cf. Gen. 17 : 10–13); and to harvest (cf. Gen. 8 : 22) and harvest of harvest, as in the text, 'when you harvest

your harvest' (cf. Lev. 23 : 10). The texts about the sabbath surely refer to the full attainment of practical, natural and theological philosophy; the texts about circumcision, to separation from things that are subject to generation and from the inner principles of these things; the texts about harvest, to the ingathering and enjoyment of more exalted spiritual principles on the part of the senses and the intellect. Through studying these three sets of texts the person of spiritual knowledge may discover the reasons why Moses, when he dies, takes his sabbath rest outside the holy land (cf. Deut. 34 : 5), why Joshua carried out the circumcisions after crossing the Jordan (cf. Josh. 5 : 3), and why those who inherited the promised land brought to God the superabundant fruits of the double harvest (cf. Lev. 23 : 11).

37. The sabbath signifies the dispassion of the deiform soul that through practice of the virtues has utterly cast off the marks of sin.

38. Sabbaths signify the freedom of the deiform soul that through the spiritual contemplation of created nature has quelled even the natural activity of sense-perception.

39. Sabbaths of sabbaths signify the spiritual calm of the deiform soul that has withdrawn the intellect even from contemplation of all the divine principles in created beings, that through an ecstasy of love has clothed it entirely in God alone, and that through mystical theology has brought it altogether to rest in God.

40. Circumcision signifies the quelling of the soul's impassioned predilection for things subject to generation.

41. Circumcision of circumcision signifies the complete discarding and stripping away also of even the soul's natural feelings for things subject to generation.

42. Harvest signifies the deiform soul's ingathering and knowledge of the more spiritual principles of created beings in a manner conforming to both virtue and nature.

43. Harvest of harvest signifies the apprehension of God which follows the mystical contemplation of noetic realities and which, inaccessible to all, is consummated in the intellect in a manner beyond understanding. Such apprehension is fittingly reaped by the person who in a worthy manner honours the Creator because of what He has created, whether visible or invisible.

44. There is another more spiritual harvest, which is said to belong to God Himself; there is another more mystical circumcision;

and there is another more hidden sabbath, which God celebrates when He rests from His own labours. This is shown in the following texts: 'The harvest is abundant, but the labourers are few' (Matt. 9 : 37); 'Circumcision of the heart in the spirit' (Rom. 2 : 29); and 'God blessed the seventh day and sanctified it, because in it God rested from all the works He had begun to do' (Gen. 2 : 3. LXX).

45. The harvest of God signifies the total dwelling and stability of the saints in God at the consummation of the ages.

46. Circumcision of the heart in the spirit signifies the utter stripping away from the senses and the intellect of their natural activities connected with sensible and intelligible things. This stripping away is accomplished by the Spirit's immediate presence, which completely transfigures body and soul and makes them more divine.

47. The sabbath rest of God signifies the complete reversion of created beings to God. It is then that God suspends in created beings the operation of their natural energy by inexpressibly activating in them His divine energy.[1] It is by virtue of this natural energy that each created being naturally acts; and God suspends its operation in each created being to the degree to which that being participates in His divine energy and so establishes its own natural energy within God Himself.

48. One should learn from those imbued with spiritual knowledge what is to be understood by the works which God began to do and what by those which He did not begin to do. For if He rested from all the works which He began to do, clearly He did not rest from those works which He did not begin to do. Perhaps, then, all that participates in being, such as the various essences of creatures, are works of God which began to be in time. For they have non-being as prior to their own being, since participant beings have not always existed. Participable beings, in which participant beings participate by grace, such as goodness and all that is included in the principle of goodness, are perhaps works of God which did not begin to be in time. Briefly, these include all life, immortality, simplicity, immutability and infinity, and all the other qualities that contemplative vision perceives as substantively appertaining to God. These are works of God, yet not begun in time. For non-being is

_____
[1] Reading *energoumenos* in place of *energoumenois*.

never prior to goodness, nor to any of the other things we have listed, even if those things which participate in them do in themselves have a beginning in time. All goodness is without beginning because there is no time prior to it: God is eternally the unique author of its being.

49. God is infinitely above all beings, whether participant or participable. For whatever belongs to the category of being is a work of God, even though participant beings had a temporal origin, whereas participable beings were implanted by grace among things that come into existence in time. In this way participable beings are a kind of innate power clearly proclaiming God's presence in all things.

50. All immortal things and immortality itself, all living things and life itself, all holy things and holiness itself, all good things and goodness itself, all blessings and blessedness itself, all beings and being itself are manifestly works of God. Some things began to be in time, for they have not always existed. Others did not begin to be in time, for goodness, blessedness, holiness and immortality have always existed. Those things which began in time exist and are said to exist by participation in the things which did not begin in time. For God is the creator of all life, immortality, holiness and goodness; and He transcends the being of all intelligible and describable beings.

51. The sixth day of creation, according to Scripture, represents the completion of the beings that are subject to nature. The seventh day marks the limit of the flow of temporal existence. The eighth day betokens the quality of that state which is beyond nature and time.

52. He who observes the sixth day only according to the Law, fleeing the active, soul-afflicting domination of the passions, passes fearlessly through the sea to the desert (cf. Exod. 16 : 1): his sabbath consists simply of rest from the passions. But when he has crossed the Jordan (cf. Josh. 3 : 17) and has left behind this state of simply resting from the passions, he enters into possession of the virtues.

53. He who observes the sixth day according to the Gospel, having already put to death the first impulses of sin, through cultivating the virtues attains a state of dispassion which, like a desert, is bare of all evil: his sabbath is a rest of his intellect even from the

merest images suggested by the passions. But when he has crossed the Jordan he passes over into the land of spiritual knowledge, where the intellect, the temple mystically built by peace, becomes in spirit the dwelling-place of God.

54. He who after the example of God has completed the sixth day with fitting actions and thoughts, and has himself with God's help brought his own actions to a successful conclusion, has in his understanding traversed the condition of all things subject to nature and time and has entered into the mystical contemplation of the aeons and the things inherent in them: his sabbath is his intellect's utter and incomprehensible abandonment and transcendence of created beings. But if he is also found worthy of the eighth day he has risen from the dead – that is, from all that is sequent to God, whether sensible or intelligible, expressible or conceivable. He experiences the blessed life of God, who is the only true life, and himself becomes god by deification.

55. The sixth day is the complete fulfilment, on the part of those practising the ascetic life, of the natural activities which lead to virtue. The seventh day is the conclusion and cessation, in those leading the contemplative life, of all natural thoughts about inexpressible spiritual knowledge. The eighth day is the transposition and transmutation of those found worthy into a state of deification. The Lord, giving perhaps a mysterious hint of the seventh and the eighth days, spoke of a day and an hour of consummation which encompasses the mysteries and the inner essences of all things. Apart from their Creator, the blessed Divinity Himself, there is no power whatsoever in heaven or on earth that can know that day and hour before the actual experience of them (cf. Matt. 24 : 36).

56. The sixth day betokens the inner essence of the being of created things. The seventh signifies the quality of the well-being of created things. The eighth denotes the inexpressible mystery of the eternal well-being of created things.

57. Since we know that the sixth day is a symbol of practical activity, let us during this day fully discharge our debt of virtuous works, so that it may also be said of us, 'And God saw everything He had made, and behold, it was very good' (Gen. 1 : 31).

58. He who exerts himself bodily in order to adorn the soul with the manifold virtues pays to God the debt of good work that is required of him.

59. He who has completed the sixth day, the day of preparation, in works of righteousness has crossed over to the repose of spiritual contemplation. During such contemplation his intellect, grasping in a divine manner the inner essences of created beings, ceases from all movement.

60. He who for our sake shared in God's rest of the seventh day also for our sake participates in God's deifying energy on the eighth day, that is, in the mystical resurrection, and leaves lying in the sepulchre His linen clothes and the napkin that was about his head (cf. John 20 : 6–7). Those who perceive this, like Peter and John, are convinced that the Lord has risen.

61. The Lord's tomb stands equally either for this world or for the heart of each faithful Christian. The linen clothes are the inner essences of sensible things together with their qualities of goodness. The napkin is the simple and homogeneous knowledge of intelligible realities, together with the vision of God, in so far as it is granted. Through these things the Logos is initially recognized, for without them any higher apprehension of what He is would be altogether beyond our capacity.

62. Those who bury the Lord with honour will also see Him risen with glory, but He is not seen by anyone else. For He can no longer be apprehended by His enemies as He does not wear those outer coverings through which He seemed to let Himself be captured by those who sought Him, and in which He endured suffering for the salvation of all.

63. He who buries the Lord with honour is revered by all who love God. For he has not allowed the Lord's body, nailed to the cross, to be left exposed to the blasphemy of unbelievers, but has befittingly delivered Him from derision and insult. Those who sealed the tomb and set soldiers to watch (cf. Matt. 27 : 66) are hateful because of their scheming. When the Logos had risen, they slandered Him, saying that His body had been stolen away. In the same way, as they bribed the false disciple with silver to betray the Lord – by false disciple I mean a pretence of holiness for the sake of display – so they bribed the soldiers to make a false accusation against the risen Saviour. Whoever possesses spiritual knowledge knows the significance of what has been said, for he is not ignorant of how and in how many ways the Lord is crucified, buried and rises again. Such a person makes corpses, as it were, of the impassioned

thoughts which have been insinuated by the demons into his heart, and which through the temptations they suggest cut in pieces the qualities of moral beauty as if they were garments (cf. Matt. 27 : 35); and he breaks like seals the impressions stamped deeply into his soul by the sins of prepossession.

64. Whenever a lover of riches who feigns virtue by an outward show of devotion finds he has procured the material possessions he desires, he repudiates the way of life that made people think he was a disciple of the Logos.

65. When you see arrogant men not able to endure praise being given to others better than themselves, and contriving to suppress the truth by denying it with countless insinuations and baseless slanders, you must understand that the Lord is again crucified by these men and buried and guarded with soldiers and seals. But the Logos rises afresh and puts them to confusion. The more the Logos is attacked, the more clearly He reveals Himself, as steeled in dispassion through His sufferings. The Logos is stronger than all else: not only is He called truth but He is truth.

66. The mystery of the incarnation of the Logos is the key to all the arcane symbolism and typology in the Scriptures, and in addition gives us knowledge of created things, both visible and intelligible. He who apprehends the mystery of the cross and the burial apprehends the inward essences of created things; while he who is initiated into the inexpressible power of the resurrection apprehends the purpose for which God first established everything.

67. All visible realities need the cross, that is, the state in which they are cut off from things acting upon them through the senses. All intelligible realities need burial, that is, the total quiescence of the things which act upon them through the intellect. When all relationship with such things is severed, and their natural activity and stimulus is cut off, then the Logos, who exists alone in Himself, appears as if risen from the dead. He encompasses all that comes from Him, but nothing enjoys kinship with Him by virtue of natural relationship. For the salvation of the saved is by grace and not by nature (cf. Eph. 2 : 5).

68. Ages, times and places belong to the category of relationship, and consequently no object necessarily associated with these things can be other than relative. But God transcends the category of relationship; for nothing else whatsoever is necessarily associated with

Him. Therefore if the inheritance of the saints is God Himself, he who is found worthy of this grace will be beyond all ages, times and places: he will have God Himself as his place, in accordance with the text, 'Be to me a God who is a defender and a fortified place of my salvation' (Ps. 71 : 3. LXX).

69. The consummation bears no resemblance whatsoever to the intermediary state, for otherwise it would not be a consummation. The intermediary state consists of everything that is sequent to the origin but falls short of the consummation. But if all ages, times and places, together with all that is necessarily associated with them, are sequent to God – since He is an unoriginate origin – and also fall far short of God – since He is an infinite consummation – then clearly they belong to the intermediary state. The consummation of those who are saved is God; in this supreme consummation no trace of the intermediary state will be observed in those who have been saved.

70. The whole world, limited as it is by its own inner principles, is called both the place and age of those dwelling in it. There are modes of contemplation natural to it which are able to engender in created beings a partial understanding of the wisdom of God that governs all things. So long as they make use of these modes to gain understanding, they cannot have more than a mediate and partial apprehension. But when what is perfect appears, what is partial is superseded: all mirrors and indistinct images pass away when truth is encountered face to face (cf. 1 Cor. 13 : 10–12). When he who is saved is perfected in God, he will transcend all worlds, ages and places in which hitherto he has been trained as a child.

71. Pilate is a type of the natural law; the Jewish crowd is a type of the written law. He who has not risen through faith above the two laws cannot therefore receive the truth which is beyond nature and expression. On the contrary, he invariably crucifies the Logos, for he sees the Gospel either, like a Jew, as a stumbling-block or, like a Greek, as foolishness (cf. 1 Cor. 1 : 23).

72. When you see Herod and Pilate making friends with each other in order to destroy Jesus (cf. Luke 23 : 12), you may discern in this the concurrence of the demons of unchastity and self-esteem, who combine together to put to death the Logos of virtue and spiritual knowledge. For the demon of self-esteem, making a pretence of spiritual knowledge, refers to the demon of unchastity, and

the demon of unchastity, putting on a hypocritical show of purity, refers back to the demon of self-esteem. Thus it is said, 'When Herod had arrayed Jesus in a gorgeous robe, he sent Him again to Pilate' (Luke 23 : 11).

73. The intellect should not yield to the flesh or cling to the passions. For, it is said, 'men do not gather figs from thorns', that is, they do not gather virtue from the passions, 'nor do they gather grapes from a bramble bush' (cf. Matt. 7 : 16), that is, they do not gather from the flesh that spiritual knowledge which gladdens the heart.

74. An ascetic tested by the patient acceptance of trials and temptations, purified by bodily training, and perfected by attention to the higher forms of contemplation, receives the blessings of divine grace. 'For the Lord', says Moses, 'came from Sinai,' that is, from trials and temptations, 'and appeared to us from Seir,' that is, from bodily hardships, 'and hastened down from mount Paran with ten thousands of Kadesh' (Deut. 33 : 2. LXX), that is, from the mountain of faith with untold sacred knowledge.

75. Herod exemplifies the will of the flesh; Pilate, the senses; Caesar, sensible things; and the Jews, the soul's thoughts. When the soul through ignorance associates with sensible things, it betrays the Logos into the hands of the senses to be put to death and proclaims within itself the kingship of perishable things. For the Jews say, 'We have no king but Caesar' (John 19 : 15).

76. Again, Herod exemplifies the activity of the passions; Pilate, a disposition that is deluded by them; Caesar, the ruler of the world of darkness; and the Jews, the soul. When the soul submits to the passions and betrays virtue into the power of an evil disposition, it manifestly denies the kingdom of God and transfers itself to the destructive tyranny of the devil.

77. The subjugation of the passions is not sufficient to ensure spiritual happiness for the soul unless the soul also acquires the virtues by keeping the commandments. Scripture says, 'Do not rejoice because the spirits are subject to you,' that is, the operations of the passions, but 'because your names are written in heaven' (Luke 10 : 20), having been transferred to the place of dispassion by the grace of sonship gained through the virtues.

78. Whoever possesses spiritual knowledge must always possess as well a rich store of virtue gained through his conduct. Scripture

says, 'He who has a purse,' that is, spiritual knowledge, 'let him take it, and his knapsack as well' (Luke 22 : 36), that is, the store from which he liberally nourishes his soul with virtue. He who does not have a purse and a knapsack, that is, knowledge and virtue, 'let him sell his garment and buy a sword' (ibid.). By this Scripture means: let him give his own flesh willingly to labours in pursuit of virtue, and for the sake of the peace of God let him wisely wage war against passions and demons, that is, let him acquire the skill of discriminating in the word of God between the lower and the higher.

79. The Lord appeared when He was thirty years old, and with this number secretly teaches those with discernment the mysteries relating to Himself. For, mystically understood, the number thirty presents the Lord as the Creator and provident ruler of time, nature, and the intelligible realities that lie beyond visible nature. The number seven signifies that He is the Creator of time, for time has a sevenfold character. The number five signifies that He is the Creator of nature, for nature has a fivefold character because of the fivefold division of the senses. The number eight signifies that He is the Creator of intelligible realities, for intelligible realities come into being outside the cycle that is measured by time. And the number ten signifies that He is the provident ruler, because it is the ten holy commandments that lead men towards perfection, and also because the symbol for ten[1] is the first letter of the name taken by the Lord when He became man. By adding up five, seven, eight and ten you obtain the number thirty. Thus he who truly knows how to follow the Lord as his master will understand why, should he attain the age of thirty, he will also be empowered to proclaim the gospel of the kingdom. For when through his ascetic practice he has irreproachably created the world of the virtues as if it were a world of visible nature, not allowing his soul to be diverted from its course by the hostile powers as he passes through time; and when he unerringly gathers spiritual knowledge through contemplation, and is providentially able to engender the same state in others, then he himself, whatever his physical age, is thirty years old in spirit and makes manifest in others the power of the blessings which he himself possesses.

[1] In Greek the number ten is indicated by the letter I, the first letter of the name Iisous.

80. He who yields to the pleasures of the body is neither diligent in virtue nor readily receptive of spiritual knowledge. For this reason he has no one – that is, no intelligent thought – to put him into the pool when the water is disturbed (cf. John 5 : 7), that is, into a state of virtue capable of receiving spiritual knowledge and of healing every sickness. On the contrary, although sick, he procrastinates because of laziness and is forestalled by someone else, who prevents him from being cured. And so he lies there with his illness for thirty-eight years. He who does not contemplate the visible creation so as to discern God's glory in it, and does not reverently raise his inner vision to the noetic world, quite fittingly remains ill for the number of years specified. For the number thirty, understood with reference to nature, signifies the sensible world, while with reference to the ascetic life it signifies the practice of the virtues. The number eight, understood mystically, denotes the intelligible nature of incorporeal beings, while understood in terms of spiritual knowledge it denotes the supreme wisdom of theology. Whoever does not advance towards God by these means remains paralysed until the Logos comes to teach him how he can obtain prompt healing, saying to him, 'Rise, take up your bed and walk' (John 5 : 8); that is to say, the Logos commands him to upraise his intellect from the love of pleasure which dominates him, to shoulder the body of the virtues and to go home, that is, to heaven. Better that the higher should raise the lower up to virtue on the shoulders of ascetic practice than that, through soft living, the lower should drag the higher down into self-indulgence.

81. Until our minds in purity have transcended our own being and that of all things sequent to God, we have not yet acquired a permanent state of holiness. When this noble state has, by means of love, been established in us, we shall know the power of the divine promise. For we must believe that where the intellect, taking the lead, has by means of love rooted its power, there the saints will find a changeless abode. He who has not transcended himself and all that is in any way subject to intellection, and has not come to abide in the silence beyond intellection, cannot be entirely free from change.

82. Every intellection has either a multiple or at least a dual aspect. For it is an intermediate relationship between two extremes – an intellective being and an intelligible being – and links the one to the other. Hence neither extreme can possess an absolute

simplicity. An intellective being is a subject, and so the capacity of apprehending some intelligible object is necessarily associated with it. And an intelligible being necessarily either is a subject or exists in a subject: as a subject it possesses the intrinsic capacity of being apprehended by an intellective being; as existing in a subject it presupposes a being in which it exists potentially. For no creature is in itself a simple being or intellection, in such a way as to constitute an indivisible unity. Thus, if we call God a being, then the capacity to be apprehended by a process of intellection is not inherent in His nature, for if it were He would be composite. Or if we call Him an intellection, then He does not possess an essence with a natural capacity for being an intellective subject, but He Himself is intellection in His very essence; the whole of God is intellection and intellection alone. But in terms of intellection He is also being: the whole of God is being and being alone. And yet the whole of God is beyond being and beyond intellection, because He is an indivisible unity, simple and without parts. Thus whoever, to whatever degree, still apprehends by means of intellection has not yet transcended duality. But he who has advanced altogether beyond intellection, and has renounced it because he has transcended it, has come to dwell to some extent in unity.

83. In the multiplicity of beings there is diversity, dissimilarity and difference. But in God, who is in an absolute sense one and alone, there is only identity, simplicity and similarity. It is therefore not safe to devote oneself to the contemplation of God before one has advanced beyond the multiplicity of beings. Moses showed this when he pitched the tent of his mind outside the camp (cf. Exod. 33 : 7) and then conversed with God. For it is dangerous to attempt to utter the inexpressible by means of the spoken word, for the spoken word involves duality or more than duality. The surest way is to contemplate pure being silently in the soul alone, because pure being is established in undivided unity and not among the multiplicity of things. The high priest, who was commanded to go into the holy of holies within the veil only once every year (cf. Lev. 16; Heb. 9 : 7), shows us that only he who has passed through what is immaterial and holy and has entered the holy of holies – that is, who has transcended the whole natural world of sensible and intelligible realities, is free from all that is specific to creatures and whose mind is unclad and naked – is able to attain the vision of God.

84. When Moses pitches his tent outside the camp (cf. Exod. 33 : 7) – that is, when he establishes his will and mind outside the world of visible things – he begins to worship God. Then, entering into the darkness (cf. Exod. 20 : 21) – that is, into the formless and immaterial realm of spiritual knowledge – he there celebrates the most sacred rites.

85. The darkness is that formless, immaterial and bodiless state which embraces the knowledge of the prototypes of all created things. He who like another Moses enters into it, although mortal by nature, understands things that are immortal. Through this knowledge he depicts in himself the beauty of divine excellence, as if painting a picture which is a faithful copy of archetypal beauty. Then he comes down from the mountain and offers himself as an example to those who wish to imitate that excellence. In this way he manifests the love and generosity of the grace he has received.

86. Those who apply themselves with a pure heart to divine philosophy derive the greatest gain from the knowledge it contains. For their will and purpose no longer change with circumstances, but readily and with firm assurance they undertake all that conforms to the standard of holiness.

87. Baptized in Christ through the Spirit, we receive the first incorruption according to the flesh. Keeping this original incorruption spotless by giving ourselves to good works and by dying to our own will, we await the final incorruption bestowed by Christ in the Spirit. No one who possesses this final incorruption fears the loss of the blessings he has obtained.

88. When God in His mercy resolved to send down from heaven the grace of His divine power to us on earth, He established the sacred tabernacle with all its contents as a symbolical image, type and imitation of wisdom.

89. The grace of the New Testament is mystically hidden in the letter of the Old. That is why St Paul says that 'the Law is spiritual' (Rom. 7 : 14). Thus the letter of the Law, superseded, grows old and decays (cf. Heb. 8 : 13), while its spirit, perpetually renewed, stays young. For grace is altogether immune from decay.

90. The Law is the shadow of the Gospel. The Gospel is the image of the blessings held in store. The Law checks the actualization of evil. The Gospel brings about the realization of divine blessings.

91. All sacred Scripture can be divided into flesh and spirit as if it were a spiritual man. For the literal sense of Scripture is flesh and its inner meaning is soul or spirit. Clearly someone wise abandons what is corruptible and unites his whole being to what is incorruptible.

92. The Law is the flesh of the spiritual man who here corresponds to sacred Scripture; the prophets are the senses; the Gospel is the noetic soul that functions through the flesh of the Law and the senses of the prophets, revealing its power in its actions.

93. The Law is a shadow and the prophets are an image of the divine and spiritual blessings contained in the Gospel. The truth itself, foreshadowed in the Law and prefigured in the prophets, is revealed in the Gospel as now present to us through actual events.

94. He who fulfils the Law in his private and public life only abstains from the actual commission of sin, sacrificing to God the outward fulfilment of his mindless passions. He is satisfied with this manner of seeking salvation because of his spiritual immaturity.

95. He who has been trained by the prophets' words not only refrains from the outward fulfilment of the passions but also renounces all assent to them in his soul. He is not content simply to appear to abstain from sin in the inferior part of himself, the flesh, while secretly allowing its free rein in his superior part, the soul.

96. He who has truly embraced the life of the Gospel has made himself immune to both the promptings and performance of evil, and pursues every virtue in action and thought. He offers a sacrifice of praise and thanksgiving (cf. Ps. 116 : 17), for he has been set free from all disturbance produced by the passions and liberated from mental warfare against them; and he feeds his soul with the hope of the blessings held in store, his one unquenchable delight.

97. To the more diligent students of Holy Scripture the Lord is clearly shown as having two forms. The first is common and more popular, and it can be perceived by many. The text 'We saw Him and He had no comeliness or beauty' (Isa. 53 : 2. LXX) refers to this form. The second is more hidden, and it can be perceived only by a few, that is, by those who have already become like the holy apostles Peter and John, before whom the Lord was transfigured with a glory that overwhelmed the senses (cf. Matt. 17 : 2). The

text 'Thou art fairer than the children of men' (Ps. 45 : 2) refers to this form. The first of these two forms is consonant to beginners; the second to those perfected in spiritual knowledge, in so far as such perfection is possible. The first is an image of the Lord's initial advent, to which the literal meaning of the Gospel refers, and which by means of suffering purifies those practising the virtues. The second prefigures the second and glorious advent, in which the spirit of the Gospel is apprehended, and which by means of wisdom transfigures and deifies those imbued with spiritual knowledge: because of the transfiguration of the Logos within them 'they reflect with unveiled face the glory of the Lord' (2 Cor. 3 : 18).

98. He who endures suffering for the sake of virtue, without being shaken in his resolve, is inspired by the first advent of the Logos, which cleanses him from all defilement. He who through contemplation has raised his intellect to the angelic state possesses the power of the second advent, which produces in him dispassion and incorruptibility.

99. Sense-perception pertains to the ascetic who is struggling to attain the virtues through enduring hardships. Freedom from sense-perception pertains to the contemplative who draws his intellect away from the flesh and the world and concentrates it on God. The first, in his ascetic struggle to loosen the natural bond linking the soul to the flesh, constantly submits his will to the hardships he undergoes. The second, who has broken that bond through contemplation, is not held back by anything at all: he has already freed himself from the domination of those who try to overpower him.

100. The manna which was given to Israel in the desert (cf. Exod. 16 : 14–35) is the Logos of God. Those who eat it find that it supplies every spiritual delight. It is blended to suit every taste in accordance with the different desires of those who eat it, for it has the quality of every kind of spiritual food. Thus, to those who through the Spirit have been born from above by means of incorruptible seed (cf. John 3 : 3–5), it comes as pure spiritual milk (cf. 1 Pet. 2 : 2); to the weak it comes as vegetables (cf. Rom. 14 : 2) sustaining the soul's passible aspect; to those in whom the soul's organs of perception have been trained by long practice to distinguish between good and evil it serves as solid food (cf. Heb. 5 : 14). The Logos of God also has other infinite powers which cannot be encompassed in this world. If at death a man is worthy to be put in

charge of many things or all things because in this world he has been faithful in small things (cf. Matt. 25 : 21), he will also receive all or some of these other powers of the Logos. For the most exalted of the divine gifts of grace bestowed in this world is scant and minimal compared with those that are held in store for us.

Second Century

1. God is one because there is one Divinity: unoriginate, simple, beyond being, without parts, indivisible. The Divinity is both unity and trinity – wholly one and wholly three. It is wholly one in respect of the essence, wholly three in respect of the hypostases or persons. For the Divinity is Father, Son and Holy Spirit, and is in Father, Son and Holy Spirit. The whole Divinity is in the whole Father and the whole Father is in the whole Divinity. The whole Divinity is in the whole Son and the whole Son is in the whole Divinity. The whole Divinity is in the whole Holy Spirit and the whole Holy Spirit is in the whole Divinity. The whole Divinity is both Father and in the whole Father; the whole Father is in the whole Divinity and the whole Divinity is the whole Father. The whole Son is in the whole Divinity and the whole Divinity is in the whole Son; the whole Son is both the whole Divinity and in the whole Divinity. The whole Divinity is both the Holy Spirit and in the whole Holy Spirit; and the whole Holy Spirit is both the whole Divinity and in the whole Divinity. For the Divinity is not partially in the Father, nor is the Father part of God. The Divinity is not partially in the Son, nor is the Son part of God. The Divinity is not partially in the Holy Spirit, nor is the Holy Spirit part of God. For the Divinity is not divisible; nor is the Father, or the Son, or the Holy Spirit incomplete God. On the contrary, the whole and complete Divinity is completely in the complete Father; the whole and complete Divinity is completely in the complete Son; and the whole and complete Divinity is completely in the complete Holy Spirit. For the whole Father is completely in the whole Son and Spirit; and the whole Son is completely in the whole Father and Spirit; and the whole Holy Spirit is completely in the whole Father and Son. Therefore the Father, the Son and the Holy Spirit are one God. The essence, power and energy of the Father, the Son and the

Holy Spirit are one, for none of the hypostases or persons either exists or is intelligible without the others.

2. Every intellection involves both an intellect that apprehends and an intelligible being that is apprehended. But God is neither an apprehending intellect nor an intelligible being: He transcends both. For if He were an apprehending intellect He would be limited by His need for a relationship with an intelligible being; and if He were an intelligible being He would be limited because naturally subject to an apprehending intellect capable of grasping Him. It follows therefore that God is not to be conceived as either an intellect or an intelligible being, and that He is beyond both intellection and intelligibility. Intellection and intelligibility appertain by nature to what is sequent to God.

3. Every intellection inheres as a quality in an apprehending being; and its activity is directed towards a being endowed with qualities. For no intellection can be directed towards a being that is absolutely independent, simple and self-subsistent, since the intellection itself is not independent and simple. But God is in both respects absolutely simple: in so far as He is being, He is independent of any apprehending subject; in so far as He is intellection, He is independent of any apprehensible object. Thus God is neither an intelligible object nor an intellective subject, for He clearly transcends both being and intellection.

4. The centre of a circle is regarded as the indivisible source of all the radii extending from it; similarly, by means of a certain simple and indivisible act of spiritual knowledge, the person found worthy to dwell in God will perceive pre-existing in God all the inner essences of created things.

5. When intellection is given form through its apprehension of intelligible objects, it ceases to be single and becomes many intellections; for it is marked by the form of each intelligible object that it apprehends. But as it passes beyond the multiplicity of the sensible and intelligible things that in this way confer their manifold forms upon it, it becomes altogether free from form. It is now that the Logos, who is beyond intellection, unites Himself to it and makes it His own, giving it rest from those things which by nature change and diversify it with the many conceptual forms that they impose upon it. He who experiences this has rested from his works, just as God did from His (cf. Gen. 2 : 2; Heb. 4 : 10).

6. He who reaches such perfection as is attainable by men in this world offers to God the fruits of love, joy, peace and long-suffering (cf. Gal. 5 : 22), and will in the age to be offer those of incorruptibility, eternity and similar gifts. The first qualities may be found in the man perfect in the practice of the virtues; the second in the man who through true spiritual knowledge has passed beyond the world of created things.

7. Just as the result of disobedience is sin, so the result of obedience is virtue. And just as disobedience leads to breaking the commandments and to separation from Him who gave them, so obedience leads to keeping the commandments and to union with Him who gave them. Thus he who through obedience has kept the commandments has achieved righteousness and, moreover, he has not cut himself off from union in love with Him who gave them; and the opposite is equally true.

8. If you are healed of the breach caused by the fall, you are severed first from the passions and then from impassioned thoughts. Next you are severed from nature and the inner principles of nature, then from conceptual images and the knowledge relating to them. Lastly, when you have passed through the manifold principles relating to divine providence, you attain through unknowing the very principle of divine unity. Then the intellect contemplates only its own immutability, and rejoices with an unspeakable joy because it has received the peace of God which transcends all intellect and which ceaselessly keeps him who has been granted it from falling (cf. Phil. 4 : 7).

9. Fear of hell causes beginners to shun evil. Desire to be rewarded with divine blessings confers on those who are advancing a readiness to practise the virtues. But the mystery of love transcends all created beings and makes the intellect blind to all that is sequent to God. Only upon those who have become blind to all that is sequent to Him does the Lord bestow wisdom, showing them what is more divine.

10. The Logos of God is like a grain of mustard seed (cf. Matt. 13 : 31): before cultivation it looks extremely small, but when cultivated in the right way it grows so large that the highest principles of both sensible and intelligible creation come like birds to revive themselves in it. For the principles or inner essences of all things are embraced by the Logos, but the Logos is not embraced by any

thing. Hence the Lord has said that he who has faith as a grain of mustard seed can move a mountain by a word of command (cf. Matt. 17 : 20), that is, he can destroy the devil's dominion over us and remove it from its foundation.

11. The grain of mustard seed is the Lord, who by faith is sown spiritually in the hearts of those who accept Him. He who diligently cultivates the seed by practising the virtues moves the mountain of earth-bound pride and, through the power he has gained, he expels from himself the obdurate habit of sin. In this way he revives in himself the activity of the principles and qualities or divine powers present in the commandments, as though they were birds.

12. Let us build on the Lord, as though on a foundation of faith, with gold, silver and precious stones, raising a temple of holiness (cf. 1 Cor. 3 : 12). Let us build, that is to say, with pure undebased theology, with a way of life that is lucid and radiant, with divine thoughts and conceptual images more precious than jewels. Let us not use wood, hay or stubble, that is, idolatry – which is a passionate desire for sensible things – or a meaningless way of life, or thoughts which are impassioned and as empty of wise understanding as straw.

13. If a man seeks spiritual knowledge, let him plant the foundations of his soul immovably before the Lord, in accordance with God's words to Moses: 'Stand here by Me' (Deut. 5 : 31). But it should be realized that there are differences among those who stand before the Lord, as is clear from the text, 'There are some standing here who will not taste death till they have seen the kingdom of God come with power' (Mark 9 : 1). For the Lord does not always appear in glory to all who stand before Him. To beginners He appears in the form of a servant (cf. Phil. 2 : 7); to those able to follow Him as He climbs the high mountain of His transfiguration He appears in the form of God (cf. Matt. 17 : 1–9), the form in which He existed before the world came to be (cf. John 17 : 5). It is therefore possible for the same Lord not to appear in the same way to all who stand before Him, but to appear to some in one way and to others in another way, according to the measure of each person's faith.

14. When the Logos of God becomes manifest and radiant in us, and His face shines like the sun, then His clothes will also look white (cf. Matt. 17 : 2). That is to say, the words of the Gospels

will then be clear and distinct, with nothing concealed. And Moses and Elijah – the more spiritual principles of the Law and the prophets – will also be present with Him.

15. It is written that the Son of Man is coming 'with His angels in the glory of the Father' (Matt. 16 : 27). Similarly, in those found worthy, the Logos of God is transfigured to the degree to which each has advanced in holiness, and He comes to them with His angels in the glory of the Father. For the more spiritual principles in the Law and the prophets – symbolized by Moses and Elijah when they appeared with the Lord at His transfiguration – manifest their glory according to the actual receptive capacity of those to whom it is revealed.

16. He who to some degree has been initiated into the inner principle of the divine unity invariably discovers the inner principles of divine providence and judgment conjoined with it. That is why, like St Peter, he thinks it good that three tabernacles should be made within himself for those who have appeared to him (cf. Matt. 17 : 4). These tabernacles represent three stages of salvation, namely that of virtue, that of spiritual knowledge and that of theology. The first requires fortitude and self-restraint in the practice of the virtues: of this the type was Elijah. The second requires right discernment in natural contemplation: Moses disclosed this in his own person. The third requires the consummate perfection of wisdom: this was revealed by the Lord. They were called tabernacles, or temporary dwellings, because beyond them there are other still more excellent and splendid stages, through which those found worthy will pass in the age to be.

17. A man engaged in the practice of the virtues is said to be 'sojourning' in the flesh (cf. Gen. 12 : 10), for by practising the virtues he is severing the soul's relationship with the flesh and stripping from himself the deceit of material things. A man of spiritual knowledge is said to be sojourning in virtue itself, for he still contemplates the truth indistinctly, as though in a mirror (cf. 1 Cor. 13 : 12): he has not yet enjoyed a face-to-face vision of the self-subsistent forms of goodness, seeing them as they are in themselves. For as regards the blessings of the age to be, every saint does no more than walk in the image of them, crying, 'I am a stranger and a sojourner as all my fathers were' (Ps. 39 : 12).

18. He who prays must never stand still on the steep ascent that

leads to God. Just as he has to progress upwards from strength to strength in the practice of the virtues (cf. Ps. 84 : 5–7), and to rise in his contemplation of spiritual truths from glory to glory (cf. 2 Cor. 3 : 18), and to pass from the letter to the spirit of Holy Scripture, so he must advance in a similar manner within the realm of prayer. He must raise his intellect and the resolve of his soul from what is human to what is divine, so that his intellect can follow Jesus the Son of God, who has passed through the heavens (cf. Heb. 4 : 14) and who is everywhere. For He has passed through all things for us by the dispensation of His incarnation, so that we, by following Him, may pass through all that is sequent to Him and so come to be with Him, provided we apprehend Him not according to the limitations to which He accommodated Himself in His incarnation but according to the majesty of His natural infinitude.

19. We should always devote ourselves to God and seek Him out as we have been commanded (cf. Matt. 6 : 33). Although when we seek Him in this present stage of life we cannot come to the limit of His depth, yet perhaps if we penetrate His depth even slightly we shall contemplate what is more holy than the holy and more spiritual than the spiritual. The high priest shows this to us typologically when he goes from the holy place, which is holier than the court, into the holy of holies, which is holier than the holy place (cf. Lev. 16).

20. The whole Logos of God is neither diffuse nor prolix but is a unity embracing a diversity of principles, each of which is an aspect of the Logos. Thus he who speaks about the truth, however fully he deals with his subject, speaks always about the one Logos of God.

21. Since Christ is God and the Logos of the Father, 'the fulness of the Godhead dwells bodily in Him' in a manner that is according to essence (Col. 2 : 9). The fulness of the Godhead dwells in us by grace when we gather into ourselves all virtue and wisdom, a wisdom which, so far as this is possible in man, does not in any way fall short of a faithful imitation of the divine archetype. For it is not incongruous that, by virtue of our relationship with the Logos, the fulness of the Godhead, embracing a diversity of spiritual principles, should come to dwell also in us.

22. The thought which springs naturally from our intellect is a messenger of the intellect's hidden activity. Similarly He who is in essence the Logos of God and knows the Father as a thought knows

the intellect which conceives it, reveals the Father whom He knows, no creature being able to approach the Father without Him. That is why He is called 'Messenger of great counsel' (Isa. 9 : 6. LXX).

23. The great counsel of God the Father is the unspoken and unknown mystery of the divine dispensation. This the only-begotten Son revealed through His incarnation, when He became the Messenger of the great pre-eternal counsel of God the Father. He who knows the inner principle of the mystery becomes a messenger of the great counsel of God, and he is exalted unceasingly by action and thought through all things until he encounters Him who has to a corresponding degree descended towards him.

24. The Logos of God providentially descended for our sakes into the lower parts of the earth, and also ascended far above all the heavens (cf. Eph. 4 : 9–10), even though by nature He is entirely unmoving. Since through the incarnation the Logos has already accomplished in Himself as man all that is to be, let him who delights in spiritual knowledge rejoice inwardly as he considers the consummation promised to those who love the Lord.

25. If the divine Logos of God the Father became son of man and man so that He might make men gods and the sons of God, let us believe that we shall reach the realm where Christ Himself now is; for He is the head of the whole body (cf. Col. 1 : 18), and endued with our humanity has gone to the Father as forerunner on our behalf. God will stand 'in the midst of the congregation of gods' (Ps. 82 : 1. LXX) – that is, of those who are saved – distributing the rewards of that realm's blessedness to those found worthy to receive them, not separated from them by any space.

26. He who still satisfies the impassioned appetites of the flesh dwells in the land of the Chaldeans as a maker and worshipper of idols. But when he has begun to discern what the situation is and has gained some insight into the mode of life which nature demands, he leaves the land of the Chaldeans and comes to Haran in Mesopotamia (cf. Gen. 11 : 31). By Haran I mean that intermediate state between virtue and vice – a state not yet purified from the delusion of the senses. But if he goes beyond that moderate understanding of goodness which he has attained through the senses, he will hasten towards the blessed land, that is, to the state free from all sin and ignorance which God, who does not lie, manifests to those who love Him, promising to give it to them as a reward for their virtue.

27. If for our sakes the Logos of God 'died on the Cross in weakness' and was raised 'by the power of God' (2 Cor. 13 : 4), then in a spiritual sense He is always doing and suffering this on our account, becoming all things to all men so that He might save all men (cf. 1 Cor. 9 : 22). Thus, since the Corinthians were weak, while with them St Paul rightly 'decided to know nothing except Jesus Christ and Him crucified' (1 Cor. 2 : 2). But since the Ephesians were perfect, he wrote to them that God 'has raised us up in union with Christ Jesus and enthroned us with Him in the heavenly realm' (Eph. 2 : 6), thus affirming that the Logos of God adapts Himself according to each person's strength. In this way, He is crucified for those taking their first steps in the ascetic life, and He nails their impassioned energies to the cross with divine fear. He rises again and ascends into heaven for those who have put off the whole of their fallen selfhood, corrupted by the desires of deceitfulness (cf. Eph. 4 : 22); who have been entirely renewed through the Holy Spirit as man created in the image of God (cf. Eph. 4 : 24); and who draw near to the Father through His grace which is in them, and so are raised 'far above every principality, power, might and dominion, and above every name that is named not only in this age but also in the age to come' (Eph. 1 : 21). For all things, all names and dignities sequent to God, are likewise inferior to him who through grace dwells in God.

28. Before His visible advent in the flesh the Logos of God dwelt among the patriarchs and prophets in a spiritual manner, prefiguring the mysteries of His advent. After His incarnation He is present in a similar way not only to those who are still beginners, nourishing them spiritually and leading them towards the maturity of divine perfection, but also to the perfect, secretly pre-delineating in them the features of His future advent as if in an ikon.

29. Just as the teachings of the Law and the prophets, being harbingers of the coming advent of the Logos in the flesh, guide our souls to Christ (cf. Gal. 3 : 24), so the glorified incarnate Logos of God is Himself a harbinger of His spiritual advent, leading our souls forward by His own teachings to receive His divine and manifest advent. He does this ceaselessly, by means of the virtues converting those found worthy from the flesh to the spirit. And He will do it at the end of the age, making manifest what has hitherto been hidden from all men.

30. As long as I remain imperfect and refractory, neither obeying God by practising the commandments nor becoming perfect in spiritual knowledge, Christ from my point of view also appears imperfect and refractory because of me. For I diminish and cripple Him by not growing in spirit with Him, since I am 'the body of Christ and one of its members' (1 Cor. 12 : 27).

31. 'The sun rises and the sun sets', says Scripture (Eccles. 1 : 5). Likewise the Logos appears sometimes as risen and sometimes as set, depending on the manner of life and the spiritual status and essence or quality of those pursuing virtue and searching for divine knowledge. Blessed is he who like Joshua (cf. Josh. 10 : 12–13) keeps the Sun of righteousness from setting in himself throughout the whole day of this present life, not allowing it to be blotted out by the dusk of sin and ignorance. In this way he will truly be able to put to flight the cunning demons that rise up against him.

32. When the Logos of God is raised up in us by our practice of the virtues and by contemplation, He draws all things to Himself (cf. John 12 : 32); He sanctifies in virtue and spiritual knowledge our thoughts and words about the flesh, the soul and the nature of beings; He sanctifies also the very members of our bodies and our senses, and He places them all under His yoke. So let the visionary of divine things eagerly ascend in pursuit of the Logos until he reaches the place where He is. For, as Ecclesiastes puts it, He 'draws to His place' (Eccles. 1 : 5) all those who follow Him, and as the great High Priest He brings them into the Holy of Holies, where He Himself, who became as we are, has entered as a forerunner on our behalf (cf. Heb. 6 : 20).

33. He who devoutly strives to attain wisdom and is on his guard against the invisible powers, should pray that both natural discrimination – whose light is but limited – and the illuminating grace of the Spirit abide with him. The first by means of practice trains the flesh in virtue, the second illuminates the intellect so that it chooses above all else companionship with wisdom; and through wisdom it destroys the strongholds of evil and pulls down 'all the self-esteem that exalts itself against the knowledge of God' (2 Cor. 10 : 5). Joshua exemplifies this both when he prays for the sun to stand still upon Gibeon, that is, for the light of the knowledge of God to remain unsetting as it shines for him over the mountain of spiritual contemplation; and when he asks for the moon to stand still in

the valley, that is, for the natural discrimination which watches over the weak flesh to remain changelessly wedded to virtue (cf. Josh. 10 : 12–13).

34. Gibeon is the spiritual intellect. The valley is the flesh humbled by death. The sun is the Logos, who illumines the intellect, supplying it with the power of contemplation and delivering it from all ignorance. The moon is the natural law, which persuades the flesh duly to submit to the spirit and accept the yoke of the commandments. The moon is the symbol of nature because of its mutability; but among the saints it remains immutable, for in them the state of virtue is unchanging.

35. Those who seek the Lord should not look for Him outside themselves; on the contrary, they must seek Him within themselves through faith made manifest in action. For He is near you: 'The word is . . . in your mouth and in your heart, that is, the word of faith' (Rom. 10 : 8) – Christ being Himself the word that is sought.

36. When we think of the height of God's infinity we should not despair of His compassion reaching us from such a height; and when we recall the infinite depth of our fall through sin we should not refuse to believe that the virtue which has been killed in us will rise again. For God can accomplish both these things: He can come down and illumine our intellect with spiritual knowledge, and He can raise up the virtue within us and exalt it with Himself through works of righteousness. For it is written: 'Do not say in your heart, "Who shall ascend into heaven?" – that is, to bring Christ down – or, "Who shall descend into the depths?" – that is, to bring Christ up again from the dead' (Rom. 10 : 6–7). Interpreted in another way, the depths stand for all that is sequent to God, in the whole of which the whole divine Logos providentially comes to dwell, as life returning to what is dead. For all things whose life depends upon their participation in life are in themselves dead. And heaven stands for God's natural hiddenness, whereby He is incomprehensible to all things. Alternatively, if anyone explains heaven as the doctrine of the Holy Trinity, and the depths as the mystery of the incarnation, he will not, I think, be far from the mark. For it is hard to grasp the meaning of either doctrine through rational demonstration; or rather, their meaning is altogether inaccessible unless explored with faith.

37. In the life of ascetic practice the Logos, adapted to the cor-

poreal action of the virtues, becomes flesh (cf. John 1 : 14). In the
contemplative life the Logos, refined by conceptual images that are
spiritual, becomes what He was in His principial state, the Logos
that was God and was with God (cf. John 1 : 1–2).

38. If you expound the teaching of the Logos from the stand-
point of the moral life, using relatively materialistic words and
examples which correspond to the capacity of your hearers, you
make the Logos flesh. Conversely, if you elucidate mystical theology
by means of the higher forms of contemplation you make the Logos
spirit.

39. If you theologize in an affirmative or cataphatic manner,
starting from positive statements about God, you make the Logos
flesh, for you have no other means of knowing God as cause except
from what is visible and tangible. If you theologize in a negative or
apophatic manner, through the stripping away of positive attributes,
you make the Logos spirit or God as He was in His principial state
with God: starting from absolutely none of the things that can be
known, you come in an admirable way to know Him who transcends unknowing.

40. When like the patriarchs we learn to dig wells of virtue and
spiritual knowledge within ourselves by means of ascetic practice
and contemplation, we will find within us Christ the spring of life
(cf. Gen. 26 : 15–18). Wisdom commands us to drink from this
spring, saying, 'Drink water from your own pitchers and from the
spring of your own wells' (Prov. 5 : 15). If we do this we shall find
that the treasures of wisdom truly are within us.

41. Those who animal-like live solely according to the senses
make the Logos flesh for themselves in a dangerous way: they misuse God's creation in order to indulge the passions. They do not
understand the principle of that wisdom which is revealed to all:
that we should know and praise God through His creation and that
by means of the visible world we should understand whence we
came, what we are, for what purpose we were made and where we
are going. On the contrary, they travel through this present age in
darkness, fumbling with both hands merely their ignorance of God.

42. Those who abide solely by the letter of Holy Scripture and
tie down the dignity of the soul to the external worship of the Law
make the Logos flesh for themselves in a reprehensible manner. They
think that God will be pleased with sacrifices of dumb animals. They

pay much attention to the body with outward purifications but neglect the soul's beauty, stained as it is by the passions. But it was for the soul that every power of the visible world was brought forth and that every divine teaching and law was proclaimed.

43. 'For the fall and resurrection of many in Israel is the Lord appointed', says the Holy Gospel (Luke 2 : 34). We should ask consequently whether He may not be appointed for the fall of those who contemplate the visible creation solely according to the senses and of those who stick to the mere letter of Holy Scripture, not being able in their folly to go further and grasp the new spirit of grace. And we should ask whether He may not be appointed for the resurrection of those who contemplate God's creatures and listen to His words in a spiritual manner, cultivating in appropriate ways only the divine image that is within the soul.

44. If the Lord's being appointed for the fall and resurrection of many is understood in the right way, then the fall will refer to that of the passions and of evil thoughts in each of the faithful, and the resurrection to that of the virtues and of every thought that enjoys God's blessing.

45. Those who think of the Lord only as the creator of things which are generated and which decay mistake Him, as Mary Magdalene did, for the gardener. It is therefore for their own good that the Master avoids contact with such persons, saying, 'Do not touch Me' (John 20 : 17); for they are not yet capable of ascending with Him to the Father. He knows that those who are predisposed to think of Him in such mean terms will suffer harm if they draw near to Him.

46. The people assembled in Galilee in the upper room with the doors locked for fear of the Jews are those who, having safely reached the height of divine contemplation in the land of revelations and having shut their senses like doors for fear of the spirits of evil, receive the presence of the divine Logos of God in a way that cannot be conceived. He is revealed to them without the activity of their senses; through His words 'Peace be with you' He bestows dispassion on them, and breathing on them He grants them participation in the Holy Spirit, giving them power to combat evil spirits and showing them the signs of His mysteries (cf. John 20 : 19–22; Mark 16 : 17–18).

47. The Lord does not ascend to the Father for those who explore

divine truth with their faculties as they are in their fallen state; but He does ascend to the Father for those who seek out the truth in the Spirit by means of the higher forms of contemplation. The Logos came down out of love for us. Let us not keep Him down permanently, but let us go up with Him to the Father, leaving the earth and earthly things behind, lest He say to us what He said to the Jews because of their stubbornness: 'I go where you cannot come' (John 8 : 21). For without the Logos it is impossible to approach the Father of the Logos.

48. The land of the Chaldeans is a way of life dominated by the passions, in which the idols of sins are fashioned and worshipped. Mesopotamia, the land between the rivers, is a way of life that vacillates between opposites. The promised land is a state filled with every blessing. Everyone, then, who like ancient Israel neglects this state, loses the freedom which he has been granted, and allows himself once more to be dragged off into slavery to the passions.

49. It should be noted that none of the saints went down to Babylon of his own accord. For it would be inept and inane for those who love God to choose what is bad rather than what is good. If some of them were taken there by force along with the people (cf. 2 Kings 25, 2 Chron. 36), they are to be understood as those who, not premeditatedly but at a time of crisis, and for the sake of saving those who needed their help, abandoned their absorption in the higher principle of spiritual knowledge in order to give instruction concerning the passions. For this reason St Paul felt that he would be more useful if he was in the flesh – that is, engaged in giving moral instruction to the disciples – although his whole desire was to be set free from moral teaching and to be with God (cf. Phil. 1 : 23) through pure intellectual contemplation which transcends the world.

50. When Saul was being choked by an evil spirit, David sang to the accompaniment of the harp and gave him relief (cf. 1 Sam. 16 : 14–23). In a similar manner every spiritual discourse, sweetened with mystical contemplation, brings relief to the intellect possessed by evil spirits and frees it from the bad conscience which chokes it.

51. David's glowing complexion and beautiful eyes (cf. 1 Sam. 16 : 12. LXX) signify a man in whom the splendour of a holy way of life is enriched by the presence of the principle of spiritual

knowledge. In this state ascetic practice and contemplation go together. Ascetic practice is given lustre by the qualities of the virtues; contemplation is illumined by divine conceptual images.

52. The reign of Saul is an image of the external worship of the Law, which the Lord abolished because it perfected nothing. 'For the Law', says Scripture, 'made nothing perfect' (Heb. 7 : 19). But the reign of the great David prefigures the worship set forth in the Gospel, for it enshrines to perfection God's most intimate purposes.

53. Saul is the natural law originally established by the Lord to rule over nature. But Saul was disobedient: he spared Agag, king of Amalek (cf. 1 Sam. 15 : 8–16 : 13), that is, the body, and slipped downward into the sphere of the passions. He was therefore deposed so that David might take over Israel. David is the law of the Spirit – the law engendering that peace which so excellently builds for God the temple of contemplation.

54. Samuel signifies obedience to God. So long as the principle of obedience exercises its priestlike office within us, even though Saul spares Agag – that is, the earthly will – yet that principle in its zeal will put him to death (cf. 1 Sam. 15 : 33): it strikes the sin-incited intellect and puts it to shame for having transgressed the divine ordinances.

55. When the intellect scorns the teaching which purifies it from the passions, and ceases to examine what should be done and what should not be done, it will through ignorance inevitably be overcome by the passions. As the intellect gradually comes to be separated from God, it is more and more involved in difficulties not of its own choosing. Obeying the demons, it makes a god of the belly and tries to find relief there from what oppresses it. Let Saul convince you of the truth of this: because he did not take Samuel for an adviser in all things he inevitably turned to idolatry, putting his trust in a ventriloquist and consulting her as if she were a god (cf. 1 Sam. 28 : 7–20).

56. He who asks to receive his daily bread (cf. Matt. 6 : 11) does not automatically receive it in its fulness as it is in itself: he receives it according to his own capacity as recipient. The Bread of Life (cf. John 6 : 35) gives Himself in His love to all who ask, but not in the same way to all; for He gives Himself more fully to those who have performed great acts of righteousness, and in smaller measure to

those who have not achieved so much. He gives Himself to each person according to that person's spiritual ability to receive Him.

57. Sometimes the Lord is absent from us; at other times He is present within us. He is absent when we contemplate Him indistinctly, as though in a mirror; He is present within us when we contemplate Him face to face (cf. 1 Cor. 13 : 12).

58. For the man living the life of ascetic practice the Lord is present through the virtues; but He is absent from the man who does not bother about virtue. Similarly, for a man engaged in the contemplative life, He is present in genuine knowledge of created beings, but absent when there is some lapse from this.

59. When a man passes from the life of ascetic practice to the stage of spiritual knowledge, he is absent from the flesh (cf. 2 Cor. 5 : 8). Caught up as on clouds by the more lofty conceptual images into the translucent air of mystical contemplation, he is able to 'be with the Lord for ever' (1 Thess. 4 : 17). A man 'is absent from the Lord' (2 Cor. 5 : 6) if he is not yet able to contemplate his conceptual images of things with a pure intellect free from the operations of the senses (so far as this is possible), and if he cannot yet embrace the knowledge of the Lord in its true simplicity, without the help of symbols.

60. The Logos of God is called flesh not only inasmuch as He became incarnate, but in another sense as well. When He is contemplated in His true simplicity, in His principial state with God the Father (cf. John 1 : 1–2), although He embraces the models of the truth of all things in a distinct and naked manner, He does not contain within Himself parables, symbols and stories needing allegorical interpretation. But when He draws near to men who cannot with the naked intellect come into contact with noetic realities in their naked state, He selects things which are familiar to them, combining together various stories, symbols, parables and dark sayings; and in this way He becomes flesh. Thus at the first encounter our intellect comes into contact not with the naked Logos but with the incarnate Logos, that is, with various sayings and stories. The incarnate Logos, though Logos by nature, is flesh in appearance. Hence most people think they see flesh and not the Logos, although in fact He is the Logos. The intellect – that is, the inner meaning – of Scripture is other than what it seems to most people. For the Logos becomes flesh in each of the recorded sayings.

61. The initial stages of learning about religious devotion are naturally related to the flesh. For in our first encounter with religion we come into contact with the letter and not the spirit. But as we get nearer to the spirit and refine the materiality of words with the more subtle forms of contemplation, we come to dwell – so far as this is possible for man – purely in the pure Christ, so that we can say with St Paul, 'Though we have known Christ according to the flesh, now we no longer know Him in this manner' (2 Cor. 5 : 16). That is to say, we no longer know Him according to the flesh because, through the intellect's naked encounter with the Logos stripped of the veils covering Him, we have advanced from knowing Him according to the flesh to knowing His 'glory as of the only-begotten Son of the Father' (John 1 : 14).

62. He who is living the life in Christ has gone beyond the righteousness of both the Law and nature. This St Paul indicated when he said, 'For in Christ Jesus there is neither circumcision nor uncircumcision' (cf. Gal. 5 : 6). By circumcision he meant righteousness according to the Law; by uncircumcision he hinted at natural justice, or equity.

63. Some are reborn through water and the spirit (cf. John 3 : 5); others receive baptism in the Holy Spirit and in fire (cf. Matt. 3 : 11). I take these four things – water, spirit, fire and Holy Spirit – to mean one and the same Spirit of God. To some the Holy Spirit is water because He cleanses the external stains of their bodies. To others He is simply spirit because He makes them active in the practice of virtue. To others He is fire because He cleanses the interior defilement which lies deep within their souls. To others, according to Daniel, He is Holy Spirit because He bestows on them wisdom and spiritual knowledge (cf. Dan. 1 : 17; 5 : 11–12). For the single identical Spirit takes His different names from the different ways in which He acts on each person.

64. The Law instituted the sabbath, says Scripture, so that your ox and your servant might rest (cf. Exod. 20 : 10). Both of these are symbols for the body. For the person engaged in the practice of the virtues, the body is an ox under the yoke of his intellect: it is forced to bear the burdens imposed in the ascetic life through the exercising of the virtues. For the contemplative the body is the servant of his intellect, because through contemplation it is now endowed with intelligence and so serves the intellect's spiritual commands

intelligently. For both the ox and the servant the sabbath signifies the final goal pursued by them throughout the ascetic and the contemplative life, and so it provides for both of them a fitting rest.

65. The man who attains virtue together with a consonant spiritual knowledge treats his body as an ox: with his intelligence he steers it to do what has to be done. The life of active virtue is his servant – the life which naturally gives rise to virtue and which is acquired through the exercise of discrimination as if bought with money. The sabbath is a virtuous, dispassionate and peaceful condition of both body and soul. It is an unchanging state.

66. For those still mainly concerned with the bodily forms of virtue, the Logos of God becomes hay and straw, sustaining the passible aspect of their souls and guiding it to the service of the virtues. For those who have advanced to the true contemplation of divine things, the Logos is bread, sustaining the intellective aspect of their souls and guiding it to a godlike perfection. That is why we find the patriarchs on their journeys providing themselves with bread and their asses with fodder (cf. Gen. 24 : 25; 42 : 25, 27). For the same reason the Levite in the Book of Judges said to the old man who questioned him in the street of Gibeah: 'There is bread for us and fodder for our asses, and for your servants there is no lack of anything' (cf. Judges 19 : 19).

67. In Scripture the Logos of God is called and actually is dew (cf. Deut. 32 : 2), water, spring (cf. John 4 : 14) and river (cf. John 7 : 38), according to the subjective capacity of the recipient. To some He is dew because He quenches the burning energy of the passions which assails the body from without. To those seared in the depths of their being by the poison of evil He is water, not only because water through antipathy destroys its opposite but also because it bestows a vivifying power conducive to well-being. To those in whom the fountain of contemplative experience is continually active He is a spring bestowing wisdom. To those from whom flows the true teaching about salvation, He is a river copiously watering men, domestic animals, wild beasts and plants. That is to say, those who have remained human are uplifted by the conceptual images they have been given and are so deified; those made like domestic animals by the passions are restored to the human state by being shown the exact character of the virtuous way of life and so they recover their natural intelligence; those made like wild beasts by

evil habits and actions are tamed by kind and tender counsel and return to their natural gentleness; those hardened like plants against divine blessings are made pliable by the Logos passing deeply through them, and they regain the sensitivity that enables them to bear fruit and to sustain the Logos within them.

68. The Logos of God is the way (cf. John 14 : 6) for those who run the course of virtue in their ascetic life nobly and vigorously, swerving neither to the right through self-esteem, nor to the left through proclivity to the passions, but directing their steps in accordance with God's will. Asa, king of Judah, did not persevere in this to the end and so it is said that in his old age he suffered from his feet (cf. 1 Kings 15 : 23), because he faltered in running the race of his life according to God's will.

69. The Logos of God is called the door (cf. John 10 : 9) because He leads to spiritual knowledge those who, in their unsullied pursuit of the ascetic life, have nobly traversed the whole way of the virtues, and because He reveals, as does light, the lustrous treasures of wisdom. For He Himself is the way, the door, the key and the kingdom. He is the way because He guides; He is the key because He both opens and is opened to those found worthy to receive divine blessings; He is the door because He gives admittance; He is the kingdom because He is inherited and because He enters by participation into all things.

70. The Lord is called light, life, resurrection and truth (cf. John 8 : 12; 11 : 25; 14 : 6). He is light because He gives lucidity to the soul, dispels the darkness of ignorance, illumines the intellect so that it can grasp what is unutterable, and reveals mysteries perceptible only to the pure. He is life because He gives souls who love Him the activity proper to the divine realm. He is resurrection because He raises the intellect from its lethal attachment to material things and purifies it from all decay and mortality. He is truth because He gives to those found worthy an unchanging state of sanctity.

71. The divine Logos of God the Father is mystically present in each of His commandments. God the Father is by nature present entirely and without division in His entire divine Logos. Thus, he who receives a divine commandment and carries it out receives the Logos of God who is in it; and he who receives the Logos through the commandments also receives through Him the Father who is by nature present in Him, and the Spirit who likewise is by nature in

Him. 'I tell you truly, he that receives whomever I send receives Me; and he that receives Me receives Him that sent Me' (John 13 : 20). In this way, he who receives a commandment and carries it out receives mystically the Holy Trinity.

72. It is not the man who worships God with words alone who glorifies God in himself but he who for God's sake bears hardship and suffering in the quest for virtue. Such a man is glorified in return by God with the glory that is in God, receiving through participation the grace of dispassion as a reward for virtue. For everyone living the life of ascetic practice who glorifies God in himself by suffering for the sake of virtue is himself glorified in God through the dispassionate illumination of divine realities perceived during contemplation. For the Lord said as He drew near to His passion, 'Now is the Son of man glorified, and God is glorified in Him. If God is glorified in Him, God will also glorify Him in Himself; and He will glorify Him at once' (John 13 : 31–32). From this it is clear that divine gifts follow sufferings endured for the sake of virtue.

73. So long as we only see the Logos of God as embodied multifariously in symbols in the letter of Holy Scripture, we have not yet achieved spiritual insight into the incorporeal, simple, single and unique Father as He exists in the incorporeal, simple, single and unique Son, according to the saying, 'He who has seen Me has seen the Father . . . and I am in the Father and the Father in Me' (John 14 : 9–10). We need much knowledge so that, having first penetrated the veils of the sayings which cover the Logos, we may with a naked intellect see – in so far as men can – the pure Logos, as He exists in Himself, clearly showing us the Father in Himself. Hence a person who seeks God with true devotion should not be dominated by the literal text, lest he unwittingly receives not God but things appertaining to God; that is, lest he feel a dangerous affection for the words of Scripture instead of for the Logos. For the Logos eludes the intellect which supposes that it has grasped the incorporeal Logos by means of His outer garments, like the Egyptian woman who seized hold of Joseph's garments instead of Joseph himself (cf. Gen. 39 : 7–13), or like the ancients who were content merely with the beauty of visible things and mistakenly worshipped the creation instead of the Creator (cf. Rom. 1 : 25).

74. It is by means of the more lofty conceptual images that the inner principle of Holy Scripture can be stripped gradually of the

complex garment of words with which it is physically draped. Then to the visionary intellect – the intellect which through the total abandonment of its natural activities is able to attain a glimpse of the simplicity that in some measure discloses this principle – it reveals itself as though in the sound of a delicate breeze. This was the case with Elijah, who was granted such a vision in the cave of Horeb (cf. 1 Kgs. 19 : 12). Horeb signifies fallow land just broken up, which is the firm possession of the virtues established through the new spirit of grace. The cave is the hidden sanctuary of wisdom within the intellect; he who enters it will mystically perceive the spiritual knowledge that is beyond perception, in which God is said to dwell. Therefore everyone who like Elijah truly seeks God will not only arrive at Horeb – that is, not only will he through ascetic practice attain the state of virtue – but will also enter the cave at Horeb – that is, as a contemplative he will enter into that hidden sanctuary of wisdom found only by those who have attained the state of virtue.

75. When our intellect has shaken off its many opinions about created things, then the inner principle of truth appears clearly to it, providing it with a foundation of real knowledge and removing its former preconceptions as though removing scales from the eyes, as happened in the case of St Paul (cf. Acts 9 : 18). For an understanding of Scripture that does not go beyond the literal meaning, and a view of the sensible world that relies exclusively on sense-perception, are indeed scales, blinding the soul's visionary faculty and preventing access to the pure Logos of truth.

76. The Apostle Paul says that he had a partial knowledge of the Logos (cf. 1 Cor. 13 : 9). The Evangelist John states that he has seen His glory: 'For we beheld His glory,' he says, 'the glory as of the only-begotten Son of the Father, full of grace and truth' (John 1 : 14). Perhaps St Paul says that he has but a partial knowledge of the divine Logos because the Logos is known from His energies only to a limited degree, while knowledge of Him as He is in essence and person is altogether inaccessible to all angels and men alike. St John, who was initiated as perfectly as a man can be into the mystery of the incarnation of the Logos, said that he saw the glory of the Logos as flesh, that is, he saw the purpose for which God, full of grace and truth, became man. For not as God in His essence and as coessential with God the Father was the only-begotten Son given to

us; only inasmuch as by virtue of God's providential dispensation He became man by nature and, for our sakes made coessential with us, He was given to us who have need of such grace. And from His fulness we always receive the grace which corresponds to each step we take along the spiritual path. Thus he who has kept the inner principle of things perfectly pure within himself will acquire the glory, full of grace and truth, of the Logos of God made flesh for us, who through His coming glorified and sanctified Himself in His human nature for our sake. For 'when He appears,' says Scripture, 'we shall be like Him' (1 John 3 : 2).

77. So long as the soul advances 'from strength to strength' (Ps. 84 : 7) and 'from glory to glory' (2 Cor. 3 : 18), that is, so long as it advances from one degree of virtue to a greater degree and from one level of spiritual knowledge to a higher level, it remains a 'sojourner', one who has no permanent home, as in the saying, 'My soul has long been a sojourner' (Ps. 120 : 6. LXX). For great is the distance and many are the levels of knowledge through which the soul must pass before it reaches 'the place of the miraculous tabernacle, the house of God itself, with the voice of exultation and thanksgiving, and the sound of feasting' (Ps. 42 : 4. LXX). It advances continually from one hymn of praise to another, from one level of divine contemplation to another, full of joy and thankfulness for what it has already seen. For all those who have received the Spirit of grace into their hearts celebrate in this festive manner, crying 'Abba, Father' (Gal. 4 : 6).

78. 'The place of the miraculous tabernacle' is a dispassionate and untroubled state of virtue in which the Logos of God adorns the soul like a tabernacle with the varied beauties of the virtues. 'The house of God' is spiritual knowledge compounded of many different forms of contemplation when God dwells in a soul, filling it from the bowl of wisdom. 'Exultation' is the soul's leap of joy at the riches of the virtues. 'Thanksgiving' is gratitude for the bountiful outpouring of wisdom. 'The sound of feasting' is the unceasing mystical hymn of glory, which exultation and thanksgiving combine to form.

79. The man who has struggled bravely with the passions of the body, has fought ably against unclean spirits, and has expelled from his soul the conceptual images they provoke, should pray for a pure heart to be given him and for a spirit of integrity to be renewed within him (cf. Ps. 51 : 10). In other words, he should pray that by

grace he may be completely emptied of evil thoughts and filled with divine thoughts, so that he may become a spiritual world of God, splendid and vast, wrought from moral, natural and theological forms of contemplation.

80. He who has made his heart pure will not only know the inner essences of what is sequent to God and dependent on Him but, after passing through all of them, he will in some measure see God Himself, which is the supreme consummation of all blessings. When God comes to dwell in such a heart, He honours it by engraving His own letters on it through the Holy Spirit, just as He did on the Mosaic tablets (cf. Exod. 31 : 18). This He does according to the degree to which the heart, through practice of the virtues and contemplation, has devoted itself to the admonition which bids us, in a mystical sense, 'Be fruitful and multiply' (Gen. 35 : 11).

81. A pure heart is perhaps one which has no natural propulsion towards anything in any manner whatsoever. When in its extreme simplicity such a heart has become like a writing-tablet beautifully smoothed and polished, God comes to dwell in it and writes there His own laws.

82. A pure heart is one which offers the mind to God free of all image and form, and ready to be imprinted only with His own archetypes, by which God Himself is made manifest.

83. According to the text, 'But we have the intellect of Christ' (1 Cor. 2 : 16), the saints are said to receive Christ's intellect. But this does not come to us through the loss of our own intellectual power; nor does it come to us as a supplementary part added to our intellect; nor does it pass essentially and hypostatically into our intellect. Rather, it illumines the power of our intellect with its own quality and conforms the activity of our intellect to its own. In my opinion the person who has Christ's intellect is he whose intellection accords with that of Christ and who apprehends Christ through all things.

84. According to the text, 'We are the body of Christ and each of us is one of its members' (cf. 1 Cor. 12 : 27), we are said to be the body of Christ. We do not become this body through the loss of our own bodies; nor again because Christ's body passes into us hypostatically or is divided into members; but rather because we conform to the likeness of the Lord's flesh by shaking off the corruption of sin. For just as Christ in His manhood was sinless by nature both

in flesh and in soul, so we too who believe in Him, and have clothed ourselves in Him through the Spirit, can be without sin in Him if we so choose.

85. According to Scripture there are temporal ages in themselves, and temporal ages which encompass the consummation of other ages. This is clear from the text: 'But now once at the consummation of the ages . . .' (Heb. 9 : 26). Again there are other ages or aeons, free of a temporal nature, after this temporal age established at the consummation of the ages. This is shown by the text: '. . . so that in the ages to come He might display the overflowing richness . . .' (Eph. 2 : 7). But we also find in Scripture a large number of past, present and future ages: there are references to 'ages of ages' (Ps. 84 : 4. LXX), 'age of age' (Ps. 9 : 5. LXX), 'agelong times' (2 Tim. 1 : 9) and 'generations joined together by the ages' (Gen. 9 : 12). But now lest we digress too far from our subject by expounding what Scripture means by temporal ages or agelong times or generations, and by explaining what are merely ages, what are ages of ages, and what is simply age, and age of age, let us leave these matters to the researches of scholars and return to the theme of our chapters.

86. We know that according to Scripture there is something which transcends the age. Scripture has indicated that this thing exists but it has not specified what it is, as the following text shows: 'The Lord rules the age, and above the age, and for ever' (Exod. 15 : 18. LXX). There is therefore something above the age, namely the inviolate kingdom of God. For it is not right to say that the kingdom of God had a beginning or that it was preceded by ages or by time. We believe the kingdom to be the inheritance of those who are saved, their abode and their place, as the true Logos has taught us. For it is the final goal of those who long for that which is the desire of all desires. Once they have reached it they are granted rest from all movement whatsoever, as there is no longer any time or age through which they need to pass. For after passing through all things they will come to rest in God, who exists before all ages and whom the nature of ages cannot attain.

87. Even though a man attains the highest degree of ascetic practice and contemplation possible in this earthly life, yet so long as he is still in this life he will possess spiritual knowledge, the power to prophesy and the pledge of the Holy Spirit only in part, not in their fulness. But when he comes, beyond the limit of the ages, to that

perfect inheritance in which those found worthy behold the truth face to face and as it really is (cf. 1 Cor. 13 : 12), he will no longer have only a part of the fulness but will acquire by participation the whole fulness of grace. For, as St Paul says, all who are saved will attain perfect manhood, according to 'the measure of the stature of the fulness of Christ' (Eph. 4 : 13), in whom all the treasures of wisdom and spiritual knowledge are hidden (cf. Col. 2 : 3). When these things are revealed, what is partial will cease to exist.

88. Some seek to discover what the state of perfection of the saints in the kingdom of God is like. Does it involve progress and change or is it a fixed condition? In what way must bodies and souls be thought to exist? Speaking conjecturally, one may suggest a parallel between the life of the body and that of the soul. In the case of physical life the reason for taking food is twofold: first for growth and second for sustenance when we have already grown up. Until we reach physical maturity we feed ourselves in order to grow; but when the body reaches its full stature it is fed no longer for growth but for sustenance. In the same way the reason for nourishing the soul is also twofold. While it is advancing along the spiritual path it is nourished by virtue and contemplation, until it transcends all created things and attains 'the measure of the stature of the fulness of Christ' (Eph. 4 : 13). Once it has entered this state it ceases from all increase and growth nourished by indirect means and is nourished directly, in a manner which passes understanding. Having now completed the stage of growth, the soul receives the kind of incorruptible nourishment which sustains the godlike perfection granted to it, and receives a state of eternal well-being. Then the infinite splendours inherent in this nourishment are revealed to the soul, and it becomes god by participation in divine grace, ceasing from all activity of intellect and sense, and at the same time suspending all the natural operations of the body. For the body is deified along with the soul through its own corresponding participation in the process of deification. Thus God alone is made manifest through the soul and the body, since their natural properties have been overcome by the superabundance of His glory.

89. Some scholars try to discover how the eternal dwelling-places and things promised differ from each other. Is there a difference in their actual locality? Or does the difference arise from our conception of the spiritual quality and quantity peculiar to each dwelling-

place? Some think the first and some the second. He who knows the meaning of 'The kingdom of God is within you' (Luke 17 : 21), and 'In my Father's house are many dwelling-places' (John 14 : 2), will prefer the second explanation.

90. Some try to discover how the kingdom of heaven differs from the kingdom of God. Is there a difference in their actual nature, or is the difference a conceptual one? The answer is that they do not differ in their actual natures, but merely in our conception of them. The kingdom of heaven consists in possessing an inviolate and pre-eternal knowledge of created things through perceiving their inner essences as they exist in God. The kingdom of God is the imparting through grace of those blessings which pertain naturally to God. The first concerns the consummation of created things, the second our conception of their state after they reach their consummation.

91. The text, 'The kingdom of heaven has drawn near' (Matt. 3 : 2; 4 : 17), does not in my judgment imply any temporal limitation. For the kingdom 'does not come in a way that can be observed: one cannot say, "Look, it is here" or "Look, it is there" ' (Luke 17 : 20–21). The phrase has reference to the relationship which the saints have with the kingdom, each according to his or her inner state. For 'the kingdom of God', says Scripture, 'is within you' (Luke 17 : 21).

92. The kingdom of God the Father is present in all believers in potentiality; it is present in actuality in those who, after totally expelling all natural life of soul and body from their inner state, have attained the life of the Spirit alone and are able to say, 'I no longer live, but Christ lives in me' (Gal. 2 : 20).

93. Some say that the kingdom of heaven is the way of life which the saints lead in heaven; others that it is a state similar to that of the angels, attained by those who are saved; others that it is the very form of the divine beauty of those who 'wear the image of Him who is from heaven' (1 Cor. 15 : 49). In my judgment each of these three views is correct. For the grace of the kingdom is given to all according to the quality and quantity of the righteousness that is in them.

94. So long as we are manfully engaged in the holy warfare of ascetic or practical philosophy we retain with us the Logos, who in the form of the commandments came from the Father into this world. But when we are released from our ascetic struggle with the passions and are declared victor over both them and the demons, we

pass, by means of contemplation, to gnostic philosophy; and in this way we allow the Logos mystically to leave the world again and make His way to the Father. Hence it is that the Lord says to His disciples: 'You have loved Me and have believed that I come from God. I came from the Father and have come into the world; again I leave the world and make My way to the Father' (John 16 : 27–28). By the world He meant perhaps the hard task of practising the virtues; by the Father, that intellectual state which transcends the world and is free from all material propensity. When we are in this state the Logos of God enters into us, putting an end to our battle with the passions and the demons.

95. He who through practice of the virtues has succeeded in mortifying whatever is earthly in him (cf. Col. 3 : 5), and who by fulfilling the commandments has triumphed over the world of the passions within him, will experience no more affliction; for he will have already left the world and come to be in Christ, the conqueror of the world of the passions and the source of all peace. He who has not severed his attachment to material things will always experience affliction, since his state of mind depends on things that are naturally changeable, and so it alters when they do. But he who has come to be in Christ will be totally impervious to such material change. That is why the Lord says, 'I have said these things to you, so that in Me you may have peace. In the world you will experience affliction; but have courage, for I have overcome the world' (John 16 : 33). In other words, 'In Me, the Logos of virtue, you have peace, for you have been released from the swirl and turmoil of material passions and objects; in the world – that is, in a state of attachment to material things – you are afflicted because of the successive changes of these things.' For both he who practises the virtues and he who loves the world experience affliction, the first because of the toil which such practice entails and the second because of the futility of material things. But the affliction of the first is salutary, that of the second corrupting and destructive. The Lord gives release to both: in the case of the first He allays the toil of ascetic practice with the contemplation attained through dispassion, and in the case of the second He rescinds attachment to corrupted things by means of repentance.

96. The charge made against the Saviour in the inscription on the Cross clearly showed that He who was crucified was Lord and king

of practical, natural and theological philosophy. For Scripture says
that the inscription was written in Latin, Greek and Hebrew (cf.
John 19 : 20). I take Latin to signify the practical branch of philosophy, since according to Daniel (cf. Dan. 2 : 40) the Roman empire was appointed to be the most resolute and manful of all the
kingdoms on earth; for the distinguishing feature of the practice of
the virtues, or practical philosophy, is resolution and manfulness. I
take Greek to signify natural contemplation, since the Greek nation
more than any other people has pursued natural philosophy. I take
Hebrew to signify initiation into the mysteries of theology, since
this nation was from the beginning clearly consecrated to God
through the patriarchs.

97. We must not only put bodily passions to death but also
destroy the soul's impassioned thoughts. Hence the psalmist says,
'Early in the morning I destroyed all the wicked of the earth, that I
might cut off all evil-doers from the city of the Lord' (Ps. 101 : 8) —
that is, the passions of the body and the soul's godless thoughts.

98. If we keep the path of virtue undefiled through devout and
true knowledge, and do not deviate to either side, we will experience the advent of God revealed to us because of our dispassion. For
'I will sing a psalm and in a pure path I will understand when Thou
wilt come to me' (cf. Ps. 101 : 1–2). The psalm stands for virtuous
conduct; understanding indicates the spiritual knowledge, gained
through virtue, by means of which we perceive God's advent, when
we wait for the Lord vigilant in the virtues.

99. He who is a beginner on the spiritual way must not be
brought to practise the commandments by kindness alone, but must
more often be induced to continue the struggle by being rigorously
reminded of God's judgment. In this way he will not only be moved
by love to desire what is divine, but will be moved by fear to avoid
what is evil. For 'I will sing to Thee, O Lord, of mercy and judgment' (Ps. 101 : 1. LXX). He will sing to God charmed by love,
and steeled by fear he will have strength for the song.

100. He who through virtue and spiritual knowledge has brought
his body into harmony with his soul has become a harp, a flute and a
temple of God. He has become a harp by preserving the harmony of
the virtues; a flute by receiving the inspiration of the Spirit through
divine contemplation; and a temple by becoming a dwelling place
of the Logos through the purity of his intellect.

Various Texts on Theology, the Divine Economy, and Virtue and Vice

First Century[1]

1. The Good that is beyond being and beyond the unoriginate is one, the holy unity of three persons, Father, Son and Holy Spirit. It is an infinite union of three infinites. Its principle of being, together with the mode, the nature and the quality of its being, is altogether inaccessible to creatures. For it eludes every intellection of intellective beings, in no way issuing from its natural hidden inwardness, and infinitely transcending the summit of all spiritual knowledge.

2. The substantive and essential Good is that which has no origin, no consummation, no cause of being and no motion whatsoever, so far as its being is concerned, towards any final cause. The goodness to which such terms apply is not substantive since it has an origin, a consummation, a cause of being, and motion, so far as its being is concerned, towards some final cause. Even if what is not being in the substantive sense is said to be, it exists and is said to be by participation, through the will of substantive being.

3. Not only is the divine Logos prior to the genesis of created beings, but there neither was nor is nor will be a principle superior to the Logos. The Logos is not without intellect or bereft of life; He possesses intellect and life because the Father is the essentially subsistent intellect that begets Him, and the Holy Spirit is His essentially subsistent and coexistent life.

[1] In the Greek *Philokalia* of St Nikodimos, this and the four following Centuries are numbered 'Third' to 'Seventh' respectively (see introductory note, p. 49 above).

4. There is one God, because the Father is the begetter of the unique Son and the fount of the Holy Spirit: one without confusion and three without division. The Father is unoriginate Intellect, the unique essential Begetter of the unique Logos, also unoriginate, and the fount of the unique everlasting life, the Holy Spirit.

5. There is one God because there is one Divinity, a Unity unoriginate, simple, beyond being, without parts and undivided. The same Unity is a Trinity, also unoriginate, simple and so on.

6. Everything that derives its existence from participation in some other reality presupposes the ontological priority of that other reality. Thus it is clear that the divine Cause of created beings – which derive their existence from participation in that Cause – is incomparably superior to all such beings in every way, since by nature its existence is prior to theirs and they presuppose its ontological priority. It does not exist as a being with accidents, because if that were the case the divine would be composite, its own existence receiving completion from the existence of created beings. On the contrary, it exists as the beyond-beingness of being. For if artists in their art conceive the shapes of those things which they produce, and if universal nature conceives the forms of the things within it, how much more does God Himself bring into existence out of nothing the very being of all created things, since He is beyond being and even infinitely transcends the attribution of beyond-beingness. For it is He who has yoked the sciences to the arts so that shapes might be devised; it is He who has given to nature the energy which produces its forms, and who has established the very is-ness of beings by virtue of which they exist.

7. God, in whose essence created beings do not participate, but who wills that those capable of so doing shall participate in Him according to some other mode, never issues from the hiddenness of His essence; for even that mode according to which He wills to be participated in remains perpetually concealed from all men. Thus, just as God of His own will is participated in – the manner of this being known to Him alone – in the surpassing power of His goodness, He freely brings into existence participating beings, according to the principle which He alone understands. Therefore what has come into being by the will of Him who made it can never be co-eternal with Him who willed it to exist.

8. The divine Logos, who once for all was born in the flesh,

always in His compassion desires to be born in spirit in those who desire Him. He becomes an infant and moulds Himself in them through the virtues. He reveals as much of Himself as He knows the recipient can accept; He does not diminish the manifestation of His own greatness out of lack of generosity but estimates the receptive capacity of those who desire to see Him. In this way the divine Logos is eternally made manifest in different modes of participation, and yet remains eternally invisible to all in virtue of the surpassing nature of His hidden activity. That is why the apostle, when wisely considering the power of this hidden activity, says, 'Jesus Christ the same yesterday, and today, and throughout the ages' (Heb. 13 : 8); for he sees the hidden activity as something which is always new and never becomes outmoded through being embraced by the intellect.

9. Christ our God is born and becomes man by adding to Himself flesh endowed with an intellective soul. He who from non-being brings created things into being is Himself born supranaturally of a Virgin who does not thereby lose her virginity. For just as He Himself became man without changing His nature or altering His power, so He makes her who bore Him a Mother while keeping her a Virgin. In this way He reveals one miracle through another miracle, at the same time concealing the one with the other. This is because in Himself, according to His essence, God always remains a mystery. He expresses His natural hiddenness in such a way that He makes it the more hidden through the revelation. Similarly, in the case of the Virgin who bore Him, He made her a Mother in such a way that by conceiving Him the bonds of her virginity became even more indissoluble.

10. Natures are changed into something new and God becomes man. Not only is divine nature, stable and unmoved, moved towards what is unstable and subject to movement, in order to stop it from being swept away; not only does human nature produce without seed, in a way that is supranatural, the flesh which is brought to perfection by the Logos, in order to prevent it too from being swept away; but a star from the east shone in the day and guided the Magi (cf. Matt. 2 : 2–10) to the place where the Logos became incarnate, in order to show in a mystical way that the inner teaching of the Law and the prophets is superior to the senses and guides the Gentiles towards the supreme light of spiritual knowledge. For

clearly the inner teaching of the Law and the prophets, when contemplated devoutly like a star, leads to knowledge of the incarnate Logos those who freely respond to the call of grace.

11. As man I deliberately transgressed the divine commandment, when the devil, enticing me with the hope of divinity (cf. Gen. 3 : 5), dragged me down from my natural stability into the realm of sensual pleasure; and he was proud to have thus brought death into existence, for he delights in the corruption of human nature. Because of this, God became perfect man, taking on everything that belongs to human nature except sin (cf. Heb. 4 : 15); and indeed sin is not part of human nature. In this way, by enticing the insatiable serpent with the bait of the flesh, He provoked him to open his mouth and swallow it. This flesh proved poison to him, destroying him utterly by the power of the Divinity within it; but to human nature it proved a remedy restoring it to its original grace by that same power of the Divinity within it. For just as the devil poured out his venom of sin on the tree of knowledge and corrupted human nature once it had tasted it, so when he wished to devour the flesh of the Master he was himself destroyed by the power of the Divinity within it.

12. The great mystery of the incarnation remains a mystery eternally. Not only is what is not yet seen of it greater than what has been revealed — for it is revealed merely to the extent that those saved by it can grasp it — but also even what is revealed still remains entirely hidden and is by no means known as it really is. What I have said should not appear paradoxical. For God is beyond being and transcends all beyond-beingness; and so, when He wished to come down to the level of being, He became being in a manner which transcends being. Thus, too, although transcending man, yet out of love for man He truly became man by taking on the substance of men; but the manner in which He became man always remains unrevealed, for He was made man in a way which transcends man.

13. Let us contemplate with faith the mystery of the divine incarnation and in all simplicity let us simply praise Him who in His great generosity became man for us. For who, relying on the power of rational demonstration, can explain how the conception of the divine Logos took place? How was flesh generated without seed? How was there an engendering without loss of maidenhood? How did a mother after giving birth remain a virgin? How did He who

was supremely perfect develop as He grew up (cf. Luke 2 : 52)? How was He who was pure baptized? How did He who was hungry give sustenance (cf. Matt. 4 : 2; 14 : 14–21)? How did He who was weary impart strength (cf. John 4 : 6)? How did He who suffered dispense healing? How did He who was dying bestow life? And, to put the most important last, how did God become man? And – what is even more mysterious – how did the Logos, while subsisting wholly, essentially and hypostatically in the Father, also exist essentially and hypostatically in the flesh? How did He who is wholly God by nature become wholly man by nature, not renouncing either nature in any way at all, neither the divine, through which He is God, nor ours, through which He became man? Faith alone can embrace these mysteries, for it is faith that makes real for us things beyond intellect and reason (cf. Heb. 11 : 1).

14. Because Adam disobeyed, human nature has come to be generated through sensual pleasure; banishing such pleasure from human nature, the Lord had nothing to do with engendering by means of seed. Because the woman transgressed the commandment, the generation of human nature begins in pain (cf. Gen. 3 : 16); expelling this from human nature through His birth, the Lord did not allow her who bore Him to lose her virginity. He did this in order to expel from human nature both pleasure deliberately sought and the resulting unsought pain, becoming the destroyer of those things which He did not create. Through this He also mystically taught us to embark of our own accord on another way of life, one perhaps begun in pain and labour but nevertheless ending in divine pleasure and everlasting gladness. That is why He who made man became a man and was born as a man, so that He might save man and, by healing our passions through His passion, might Himself supranaturally destroy the passions that were destroying us, in His compassion renewing us in the spirit through His privations in the flesh.

15. He who longing for the divine has overcome the soul's predilection for the body is free from physical limitations even though he is in a body. For God, who attracts the desire of the person who longs for Him, is incomparably higher than all things, and does not allow anyone who longs for Him to direct his desire towards anything sequent to Him. Let us therefore long for God with all the strength of our nature and let us keep our resolution unfettered by any bodily needs. Let us rise above all sensible and intelligible

realities, and let us not allow any physical limitation to compromise our resolve to be with God, who is by nature beyond all limitation.

16. The suffering of the saints lies in the struggle between malice and virtue, the former fighting to win control, the latter enduring all things to avoid defeat. The first struggles to nurture sin by chastising the righteous; the second to hold good men firm although they experience more than their share of misfortunes.

17. The task of virtue is to contend against hardship and suffering. The prize for victory, given to those who stand their ground, is the soul's dispassion. In this state the soul is united with God through love, and in inward resolution it is separated from the body and the world. Those who stand their ground find that the soul's strength lies in the body's affliction.

18. Beguiled from our original state by the deceitfulness of sensual pleasure, we chose death rather than true life. Let us then gladly endure the bodily hardship which puts such pleasure to death. In this way the death of pleasure will destroy the death which came about through pleasure, and we shall receive back, purchased with but slight bodily hardship, the life which we sold for the sake of sensual pleasure.

19. If when the flesh has an easy life the force of sin tends to grow stronger, it is clear that when the flesh suffers affliction the force of virtue will also increase. So let us bravely endure the affliction of the flesh, which cleanses the soul's stains and brings us future glory. For 'the sufferings of this present time are not worthy to be compared with the glory which shall be revealed in us' (Rom. 8 : 18).

20. When physicians are treating the body they do not administer the same remedy in all cases. Neither does God, when treating the illnesses of the soul, regard a single kind of therapy as suitable for all conditions; but He allots to each soul what is suitable for it and effects its cure. So let us give thanks while we are being treated, however great our suffering, for the result is blessed.

21. Nothing disciplines the disposition of the soul so well as the protests of the afflicted flesh. If the soul gives way to them, it will be evident that it loves the flesh more than God. But if it remains unshaken by these disturbances, it will be shown to honour virtue more than the flesh. Through virtue God will come to dwell in it – God who for the soul's sake patiently bears our human suffering –

and will say to it as He once did to the disciples, 'Have courage, for
I have overcome the world' (John 16 : 33).

22. If all the saints had their share of discipline, we too should
thank God that we are disciplined with them, so that we may be
found worthy to partake of their glory. 'For whom the Lord loves He
disciplines; He chastens every son He accepts' (Prov. 3 : 12. LXX).

23. When Adam accepted the sensual pleasure offered to him by
Eve, who had come from his side, he expelled humanity from
paradise (cf. Gen. 3 : 24). But when the Lord in His agony was
pierced in his side by the lance, He brought the robber into paradise
(cf. Luke 23 : 43). Let us, then, love the suffering of the flesh and
hate its pleasure; for the first brings us in and restores God's blessings to us, while the second drives us out and separates us from those
blessings.

24. If God suffers in the flesh when He is made man, should we
not rejoice when we suffer, for we have God to share our sufferings? This shared suffering confers the kingdom on us. For he spoke
truly who said, 'If we suffer with Him, then we shall also be glorified
with Him' (Rom. 8 : 17).

25. If we have to suffer because our ancestor involved our nature
with sensual pleasure, let us endure our temporary sufferings
bravely; for they blunt the sharp point of such pleasure for us, and
free us from the eternal torment which it brings upon us.

26. Love is the consummation of all blessings, since all who walk
in it love leads and guides towards God, the supreme blessing and
cause of every blessing, and unites them with Him; for love is faithful and never fails (cf. 1 Cor. 13 : 8). Faith is the foundation of what
comes after it, namely hope and love, since it provides a firm basis
for truth. Hope is the strength of the two pre-eminent gifts of love
and faith, since hope gives us glimpses both of that in which we believe
and of that for which we long, and teaches us to make our way
towards our goal. Love is the completion of the other two, embracing entirely the entire desire of all desires, and satisfying the
yearning of our faith and hope for it; for that which we believe to
be and which we hope will come to pass, love enables us to enjoy
as a present reality.

27. The most perfect work of love, and the fulfilment of its
activity, is to effect an exchange between those it joins together,
which in some measure unites their distinctive characteristics and

adapts their respective conditions to each other. Love makes man god, and reveals and manifests God as man, through the single and identical purpose and activity of the will of both.

28. If we are made, as we are, in the image of God (cf. Gen. 1 : 27), let us become the image both of ourselves and of God; or rather let us all become the image of the one whole God, bearing nothing earthly in ourselves, so that we may consort with God and become gods, receiving from God our existence as gods. For in this way the divine gifts and the presence of divine peace are honoured.

29. Love is a great blessing and of all blessings the first and supreme, since it joins God and men together around him who has love, and it makes the Creator of men manifest Himself as man through the exact likeness of the deified man to God, in so far as this is possible for man. This is what I take to be the actualization of the commandment, 'You shall love the Lord your God with all your heart, and with all your soul, and with all your might, and your neighbour as yourself' (cf. Lev. 19 : 18; Deut. 6 : 5; Matt. 22 : 37–39).

30. The devil has deceived us by guile in a malicious and cunning way, provoking us through self-love to sensual pleasure (cf. Gen. 3 : 1–5). He has separated us in our wills from God and from each other; he has perverted straightforward truth and in this manner has divided humanity, cutting it up into many opinions and fantasies.

31. The greatest authors and instigators of evil are ignorance, self-love and tyranny. Each depends on the other two and is supported by them: from ignorance of God comes self-love, and from self-love comes tyranny over one's own kind. The devil establishes these in us when we misuse our own powers, namely our intelligence, our desire and our incensive power.

32. By intelligence we should be stimulated to overcome our ignorance and to seek the one and only God by means of spiritual knowledge; through desire – through a passion of self-love which has been purified – we should be drawn in longing to the one God; and with an incensive power divorced from all tyrannical propensity we should struggle to attain God alone. From these three powers of the soul we should actualize that divine and blessed love on account of which they exist, that love which joins the devout man to God and reveals him to be a god.

33. Since self-love is, as I have said, the origin and mother of evil, when this is eradicated all the things which derive from it are eradicated as well. For when self-love is absent, not the slightest trace or form of evil can exist in any way at all.

34. We should care for ourselves and each other in the way that Christ Himself, who patiently suffered for us, has already shown us in His own person.

35. For the sake of love all the saints resisted sin, not showing any regard for this present life. And they endured many forms of death, in order to be separated from the world and united with themselves and with God, joining together in themselves the broken fragments of human nature. For this is the true and undefiled theosophy of the faithful. Its consummation is goodness and truth – if indeed goodness as compassion and truth as devotion to God in faith are the marks of love. It unites men to God and to one another, and on this account contains the unchanging permanence of all blessings.

36. The actualization and proof of perfect love for God is a genuine and willing attitude of goodwill towards one's neighbour. 'For he who does not love his brother whom he has seen', says St John, 'cannot love God whom he has not seen' (1 John 4 : 20).

37. The way of truth is love. The Logos of God called Himself the way (cf. John 14 : 6, 1 John 4 : 8); and those who travel on this way He presents, purified from every stain, to God the Father.

38. This is the door through which a man enters into the Holy of Holies and is brought to the vision of the unapproachable beauty of the Holy and Royal Trinity.

39. It is a fearful and heinous thing for us, because of our love for things corruptible, deliberately to kill the life that was given to us by God as the gift of the Holy Spirit. Those who have trained themselves to prefer truth to self-love will certainly know this fear.

40. Let us use peace in the right way: repudiating our evil alliance with the world and its ruler, let us at last break off the war which we wage against God through the passions. Concluding an unbreakable covenant of peace with Him by destroying the body of sin within us (cf. Rom. 6 : 6), let us put an end to our hostility towards Him.

41. Rebelling as we do against God through the passions and agreeing to pay tribute in the form of evil to that cunning tyrant

and murderer of souls, the devil, we cannot be reconciled with God until we have first begun to fight against the devil with all our strength. For even though we assume the name of faithful Christians, until we have made ourselves the devil's enemies and fight against him, we continue by deliberate choice to serve the shameful passions. And nothing of profit will come to us from our peace in the world, for our soul is in an evil state, rebelling against its own Maker and unwilling to be subject to His kingdom. It is still sold into bondage to hordes of savage masters, who urge it towards evil and treacherously contrive to make it choose the way which leads to destruction instead of that which brings salvation.

42. God made us so that we might become 'partakers of the divine nature' (2 Pet. 1 : 4) and sharers in His eternity, and so that we might come to be like Him (cf. 1 John 3 : 2) through deification by grace. It is through deification that all things are reconstituted and achieve their permanence; and it is for its sake that what is not is brought into being and given existence.

43. If we desire to belong to God in both name and reality, let us struggle not to betray the Logos to the passions, as Judas did (cf. Matt. 26 : 14–16), or to deny Him as Peter did (cf. Matt. 26 : 69–75). To deny the Logos is to fail through fear to do what is good; to betray Him is deliberately to choose and commit sin.

44. The outcome of every affliction endured for the sake of virtue is joy, of every labour rest, and of every shameful treatment glory; in short, the outcome of all sufferings for the sake of virtue is to be with God, to remain with Him for ever and to enjoy eternal rest.

45. Because He wishes to unite us in nature and will with one another, and in His goodness urges all humanity towards this goal, God in His love entrusted His saving commandments to us, ordaining simply that we should show mercy and receive mercy (cf. Matt. 5 : 7).

46. The self-love and cleverness of men, alienating them from each other and perverting the law, have cut our single human nature into many fragments. They have so extended the insensibility which they introduced into our nature and which now dominates it, that our nature, divided in will and purpose, fights against itself. Thus anyone who has succeeded by sound judgment and nobility of intelligence in resolving this anomalous state of our nature has shown

mercy to himself prior to showing it to others; for he has moulded his will and purpose in conformity to nature, and through them he has advanced towards God by means of nature; he has revealed in himself what it means to be 'in the image' and shown how excellently in the beginning God created our nature in His likeness and as a pure copy of His own goodness, and how He made our nature one with itself in every way – peaceable, free from strife and faction, bound to God and to itself by love, making us cleave to God with desire and to each other with mutual affection.

47. In His love for man God became man so that He might unite human nature to Himself and stop it from acting evilly towards itself, or rather from being at strife and divided against itself, and from having no rest because of the instability of its will and purpose.

48. Nothing sequent to God is more precious for beings endowed with intellect, or rather is more dear to God, than perfect love; for love unites those who have been divided and is able to create a single identity of will and purpose, free from faction, among many or among all; for the property of love is to produce a single will and purpose in those who seek what pertains to it.

49. If by nature the good unifies and holds together what has been separated, evil clearly divides and corrupts what has been unified. For evil is by nature dispersive, unstable, multiform and divisive.

50. The true love of God, grounded in real knowledge, together with the total repudiation of the soul's affection for the body and this world, is the short road to salvation and brings deliverance from all sins. In this way, casting off desire for pleasure and fear of pain, we are freed from evil self-love and are raised to a spiritual knowledge of the Creator. In the place of the evil self-love, we receive an uncorrupt and spiritual self-love, separated from affection for the body; and we do not cease to worship God through this uncorrupt self-love, always seeking from Him sustenance for our souls. For true worship, genuinely pleasing to God, is the strict cultivation of the soul through the virtues.

51. If you do not long for bodily pleasure and have not the slightest fear of pain, you have attained dispassion. For by overcoming such longing and fear, together with the self-love which has engendered them, you have killed at a single blow all the passions which have come into being through them and from them, as well as the principal source of all evil, ignorance. You have become full of

that goodness which is stable and permanent and always remains the same by nature; and in that goodness you stand absolutely immovable, 'with unveiled face reflecting the glory of the Lord' (2 Cor. 3 : 18) and contemplating through the radiant brightness within you the divine and unapproachable glory.

52. Let us reject the pleasure and pain of this present life with what strength we have, and so free ourselves entirely from all thoughts of the passions and all machinations of the demons. For we love the passions because of pleasure and avoid virtue because of pain.

53. Since it is the nature of every evil to destroy itself along with the habits which brought it into being, man finds by experience that every pleasure is inevitably succeeded by pain, and so directs his whole effort towards pleasure and does all he can to avoid pain. He struggles with all his might to attain pleasure and he fights against pain with immense zeal. By doing this he hopes to keep the two apart from each other – which is impossible – and to indulge his self-love in ways which bring only pleasure and are entirely free from pain. Dominated by the passion of self-love he is, it appears, ignorant that pleasure can never exist without pain. For pain is intertwined with pleasure, even though this seems to escape the notice of those who suffer it. It escapes their notice because desire for pleasure is the dominating force in self-love, and what dominates is naturally always more conspicuous and obscures one's sense of what is present with it. Thus because in our self-love we pursue pleasure, and because – also out of self-love – we try to escape pain, we generate untold corrupting passions in ourselves.

54. A man no longer experiences pleasure and pain when, freeing his intellect from its relationship with the body, he binds or rather unites it to God, the real goal of love, longing and desire.

55. Just as one cannot worship God in a pure way without utterly purifying the soul, so one cannot worship creation without pampering the body. By fulfilling, out of concern for the body, that worship which causes corruption, and by thus acquiring self-love, man became subject to the unceasing action of pleasure and pain; eating always from the tree of disobedience – the tree of the knowledge of good and evil – in this way he acquired experientially through sense-perception a knowledge in which good and evil were intermingled. And it would not be untrue to say that the tree of the knowledge of

good and evil is the visible created world. For this world is by nature subject to that alternation which produces pleasure and pain.

56. Where intelligence does not rule, the senses naturally assume the dominant role. The power of sin is somehow mingled with the senses and induces the soul by means of sensual pleasure to have pity for the flesh, to which it is joined. When the soul pursues the impassioned and pleasurable cultivation of the flesh as its natural task, it is diverted from a life lived in accordance with nature and is impelled to become the author of evil, which has no substantial existence.

57. Evil is the noetic soul's forgetfulness of what is good according to nature; and this forgetfulness results from an impassioned relationship with the flesh and the world. When the intelligence is in control it dispels this forgetfulness through spiritual knowledge, since intelligence, having investigated the nature of the world and the flesh, draws the soul to the realm of spiritual realities which is its true home. Into this realm the law of sin cannot penetrate; for the link between the soul and the senses has now been broken, and the senses, limited to the world of sensible objects, can no longer function as a bridge conveying the law of sin into the intellect. When the intellect transcends its relationship with sensible objects and the world to which they pertain, it becomes utterly free from the sway of the senses.

58. When the intelligence dominates the passions it makes the senses instruments of virtue. Conversely, when the passions dominate the intelligence they conform the senses to sin. One must watchfully study and reflect how the soul can best reverse the situation and use those things through which it had formerly sinned to generate and sustain the virtues.

59. The holy Gospel teaches men to reject life according to the flesh and to embrace life according to the Spirit. I am speaking of those who are always dying to what is human – I mean human life in the flesh according to this present age – and living for God in the Spirit alone, after the example of St Paul and his followers. They do not in any way live their own life but have Christ living in them in the soul alone (cf. Gal. 2 : 20). Those, then, who in this age are truly dead to the flesh can be distinguished in this way: even though they suffer much affliction, torment, distress and persecution, and

experience innumerable forms of trial and temptation, nevertheless they bear everything with joy.

60. Every passion always consists of a combination of some perceived object, a sense faculty and a natural power – the incensive power, desire or the intelligence, as the case may be – whose natural function has been distorted. Thus, if the intellect investigates the final result of these three inter-related factors – the sensible object, the sense faculty and the natural power involved with the sense faculty – it can distinguish each from the other two, and refer each back to its specific natural function. It can, that is to say, view the sensible object in itself, apart from its relationship to the sense faculty, and the sense faculty in itself, apart from its connexion with the sensible object, and the natural power – desire, for example – apart from its impassioned alliance with the sense faculty and the sensible object. In this way, the intellect reduces to its constituent parts whatever passion it investigates, in much the same way as the golden calf of Israel in Old Testament days was ground into powder and mixed with water (cf. Exod. 32 : 20): it dissolves it with the water of spiritual knowledge, utterly destroying even the passion-free image of the passions, by restoring each of its elements to its natural state.

61. A life stained with many faults arising from the passions of the flesh is a soiled garment. For from his mode of life, as if from some garment, each man declares himself to be either righteous or wicked. The righteous man has a holy life as a clean garment; the wicked man has a life soiled with evil actions. Thus a 'garment stained by the flesh' (Jude, verse 23) is the inner state and disposition of the soul when its conscience is deformed by the recollection of evil impulses and actions arising from the flesh. When this state or disposition constantly envelops the soul like a garment, it is filled with the stink of the passions. But when the virtues, through the power of the Spirit, are interwoven in accordance with the intelligence, they form a garment of incorruption for the soul: dressed in this the soul becomes beautiful and resplendent. Conversely, when the passions are interwoven under the influence of the flesh, they form a filthy, soiled garment, which reveals the character of the soul, imposing on it a form and image contrary to the divine.

62. A sure warrant for looking forward with hope to the deification of human nature is provided by the incarnation of God, which

makes man god to the same degree as God Himself became man. For it is clear that He who became man without sin (cf. Heb. 4 : 15) will divinize human nature without changing it into the divine nature, and will raise it up for His own sake to the same degree as He lowered Himself for man's sake. This is what St Paul teaches mystically when he says, '. . . that in the ages to come He might display the overflowing richness of His grace' (Eph. 2 : 7).

63. When the intelligence is in control of the incensive power and desire, it produces the virtues. When the intellect devotes its attention to the inner essences of created things, it reaps genuine spiritual knowledge. Thus the intelligence, after rejecting everything alien, discovers what is desirable according to our true nature; and the intellect, after passing beyond the things that are known, apprehends the Cause of created things that transcends being and knowledge. Then the passion of deification is actualized by grace: the intelligence's power of natural discrimination is suspended, for there is no longer anything to discriminate about; the intellect's natural intellection is brought to a halt, for there is no longer anything to be known; and the person found worthy to participate in the divine is made god and brought into a state of rest.

64. Suffering cleanses the soul infected with the filth of sensual pleasure and detaches it completely from material things by showing it the penalty incurred as a result of its affection for them. This is why God in His justice allows the devil to afflict men with torments.

65. Pleasure and distress, desire and fear, and what follows from them, were not originally created as elements of human nature, for in that case they would form part of the definition of that nature. I follow in this matter St Gregory of Nyssa,[1] who states that these things were introduced as a result of our fall from perfection, being infiltrated into that part of our nature least endowed with intelligence. Through them the blessed and divine image in man was at the time of our transgression immediately replaced by a clear and obvious likeness to animals. Once the true dignity of the intelligence had been obscured, it was inevitable and just that human nature should be chastised by those witless elements which it had introduced into itself. In this way God in His providence wisely made man conscious of the nobility of his intellect.

---

[1] See On the Creation of Man 18 (P.G. xliv, 192B).

66. Even the passions become good if we wisely and diligently detach them from what is bodily and direct them towards the acquisition of what is heavenly. This happens, for example, when we turn desire into a noetic yearning for heavenly blessings; or when we turn pleasure into the gentle delight which the volitive energy of the intellect finds in divine gifts; or when we turn fear into protective concern to escape punishments threatening us because of our sins; or when we turn distress into corrective remorse for present sin. In short, the passions become good if – like wise physicians who use the body of the viper as a remedy against present or expected harm resulting from its bite – we use them to destroy present or expected evil, and in order to acquire and safeguard virtue and spiritual knowledge.

67. The law of the Old Testament through practical philosophy cleanses human nature of all defilement. The law of the New Testament, through initiation into the mysteries of contemplation, raises the intellect by means of spiritual knowledge from the sight of material things to the vision of spiritual realities.

68. Those who are beginners and stand at the gate of the divine court of the virtues (cf. Exod. 27 : 9) are called 'God-fearing' by Scripture (cf. Acts 10 : 2; 13 : 16, 26). Those who with some measure of stability have acquired the principles and qualities of the virtues, it describes as 'advancing'. Those who in their pursuit of holiness have by means of spiritual knowledge already attained the summit of that truth which reveals the virtues, it entitles 'perfect'. Thus he who has abandoned his former passion-dominated way of life, and out of fear has submitted his entire will to the divine commandments, will lack none of the blessings which are appropriate to beginners, even though he has not yet acquired stability in the practice of the virtues or come to share in the wisdom spoken among those who are perfect (cf. 1 Cor. 2 : 6). And he who is advancing will not lack any of the blessings which belong to his degree, even though he has not yet acquired the transcendent knowledge of divine realities possessed by the perfect. For the perfect have already been initiated mystically into contemplative theology: having purified their intellects of every material fantasy and bearing always the stamp of the image of divine beauty in all its fulness, they manifest the divine love present in their hearts.

69. Fear is twofold; one kind is pure, the other impure. That

which is pre-eminently fear of punishment on account of offences committed is impure, for it is sin which gives rise to it. It will not last for ever, for when the sin is obliterated through repentance it too will disappear. Pure fear, on the other hand, is always present even apart from remorse for offences committed. Such fear will never cease to exist, because it is somehow rooted essentially by God in creation and makes clear to everyone His awe-inspiring nature, which transcends all kingship and power.

70. He who does not fear God as judge but holds Him in awe because of the surpassing excellence of His infinite power will not justly lack anything; for having reached perfection in love, he loves God with awe and fitting reverence. He has acquired the fear that endures for ever and he will lack for nothing (cf. Ps. 19 : 9; 34 : 9–10).

71. From created beings we come to know their Cause; from the differences between created beings we learn about the indwelling Wisdom of creation; and from the natural activity of created beings we discern the indwelling Life of creation, the power which gives created beings their life – the Holy Spirit.

72. The Holy Spirit is not absent from any created being, especially not from one which in any way participates in intelligence. For being God and God's Spirit, He embraces in unity the spiritual knowledge of all created things, providentially permeating all things with His power, and vivifying their inner essences in accordance with their nature. In this way He makes men aware of things done sinfully against the law of nature, and renders them capable of choosing principles which are true and in conformity with nature. Thus we find many barbarians and nomadic peoples turning to a civilized way of life and setting aside the savage laws which they had kept among themselves from time immemorial.

73. The Holy Spirit is present unconditionally in all things, in that He embraces all things, provides for all, and vivifies the natural seeds within them. He is present in a specific way in all who are under the Law, in that He shows them where they have broken the commandments and enlightens them about the promise given concerning Christ. In all who are Christians He is present also in yet another way in that He makes them sons of God. But in none is He fully present as the author of wisdom except in those who have understanding, and who by their holy way of life have made them-

selves fit to receive His indwelling and deifying presence. For everyone who does not carry out the divine will, even though he is a believer, has a heart which, being a workshop of evil thoughts, lacks understanding, and a body which, being always entangled in the defilements of the passions, is mortgaged to sin.

74. God, who yearns for the salvation of all men and hungers after their deification, withers their self-conceit like the unfruitful fig tree (cf. Matt. 21 : 19–21). He does this so that they may prefer to be righteous in reality rather than in appearance, discarding the cloak of hypocritical moral display and genuinely pursuing a virtuous life in the way that the divine Logos wishes them to. They will then live with reverence, revealing the state of their soul to God rather than displaying the external appearance of a moral life to their fellow-men.

75. The principle of active accomplishment is one thing and that of passive suffering is another. The principle of active accomplishment signifies the natural capacity for actualizing the virtues. The principle of passive suffering signifies experiencing either the grace of what is beyond nature or the occurrence of what is contrary to nature. For just as we do not have a natural capacity for what is above being, so we do not by nature have a capacity for what lacks being. Thus we passively experience deification by grace as something which is above nature, but we do not actively accomplish it; for by nature we do not have the capacity to attain deification. Again, we suffer evil as something contrary to nature which occurs in the will; for we do not have a natural capacity for generating evil. Thus while we are in our present state we can actively accomplish the virtues by nature, since we have a natural capacity for accomplishing them. But, when raised to a higher level, we experience deification passively, receiving this experience as a free gift of grace.

76. We accomplish things actively in so far as our intelligence, whose natural task is to accomplish the virtues, is active within us, and in so far as there is also active within us our intellect, which is capable of receiving unconditionally all spiritual knowledge, of transcending the entire nature of created beings and all that is known, and of leaving all ages behind it. We experience things passively when, having completely transcended the inner essences of created beings, we come in a manner which is beyond conception to

the Cause itself of created beings, and there suspend the activity of our powers, together with all that is by nature finite. Then we become something that is in no sense an achievement of our natural capacities, since nature does not possess the power to grasp what transcends nature. For created things are not by nature able to accomplish deification since they cannot grasp God. To bestow a consonant measure of deification on created beings is within the power of divine grace alone. Grace irradiates nature with a supranatural light and by the transcendence of its glory raises nature above its natural limits.

77. We cease to accomplish the virtues after this present stage of life. But, on a higher level than that of the virtues, we never cease to experience deification by grace. For an experience, or passion, which transcends nature is limitless, and so is always active and effective; while an experience, or passion, which is contrary to nature is without real existence, and so is impotent.

78. The qualities of the virtues and the inner principles of created beings are both images of divine blessings, and in them God continually becomes man. As His body He has the qualities of the virtues, and as His soul the inner principles of spiritual knowledge. In this way He deifies those found worthy, giving them the true stamp of virtue and bestowing on them the essence of infallible knowledge.

79. An intellect faithful in the practice of the virtues is like St Peter when he was taken captive by Herod (cf. Acts 12 : 3-18). The name 'Herod' means 'made of skins or leather', and so Herod signifies the law of leather, that is, the will of the flesh. St Peter is guarded by two squads of soldiers and shut in by an iron gate. The two squads signify the attacks suffered by the intellect from the activity of the passions and from the mind's assent to the passions. When through the teaching of practical philosophy, as though with the help of an angel, the intellect has passed safely through these two squads or prisons, it comes to the iron gate which leads into the city. By this I mean the obdurate and stubborn attachment of the senses to sensible things. None the less, the gate is opened automatically through spiritual contemplation of the inner essences of created beings; and such contemplation then fearlessly impels the intellect, now liberated from Herod's madness, towards the spiritual realities where it truly belongs.

80. The devil is both God's enemy and His avenger (cf. Ps. 8 : 2). He is God's enemy when he seems in his hatred for God somehow to have acquired a destructive love for us men, persuading us by means of sensual pleasure to assent to the passions within our control, and to value what is transitory more than what is eternal. In this way he seduces all our soul's desire, separating us utterly from divine love and making us willing enemies of Him who made us. He is God's avenger when – now that we have become subject to him through sin – he lays bare his hatred for us and demands our punishment. For nothing pleases the devil more than punishing us. When he has been given leave to carry this out, he contrives successive attacks of passions inflicted against our will, and like a tempest he pitilessly assails us over whom, by God's permission, he has acquired authority. He does this, not with the intention of fulfilling God's command, but out of the desire to feed his own passion of hatred towards us, so that the soul, sinking down enervated by the weight of such painful calamities, may cut itself off from the power of divine hope, regarding the onslaught of these calamities not as a divine admonition but as a cause for disbelief in God.

81. When those who have acquired moral stability and contemplative knowledge employ these for the sake of human glory, merely conveying an outward impression of the virtues, and uttering words of wisdom and knowledge without performing the corresponding actions; and when in addition they display to others their vanity because of this supposed virtue and knowledge, then they are rightly handed over to commensurate hardships, in order to learn through suffering that humility which was unknown to them before because of their empty conceit.

82. Each demon promotes the attack of this or that particular temptation according to his innate propensity. For one demon is productive of one kind of evil, while another is clearly more abominable than his fellow and has a greater propensity for some other form of evil.

83. Without divine permission even the demons themselves cannot assist the devil in any way at all. For it is God Himself in His loving providence who allows the devil, in appropriate ways, to inflict various sufferings through his ministers. The book of Job shows this plainly, describing as it does how the devil was utterly unable to approach Job unless God willed it (cf. Job 1 : 11–12).

84. Real faith is faith which is manifest and active. Accordingly, to those engaged in the practice of the virtues the Logos of God is revealed embodied in the commandments, and as Logos He leads them by means of these commandments up to the Father, in whom He subsists by nature.

85. Reformation of life, angelic worship, the willing separation of the soul from the body, and the beginning of divine renewal in spirit – these are proclaimed in the veiled language of the New Testament. For instance, by the term 'spiritual circumcision' Scripture denotes the excision of the soul's impassioned attachment to the body (cf. Phil. 3 : 3; Col. 2 : 11).

86. Since God is full of goodness and wishes utterly to eradicate from us the seed of evil – that is to say, the sensual pleasure which draws our intellect away from divine love – He allows the devil to afflict us with suffering and chastisement. In this way He scrapes the poison of past pleasure from our souls; and He seeks to implant in us a hatred and complete revulsion for the things which belong to this world and pander to the senses alone, by making us realize that once we have acquired them we gain nothing from their use save chastisement. For He wishes to make the devil's power of chastisement and hatred of men the contingent cause of the return to virtue of those who have by their own free choice lapsed from it.

87. It is entirely fitting and just that those who gladly accept the devil's cunning suggestions to commit sins through their own volition should also be chastised by him. For through the passions to which we willingly accede the devil is the begetter of pleasure, and through the experiences that we suffer against our will he is the inflicter of pain.

88. The contemplative and gnostic intellect is often committed for punishment to the devil, deservedly suffering hardship and affliction at his hands. This is so that by suffering it may learn patiently to endure affliction rather than to trifle arrogantly to no purpose with things that do not exist.

89. If he who suffers for having transgressed one of God's commandments recognizes the principle of divine providence which is healing him, he accepts the affliction with joy and gratitude, and corrects the fault for which he is being disciplined. But if he is insensitive to this treatment, he is justly deprived of the grace that was once given him and is handed over to the turbulence of the

passions; he is abandoned so that he may acquire by ascetic labour those things for which he inwardly longs.

90. A person who, knowing what faults he has committed, willingly and with due thankfulness endures the trials painfully inflicted on him as a consequence of these faults, is not exiled from grace or from his state of virtue; for he submits willingly to the yoke of the king of Babylon (cf. Jer. 27 : 17) and pays off his debt by accepting the trials. In this way, while remaining in a state of grace and virtue, he pays tribute to the king of Babylon not only with his enforced sufferings, which have arisen out of the impassioned side of his nature, but also with his mental assent to these sufferings, accepting them as his due on account of his former offences. Through true worship, by which I mean a humble disposition, he offers to God the correction of his offences.

91. If you do not accept gratefully the trials which, by God's permission, are inflicted on you for your correction, and do not repent and rid yourself of your conceited opinion that you are righteous, you are given up to captivity, manacles, chains, hunger, death and the sword, and dwell a complete exile from your native land; for you resist the just penalties decreed by God and refuse to submit willingly to the yoke of the king of Babylon, as God has commanded. Banished in this way from your state of virtue and spiritual knowledge as if from your native land, you suffer all these things and more besides, because in your pride and vain conceit you refuse to make full satisfaction for your offences and to 'take delight in afflictions, calamities and hardships' (cf. 2 Cor. 12 : 10), as St Paul did. For he knew that the humility produced by bodily sufferings safeguards the divine treasures of the soul; and for this reason he was content and endured patiently, both for his own sake and for the sake of those to whom he served as an example of virtue and faith, so that if they suffered when guilty, like the Corinthian who was censured (cf. 1 Cor. 5 : 1–5), they might have him who suffers innocently as an encouragement and as a model of patience.

92. If, instead of stopping short at the outward appearance which visible things present to the senses, you seek with your intellect to contemplate their inner essences, seeing them as images of spiritual realities or as the inward principles of sensible objects, you will be taught that nothing belonging to the visible world is unclean. For by nature all things were created good (cf. Gen. 1 : 31; Acts 10 : 15).

93. He who is not affected by changes in sensible things practises the virtues in a manner that is truly pure. He who does not permit the outward appearances of sensible things to imprint themselves on his intellect has received the true doctrine of created beings. He whose mind has outstripped the very being of created things has come, as a true theologian, close to the One through unknowing.

94. Every contemplative intellect that has 'the sword of the Spirit, which is the word of God' (Eph. 6 : 17), and that has cut off in itself the activity of the visible world, has attained virtue. When it has excised from itself the image of sensible appearances it finds the truth existing in the inner essences of created beings, which is the foundation of natural contemplation. And when it has transcended the being of created things, it will receive the illumination of the divine and unoriginate Unity who is the foundation of the mystery of true theology.

95. God reveals Himself to each person according to each person's mode of conceiving Him. To those whose aspiration transcends the complex structure of matter, and whose psychic powers are fully integrated in a single unceasing gyration around God, He reveals Himself as Unity and Trinity. In this way He both shows forth His own existence and mystically makes known the mode in which that existence subsists. To those whose aspiration is limited to the complex structure of matter, and whose psychic powers are not integrated, He reveals Himself not as He is but as they are, showing that they are completely caught in the material dualism whereby the physical world is conceived as composed of matter and form.

96. St Paul refers to the different energies of the Holy Spirit as different gifts of grace, stating that they are all energized by one and the same Holy Spirit (cf. 1 Cor. 12 : 11). The 'manifestation of the Spirit' (1 Cor. 12 : 7) is given according to the measure of every man's faith through participation in a particular gift of grace. Thus every believer is receptive to the energy of the Spirit in a way that corresponds to his degree of faith and the state of his soul; and this energy grants him the capacity needed to carry out a particular commandment.

97. One person is given the quality of wisdom, another the quality of spiritual knowledge, another the quality of faith, and someone else one of the other gifts of the Spirit enumerated by St

Paul (cf. 1 Cor. 12 : 8–11). In the same way, one person receives through the Spirit, according to the degree of his faith, the gift of that perfect and direct love for God which is free from all materiality; another through the same Spirit receives the gift of perfect love for his neighbour; and another receives something else from the same Spirit. In each, as I have said, the gift that conforms with his state is energized. For every capacity for fulfilling a commandment is called a gift of the Spirit.

98. The baptism of the Lord (cf. Matt. 20 : 22) is the utter mortification of our propensity for the sensible world; and the cup is the disavowal of our present mode of life for the sake of truth.

99. The baptism of the Lord typifies the sufferings we willingly embrace for the sake of virtue. Through these sufferings we wash off the stains in our conscience and readily accept the death of our propensity for visible things. The cup typifies the involuntary trials which attack us in the form of adverse circumstances because of our pursuit of the truth. If throughout these trials we value our desire for God more than nature, we willingly submit to the death of nature forced on us by these circumstances.

100. The baptism and the cup differ in this way: baptism for the sake of virtue mortifies our propensity for the pleasures of this life; the cup makes the devout value truth above even nature itself.

Second Century

1. Christ mentioned the cup before the baptism (cf. Matt. 20 : 22) because virtue exists for the sake of truth but truth does not exist for the sake of virtue. Thus he who practises virtue for the sake of truth is not wounded by the arrows of self-esteem; but he who pursues truth for the sake of virtue does harbour the conceit which self-esteem generates.

2. Truth is divine knowledge, and virtue the struggles for truth on the part of those who desire it. A man who endures the labours of virtue for the sake of such knowledge is not vainglorious, because he knows that truth cannot be grasped naturally through human effort. For it is not in the nature of things for what is primary to be circumscribed by what is secondary. But a man who expects to attain knowledge by means of the struggles he makes for the sake of virtue invariably suffers from self-esteem, because he imagines he has gained the victor's crown before he has sweated for it. He does not know that labours exist for the sake of crowns, but crowns do not exist for the sake of labours. For by nature every spiritual method ceases to be practised once the purpose for which it was intended has been achieved or is thought to have been achieved.

3. He who seeks only the outward form of knowledge, that is, knowledge which is merely theoretical, and pursues the semblance of virtue, that is, a merely theoretical morality, is puffed up, Judaic-wise, with the images of truth.

4. He who does not view the ritual of the Law with his senses alone, but noetically penetrates every visible symbol and thoroughly assimilates the divine principle which is hidden in each, finds God in the Law. For rightly he uses his intellect to grope among the material forms of the Law, as among litter, in the hope of finding

hidden somewhere in its body that pearl or principle which utterly escapes the senses (cf. Matt. 13 : 45–46).

5. Again, he who does not limit his perception of the nature of visible things to what his senses alone can observe, but wisely with his intellect searches after the essence which lies within every creature, also finds God; for from the manifest magnificence of created beings he learns who is the Cause of their being.

6. Discrimination is the distinctive characteristic of one who probes. He then who examines the symbols of the Law in a spiritual manner, and who contemplates the visible nature of created beings with intelligence, will discriminate in Scripture between letter and spirit, in creation between inner essence and outward appearance, and in himself between intellect and the senses; and in Scripture he will choose the spirit, in creation the inner essence or *logos*, and in himself the intellect. If he then unites these three indissolubly to one another, he will have found God: he will have come to recognize, as he should and as is possible, the God who is Intellect, Logos and Spirit. In this way he will be delivered from all the things which deceive man and seduce him into innumerable errors – delivered, that is to say, from the letter, the outward appearance of things, and the senses, all of which possess quantitative distinctions and are the negation of unity. But if a man compounds the letter of the Law, the outward appearance of visible things, and his own senses with each other, he is 'so short-sighted as to be blind' (2 Pet. 1 : 9), sick through his ignorance of the Cause of created beings.

7. The apostle gives us the following definition of faith: 'Faith makes real for us things hoped for, gives assurance of things not seen' (Heb. 11 : 1). One may also justly define it as an engrained blessing or as true knowledge disclosing unutterable blessings.

8. Faith is a relational power or a relationship which brings about the immediate, perfect and supranatural union of the believer with the God in whom he believes.

9. Since man is composed of body and soul, he is moved by two laws, that of the flesh and that of the Spirit (cf. Rom. 7 : 23). The law of the flesh operates by virtue of the senses; the law of the Spirit operates by virtue of the intellect. The first law, operating by virtue of the senses, automatically binds one closely to matter; the second law, operating by virtue of the intellect, brings about direct union with God. Suppose there is someone who does not doubt in

his heart (cf. Mark 11 : 23) – that is to say, who does not dispute in his intellect – and through such doubt sever that immediate union with God which has been brought about by faith, but who is dispassionate or, rather, has already become god through union with God by faith: then it is quite natural that if such a person says to a mountain, 'Go to another place', it will go (cf. Matt. 17 : 20). The mountain here indicates the will and the law of the flesh, which is ponderous and hard to shift, and in fact, so far as our natural powers are concerned, is totally immovable and unshakeable.

10. The capacity for unintelligence is rooted so deeply in human nature through the senses that the majority think that man is nothing more than flesh, which possesses sense faculties so that he can enjoy this present life.

11. 'All things are possible', says Scripture, 'for the person who believes' (Mark 9 : 23) and does not doubt – that is to say, for the person who is not dominated by his soul's attachment to the body through the senses, and so does not separate himself from the union with God which faith has brought about in him through the intellect. Whatever alienates the intellect from the world and the flesh brings it, perfected by its spiritual achievements, close to God. That is what should be understood as implied in the saying, 'All things are possible for the person who believes.'

12. Faith is knowledge that cannot be rationally demonstrated. If such knowledge cannot be rationally demonstrated, then faith is a supranatural relationship through which, in an unknowable and so undemonstrable manner, we are united with God in a union which is beyond intellection.

13. When the intellect is in direct union with God, that quality in it by virtue of which it apprehends and is apprehended is completely in abeyance. As soon as it activates this quality by apprehending something sequent to God, it experiences doubt and severs the union which is beyond intellection. So long as the intellect is joined to God in this union, and has passed beyond nature and become god by participation, it will have transposed the law of its nature as though shifting an immovable mountain.

14. He who has just begun to follow a holy way of life, and has received instruction about how to act righteously, devotes himself wholly to the practice of the virtues in all obedience and faith, nourishing himself, as if on meat, on their manifest aspects, that is

to say, on moral training. The inner principles of the commandments, which constitute the knowledge of the perfect, in his faith
he leaves to God, for he cannot as yet embrace the full magnitude
of faith.

15. The perfect man, who has passed beyond the category not
only of beginners but also of those who are advancing, is not ignorant of the inner principles of the actions he performs in carrying out
the commandments. On the contrary, he first spiritually imbibes
those principles and then by means of his actions feeds upon the
whole body of the virtues. In this way he transposes to the plane of
spiritual knowledge actions which take place in the sensible realm.

16. The Lord said, 'First seek the kingdom of God and His
righteousness' (Matt. 6 : 33), that is, seek the knowledge of truth
before all things, and therefore seek training in appropriate methods
of attaining it. In saying this, He showed clearly that believers must
seek only divine knowledge and the virtue which adorns it with
corresponding actions.

17. Many are the things of which the believer has need in order
to attain knowledge of God and virtue: deliverance from passions,
patient acceptance of trials, the inner principles of virtues, the
practice of methods of spiritual warfare, the uprooting of the soul's
predilection for the flesh, the breaking of the senses' attachment to
sensible objects, the utter withdrawal of the intellect from all
created things; and, in short, there are countless other things which
help us to reject sin and ignorance and to attain knowledge and
virtue. It was surely because of this that the Lord said, 'Whatever
you ask for in prayer, believing, you will receive' (Matt. 21 : 22),
stating simply that the devout must seek and ask with understanding
and faith for all those things, and for those alone, which lead to
virtue and knowledge of God. For all these things are profitable,
and unquestionably the Lord gives them to those who ask.

18. Thus he who for the sake of faith alone – that is to say, for
the sake of direct union with God – seeks all the things that contribute towards this union will unquestionably receive them. He who
seeks either the things which we have mentioned or other things
without this motive will not receive them. For he has no faith, but
like an unbeliever uses divine things to boost his own glory.

19. He who purges his will from the corruption of sin destroys
the corrupting activity of what causes corruption. For when one's

free will is itself free from corruption, it prevents nature from being corrupted by hostile forces and keeps it incorrupt through the providential grace of the Spirit within it.

20. Since the principles of nature and of grace are not one and the same, we should not be surprised if certain of the saints sometimes resisted the passions and sometimes succumbed to them; for we know that the miracle of resistance is due to grace, while the passion belongs to nature.

21. He who keeps in mind the way of the saints by imitating them not only shakes off the deadly paralysis of the passions but also takes up the life of the virtues.

22. God, who before all ages set the bounds of each man's life, in the manner which He wills, leads every man, whether righteous or unrighteous, towards the final end he deserves.

23. As I take it, the dark storm which befell St Paul (cf. Acts 28 : 1-4) is the weight of involuntary trials and temptations. The island is the firm unshakeable state of divine hope. The fire is the state of spiritual knowledge. The sticks are the nature of visible things. Paul gathered these with his hand, which I take to mean with the exploratory capacity of the intellect during contemplation. He fed the state of spiritual knowledge with conceptual images derived from the nature of visible things, for the state of spiritual knowledge heals the mental dejection produced by the storm of trials and temptations. The viper is the cunning and destructive power hidden secretly in the nature of sensible things. It bites the hand, that is, the exploratory noetic activity of contemplation, but without harming the visionary intellect; and this, with the light of spiritual knowledge, as if with fire, at once destroys the destructive power that arises from the contemplation of sensible things and that attaches itself to the practical activity of the intellect.

24. St Paul was a 'scent of life, leading to life' (2 Cor. 2 : 16) because he inspired the faithful by his own example to experience the fragrance of the virtues by putting them into practice, or because like a preacher he led those who had been converted by the word of grace away from life in the senses to life in the spirit. 'The scent of death, leading to death' (ibid.) gives a taste of their future condemnation to those who go from the death of ignorance to the death of unbelief. Or, alternatively, the 'scent of life, leading to life' refers to those who have advanced from the life of ascetic prac-

tice to that of contemplation, and the 'scent of death, leading to death' refers to those who have passed from the mortification of whatever is earthly in their nature (cf. Col. 3 : 5) to the blessed mortification of impassioned conceptual images and fantasies.

25. The soul has three powers: the intelligence, the incensive power and desire. With our intelligence we direct our search; with our desire we long for that supernal goodness which is the object of our search; and with our incensive power we fight to attain our object. With these powers those who love God cleave to the divine principle of virtue and spiritual knowledge. Searching with the first power, desiring with the second, and fighting by means of the third, they receive incorruptible nourishment, enriching the intellect with the spiritual knowledge of created beings.

26. When the Logos of God became man, He filled human nature once more with the spiritual knowledge that it had lost; and steeling it against changefulness, He deified it, not in its essential nature but in its quality. He stamped it completely with His own Spirit, as if adding wine to water so as to give the water the quality of wine. For He becomes truly man so that by grace He may make us gods.

27. When God created human nature, at the same time as He gave it being and free will He joined to it the capacity for carrying out the duties laid upon it. By this capacity I mean the impulse implanted in human nature on the level of both being and free will: on the level of being, so that man has the power to achieve the virtues; on the level of free will, so that he may use this power in the right way.

28. We have as a natural criterion the law of nature. This teaches us that, before we can acquire the wisdom that lies in all things, we must through mystical initiation seek their Maker.

29. Jacob's well (cf. John 4 : 5–15) is Scripture. The water is the spiritual knowledge found in Scripture. The depth of the well is the meaning, only to be attained with great difficulty, of the obscure sayings in Scripture. The bucket is learning gained from the written text of the word of God, which the Lord did not possess because He is the Logos Himself; and so He does not give believers the knowledge that comes from learning and study, but grants to those found worthy the ever-flowing waters of wisdom that spill from the fountain of spiritual grace and never run dry. For the bucket – that is to

say, learning – can only grasp a very small amount of knowledge and leaves behind all that it cannot lay hold of, however it tries. But the knowledge which is received through grace, without study, contains all the wisdom that man can attain, springing forth in different ways according to his needs.

30. There is a great and unutterable difference between the tree of life and the one which is not the tree of life. This is clear simply from the fact that the one is called the tree of life while the other is merely called the tree of the knowledge of good and evil (cf. Gen. 2 : 9). Unquestionably, the tree of life is productive of life; the tree that is not called the tree of life, and so is not productive of life, is obviously productive of death. For only death is the opposite of life.

31. The tree of life, when understood as symbolizing wisdom, likewise differs greatly from the tree of the knowledge of good and evil, in that the latter neither symbolizes wisdom nor is said to do so. Wisdom is characterized by intellect and intelligence, the state which is opposite to wisdom by lack of intelligence and by sensation.

32. Since man came into being composed of noetic soul and sentient body, one interpretation could be that the tree of life is the soul's intellect, which is the seat of wisdom. The tree of the knowledge of good and evil would then be the body's power of sensation, which is clearly the seat of mindless impulses. Man received the divine commandment not to involve himself actively and experientially with these impulses; but he did not keep the commandment.

33. Both trees in Scripture symbolize the intellect and the senses. Thus the intellect has the power to discriminate between the spiritual and the sensible, between the eternal and the transitory. Or rather, as the soul's discriminatory power, the intellect persuades the soul to cleave to the first and to transcend the second. The senses have the power to discriminate between pleasure and pain in the body. Or rather, as a power existing in a body endowed with soul and sense-perception, they persuade the body to embrace pleasure and reject pain.

34. If a man exercises only sensory discrimination between pain and pleasure in the body, thus transgressing the divine commandment, he eats from the tree of the knowledge of good and evil, that is to say, he succumbs to the mindless impulses that pertain to the senses; for he possesses only the body's power of discrimination,

which makes him embrace pleasure as something good and avoid pain as something evil. But if he exercises only that noetic discrimination which distinguishes between the eternal and the transitory, and so keeps the divine commandment, he eats from the tree of life, that is to say, from the wisdom that appertains to his intellect; for he exercises only the power of discrimination associated with the soul, which makes him cleave to the glory of what is eternal as something good, and avoid the corruption of what is transitory as something evil.

35. Goodness so far as the intellect is concerned is a dispassionate predilection for the spirit; evil is an impassioned attachment to the senses. Goodness so far as the senses are concerned is the impassioned activity of the body under the stimulus of pleasure; evil is the state destitute of such activity.

36. He who persuades his conscience to regard the evil he is doing as good by nature reaches out with his moral faculty as with a hand and grasps the tree of life in a reprehensible manner; for he thinks that what is thoroughly evil is by nature immortal. Therefore God, who has implanted in man's conscience a natural hatred of evil, cuts him off from life, for he has now become evil in his will and intention. God acts in this way so that when a man does wrong he cannot persuade his own conscience that what is thoroughly evil is good by nature.

37. The vine produces wine, the wine drunkenness and drunkenness an evil form of ecstasy. Similarly the intelligence – which is the vine – when well-nurtured and cultivated by the virtues, generates spiritual knowledge; and such knowledge produces a good form of ecstasy which enables the intellect to transcend its attachment to the senses.

38. It is the devil's practice maliciously to confound the forms and shapes of sensible things with our conceptual images of them. Through these forms and shapes are generated passions for the outward aspects of visible things; and our intellectual energy, being halted at the level of what pertains to sense-perception, cannot raise itself to the realm of intelligible realities. In this way the devil despoils the soul and drags it down into the turmoil of the passions.

39. The Logos of God is at the same time both a lamp and a light (cf. Ps. 119 : 105; Prov. 6 : 23). For He illumines those thoughts of the faithful which are in accordance with nature, but burns those

which are contrary to nature; He dispels the darkness of sensory
life for those who press forward by means of the commandments
towards the life that they hope for, but punishes with the fire of
judgment those who wilfully cleave to the dark night of this present
life because of their love for the flesh.

40. It is said that he who does not first reintegrate himself with
his own being by rejecting those passions which are contrary to
nature will not be reintegrated with the Cause of his being – that is,
with God – by acquiring supranatural blessings through grace. For
he who would truly unite himself with God must first separate himself mentally from created things.

41. The function of the written Law is to deliver men from
passions; that of the natural law is to grant equal rights to all men in
accordance with natural justice. The fulfilment of the spiritual law
is to attain similitude to God, in so far as this is possible for man.

42. The intellect has by nature the capacity to receive a spiritual
knowledge of corporeal and incorporeal things; but by grace alone
does it receive revelations of the Holy Trinity. While believing that
the Trinity exists, the human intellect can never presume to grasp
what the Trinity is in Its essence, in the way that this is known to the
divine Intellect. The person without spiritual knowledge is completely ignorant of the way in which sin is purged by virtue.

43. He who loves falsehood is handed over to be harrowed by it,
so that by suffering he may come to know what it is he willingly
pursued, and may learn by experience that he mistakenly embraced
death instead of life.

44. God has knowledge only of what is good, because He is in
essence the nature and the knowledge of what is good. He is ignorant of evil because He has no capacity for evil. Only of those things
for which by nature He possesses the capacity does He also possess
the essential knowledge.

45. The breast mentioned in Leviticus (cf. Lev. 7 : 30, 34) indicates the higher form of contemplation. The shoulder (cf. Lev.
7 : 32, 34) stands for the mental state and activity concordant with
the life of ascetic practice. Thus the breast and the shoulder denote
respectively spiritual knowledge and virtue. For spiritual knowledge
leads the intellect directly to God Himself, while virtue in the life of
ascetic practice separates it from all involvement in generation. In
the text in question, breast and shoulder were set aside for the

priests, who alone possessed the Lord as their inheritance for ever and had no share at all in earthly things.

46. Those fully endowed by the Spirit with spiritual knowledge and virtue are able, through preaching and instruction, to make the hearts of others receptive of true devotion and faith, withdrawing their disposition and capacity from its preoccupation with corruptible nature and directing it towards the actualization of supranatural and incorruptible blessings. It is therefore fitting that in this same text the breast of the victims offered in sacrifice to God – that is, the hearts of those who offer themselves to God – and the shoulder – that is, their life of ascetic practice – should be set aside for the priests.

47. Compared with the righteousness of the age to be, all earthly righteousness fulfils the role of a mirror: it contains the image of archetypal realities, not the realities themselves as they subsist in their true and universal nature. And compared with knowledge there, all spiritual knowledge in this world is an indistinct image: it contains a reflection of the truth but not the truth itself as it is destined to be revealed (cf. 1 Cor. 13 : 12).

48. Since what is divine consists in virtue and spiritual knowledge, the mirror displays the archetypes of virtue and the indistinct image reveals the archetypes of spiritual knowledge.

49. He who has conformed his life to God's will through practice of the virtues transposes his intellect to the realm of intelligible realities by means of contemplation. By so doing he places himself utterly beyond the reach of everything that seeks to entrap him, and so is not attracted through some sensory image towards the death that lies in the passions.

50. The person who with the clear eye of faith beholds the beauty of the blessings of the age to be readily obeys the command to leave his country and his kindred and his father's house (cf. Gen. 12 : 1), and he abandons the flesh, the senses and sensory things, together with passionate attachments and inclinations. In times of temptation and conflict he rises above nature because he has put the Cause of nature first, just as Abraham put God before Isaac (cf. Gen. 22 : 1– 14).

51. So long as you do not pursue virtue or study Holy Scripture for the sake of glory, or as a cloak for greed (cf. 1 Thess. 2 : 5), or from love of flattery and popularity, or for self-display, but do and

say and think all things for the sake of God, then you are walking
with spiritual knowledge in the way of truth. If, however, you have
in some respects 'prepared the way for the Lord', yet have not
'made His paths straight', He will not come to dwell within you
(cf. Isa. 40 : 3. LXX; Mark 1 : 3).

52. If you fast and avoid a mode of life which excites the passions,
and in general do whatever contributes to your deliverance from
evil, then you have 'prepared the way for the Lord'. But if you do
these things out of self-esteem, or greed, or love of flattery, or for
some similar motive, and not with a desire to perform God's will,
then you have not 'made His paths straight'. You have endured the
labour of preparing the way but do not have God walking in your
paths.

53. 'Every valley shall be filled' – yet not 'every' without quali-
fication, or 'everyone's valley', for the text does not refer to the
valley of those who have not prepared the way of the Lord and made
His paths straight. By a valley is meant the flesh or soul of those who
have prepared the way of the Lord and made His paths straight in the
manner I have explained. When such a valley has been filled with
spiritual knowledge and virtue by the divine Logos who, present in
His commandments, walks in its paths, then all the spirits of false
knowledge and evil are 'abased'; for the Logos treads them down
and brings them into subjection. He overthrows that cunning power
which has raised itself up against human nature; He levels it as if it
were high and massive mountains and hills which He uses to fill in
the valleys. For the rejection of passions which are contrary to
nature, and the reception of virtues which are in accordance with
nature, fills up the valley-like soul and abases the exalted lordship of
the evil spirits (Isa. 40 : 4. LXX).

54. The 'rough places' – that is to say, the attacks of trials and
temptations suffered against our will – shall be made 'smooth',
above all when the intellect, rejoicing and delighting in weakness,
affliction and calamity, through its unsought sufferings deprives of all
their lordship the passions in which we deliberately indulge. For by
'rough places' Scripture means those experiences of unsought trials
and temptations which change to smooth ways when endured with
patience and thankfulness (cf. Isa. 40 : 4. LXX).

55. He who longs for the true life knows that all suffering,
whether sought or unsought, brings death to sensual pleasure, the

mother of death; and so he gladly accepts the harsh attacks of trials and temptations suffered against his will. By patiently enduring them he turns afflictions into smooth untroubled paths, unerringly leading whoever devoutly runs the divine race along them towards 'the prize of the high calling' (Phil. 3 : 14). For sensual pleasure is the mother of death and the death of such pleasure is suffering, whether freely chosen or not.

56. Everyone, then, who through self-restraint does away with sensual pleasure, which is intricate, convoluted and intertwined in many ways with every sensible object, makes the crooked straight. And he who with patience withstands and defeats the harsh implacable bouts of suffering turns the rough places into smooth ways. Thus, when a person has well and truly struggled, has defeated sensual pleasure with desire for virtue, has overcome pain with love for spiritual knowledge, and through both virtue and knowledge has bravely persevered to the end of the divine contest, he will see, according to Scripture, 'the salvation of God'; and this will be his reward for virtue and for the efforts he has made to attain it (Isa. 40 : 4–5. LXX).

57. The lover of virtue willingly puts out the fire of sensual pleasure. And if a man has dedicated his intellect to the knowledge of truth, he will not allow unsought sufferings to thwart the ceaseless aspiration that leads him towards God.

58. When through self-control you have straightened the crooked paths of the passions in which you deliberately indulged – that is to say, the impulses of sensual pleasure – and when, by enduring patiently the harsh and painful afflictions produced by trials and temptations suffered against your will, you have made the rough ways smooth and even, then you may expect to see God's salvation, for you will have become pure in heart. In this state of purity, through the virtues and through holy contemplation, you will at the end of your contest behold God, in accordance with Christ's words: 'Blessed are the pure in heart, for they shall see God' (Matt. 5 : 8). And because of the sufferings you have endured for the sake of virtue you will receive the gift of dispassion. To those who possess this gift there is nothing which reveals God more fully.

59. In Scripture hearts capable of receiving the heavenly gifts of holy knowledge are called cisterns (cf. 2 Chr. 26 : 10). They have been hewn out by the firm principle of the commandments; they

have been cleared, as if of earth, of self-indulgence in the passions and of natural attachment to sensible things; and they have been filled with that spiritual knowledge which purges the passions and gives life and sustenance to the virtues.

60. The Lord hews out cisterns in the desert, that is to say, in the world and in human nature. He excavates the hearts of those who are worthy, clears them of their material sordidness and arrogance, and makes them deep and wide in order to receive the divine rains of wisdom and knowledge. He does this so that they may water Christ's flocks, those who need moral instruction because of the immaturity of their souls.

61. Scripture refers to the higher form of the spiritual contemplation of nature as 'hill-country' (Deut. 11 : 11). Its cultivators are those who have rejected the images derived from sensible objects, and have advanced to a perception of the noetic essences of these objects through the acquisition of the virtues.

62. So long as the intellect continuously remembers God, it seeks the Lord through contemplation, not superficially but in the fear of the Lord, that is, by practising the commandments. For he who seeks Him through contemplation without practising the commandments does not find Him: he has not sought Him in the fear of the Lord and so the Lord does not guide him to success. The Lord guides to success all who combine the practice of the virtues with spiritual knowledge: He teaches them the qualities of the commandments and reveals to them the true inner essences of created beings.

63. Sublime knowledge about God stands in the soul like a tower, fortified with the practice of the commandments. That is the meaning of the text, 'Uzziah built towers in Jerusalem' (2 Chr. 26 : 9). A man builds towers in Jerusalem when he is blessed with success in his search for the Lord through contemplation accompanied by the requisite fear, that is, by observing the commandments; for he then establishes the principles of divine knowledge in the undivided and tranquil state of his soul.

64. When the inner principles of particulars combine with those of universals, they bring about the union of what is divided. This is because the more universal a principle is, the greater the degree to which it embraces and unifies the more particular principles. Particulars have a natural affinity with universals. But there is also a

certain spiritual principle which relates the intellect to the senses, heaven to earth, sensibles to intelligibles, and nature to the principle of nature, uniting them one with another.

65. If you have been able to free your senses from the passions and have separated your soul from its attachment to the senses, you will have succeeded in barring the devil from entering the intellect by means of the senses. It is to this end that you should build safe towers in the desert (cf. 2 Chr. 26 : 10). By 'desert' is meant natural contemplation; by 'safe towers' a true understanding of the nature of created beings. If you take refuge in these towers, you will not fear the demons who raid this desert – that is, who insinuate themselves into the nature of visible things, deceiving the intellect through the senses and dragging it off into the darkness of ignorance. If you acquire a true understanding of each thing, you will not be afraid of the demons who deceive men by means of the external appearance of sensible objects.

66. Every intellect that has the power to contemplate is a true cultivator: so long as it has the remembrance of God to sustain it, it keeps the seeds of divine goodness clear of tares through its own diligence and solicitude. For it is said, 'And with fear of the Lord he sought God in the days of Zechariah' (2 Chr. 26 : 5. LXX). 'Zechariah' means 'remembrance of God'. So let us always pray to God to keep this saving remembrance alive in us, lest what our intellect has achieved corrupts our soul, filling it with pride and encouraging it to aspire presumptuously, like Uzziah, to what is above nature (cf. 2 Chr. 26 : 16).

67. Only a soul which has been delivered from the passions can without error contemplate created beings. Because its virtue is perfect, and because its knowledge is spiritual and free from materiality, such a soul is called 'Jerusalem'. This state is attained through exclusion not only of the passions but also of sensible images.

68. Without faith, hope and love (cf. 1 Cor. 13 : 13) nothing sinful is totally abolished, nor is anything good fully attained. Faith urges the beleaguered intellect to press on towards God and encourages it by equipping it with a full range of spiritual weapons. Hope is the intellect's surest pledge of divine help and promises the destruction of hostile powers. Love makes it difficult or, rather, makes it utterly impossible for the intellect to estrange itself from

the tender care of God; and when the intellect is under attack, love impels it to concentrate its whole natural power into longing for the divine.

69. Faith encourages the beleaguered intellect and strengthens it with the hope of assistance. Hope brings before its eyes this help promised by faith and drives off the enemy's attack. Love kills the enemy's provocations within the devout intellect, utterly obliterating them with deep longing for the divine.

70. The first and unique effect of the divine gift of genuine spiritual knowledge is to produce within us by faith the resurrection of God. Faith needs to be accompanied by the right ordering of our will and purpose – that is to say, by discrimination – which makes it possible for us bravely to withstand the spate of trials and temptations, sought or unsought. Thus faith, rightfully expressing itself through the fulfilment of the commandments, is the first resurrection within us of the God whom we have slain through our ignorance.

71. The return to God clearly implies the fullest affirmation of hope in Him, for without this nobody can accept God in any way at all. For it is characteristic of hope that it brings future things before us as if they were present, and so it assures those who are attacked by hostile powers that God, in whose name and for whose sake the saints go into battle, protects them and is in no way absent. For without some expectation, pleasant or unpleasant, no one can ever undertake a return to the divine.

72. Nothing so much as love brings together those who have been sundered and produces in them an effective union of will and purpose. Love is distinguished by the beauty of recognizing the equal value of all men. Love is born in a man when his soul's powers – that is, his intelligence, incensive power and desire – are concentrated and unified around the divine. Those who by grace have come to recognize the equal value of all men in God's sight and who engrave His beauty on their memory, possess an ineradicable longing for divine love, for such love is always imprinting this beauty on their intellect.

73. Every intellect girded with divine authority possesses three powers as its counsellors and ministers. First, there is the intelligence. It is intelligence which gives birth to that faith, founded upon spiritual knowledge, whereby the intellect learns that God is always

present in an unutterable way, and through which it grasps, with the aid of hope, things of the future as though they were present. Second, there is desire. It is desire which generates that divine love through which the intellect, when of its own free will it aspires to pure divinity, is wedded in an indissoluble manner to this aspiration. Third, there is the incensive power. It is with this power that the intellect cleaves to divine peace and concentrates its desire on divine love. Every intellect possesses these three powers, and they co-operate with it in order to purge evil and to establish and sustain holiness.

74. Without the power of intelligence there is no capacity for spiritual knowledge; and without spiritual knowledge we cannot have the faith from which springs that hope whereby we grasp things of the future as though they were present. Without the power of desire there is no longing, and so no love, which is the issue of longing; for the property of desire is to love something. And without the incensive power, intensifying the desire for union with what is loved, there can be no peace, for peace is truly the complete and undisturbed possession of what is desired.

75. Until you have been completely purified from the passions you should not engage in natural contemplation through the images of sensible things; for until then such images are able to mould your intellect so that it conforms to passion. An intellect which, fed by the senses, dwells in imagination on the visible aspects of sensible things becomes the creator of impure passions, for it is not able to advance through contemplation to those intelligible realities cognate with it.

76. When faced with the eruption of the passions, you should courageously close your senses and totally reject the images and memories of sensible things, and in every way restrict the intellect's natural tendency to investigate things in the external world. Then, with God's help, you will abase and overcome the cunning tyrannical power which rises up against you.

77. When intelligence is stupefied, the incensive power precipitate and desire mindless, and when ignorance, a domineering spirit and licentiousness govern the soul, then sin becomes a habit, actively entangling one in the various pleasures of the senses.

78. The mature intellect must with spiritual knowledge escape from invisible entanglements. While it is being provoked by evil

powers it must not engage in natural contemplation or do anything but pray, tame the body with hardship, diligently bring the earthly will into subjection, and guard the walls of the city, that is, the virtues which protect the soul or the qualities which guard the virtues, namely, self-control and patience. Otherwise he who proffers the soul a foul potion may deceive the intellect with what seems to be good and secretly turn its desire away from God, drawing its understanding, which seeks what is good, towards what is bad, because it has mistaken the bad for the good.

79. The person who courageously closes his senses by means of the deliberate and all-embracing practice of self-control and patience, and prevents sensory forms from entering the intellect through the soul's faculties, easily frustrates the wicked schemes of the devil and turns him back, abased, along the way by which he came. The way by which the devil comes consists of material things which seem to be needed for sustaining the body.

80. The intellect reaps true knowledge from natural contemplation when, in a way that conforms to nature, it unites the senses to itself by means of the intelligence.

81. When Scripture speaks of the springs blocked up by Hezekiah outside the city (cf. 2 Chr. 32 : 3–4. LXX), the city signifies the soul and the springs the totality of sensible things. The waters of these springs are conceptual images of sensible things. The river that flows through the middle of the city is knowledge gathered in natural contemplation from these conceptual images of sensible things. This knowledge passes through the middle of the soul because it links the intellect and the senses. For the knowledge of sensible things is not entirely unconnected with the noetic faculty, nor does it depend altogether on the activity of the senses. On the contrary, it is as it were the intermediary between the intellect and the senses and between the senses and the intellect, and itself brings about the union of the two with each other. So far as the senses are concerned, it impresses on them the forms of sensible things, each according to its own kind; so far as the intellect is concerned, it transmutes these impressions into the inner essences of the forms. It is therefore fitting that the knowledge of visible things should be described as a river flowing through the middle of the city, for it occupies the middle ground between the intellect and the senses.

82. If during periods of temptation and trial you refrain from natural contemplation and hold fast to prayer, withdrawing your intellect from all things and focusing it on itself and on God, you will put to death the inward disposition which produces evil and you will send the devil packing with his tail between his legs. For it was the devil who insinuated this habit into you and, relying on it, he boastfully approached your soul, vilifying truth with proud thoughts. David, who had vast experience in the front line of every kind of spiritual battle, was most likely not simply familiar with these tactics but actually put them into practice; for he says: 'While the wicked one stood before me I was dumb and humbled myself and refrained from uttering even good words' (Ps. 39 : 1–2. LXX). Jeremiah, in the same spirit, warned the people not to go out of the city because the sword of the enemy lay about it (cf. Jer. 6 : 25).

83. We may apply this also to Cain and Abel (cf. Gen. 4 : 8). Cain is the law of the flesh, and the field into which Cain and Abel went is the realm of natural contemplation. Had Abel kept guard over himself and had he not gone out with Cain into the field before attaining dispassion, then the law of the flesh would not have risen up and killed him, cleverly deceiving him when he was engaged in the contemplation of created beings before being fully prepared.

84. Similarly, if Dinah the child of Jacob had not gone out to the daughters of the land – that is, into the world of sensible images – Shechem the son of Hamor would not have risen up and humiliated her (cf. Gen. 34 : 1–2).

85. We should abstain from natural contemplation until we are fully prepared, lest in trying to perceive the spiritual essences of visible creatures we reap passions by mistake. For the outward forms of visible things have greater power over the senses of those who are immature than the essences hidden in the forms of things have over their souls. Of course, those who confine their minds Judaic-wise to the letter alone expect the promises of divine blessings to be fulfilled in this present age, for they are ignorant of the qualities naturally inherent in the soul.

86. He who 'wears the image of Him who is from heaven' (1 Cor. 15 : 49) tries to follow the spirit of Holy Scripture in all things, for it is the spirit which, by promoting virtue and spiritual knowledge, sustains the soul. He who 'wears the image of him who is from earth' pays heed only to the letter, for the cultivation of the body by

means of the senses is promoted by the letter. Such cultivation in its turn generates the passions.

87. By the power of God is meant the virtue that destroys the passions and safeguards holy thoughts. Such virtue is generated by the practice of the commandments: in this way, with God's co-operation or, rather, by His strength alone, we destroy the forces of evil that are opposed to sanctity. By God's sublimity is meant the spiritual knowledge of the truth, realized through our efforts to attain the contemplation of created beings and the practice of the virtues. Through spiritual knowledge we utterly annihilate the truth-opposing power of falsehood, abasing and demolishing the vaunting self-assertion of the evil spirits that exalt themselves against the knowledge of God (cf. 2 Cor. 10 : 5). For just as ascetic practice gives birth to virtue, so contemplation engenders spiritual knowledge.

88. Ineffaceable knowledge, whose spiritual gyration around God's infinitude is unconditioned and beyond intellection, images in its unconditionality the more than infinite glory of the truth. The voluntary imitation of divine wisdom and goodness brings as its reward the intellect's longing for and glorious attainment of likeness to God, in so far as this is possible for man.

89. The tongue is a symbol of the soul's spiritual energy and the larynx a symbol of natural self-love for the body. Thus he who ignobly welds the one to the other cannot give his attention to the tranquil state of virtue and spiritual knowledge, for he sedulously indulges in the confusion of bodily passions.

90. Appetites and pleasures which are in accordance with nature are not reprehensible, since they are a necessary consequence of natural appetency. For our ordinary food, whether we wish it or not, naturally produces pleasure, since it satisfies the hunger which precedes a meal. Drink also produces pleasure, since it relieves the discomfort of thirst; so does sleep, since it renews the strength expended in our waking hours; and so, too, do all our other natural functions necessary for maintaining life and conducive to the acquisition of virtue. But every intellect that is trying to escape from the confusion of sin transcends such passions, lest through them it remains a slave to passions which are subject to our control, contrary to nature and reprehensible; for these have no ground in us other than the activity of the passions which are in accordance with nature,

although not on that account destined to accompany us into immortal and everlasting life.

91. If the words of God are uttered merely as verbal expressions, and their message is not rooted in the virtuous way of life of those who utter them, they will not be heard. But if they are uttered through the practice of the commandments, their sound has such power that they dissolve the demons and dispose men eagerly to build their hearts into temples of God through making progress in works of righteousness.

92. Just as God in His essence cannot be the object of man's spiritual knowledge, so not even His teaching can be fully embraced by our understanding. For though Holy Scripture, being restricted chronologically to the times of the events which it records, is limited where the letter is concerned, yet in spirit it always remains unlimited as regards the contemplation of intelligible realities.

93. If you want to absorb the precise spiritual sense of Holy Scripture in a way that accords with Christ's wishes, you must train yourself diligently in the interpretation of names, for in this way you can elucidate the meaning of all that is written. But you must not Judaic-wise drag the sublimity of the Spirit down to the level of the body and the earth, and limit the divine inviolate promise of spiritual blessings to things corrupt and transitory.

94. Since a vow is a promise of some good thing offered by man to God, it may clearly be inferred that prayer is petition for the blessings bestowed by God on man with a view to his salvation and as a reward for the good inner state of those who make the prayer. Succour is the gift and growth, in the face of demonic attack, of virtuous qualities pursued through the practice of the ascetic life and of spiritual vision pursued through the life of contemplation. In the cry for such succour God naturally pays heed above all not to the loudness with which it is uttered but to the inner state of virtue and spiritual knowledge possessed by those who utter it.

95. The evil and destructive kingdom of the devil – typified by the kingdom of the Assyrians (cf. 2 Kgs. 18 : 11) – has organized a war against virtue and spiritual knowledge, plotting to pervert the soul through the soul's innate powers. First it stimulates the soul's desire to develop an appetite for what is contrary to nature, and persuades it to prefer sensible to intelligible things. Then it rouses the soul's incensive power to struggle with all its might in order to

attain the sensible object which it desires. Finally it teaches the soul's intelligence how to contrive opportunities for sensual pleasure.

96. In His supreme goodness God has not only made the divine and incorporeal essences of noetic realities images of His unutterable glory, each in its own way reflecting, in so far as this is granted, the supra-noetic splendour of His unapproachable beauty; He also permeates with echoes of His majesty things that are sensory and far inferior to noetic essences. These enable the human intellect, mounted upon them and carried above all visible things, to journey towards God and to attain the summit of blessedness.

97. Every intellect crowned with virtue and spiritual knowledge is appointed like the great Hezekiah to rule over Jerusalem (cf. 2 Kgs. 18 : 1–2) – that is to say, over the state in which one beholds only peace and which is free from all passions. For Jerusalem means 'vision of peace'. Through the forms which fill creation, such an intellect has the whole of creation under its sovereignty. Through the intellect creation offers as gifts to God the spiritual principles of knowledge that lie within it; and as gifts to the intellect it presents the qualities conducive to virtue which exist within it in accordance with the law of nature. Both through the principles of spiritual knowledge and through the qualities of virtue creation honours the intellect so admirably fitted to make right use of both – the philosophic intellect perfected in both intelligence and action through contemplation and the practice of the ascetic life.

98. He who has attained the summit of virtue and spiritual knowledge through the practice of the ascetic life and contemplation naturally transcends every carnal and reprehensible passion; he also surmounts the condition of so-called natural bodies, that is, of beings subject to generation and corruption. In short, through contemplation he gains spiritual knowledge of the inner essences of all sensible forms and passes beyond them, raising his intellect to the divine realities that are akin to it.

99. When, thanks to the hardships you have undergone in the practice of the virtues, you are appointed to dwell in the state of dispassion as though in Jerusalem and, freed from all the disturbance of sin, you practise, speak, hear and think nothing but peace; and when, after that, you have received through natural contemplation an understanding of the nature of visible things – a nature which

offers through you as gifts to the Lord the divine essences dwelling within it, and presents to you, as if presenting gifts to a king, the laws that lie within it – then you are 'magnified in sight of all nations' (2 Chr. 32 : 23). For you are now above all things: through the practice of the virtues you have risen above natural bodies and the passions of the flesh, and through contemplation you have passed beyond the indwelling spiritual essences and qualities of all sensible forms.

100. Practical philosophy sets above the passions the man who practises the virtues. Contemplation establishes above visible things the man who attains spiritual knowledge, raising his intellect to the noetic realities akin to it.

Third Century

1. The person who combines spiritual knowledge with the practice of the virtues and practice of the virtues with spiritual knowledge is a throne and a footstool of God (cf. Isa. 66 : 1) – a throne because of his spiritual knowledge and a footstool because of his ascetic practice. And the human intellect, purified of all material images and occupied or, rather, adorned with the divine principles of the noetic world, is a heaven itself.

2. When any philosopher – any devout philosopher – fortified with virtue and spiritual knowledge, or with ascetic practice and contemplation, sees the power of evil rising up against him through the passions, like the king of the Assyrians rising up against Hezekiah (cf. 2 Kgs. 18 : 13–16; Isa. 36 : 1–2), he is aware that only with God's help can he escape. He invokes God's mercy by crying out silently and by striving to advance still further in virtue and knowledge; and he receives as an ally, or rather as his salvation, an angel, that is, one of the higher principles of wisdom and knowledge, who cuts off 'every mighty man, warrior, leader and commander in the camp' (2 Chr. 32 : 21).

3. Every passion has its origin in the corresponding sensible object. For without some object to attract the powers of the soul through the medium of the senses, no passion would ever be generated. In other words, without a sensible object a passion does not come into being: without a woman there is no unchastity; without food there is no gluttony; without gold there is no love of money, and so on. Thus at the origin of every impassioned stimulation of our natural powers there is a sensible object or, in other terms, a demon inciting the soul to commit sin by means of the sensible object.

4. Attrition suppresses the actualization of sin; obliteration destroys even the thought of it. For attrition prevents the realization

of the impassioned act, while obliteration completely annihilates all demonic motivation in the mind itself.

5. Sensible and noetic realities lie between God and man. When the human intellect moves towards God it transcends them, provided that it is not enslaved to sensible realities through outward activity and is not dominated in any way by the noetic realities it beholds during contemplation.

6. Creation is the accuser of the ungodly. For through its inherent spiritual principles creation proclaims its Maker; and through the natural laws intrinsic to each individual species it instructs us in virtue. The spiritual principles may be recognized in the unremitting continuance of each individual species, the laws in the consistency of its natural activity. If we do not ponder on these things, we remain ignorant of the cause of created being and we cling to all the passions which are contrary to nature.

7. Scripture exhorts us to offer gifts to God so that we may become conscious of His infinite goodness. For God receives our offerings as if they were entirely our own gifts and He had not already given us anything. In this way God's untold goodness towards us is fully evident, for when we offer Him things which in reality are His own He accepts them as if they were ours, and He makes Himself our debtor as though they were not already His.

8. If we perceive the spiritual principles of visible things we learn that the world has a Maker. But we do not ask what is the nature of that Maker, because we recognize that this is beyond our scope. Visible creation clearly enables us to grasp that there is a Maker, but it does not enable us to grasp His nature.

9. The wrath of God is the painful sensation we experience when we are being trained by Him. Through this painful experience of unsought sufferings God often abases and humbles an intellect conceited about its knowledge and virtue; for such sufferings make it conscious of itself and its own weakness. When the intellect perceives its own weakness it rejects the vain pretensions of the heart.

10. The wrath of God is the suspension of gifts of grace – a most salutary experience for every self-inflated intellect that boasts of the blessings bestowed by God as if they were its own achievements.

11. The intellect of every true philosopher and gnostic possesses both Judah and Jerusalem; Judah is practical philosophy and Jerusalem is contemplative initiation. Whenever by the grace of God

such an intellect repels the powers of evil with virtue and spiritual knowledge, and wins a complete victory over them, yet does not thank God, the true author of this victory, but boasts that the achievement is its own, it brings down the wrath of God's abandonment not only on itself but also on Judah and Jerusalem (cf. 2 Chr. 32 : 25), that is, on both its practice of the virtues and its contemplative life; it has failed to 'give thanks to God for the gifts that He has given' (ibid.). God at once permits shameful passions to vitiate its practice of the virtues and to sully its conscience, which until then was pure; He also permits false concepts to insinuate themselves into its contemplation of created beings and to pervert its spiritual knowledge, which until then had been sound. For ignoble passions immediately attack an intellect conceited about its virtue, just as an intellect over-elated because of its spiritual knowledge will be permitted by God's just judgment to lapse from true contemplation.

12. Providence has implanted a divine standard or law in created beings, and in accordance with this law when we are ungrateful for spiritual blessings we are schooled in gratitude by adversity, and brought to recognize through this experience that all such blessings are produced through the workings of divine power. This is to prevent us from becoming irrepressibly conceited, and from thinking in our arrogance that we possess virtue and spiritual knowledge by nature and not by grace. If we did this we would be using what is good to produce what is evil: the very things which should establish knowledge of God unshaken within us will instead be making us ignorant of Him.

13. We know that the providence which sustains created beings exists in them as a divine rule and law. In accordance with God's justice, when those rich in blessings are ungrateful to Him who bestows them, they are schooled in gratitude by this richness being drastically curtailed; and through this adversity they are led to recognize the true source of the blessings they receive. For when conceit about one's virtue is left undisciplined it naturally generates arrogance, and this induces a sense of hostility to God.

14. He who thinks that he has achieved perfection in virtue will never go on to seek the original source of blessing, for he has limited the scope of his aspiration to himself and so of his own accord has deprived himself of the condition of salvation, namely

God. The person aware of his natural poverty where goodness is concerned never relaxes his impetus towards Him who can fully supply
what he lacks.

15. He who has perceived how limitless virtue is never ceases
from pursuing it, so as not to be deprived of the origin and consummation of virtue, namely God, by confining his aspiration to himself. For by wrongly supposing that he had achieved perfection he
would forfeit true being, towards which every diligent person
strives.

16. The arrogant intellect is justly made the object of wrath, that
is to say, it is abandoned by God, as I have already described, and the
demons are permitted to plague it during contemplation. This
happens so that it may become aware of its own natural weakness
and recognize the grace and divine power which shields it and which
accomplishes every blessing; and so that it may also learn humility,
utterly discarding its alien and unnatural pride. If this indeed
happens, then the other form of wrath – the withdrawal of graces
previously given – will not visit it, because it has already been
humbled and is now conscious of Him who provides all blessings.

17. The person who has not been recalled to humility by the first
form of wrath, namely abandonment, and does not through this
humility learn true awareness, inevitably brings on himself the other
form of wrath, which deprives him of the operation of the graces
and leaves him destitute of the power that until then had protected
him. For 'I will take away its protection', says God of an ungrateful
Israel, 'and it will be plundered; I will break down its wall and it
will be trampled under foot; I will destroy My vineyard, it will not
be pruned or dug, and briars will grow in it as in ground that is
waste; and I will command the clouds not to rain on it' (Isa.
5 : 5–6. LXX).

18. Complete unawareness of the loss of the virtues marks the
downward path to godlessness. For the person who habitually disobeys God, through indulging in the pleasures of the flesh, will deny
God Himself when the occasion arises. In preferring the life of the
flesh to God, he places a higher value on sensual pleasures than on
the divine will.

19. When we think that our intellect has experienced something
we must surely believe that its powers of ascetic practice and of
contemplation have also shared in this experience in accordance

with their natural principles. For a subject cannot experience something without the things within the subject also sharing in the experience. I call the intellect a subject because it is capable of receiving virtue and spiritual knowledge. By the phrase 'within the
subject' I refer to the life of ascetic practice and the contemplative
life, which in relation to the intellect are accidents or attributes.
Hence they share completely in the experience of the intellect,
because it is the intellect's mobility that produces in them any
modification which they undergo.

20. Suppose the demons invisibly attack the intellect of a virtuous, God-loving man who, like Hezekiah, has girded himself
spiritually with power against them, and who through prayer has
received an angel sent to him from God (cf. 2 Chr. 32 : 21), that is
to say, has received one of the higher principles of wisdom, and so
scatters and destroys the whole army of the devil; and suppose this
man ascribes this victory and deliverance not to God but entirely to
himself, then he has failed to 'give thanks to God for the gifts He
has given' (2 Chr. 32 : 25). His gratitude does not match the greatness of his deliverance, nor does his inner attitude measure up to the
bounty of his deliverer.

21. Let us illumine our intellect with intellections of the divine
world and make our body refulgent with the quality of the spiritual
principles we have perceived, so that through the rejection of the
passions it becomes a workshop of virtue, controlled by the intelligence. If the natural passions of the body are governed by the intelligence there is no reason to censure them. But when their activity is
not controlled by the intelligence, they do deserve censure. This is
why it is said that such passions must be rejected, for although their
activity is natural, they may often be used, when not governed by
the intelligence, in a way that is contrary to nature.

22. Anyone whose heart exults because of the divine gifts he has
received, and who preens himself as though those gifts were his own
and had not been received (cf. 1 Cor. 4 : 7), justly calls down wrath
on himself. God permits the devil to entangle his intellect, to undermine the virtuous quality of his conduct, and to obscure the luminous principles of spiritual knowledge during his contemplation. This
is to make him realize his own weakness and recognize the one power
capable of defeating the passions in us. If this happens, he may repent
and be brought to a state of humility, discarding his load of conceit

and being reconciled with God. Then he will avert the wrath that falls on those who do not repent, that takes away the grace which guards their souls, and leaves their ungrateful minds destitute.

23. When wrath takes the form of God allowing the demons to attack an arrogant intellect through the passions, it is a means of deliverance. For through suffering these shameful attacks the person that boasts of his virtues is enabled to learn who is the giver of these virtues. Otherwise he will be stripped of those things that are not in fact his, though he regarded them as such, forgetting that he had received them as a gift.

24. Truly blessed is the intellect that dies to all created beings: to sensible beings by quelling the activity of the senses, and to intelligible beings by ceasing from noetic activity. Through such a death of the intellect the will dies to all things. The intellect is then able to receive the life of divine grace and to apprehend, in a manner that transcends its noetic power, not simply created beings, but their Creator.

25. Blessed is he who has united his practice of the virtues to natural goodness and his contemplative life to natural truth. For all practice of the virtues is for the sake of goodness and all contemplation seeks spiritual knowledge solely for the sake of truth. When goodness and truth are attained, nothing can afflict the soul's capacity for practising the virtues, or disturb its contemplative activity with outlandish speculations; for the soul will now transcend every created and intelligible reality, and will enter into God Himself, who alone is goodness and truth and who is beyond all being and all intellection.

26. Goodness, which is the full expression of divine activity within us, is said to be the consummation of practical virtue. The soul's intelligent power is drawn towards goodness when it uses its incensive and desiring aspects in accordance with nature. In goodness the beauty that is according to God's likeness is made manifest. The consummation of contemplative philosophy is said to be the truth. Truth is the simple, undivided knowledge of all the qualities that appertain to God. A pure intellect is drawn towards this knowledge when it has nullified all judgment based on the senses. Such knowledge makes manifest the dignity of the divine image in a wholly unsullied state.

27. No one can truly bless God unless he has sanctified his body

with the virtues and made his soul luminous with spiritual knowledge. For a virtuous disposition constitutes the face of a contemplative intellect, its gaze turned heavenwards to the height of true knowledge.

28. Blessed is he who knows in truth that we are but tools in God's hands; that it is God who effects within us all ascetic practice and contemplation, virtue and spiritual knowledge, victory and wisdom, goodness and truth; and that to all this we contribute nothing at all except a disposition that desires what is good. Zerubbabel had this disposition when he said to God: 'Blessed art Thou who hast given me wisdom; I give thanks to Thee, O Lord of our fathers; from Thee comes victory and wisdom; and Thine is the glory and I am Thy servant' (1 Esd. 4 : 59–60). As a truly grateful servant he ascribed all things to God, who had given him everything. He possessed wisdom as a gift from God and attributed to Him as Lord of his fathers the efficacy of the blessings bestowed on him. These blessings are, as we have said, the union of victory and wisdom, virtue and spiritual knowledge, ascetic practice and contemplation, goodness and truth. For when these are united together they shine with a single divine glory and brightness.

29. All the achievements of the saints were clearly gifts of grace from God. None of the saints had the least thing other than the goodness granted to him by the Lord God according to the measure of his gratitude and love. And what he acquired he acquired only in so far as he surrendered himself to the Lord who bestowed it.

30. When a man's intellect is pre-eminent in virtue and spiritual knowledge, and he is determined to keep his soul free from evil slavery to the passions, he says, 'Women are extremely strong but truth conquers all' (1 Esd. 3 : 12). By women he means the divinizing virtues which give rise to the love that unites men with God and with one another. This love wrests the soul away from all that is subject to generation and decay and from all intelligible beings that are beyond generation and decay, and – in so far as this can happen to human nature – it intermingles the soul with God Himself in a kind of erotic union, mystically establishing a single shared life, undefiled and divine. By truth he means the sole and unique cause, origin, kingdom, power and glory of created beings, from which and through which all things were made and are being made, by which and through which the being of all things is sustained,

and to which the lovers of God dedicate all their diligence and activity.

31. Women signify the supreme realization of the virtues, which is love. Love is the unfailing pleasure and indivisible union of those who participate through their longing in what is good by nature. Truth signifies the fulfilment of all spiritual knowledge and of all the things that can be known. For the natural activities of all created things are drawn by a certain universal intelligence to this truth as their origin and fulfilment. For the Origin and Cause of created beings has as truth conquered all things naturally, and has drawn their activity to Himself.

32. Because it transcends all things, truth admits of no plurality, and reveals itself as single and unique. It embraces the spiritual potentialities of all that is intellective and intelligible, since it transcends both intellective and intelligible beings; and by an infinite power it encompasses both the ultimate origin and the ultimate consummation of created beings and draws the entire activity of each to itself. On some it bestows lucid spiritual knowledge of the grace they have lost, and to others it grants, through an indescribable mode of perception and by means of participation, clear understanding of the goodness for which they long.

33. The intellect is the organ of wisdom, the intelligence that of spiritual knowledge. The natural sense of assurance common to both intellect and intelligence is the organ of the faith established in each of them, while natural compassion is the organ of the gift of healing. For, corresponding to every divine gift, there is in us an appropriate and natural organ capable of receiving it – a kind of capacity, or intrinsic state or disposition. Thus he who purges his intellect of all sensible images receives wisdom. He who makes his intelligence the master of his innate passions – that is to say, of his incensive and desiring powers – receives spiritual knowledge. He whose intellect and intelligence possess an unshakeable assurance concerning divine realities receives that faith with which all things are possible. He who has acquired natural compassion receives, after the utter annihilation of self-love, the gifts of healing.

34. In each of us the energy of the Spirit is made manifest according to the measure of his faith (cf. Rom. 12 : 6). Therefore each of us is the steward of his own grace and, if we think logically, we should never envy another person the enjoyment of his gifts, since

the disposition which makes us capable of receiving divine blessings depends on ourselves.

35. In other words, divine blessings are bestowed according to the measure of faith in each man. Similarly, the strength of our faith is revealed by the zeal with which we act. Thus our actions disclose the measure of our faith, and the strength of our faith determines the measure of grace that we receive. Conversely, the extent to which we fail to act reveals the measure of our lack of faith, and our lack of faith in turn determines the degree to which we are deprived of grace. Hence the person who out of jealousy envies those who practise the virtues is more than misguided, for the choice of believing and acting, and of receiving grace according to the measure of his faith, clearly depends on him and not on anybody else.

36. He who aspires to divine realities willingly allows providence to lead him by principles of wisdom towards the grace of deification. He who does not so aspire is drawn, by the just judgment of God and against his will, away from evil by various forms of discipline. The first, as a lover of God, is deified by providence; the second, although a lover of matter, is held back from perdition by God's judgment. For since God is goodness itself, He heals those who desire it through the principles of wisdom, and through various forms of discipline cures those who are sluggish in virtue.

37. Real faith is truth which is all-embracing, all-sustaining and free from all falsehood. A good conscience confers on us the power of love, since it is not guilty of any transgression of the commandments.

38. Scripture says that seven spirits will rest upon the Lord: the spirit of wisdom, the spirit of understanding, the spirit of spiritual knowledge, the spirit of cognitive insight, the spirit of counsel, the spirit of strength, and the spirit of the fear of God (cf. Isa. 11 : 2). The effects produced by these spiritual gifts are as follows: by fear, abstention from evil; by strength, the practice of goodness; by counsel, discrimination with respect to the demons; by cognitive insight, a clear perception of what one has to do; by spiritual knowledge, the active grasping of the divine principles inherent in the virtues; by understanding, the soul's total empathy with the things that it has come to know; and by wisdom, an indivisible union with God, whereby the saints attain the actual enjoyment of the things for which they long. He who shares in wisdom becomes god by partici-

pation and, immersed in the ever-flowing, secret outpouring of God's mysteries, he imparts to those who long for it a knowledge of divine blessedness.

39. The spirit of the fear of God is abstention from evil deeds. The spirit of strength is an impulse and disposition prompt to fulfil the commandments. The spirit of counsel is the habit of discrimination according to which we fulfil the divine commandments intelligently and distinguish what is good from what is bad. The spirit of cognitive insight is an unerring perception of the ways in which virtue is to be practised; if we act in accordance with this perception we will not deviate at all from the true judgment of our intelligence. The spirit of spiritual knowledge is a grasping of the commandments and the principles inherent in them, according to which the qualities of the virtues are constituted. The spirit of understanding is acceptance of the qualities and principles of the virtues or, to put it more aptly, it is a transmutation by which one's natural powers commingle with the qualities and principles of the commandments. The spirit of wisdom is ascension towards the Cause of the higher spiritual principles inherent in the commandments, and union with it. Through this ascension and union we are initiated, in so far as this is possible for human beings, simply and through unknowing into those inner divine principles of created beings, and in different ways we present to men, as if from a spring welling up in our heart, the truth which resides in all things.

40. We ascend step by step from what is remotest from God, but near to us, to the primal realities which are furthest from us but near to God. For we begin by abstaining from evil because of fear, and from this we advance to the practice of virtue through strength; from the practice of virtue we advance to the discrimination conferred by the spirit of counsel; from discrimination to a settled state of virtue, which is cognitive insight; from the settled state of virtue to the spiritual knowledge of the divine principles inherent in the virtues; from this knowledge to a state of understanding, that is, to the transmuted state in which we conform to the divine principles of virtue that we have come to know; and from this we advance to the simple and undistorted contemplation of the truth that is in all things. From this point of vantage, as a result of our wise contemplation of sensible and noetic beings, we will be enabled to speak about the truth as we should.

41. The first good which actively affects us, namely fear, is reckoned by Scripture as the most remote from God, for it is called 'the beginning of wisdom' (Ps. 111 : 10; Prov. 1 : 7; 9 : 10). Setting out from this towards our ultimate goal, wisdom, we come to understanding, and this enables us to draw close to God Himself, for we have only wisdom lying between us and our union with Him. Yet it is impossible for a man to attain wisdom unless first, through fear and through the remaining intermediary gifts, he frees himself completely from the mist of ignorance and the dust of sin. That is why, in the order established by Scripture, wisdom is placed close to God and fear close to us. In this way we can learn the rule and law of good order.

42. Ascending therefore with these eyes of faith, that is to say, with this enlightenment, we are drawn towards the divine unity of wisdom, which is divided into different gifts for our benefit; and by mounting from one virtue to another we unite with the source of those gifts. But with God's help we do not omit any of the stages we have already mentioned, lest by gradually growing neglectful we allow our faith to become blind and sightless because it is deprived of the enlightenment of the Spirit that comes through works. If this happened, we would be punished for endless ages because we have blinded in ourselves the divine eyes which had opened within us according to the measure of our faith.

43. When by neglecting the commandments a person blinds the eyes of faith that are within him, then he is certainly doomed, for he no longer has God watching over him. For if Scripture calls the energies of the Spirit the 'eyes of the Lord' (Deut. 11 : 12), the person who does not open those eyes by fulfilling the commandments does not have God watching over him. God watches us only when through fulfilling the commandments we are illumined by the energies of the Spirit, for He has no other eyes by which He looks down on those who dwell on earth.

44. Wisdom is a unity contemplated indivisibly in the various virtues which arise from it; and it is perceived in a single form in the operations of the virtues. Again, it appears as a simple unity when the virtues which issued from it are reintegrated with it. This happens when we, for whose sake wisdom has produced from itself each individual virtue, are drawn upwards towards it by means of each virtue.

45. When you fail to carry out the divine precepts of faith, your faith is blind. For if the precepts of God are light (cf. Isa. 26 : 9. LXX), it is clear that when you fail to put the divine precepts into practice you are without divine light. You are God's servant merely in name, not in reality.

46. No one can plead the weakness of the flesh as an excuse when he sins; for the union of our humanity with the divine Logos through the incarnation has renewed the whole of nature by lifting the curse, and so we have no excuse if our will remains attached to the passions. For the divinity of the Logos, which always dwells by grace in those who believe in Him, withers the rule of sin in the flesh.

47. He who through faith in God and love for Him has conquered the witless desires or impulses of the passions which are contrary to nature, moves out of the sphere of natural law and enters wholly into the noetic realm. And, together with himself, he delivers from alien servitude his fellow-men and their concerns.

48. Unless curbed by the fear of God that accompanies the practice of the virtues, spiritual knowledge leads to vanity; for it encourages the person puffed up by it to regard as his own what has merely been lent to him, and to use his borrowed intelligence to win praise for himself. But when his practice of the virtues increases concomitantly with his longing for God, and he does not arrogate to himself more spiritual knowledge than is needed for the task in hand, then he is made humble, reduced to himself by principles which are beyond his capacity.

49. Man's heavenly abode is a dispassionate state of virtue, combined with a spiritual knowledge that has overcome all delusory notions.

50. Plurality is the consummation of unity manifested, and unity is the origin of non-manifest plurality. For the origin of every consummation is clearly its non-manifest state, and the consummation of every origin is the full development of its potentiality for manifestation. Thus, since faith is the natural origin of the virtues, its consummation is the full development of the goodness realized through the virtues; and since natural goodness is the consummation of the virtues, its origin is faith. In this way there is an intrinsic reciprocity between faith and goodness: faith is implicit goodness and goodness is faith manifested. God is by nature both faithful and good (cf.

Matt. 19 : 17); He is faithful as the primal good and good as the desire of all desires. These attributes are in every way identical with each other; and, except in our conception of them, they are not divided from each other in any way by any act of manifestation that takes its start from Him and ends in Him. Thus plurality, being the manifestation of God as the desire of all desires, brings to perfect fulfilment the longing of all that aspires towards Him; while unity, being a symbol of God as the primal good, constitutes the perfect ground of all that is made manifest from Him.

51. The first type of dispassion is complete abstention from the actual committing of sin, and it may be found in those beginning the spiritual way. The second is the complete rejection in the mind of all assent to evil thoughts; this is found in those who have achieved an intelligent participation in virtue. The third is the complete quiescence of passionate desire; this is found in those who contemplate noetically the inner essences of visible things through their outer forms. The fourth type of dispassion is the complete purging even of passion-free images; this is found in those who have made their intellect a pure, transparent mirror of God through spiritual knowledge and contemplation. If, then, you have cleansed yourself from the committing of acts prompted by the passions, have freed yourself from mental assent to them, have put a stop to the stimulation of passionate desire, and have purged your intellect of even the passion-free images of what were once objects of the passions, you have attained the four general types of dispassion. You have emerged from the realm of matter and material things, and have entered the sphere of intelligible realities, noetic, tranquil and divine.

52. The first type of dispassion, in other words, is abstention from the body's impulsion towards the actual committing of sin. The second is the complete rejection of impassioned thoughts in the soul; through this rejection the impulsion of the passions mentioned in the first type of dispassion is quelled, since there are now no impassioned thoughts to incite it to action. The third is the complete quiescence of passionate desire, and through this the second type is generated, since it is brought into being by purity of thought. The fourth type of dispassion is the complete exclusion from the mind of all sensible images. This also produces the third type, since the mind no longer possesses those images of sensible things which produce imaginings of the passions in it.

53. Intelligence and reason are to be treated like the bond-servants of Hebrew stock who are set free at the end of six years (cf. Deut. 15 : 12). They labour like a servant and a handmaid for everyone who practises the virtues, since they conceive and realize the qualities of active virtue, and their whole strength is as it were drawn up against the demons that oppose the practice of the virtues. When they have completed the stage of practical philosophy – and this completion is represented by the sixth year, for the number six signifies practical philosophy – intelligence and reason are set free to devote themselves to spiritual contemplation, that is to say, they contemplate the inner essences of created beings.

54. The incensive power and desire, on the other hand, are to be treated like the servant and the handmaid of another tribe (cf. Lev. 25 : 41–42).[1] The contemplative intellect, through fortitude and self-restraint, subjugates them for ever to the lordship of the intelligence, so that they serve the virtues. It does not give them their complete freedom until the law of nature is totally swallowed up by the law of the spirit, in the same way as the death of the unhappy flesh is swallowed up by infinite life (cf. 2 Cor. 5 : 4), and until the entire image of the unoriginate kingdom is clearly revealed, mimetically manifesting in itself the entire form of the archetype. When the contemplative intellect enters this state it gives the incensive power and desire their freedom, transmuting desire into the un-sullied pleasure and pure enravishment of an intense love for God and the incensive power into spiritual fervour, an ever-active fiery élan, a self-possessed frenzy.

55. The intellect's unwavering concentration on spiritual knowledge, and the incorruption of the senses when hallowed by virtue, constitute an image of the unoriginate kingdom. This occurs when soul and body, through the spiritual transmutation of the senses into the intellect, are united with each other solely by the divine law of the Spirit. In this state, the ever-active vital energy of the Logos always pervades them, and all unlikeness to the divine utterly vanishes.

---

[1] Servants of non-Hebrew stock, in the text of Leviticus, are kept in bondage until the year of jubilee, which occurs every fifty years. Maximos takes the period of fifty years to signify the 'age' (aeon) (see Glossary). The incensive power and desire are to be kept in bondage 'until the aeon', that is, 'for ever' or, more exactly, until a person develops spiritually from the 'present age' to the 'age to be'.

56. Pleasure has been defined as desire realized, since pleasure presupposes the actual presence of something regarded as good. Desire, on the other hand, is pleasure that is only potential, since desire seeks the realization in the future of something regarded as good. Incensiveness is frenzy premeditated, and frenzy is incensiveness brought into action. Thus he who has subjected desire and incensiveness to the intelligence will find that his desire is changed into pleasure through his soul's unsullied union in grace with the divine, and that his incensiveness is changed into a pure fervour shielding his pleasure in the divine, and into a self-possessed frenzy in which the soul, ravished by longing, is totally rapt in ecstasy above the realm of created beings. But so long as the world and the soul's willing attachment to material things are alive in us, we must not give freedom to desire and incensiveness, lest they commingle with the sensible objects that are cognate to them, and make war against the soul, taking it captive with the passions, as in ancient times the Babylonians took Jerusalem (cf. 2 Kgs. 25 : 4). For when Scripture, exhibiting the world of intelligibles through the literal narrative, speaks of an age during which the Law commands servants of another tribe to remain in bondage (cf. Lev. 25 : 40–41), it means by 'age' the attachment of the soul's will and purpose to this world, that is, to this present life.

57. Evil has a beginning, for it has its origin in activity on our part which is contrary to nature. But goodness does not have a beginning, for it exists by nature before time and before all ages. Goodness is intelligible because it can be grasped by intellection. Evil is not intelligible because it cannot be grasped by intellection. Goodness can be spoken about – indeed, it is the only thing we should speak about. It also comes into being – it is, in fact, the only thing that should come into being; for although by nature it is uncreated, yet because of God's love for us it allows itself to come into being through us by grace, so that we who create and speak may be deified. Evil – which is the only thing that should not come into being – we cannot create. Evil is corruptible because corruption is the nature of evil, which does not possess any true existence whatsoever. Goodness is incorruptible because it exists eternally and never ceases to be, and watches over everything in which it dwells. Goodness, then, is what we should seek with our intelligence, long for with our desire, and keep inviolate with our incensive power.

With our cognitive insight we should prevent it from being adulterated by anything that is contrary to it. With our voice we should make it manifest in speech to those who are ignorant of it. And with our generative power we should make it increase or, to put it more accurately, we should be increased by it.

58. The contemplative intellect, if it is to rule over conceptual images of created things, as well as over its own activities, must be in a state barren of evil, that is, one which neither conceives evil in any way nor gives birth to it. It must be in this state when it embarks on contemplation lest, in scrutinizing created beings spiritually, it inadvertently falls into the power of one of the demons whose nature it is to corrupt the heart's pure vision by means of some sensible object.

59. He who on account of his virtue or spiritual knowledge falls victim to self-esteem grows his hair like Absalom, to no good purpose (cf. 2 Sam. 14 : 26; 18 : 9). Outwardly he appears to pursue a moral way of life, but it is carefully contrived and mixed (like a mule) with conceit, and designed to deceive onlookers. Puffed up with his vainglory, he tries to supplant the spiritual father who gave him birth through the teaching of the Logos; for in his pride he wants, like a usurper, to arrogate to himself all the splendour of the virtue and spiritual knowledge which his spiritual father possessed as a gift from God. But when such a man begins to engage in the spiritual contemplation of created beings and to fight with his intelligence for truth, because his sensual nature is still full of life he is caught by his hair in the oak tree of material appearances; and thus his empty conceit, entangled as it is with death, suspends him between heaven and earth (cf. 2 Sam. 18 : 9). For the victim of self-esteem does not possess spiritual knowledge, which like heaven would draw him up out of his degrading conceit, nor does he possess earth, that basis, rooted in humility, of practical endeavour which would draw him down from the heights to which his arrogance has raised him. The spiritual teacher who gave him birth grieves compassionately on seeing him die (cf. 2 Sam. 18 : 33). In this way his teacher imitates God, who desires not the death of a sinner but rather that he should repent and live (cf. Ezek. 33 : 11).

60. The origin and consummation of every man's salvation is wisdom, which initially produces fear but when perfected gives rise to loving desire. Or, rather, initially and providentially wisdom

manifests itself for our sake as fear, so as to make us who aspire to wisdom desist from evil; but ultimately it exists in its natural state for its own sake as loving desire, so as to fill with spiritual mirth those who have abandoned all existing things in order to dwell with it.

61. To those who do not long for it, wisdom is fear, because of the loss which they suffer through their flight from it; but in those who cleave to it, wisdom is loving desire, promoting an inner state of joyous activity. For wisdom creates fear, delivering a person from the passions by making him apprehensive of punishment; and it also produces loving desire, accustoming the intellect through the acquisition of the virtues to behold the blessings held in store for us.

62. Every genuine confession humbles the soul. When it takes the form of thanksgiving, it teaches the soul that it has been delivered by the grace of God. When it takes the form of self-accusation, it teaches the soul that it is guilty of crimes through its own deliberate indolence.

63. Confession takes two forms. According to the one, we give thanks for blessings received; according to the other, we bring to light and examine what we have done wrong. We use the term confession both for the grateful appreciation of the blessings we have received through divine favour, and for the admission of the evil actions of which we are guilty. Both forms produce humility. For he who thanks God for blessings and he who examines himself for his offences are both humbled. The first judges himself unworthy of what he has been given; the second implores forgiveness for his sins.

64. The passion of pride arises from two kinds of ignorance, and when these two kinds of ignorance unite together they form a single confused state of mind. For a man is proud only if he is ignorant both of divine help and of human weakness. Therefore pride is a lack of knowledge both in the divine and in the human spheres. For the denial of two true premises results in a single false affirmation.

65. Self-esteem is the replacing of a purpose which accords with God by another purpose which is contrary to the divine. For a man full of self-esteem pursues virtue not for God's glory but for his own, and so purchases with his labours the worthless praise of men.

66. The person who likes to be popular attends solely to the outward show of morality and to the words of the flatterer. With the first he hopes to attract the eyes and with the second the ears of those

who are charmed and impressed only by what is visible and audible, and who judge virtue only with their senses. Hence the desire to be popular may be described as an outward display of moral acts and language, as though for the sake of virtue but really to impress other people.

67. Hypocrisy is the pretence of friendship, or hatred hidden in the form of friendship, or enmity operating under the guise of affection, or envy simulating the character of love, or a style of life adorned with the fiction but not the reality of virtue, or the pretence of righteousness maintained only in external appearance, or deceit with the outer form of truth. Hypocrisy is the trade of those who emulate the serpent in their twistings and twinings.

68. God is the cause of created beings and of their inherent goodness. Thus he who is puffed up with his virtue and knowledge, and whose grace-given progress in virtue is not matched by a corresponding recognition of his own weakness, falls inevitably into the sin of pride. He who seeks goodness for the sake of his own reputation prefers himself to God, for he has been pierced by the nail of self-esteem. By doing or speaking what is virtuous in order to be seen by men, he sets a much higher value on the approbation of men than on that of God. In short, he is a victim of the desire to be popular. And he who immorally makes use of morality solely to deceive by his solemn display of virtue, and hides the evil disposition of his will under the outward form of piety, barters virtue for the guile of hypocrisy. He aims at something other than the cause of all things.

69. The demons of pride, self-esteem, desire for popularity, and hypocrisy, never act by trying to dampen the ardour of the virtuous man. Instead, they cunningly reproach him for his shortcomings where the virtues are concerned, and suggest that he intensifies his efforts, encouraging him in his struggle. They do this in order to entice him to give his full attention to them; in this way they make him lose a proper balance and moderation, and lead him imperceptibly to a destination other than the one to which he thought he was going.

70. Neither do these demons hate self-restraint, fasting, almsgiving, hospitality, the singing of psalms, spiritual reading, stillness, the most sublime doctrines, sleeping on the ground, vigils, or any of the other things which characterize a life lived according to God,

so long as the aim and purpose of a person trying to live such a life are tilted in their direction.

71. A person pursuing the spiritual way is perhaps quicker to recognize the other demons, and so he more easily escapes the harm that they do; but in the case of the demons that appear to co-operate with the progress of virtue and pretend they want to help in building a temple to the Lord, surely no intellect is so sublime as to recognize them without the assistance of the active and living Logos who pervades all things and pierces 'even to the dividing asunder of soul and spirit' (Heb. 4 : 12) – who discerns, in other words, which acts or conceptual images pertain to the soul, that is, are natural forms or expressions of virtue, and which are spiritual, that is, are supranatural and characteristic of God, but bestowed on nature by grace. It is only the Logos who knows whether 'the joints and marrow', that is, the qualities of virtue and spiritual principles, have been united harmoniously or not, and who judges the intentions and thoughts of the heart (*ibid.*), that is, judges from what is said the invisible underlying disposition and the motives hidden in the soul. For to Him nothing in us is unseen: however we think we may escape notice, to Him 'all things are naked and open' (Heb. 4 : 13), not only what we do or think, but even what we will do or will think.

72. By 'dividing asunder of soul and spirit' is meant distinguishing between innate virtues, the principles of which we possess by nature, and virtues which are from the Spirit, the grace of which we receive as a free gift. The Logos discriminates with exactness between the two.

73. The intentions and thoughts which the Logos discerns are the soul's relationships with divine principles and thoughts, and the causes of these relationships. For an intention moves the mind, which has such a relationship; and a thought is directed towards a specific end, which in this way acts as a cause.

74. If God is essential knowledge, then God is subordinate to the intellect, for clearly the intellect is prior to all knowledge that it embraces. Therefore God is beyond knowledge because He is infinitely beyond every intellect, whatever the knowledge it embraces.

75. What man without the divine Logos dwelling in the depths of his heart can overcome the invisible wiles of the dissembling

demons? How can he on his own, keeping himself free of all concourse with them, found and build the temple of the Lord, like
Zerubbabel and Joshua and the heads of the clans, who expressly
announced to the deceitful spirits of pride, self-esteem, desire for
popularity and hypocrisy: 'You cannot share with us in the building
of the house for the Lord our God; we alone will build for the Lord
of Israel' (1 Esd. 5 : 70–71)? For concourse with the demons brings
about the decay and destruction of the whole building, and strips
the grace of beauty from divine offerings.

76. Nobody who accepts, as partners in his struggle for virtue,
any of the four demons we have mentioned can build for the Lord.
If he does accept any of them, as a result of his efforts he will not
find God, but will be confirmed in the passion that he consolidates
through his virtue.

77. The demons that wage war on us through our shortcomings
in virtue are those that teach unchastity, drunkenness, avarice and
envy. Those that wage war on us through our excessive zeal for
virtue teach conceit, self-esteem and pride; they secretly pervert
what is commendable into what is reprehensible.

78. When the demons attack us invisibly in the guise of spiritual
friendship, pretending that they want to accomplish the death of sin
by means which in themselves are good, and when they say, 'Let us
build with you the temple of your Lord', would that we might always
reply, 'You cannot share with us in the building of the house for the
Lord our God; we alone will build for the Lord of Israel' (1 Esd.
5 : 70–71). 'We alone' because, having been freed from the spirits
that fight against us through our shortcomings in virtue, and having
escaped from them, we do not now want to be pierced by those that
excite our pride by encouraging us to excessive zeal; because if that
happened our fall would be far worse than if we had fallen on
account of our shortcomings. For had we fallen for this latter
reason, there would have been a good chance of recovering, since
we would be forgiven because of our weakness. But recovery is impossible, or at least difficult, if we fall because we have made ourselves hateful through our pride, and in place of what is right have
set up something else which we regard as better. Yet in another
sense we are not building the temple alone because we have the
holy angels to help us to do what is good; indeed, we even have
God Himself, who reveals Himself to us through our works of

righteousness and builds us as a holy temple, fit for Himself and free from every passion.

79. Virtue may be defined as the conscious union of human weakness with divine strength. Thus the person who makes no effort to transcend the weakness of human nature has not yet attained the state of virtue. And that is why he goes astray, because he has not yet received the power which makes what is weak strong. On the other hand, he who wilfully relies on his own weakness instead of on divine power, regarding this weakness as strength, has completely overshot the bounds of virtue. And that is why he goes astray, because he is unaware that he has left goodness behind; indeed, he mistakes his error itself for virtue. Thus the person who makes no effort to transcend the limits of his natural weakness is more easily forgiven, because indolence is the main reason for his lapse. But he who relies on his own weakness instead of on divine strength in order to do what is right, is likely to have lapsed because of wilfulness.

80. When it is said that 'the just man's prayer, made active, has great strength' (Jas. 5 : 16), I understand such prayer to be made active in two ways. The first is when the person who offers prayer to God supports it with works performed in accordance with the commandments. When he does this his prayer is not merely a matter of words and of the hollow sound of the tongue, and therefore ineffectual and without real substance, but it is effectual and living, animated with the actual fulfilling of the commandments. For prayer and supplication are given real substance when the commandments are fulfilled through the practice of the virtues. That is why the just man's prayer is strong and has the power to do all things, for it has been made active in this manner. The second way in which a just man's prayer is made active is when another person asks for his prayers and then actually carries out in practice those things for which he requested the just man to pray; for in such a case this other person not only corrects his former mode of life but also, through his turn for the better, fills the just man's prayer with dynamic strength.

81. No benefit comes from a just man's prayer if he who asks for it finds more pleasure in sin than in virtue. For Samuel mourned over Saul when he sinned, but he was not able to obtain God's mercy, for his grief was not supported by the necessary change of

life on the part of the sinner. Hence God put an end to the pointless grief of His servant, saying to him, 'How long will you mourn for Saul, seeing I have rejected him from reigning over Israel?' (1 Sam. 16 : 1).

82. Again, when the compassionate Jeremiah appealed to God on behalf of the Jewish people because in their madness they deludedly worshipped the demons, his prayer was not heard; for it was not supported by the actual conversion of the godless Jews from their errors. Hence God also made him desist from his profitless prayer, saying: 'Do not pray for this people, do not ask for them to be shown mercy, and do not approach Me with further intercessions on their account, for I will not hear you' (Jer. 7 : 16. LXX).

83. It is indeed the height of folly, not to say of madness, for a person who deliberately takes pleasure in destructive sins to seek salvation through the prayers of the just and to ask them to obtain forgiveness for what he actively glories in, defiled as he is by his own free choice. If he really hates what is evil, he should not ask for the prayers of a just man and then allow them to become void and ineffectual; but he should make them active and strong, so that winged with his own virtues they may reach Him who has power to grant forgiveness for sins.

84. The prayer of a just man has great strength when it is made active either by the just man who offers it or by the person who asks the just man to offer it for him. When it is made active by the just man, his prayer gives him direct communion with God who has the power to grant what he asks. When the prayer is made active by the person who has asked the just man to pray for him, it delivers him from his evil ways and disposes him to virtue.

85. St Peter says, 'In which you rejoice, even though for a short while you may have to suffer distress from various trials' (1 Pet. 1 : 6). But how can a person in distress because of such trials rejoice in what distresses him?

86. There are two kinds of distress. The first is produced imperceptibly in the soul, the second palpably in the senses. The first embraces the full depth of the soul, tormenting it with the lash of conscience; the second pervades all the senses when their natural tendency to turn towards external things is checked by pain. The first kind is the result of sensual pleasure, the second of the soul's felicity. Or rather, the first results from sense experiences that we

deliberately embrace, the second from those we suffer against our
will.

87. Distress, in my opinion, is a state devoid of pleasure. Absence of pleasure means the presence of pain. Pain is clearly a defect
in, or a withdrawal of, some natural condition. A defect in some
natural condition is a disorder or passion in the faculty that functions
naturally in that condition. Such a disorder involves the misuse of
the natural function of that faculty in question. To misuse the
natural function is to direct the faculty towards what does not exist
by nature and lacks substantial being.

88. The soul's distress is the result of sensual pleasure. For it is
sensual pleasure that produces distress of soul. Similarly, distress in
the flesh is the result of the soul's pleasure. For the soul's felicity
is the flesh's distress.

89. There are two kinds of distress. The first involves the senses
and consists in the absence of bodily pleasures; the second involves
the intellect and consists in the absence of the soul's blessings.
Trials, or temptations, are likewise of two kinds, the first subject to
our will and the second not subject to our will. Those subject to
our will beget bodily pleasure in the senses but distress in the soul.
For sin when committed produces distress of soul. Those that are
not subject to our will become apparent in sufferings undergone un-
willingly; they beget pleasure in the soul but distress in the senses.

90. Just as there are two kinds of distress, as I have already explained, so also there are two kinds of trial or temptation, the one
willingly accepted and the other contrary to our wishes. The first
produces intended pleasure; the second inflicts unintended pain.
For temptation willingly accepted leads to pleasures clearly intended
by deliberate choice. But a trial undergone contrary to our wishes
produces sufferings which are obviously not intended by deliberate
choice. The first produces distress in the soul, the second in the
senses.

91. Temptation willingly accepted creates distress in the soul, but
clearly produces pleasure in the senses. A trial undergone contrary
to our wishes produces pleasure in the soul but distress in the flesh.

92. I think that when our Lord and God was teaching His disciples how to pray and said, 'Lead us not into temptation' (Matt.
6 : 13), He was teaching them to pray that they should reject the
kind of temptation which we accept willingly, that is, to pray that

they should not be abandoned to the experience of temptations which, when willingly accepted, lead to intended pleasures. But I think that when St James, called the brother of the Lord, was teaching those struggling for truth not to be afraid, and said, 'My brethren, regard it as a great joy when various trials befall you' (Jas. 1 : 2), he was speaking with reference to the kind of trial which is not subject to our will, that is, to trials which are contrary to our wishes and produce suffering. That both these interpretations are correct is clear from the fact that the Lord at once adds, 'But deliver us from the evil one', and that James continues: 'Knowing that the testing of your faith produces patient endurance; and let this endurance come to fruition, so that you may be perfect and entire, lacking nothing' (Jas. 1 : 3–4).

93. The Lord teaches us to pray that we may reject temptations subject to our will because these produce pleasure in the flesh and pain in the soul. St James urges us to rejoice in trials contrary to our wishes because these banish pleasure from the flesh and pain from the soul.

94. A perfect man is one who by means of self-control fights against temptations subject to his will, and who endures with patience trials that are contrary to his wishes. And an entire man is one whose practice of the virtues is completed by spiritual knowledge, and whose contemplation does not remain without practical effect.

95. Since distress and pleasure each affect both the soul and the senses, he who cultivates the soul's pleasure and patiently accepts the distress of the senses becomes tested, perfect and entire. He is tested by experiencing the contrasting effects of pleasure and distress in the senses. He becomes perfect because he fights unremittingly against pleasure and distress in the senses with self-control and patience. He becomes entire because, through constant obedience to the intelligence, he maintains the conditions that combat the mutually conflicting experiences of pleasure and distress in the senses. By these conditions I mean the practice of the virtues and contemplation, which he holds together without allowing the one to be in the least disjoined from the other: his actions manifest his contemplative knowledge and his contemplation is protected equally by the intelligence and by the practice of the virtues.

96. He who has had experience of the distress and pleasure of the

flesh may be described as tested because he has experienced both the pleasant and the unpleasant aspects of the flesh. A perfect man is one who with the power of his intelligence has struggled against the pleasure and pain of the flesh and has overcome them. An entire man is one who keeps both his practice of the virtues and his contemplative life unvarying through the intensity of his longing for God.

97. Distress of soul is of two kinds. The first is distress for one's own sins; the second is distress for the sins of others. The cause of such distress is clearly the sensual pleasure either of the man who feels distress or of those about whom he is distressed. For strictly speaking there is scarcely ever any sin in man that is not first generated by the soul's witless attachment to the senses for the sake of pleasure. And the cause of pleasure in a man's soul is obviously the distress which he feels in his senses when he delights and rejoices in his own virtues or in those of others. For again strictly speaking there is scarcely any virtue in man unless it is first generated by the soul's deliberate detachment from the senses.

98. When the soul is free of all impassioned attachment to the senses, there is no sin whatsoever in man. Moreover, all distress of soul is preceded by pleasure in the flesh.

99. The true origin of virtue lies in the soul's voluntary estrangement from the flesh. And the person who subdues the flesh with voluntary sufferings imbues his soul with spiritual delight.

100. When the soul has achieved detachment from the senses for the sake of virtue, the senses will of necessity suffer, for the soul's capacity for devising pleasure will no longer be conjoined with them in a deliberately chosen relationship. On the contrary, the soul will now bravely repulse the assaults of natural sensual pleasure with self-control; through patient endurance it will implacably resist the attacks of unnatural and involuntary suffering; it will not abandon the godlike dignity and glory of virtue for pleasure which has no real substance; and it will not fall from the heights of virtue in order to spare the flesh by relieving it of the sufferings induced by the pain of the senses. For the cause of distress in the senses is the soul's complete concentration on what accords with nature; and the pleasure of the senses is clearly supported by whatever activity of the soul is contrary to nature, for such pleasure can have no principle of existence other than the soul's rejection of what accords with nature.

Fourth Century

1. The soul has an intellectual capacity that is purposeful and inventive. When this capacity is separated from its attachment to the senses, it no longer seeks to satisfy the longing of the flesh for pleasure, as it did previously by virtue of their deliberately chosen relationship. Since its entire attention and intention are now fixed on divine realities, it refuses to assuage the flesh's suffering.

2. The natural energies of the intellect and those of the senses are opposed to one another because of the extreme dissimilarity between their objects. The intellect has as its object noetic and incorporeal beings, whose essence it is by nature fitted to apprehend; the senses have as object sensible and corporeal entities, which they likewise apprehend by virtue of their natural powers.

3. The origin of sensual pleasure lies in the soul's rejection of what accords with nature. For when the soul devotes its whole strength to the realization of blessings which accord with nature, it has no capacity for seeking out sensual pleasure.

4. When the intelligence takes precedence over the senses in the contemplation of visible things, the flesh is deprived of all natural pleasures, because the senses are then kept under control by the intelligence and so are not free to pursue their own pleasures. Once the intelligence is dominant in us, the flesh necessarily suffers, because the intelligence compels it into the service of virtue.

5. When the intellect regards the senses as its own natural power, it becomes entangled in the superficial aspects of sensible things and devises ways of enjoying the pleasures of the flesh. It is unable to transcend the nature of visible things because it is held back by its impassioned attachment to the senses.

6. It can sometimes happen that the intellect is unable to advance to the apprehension of the noetic realities akin to it except by

way of the contemplation of the intervening sensible objects. But such contemplation is impossible without the senses, which are linked to the intellect, yet are naturally akin to sensible objects. As a result the intellect, on encountering the superficial aspects of visible things, may well become entangled with them, thinking that the sense-perception linked with it is its own natural activity. If this occurs, the intellect will fall away from the noetic realities which accord with its nature and will grasp with both hands, so to speak, the corporeal entities which are contrary to its intelligence; and, because of the victory which the senses have gained over it, the intellect will fill the soul with distress. For it will be seared by the whips of conscience because it has become the author of sensual pleasure and coarsened itself with thoughts of how to pamper the flesh. But if on the other hand the intellect cuts through the superficial aspects of visible things as soon as they strike the senses, it will contemplate the spiritual essences of created things stripped of their outer forms. Then it will produce pleasure in the soul, because the soul will not be dominated by any of the sensible objects which are contemplated; but in the senses it will produce distress, because they will be deprived of every natural sensible object.

7. Sense-pleasure produces distress or suffering in the soul – the two terms mean the same. The soul's pleasure, on the other hand, produces distress or suffering in the senses. Thus he who longs in hope for life in our Lord and Saviour Jesus Christ, through the resurrection of the dead 'to an inheritance which is incorruptible, pure and unfading, kept in heaven' (1 Pet. 1 : 4), will exult and feel unutterable joy in his soul, for he will be unceasingly full of gladness because of his hope for the blessings held in store; but in his flesh and senses he will experience distress, that is to say, the suffering produced by various trials and temptations, and the pain which goes with them. For pleasure and suffering accompany every virtue – suffering in the flesh when it is deprived of its agreeable lubricious sensuality, and pleasure in the soul, as it delights in spiritual essences stripped of everything sensible.

8. In this present life – for that is what I take 'this present time' to mean – the intellect must feel distress with respect to the flesh, because of the many sufferings resulting from the trials and temptations that beset it in its struggle for virtue; but it must always rejoice with respect to the soul, and delight in the hope of eternal

blessings, even though its senses are burdened with suffering. For 'the sufferings of this present time are not worthy to be compared with the glory which shall be revealed in us' (Rom. 8 : 18), says St Paul.

9. The flesh belongs to the soul, but the soul does not belong to the flesh. For the lesser belongs to the greater, not the greater to the lesser. But the law of sin – which is sensual pleasure – has become interlaced with the flesh through the fall. Because of this the flesh has been condemned to suffer death, for the purpose of death is to destroy the law of the flesh. Hence the man who knows that because of sin death was introduced, in order to destroy sin, always rejoices in his soul when he sees that, as a result of his many sufferings, the law of sin is withdrawing from his flesh, thus preparing him to receive in the spirit the blessed life that is held in store. For unless in this present life the law of sin, evidenced in the will's attachment to the flesh, is drained from the flesh as though from some vessel, no one can receive that blessed life.

10. He who is full of distress with respect to his flesh because of the sufferings he endures for the sake of virtue, rejoices in his soul because of that very virtue; for he beholds as a present reality the beauty of the blessings held in store. For the sake of virtue he severs his will from the flesh, and so dies daily, like David (cf. Ps. 44 : 22). At the same time, he is continually renewed through his soul's spiritual regeneration; for he possesses both salutary pleasure and profitable distress. By this distress I do not mean that witless distress felt by most people, which torments their soul because, after developing unnatural impulses towards what it should reject and an aversion for what it should not reject, it then finds itself bereft of passions and material things. On the contrary, I have in mind the distress which is purposive and approved by those endowed with divine wisdom, and which indicates the presence of something evil. For distress is defined as evil present; and it is produced in the soul when sensual pleasure predominates over intelligent discrimination. But it is produced in the senses when the soul pursues the path of virtue unhindered; indeed, it induces as much suffering in the senses as it creates pleasure and joy in the soul that is brought near to God through the illumination conferred upon it by virtue and spiritual knowledge.

11. Salutary pleasure is the soul's joy on account of virtue,

while profitable distress is the pain the flesh suffers for the sake of virtue. Moreover, he who has given himself up to passions and material things generates impulses towards what he should not desire; while he who does not welcome the calamities that deprive him of passions and material things creates an aversion for what he should desire.

12. Divine grace cannot actualize the illumination of spiritual knowledge unless there is a natural faculty capable of receiving the illumination. But that faculty itself cannot actualize the illumination without the grace which God bestows.

13. Not even the grace of the Holy Spirit can actualize wisdom in the saints unless there is an intellect capable of receiving it; or spiritual knowledge unless there is a faculty of intelligence that can receive it; or faith unless there is in the intellect and the intelligence full assurance about the realities to be disclosed hereafter and until then hidden from everyone; or gifts of healing unless there is natural compassion; or any other gift of grace without the disposition and faculty capable of receiving it. On the other hand, a man cannot acquire a single one of these gifts with his natural faculties unless aided by the divine power that bestows them. All the saints show that God's grace does not suspend man's natural powers; for, after receiving revelations of divine realities, they inquired into the spiritual principles contained in what had been revealed to them.

14. If a person asks without passion, he will receive the grace to enable him to practise the virtues. And if he seeks with dispassion, he will through natural contemplation find the truth inherent in created beings. And if he dispassionately knocks on the door of spiritual knowledge, he will without hindrance attain the hidden grace of mystical theology (cf. Matt. 7 : 7–8).

15. He who dispassionately seeks for what is divine will certainly receive what he seeks. He who seeks with any passion will fail to find what he seeks. For Scripture says, 'You ask, and do not receive, because you ask wrongly' (Jas. 4 : 3).

16. The Holy Spirit within us searches out the spiritual knowledge of created beings. But He does not search it out for Himself, because He is God and beyond all knowledge; on the contrary, He searches it out for our sakes, who are in need of such knowledge. Similarly the Logos, when He accomplished His mystery through the flesh, became flesh not for Himself but for us. Yet just as the Logos,

as befits God, did not actualize what naturally pertains to the flesh without assuming flesh endowed with soul and intellect, so the Holy Spirit does not actualize in the saints a spiritual knowledge of the mysteries apart from that faculty in them which naturally searches out such knowledge.

17. Just as it is impossible for the eye to perceive sensible objects without the light of the sun, so the human intellect cannot engage in spiritual contemplation without the light of the Spirit. For physical light naturally illuminates the senses so that they may perceive physical bodies; while spiritual light illumines the intellect so that it can engage in contemplation and thus grasp what lies beyond the senses.

18. The faculties which search out divine realities were implanted by the Creator in the essence of human nature at its very entrance into being; but divine realities themselves are revealed to man through grace by the power of the Holy Spirit descending upon him. When, as a result of the fall, the devil had riveted the attention of these faculties to visible things, nobody understood or sought out God, because in all who participated in human nature intellect and intelligence were confined to the superficial aspects of sensible things, and so they acquired no understanding of what lies beyond the senses. But then, in those who had not of their own free will become inwardly subject to deceit, the grace of the Holy Spirit broke the attachment of these faculties to material things and restored them to their original state. On receiving them back thus purified, men again sought out divine realities, and they have continued to search them out through the same grace of the Holy Spirit.

19. The soul's salvation is the consummation of faith (cf. 1 Pet. 1 : 9). This consummation is the revelation of what has been believed. Revelation is the inexpressible interpenetration of the believer with the object of belief and takes place according to each believer's degree of faith (cf. Rom. 12 : 6). Through that interpenetration the believer finally returns to his origin. This return is the fulfilment of desire. Fulfilment of desire is ever-active repose in the object of desire. Such repose is eternal uninterrupted enjoyment of this object. Enjoyment of this kind entails participation in supranatural divine realities. This participation consists in the participant becoming like that in which he participates. Such likeness involves,

so far as this is possible, an identity with respect to energy between
the participant and that in which he participates by virtue of the
likeness. This identity with respect to energy constitutes the deification of the saints. Deification, briefly, is the encompassing and
fulfilment of all times and ages, and of all that exists in either. This
encompassing and fulfilment is the union, in the person granted
salvation, of his real authentic origin with his real authentic consummation. This union presupposes a transcending of all that by
nature is essentially limited by an origin and a consummation. Such
transcendence is effected by the almighty and more than powerful
energy of God, acting in a direct and infinite manner in the person
found worthy of this transcendence. The action of this divine energy
bestows a more than ineffable pleasure and joy on him in whom the
unutterable and unfathomable union with the divine is accomplished. This, in the nature of things, cannot be perceived, conceived or expressed.

20. Nature does not contain the inner principles of what is beyond nature any more than it contains the laws of what is contrary
to nature. By what is beyond nature I mean the divine and inconceivable pleasure which God naturally produces in those found
worthy of being united with Him through grace. By what is contrary to nature I mean the indescribable pain brought about by the
privation of such pleasure. This pain God naturally produces in the
unworthy when He is united to them in a manner contrary to grace.
For God is united with all men according to the underlying quality
of their inner state; and, at the creation of each person, He provides
each person with the capacity to perceive and sense Him when He
is united in one way or another with all men at the end of the
ages.

21. The Holy Spirit leads those who seek the spiritual principles
and qualities of salvation to an understanding of them; for He does
not allow the power with which they naturally seek divine things to
remain inactive and unproductive in them.

22. First a man seeks to make his will dead to sin and sin dead to
his will, and to this end he investigates how and by what means he
should make these two dead to one another. When that has been
done, he seeks to make his will alive in virtue and virtue alive in his
will; and to this end he investigates how and by what means he
should vivify each in the other. To seek is to have an appetite for

some object of desire; to investigate is to employ effective means by which the appetite can attain that object.

23. He who is to be saved must make not only sin dead to his will but also his will dead to sin. He must resurrect not only his will by means of virtue but also virtue by means of his will. In this way the will, being put to death and entirely disjoined from the totality of sin, which likewise has been put to death, becomes impervious to sin, while as revivified it becomes wholly conscious, through its unbroken union with it, of the totality of virtue, which itself has been revivified. For he who has made his will dead to sin has been united with the likeness of the death of Christ; and he who has given his will new life through righteousness has also become one with His resurrection (cf. Rom. 6 : 5).

24. When sin and will become dead to each other they become mutually impervious to each other; and when righteousness and will have life in each other they become mutually conscious of each other.

25. Christ is by nature both God and man. In an ineffable and supranatural manner we participate by grace in Him as God, while He in His incomprehensible love for men shares as man in our lot for our sake by making Himself one with us with a form like ours. The saints foresaw Him mystically in the Spirit and were taught that the glory to be revealed in Christ in the future because of His virtue must be preceded by the sufferings which He would endure for the sake of virtue (cf. 1 Pet. 1 : 11).

26. When the intellect in its longing is drawn in a manner beyond its understanding towards the source of created beings, it simply seeks; when the intelligence explores in various ways the true essences in created beings, it investigates.

27. Seeking is the intellect's first, simple, fervent movement towards its own cause. Investigating is the intelligence's first, simple discernment of its own cause with the help of some concept. Again, seeking occurs when the intellect, spurred on by intense longing, moves spiritually, and in cognitive awareness, towards its own cause. Investigating occurs when the intelligence, through the operation of the virtues, discerns its own cause with the help of some wise and profound concept.

28. While the holy and divine prophets were seeking out and investigating all that is connected with the salvation of souls, the

movement of their intellects towards God was spurred on by their
longing and kept fervent with cognitive insight and spiritual knowledge; and the discriminative power of their intelligence, in its
active discernment of divine realities, was full of understanding and
wisdom. Those who imitate them will also seek the salvation of
souls with cognitive insight and spiritual knowledge; and by investigating with understanding and wisdom they will be able to discern
the works of God.

29. The intelligence recognizes two kinds of knowledge of divine
realities. The first is relative, because it is confined to the intelligence and its intellections, and does not entail any real perception,
through actual experience, of what is known. In our present life we
are governed by this kind of knowledge. The second is true and
authentic knowledge. Through experience alone and through grace
it brings about, by means of participation and without the help of the
intelligence and its intellections, a total and active perception of
what is known. It is through this second kind of knowledge that,
when we come into our inheritance, we receive supranatural and
ever-activated deification. The relative knowledge that resides in the
intelligence and its intellections is said to stimulate our longing for
the real knowledge attained by participation. This real knowledge,
which through experience and participation brings about a perception of what is known, supersedes the knowledge that resides in the
intelligence and the intellections.

30. Knowledge, that is to say, is of two kinds. The first resides in
the intelligence and its divine intellections, and does not include, in
terms of actual vision, a perception of what is known. The second
consists solely in the actual enjoyment of divine realities through
direct vision, without the help of the intelligence and its intellections. But the intelligence is capable of giving us an intimation of
what can be known through true knowledge and so of arousing in us
a longing for such knowledge.

31. According to the wise, we cannot use our intelligence to
think about God at the same time as we experience Him, or have an
intellection of Him while we are perceiving Him directly. By 'think
about God' I mean speculate about Him on the basis of an analogy
between Him and created beings. By 'perceiving Him directly' I
mean experiencing divine or supranatural realities through participation. By 'an intellection of Him' I mean the simple and unitary

knowledge of God which is derived from created beings. What we have said is confirmed by the fact that, in general, our experience of a thing puts a stop to our thinking about it, and our direct perception of it supersedes our intellection of it. By 'experience' I mean spiritual knowledge actualized on a level that transcends all thought; and by 'direct perception' I mean a supra-intellective participation in what is known. Perhaps this is what St Paul mystically teaches when he says, 'As for prophecies, they will pass away; as for speaking in tongues, this will cease; as for knowledge, it too will vanish' (1 Cor. 13 : 8); for he is clearly referring here to the knowledge gained by the intelligence through thought and intellection.

32. It was indeed indispensable that He who is by nature the Creator of the being of all things should Himself, through grace, accomplish their deification, and in this way reveal Himself to be not only the author of being but also the giver of eternal well-being. Every creature is totally ignorant both of its own essential being and of that of every other created thing; in consequence no created thing has by nature foreknowledge of anything that will come into existence. Only God has such foreknowledge, and He transcends created things. For He knows what He is in His essence and He knows of the existence of everything made by Him before it comes into being; and it is His purpose to endow created things through grace with a knowledge both of their own essential being and of that of other things; for He will reveal to them the inner principles of their creation, pre-existent in a unified manner within Himself.

33. When God the Logos created human nature He did not make the senses susceptible either to pleasure or to pain; instead, He implanted in it a certain noetic capacity through which men could enjoy Him in an inexpressible way. By this capacity I mean the intellect's natural longing for God. But on his creation the first man, through an initial movement towards sensible objects, transferred this longing to his senses, and through them began to experience pleasure in a way which is contrary to nature. Whereupon God in His providential care for our salvation implanted pain in us as a kind of chastising force; and so through pain the law of death was wisely rooted in the body, thus setting limits to the intellect's manic longing, directed, in a manner contrary to nature, towards sensible objects.

34. Pleasure and pain were not created simultaneously with the flesh. On the contrary, it was the fall that led man to conceive and pursue pleasure in a way that corrupted his power of choice, and that also brought upon him, by way of chastisement, the pain that leads to the dissolution of his nature. Thus because of pleasure sin became the freely chosen death of the soul; and pain, by means of this dissolution, brought about the disintegration of the material form of the flesh. For God has providentially given man pain he has not chosen, together with the death that follows from it, in order to chasten him for the pleasure he has chosen.

35. Because of the meaningless pleasure which invaded human nature, a purposive pain, in the form of multiple sufferings, also gained entrance. It is in and from these sufferings that death takes its origin. Such pain drives out unnatural pleasure, but does not totally destroy it. Its total destruction is effected by the grace of divine pleasure when this is active in the intellect.

36. Sufferings freely embraced and those that come unsought drive out pleasure and allay its impetus. But they do not destroy the capacity for pleasure which resides in human nature like a natural law. For the cultivation of virtue produces dispassion in one's will but not in one's nature. But when dispassion has been attained in one's will the grace of divine pleasure becomes active in the intellect.

37. All suffering has as its cause some pleasure which has preceded it. Hence all suffering is a debt which those who share in human nature pay naturally in return for pleasure. For suffering naturally follows unnatural pleasure in all men whose generation has been preceded by submission to the rule of causeless pleasure. I describe the pleasure that derives from the fall as 'causeless' because clearly it has not come about as the result of any previous suffering.

38. Once human nature had submitted to the syndrome of pleasure freely chosen followed by pain imposed against one's will, it would have been completely impossible for it to be restored to its original life had the Creator not become man and accepted by His own free choice the pain intended as a chastisement for man's freely chosen pleasure. But in His case the pain was not preceded by generation according to the rule of pleasure. In this way, by accepting a birth which did not originate in pleasure, it was possible for Him to liberate birth from the penalty imposed on it.

39. After the fall the generation of every man was by nature impassioned and preceded by pleasure. From this rule no one was exempt. On the contrary, as if discharging a natural debt, all underwent sufferings and the death that comes from them. None could find the way to freedom, for all were under the tyranny of ill-gotten pleasure, and so subject to justly deserved sufferings and the still more justly deserved death which they engender. Because of this, another kind of suffering and death had to be conceived, first to destroy the ill-gotten pleasure and the justly deserved sufferings consequent on it – sufferings which have pitiably brought about man's disintegration, since his life originates in the corruption that comes from his generation through pleasure and ends in the corruption that comes through death; and, second, to restore suffering human nature. This other kind of suffering and death was both unjust and undeserved: undeserved because it was in no way generated by preceding pleasure, and unjust because it was not the consequence of any passion-dominated life. This other kind of suffering and death, however, had to be devised so that, intervening between ill-gotten pleasure and justly deserved suffering and death, it could completely abolish the pleasure-provoked origin of human life and its consequent termination in death, and thus free it from the pleasure-pain syndrome. It would then recover its original blessedness, unpolluted by any of the characteristics inherent in beings subject to generation and decay.

That is why the Logos of God, being by nature fully God, became fully man, with a nature constituted like ours of a soul endowed with intellect and a body capable of suffering; only in His case this nature was without sin, because His birth in time from a woman was not preceded by the slightest trace of that pleasure arising from the primal disobedience. In His love He deliberately accepted the painful death which, because of pleasure, terminates human life, so that by suffering unjustly He might abolish the pleasure-provoked and unjust origin by which this life is dominated. For, unlike that of everyone else, the Lord's death was not the payment of a debt incurred because of pleasure, but was on the contrary a challenge thrown down to pleasure; and so through this death He utterly destroys that justly deserved death which ends human life. For the cause of His being was not the illicit pleasure, justly punished by death, through which death entered into human life.

40. The Lord is wise, just and mighty by nature. Because He is wise, He could not be ignorant of the way in which to heal human nature. Because He is just, He could not save man, whose will was in the grip of sin, in a tyrannical fashion. Because He is almighty, He could not prove unequal to the task of completing His healing mission.

41. The wisdom of God is revealed in His becoming by nature a true man. His justice is shown by His assumption, at His nativity, of a passible nature identical to our own. His might is shown by His creation, through His suffering and death, of a life that is by nature eternal and of a state of dispassion that is immutable.

42. The Lord revealed His wisdom by the way in which He healed man, becoming man without the slightest change or mutation. He demonstrated the equity of justice when in His self-abasement He submitted deliberately to the sentence to which what is passible in human nature is subject, and made that sentence a weapon for the destruction of sin and of the death which comes through sin – that is, for the destruction of pleasure and of the pain which pleasure engenders. It was in this pleasure–pain syndrome that the dominion of sin and death lay: the tyranny of sin committed in pursuit of pleasure, and the lordship of the painful death consequent upon sin. For the dominion of pleasure and pain clearly applies to what is passible in human nature. And we seek how to alleviate through pleasure the penalty of pain, thus in the nature of things increasing the penalty. For in our desire to escape pain we seek refuge in pleasure, and so try to bring relief to our nature, hard pressed as it is by the torment of pain. But through trying in this way to blunt pain with pleasure, we but increase our sum of debts, for we cannot enjoy pleasure that does not lead to pain and suffering.

43. The Lord gave clear evidence of His supreme power in what He endured from hostile forces when He endowed human nature with an incorruptible form of generation. For through His passion He conferred dispassion, through suffering repose, and through death eternal life. By His privations in the flesh He re-established and renewed the human state, and by His own incarnation He bestowed on human nature the supranatural grace of deification.

44. God became true man and bestowed on human nature a new or second form of generation leading us through suffering to the pleasure of the life held in store for us. For when our forefather

Adam broke the divine commandment, in the place of the original form of generation he conceived and introduced into human nature, at the prompting of the serpent, another form, originating in pleasure and terminating through suffering in death. This pleasure was not the consequence of antecedent suffering but, rather, resulted in suffering. And because he introduced this ill-gotten pleasure-provoked form of generation, he deservedly brought on himself, and on all men born in the flesh from him, the doom of death through suffering. Thus, when the Lord became man and created in human nature a new form of generation, accomplished by the Holy Spirit, He accepted that death through suffering, justly deserved in the case of Adam, but in His case not deserved at all because His own generation was not provoked by the ill-gotten pleasure introduced by our forefather through his disobedience; and by doing so He destroyed whatever in the origin and doom of human generation according to Adam was not initially from God, and made all those who were reborn spiritually from Him free from its guilt.

45. The Lord removed the pleasure which arises from the law of sin, in order to nullify the effects of generation according to the flesh in those reborn in Him by grace through the Spirit. For when the pleasure of generation inherited from Adam is no longer active within them, but only the pain that arose because of Adam, He allows them to experience death, which was originally a sentence imposed on human nature as a penalty for sin; but in their case it is not a debt payable for sin, but an event that God in His providence permits, because of their natural condition, for the purpose of destroying sin. For when death is not born of that pleasure whose chastisement is its natural function, it begets eternal life. For just as Adam's life of pleasure gave birth to death and corruption, so the Lord's death on account of Adam, being unconditioned by the pleasure that originated in Adam, was the genitor of eternal life.

46. After the fall human life was generated by means of pleasure-provoked conception through sperm and of birth into the world of transience; and it ended in painful death through corruption. But the Lord was not generated in the flesh in the same manner, nor was He conquered by death.

47. Sin first enticed Adam and tricked him into breaking the commandment; and by giving substance to sensual pleasure and by

attaching itself through such pleasure to the very root of nature, it brought the sentence of death on all nature, since through man it impels all created things towards death. All this was contrived by the devil, that spawn of sin and father of iniquity who through pride expelled himself from divine glory, and through envy of us and of God expelled Adam from paradise (cf. Wisd. 2 : 24), in order to destroy the works of God and dissolve what had been brought into existence.

48. Since the devil is jealous both of us and of God, he persuaded man by guile that God was jealous of him (cf. Gen. 3 : 5), and so made him break the commandment. The devil is jealous of God lest His power should be seen actually divinizing man: and he is jealous of man lest through the attainment of virtue man should become a personal participant in divine glory. The foul thing is jealous not only of us, because of the glory which we attain with God through virtue, but also of God, because of that power, worthy of all praise, with which He accomplishes our salvation.

49. In Adam the sentence of death was imposed on nature (cf. Gen. 2 : 17), since sensual pleasure had become the principle of its generation. In Christ it was on sin that the sentence of death was imposed (cf. Rom. 8 : 3), for in Christ nature was given a new form of generation, unconditioned by sensual pleasure.

50. If we who have been given the honour of becoming the house of God (cf. Heb. 3 : 6) by grace through the Spirit must patiently endure suffering for the sake of righteousness (cf. Heb. 10 : 36) in order to condemn sin, and must readily submit like criminals to insolent death even though we are good, 'what will be the fate of those who refuse to obey the Gospel of God?' (1 Pet. 4 : 17). That is to say, what will be the fate or sentence of those who not only have diligently kept that pleasure-provoked, nature-dominating Adamic form of generation alive and active in their soul and body, will and nature, right up to the end; but who also accept neither God the Father, who summons them through His incarnate Son, nor the Son and Mediator Himself, the ambassador of the Father (cf. 1 Tim. 2 : 5)? To reconcile us with the Father, at His Father's wish the Son deliberately gave Himself to death on our behalf so that, just as He consented to be dishonoured for our sake by assuming our passions, to an equal degree He might glorify us with the beauty of His own divinity.

51. God is the limitless, eternal and infinite abode of those who attain salvation. He is all things to all men according to their degree of righteousness; or, rather, He has given Himself to each man according to the measure in which each man, in the light of spiritual knowledge, has endured suffering in this life for the sake of righteousness. Thus He resembles the soul that reveals its activity in the members of the body according to the actual capacity of each member, and that itself keeps the members in being and sustains their life. This being the case, 'where will the ungodly and the sinner appear' (1 Pet. 4 : 18) if he is deprived of such grace? For if a man cannot receive the active presence of God on which his well-being depends, and so fails to attain the divine life that is beyond age, time and place, where will he be?

52. If a person refuses to allow God, the abode of all who are saved and source of their well-being, to sustain his life and to assure his well-being, what will become of him? And if the righteous man will be saved only with much difficulty (cf. Prov. 11 : 31. LXX; 1 Pet. 4 : 18), what will become of the man who has not attained any principle of devotion and virtue in this present life?

53. By a single infinitely powerful act of will God in His goodness will gather all together, angels and men, the good and the evil. But, although God pervades all things absolutely, not all will participate in Him equally: they will participate in Him according to what they are.

54. All, whether angels or men, who in everything have maintained a natural justice in their disposition, and have made themselves actively receptive to the inner principles of nature in a way that accords with the universal principle of well-being, will participate totally in the divine life that irradiates them; for they have submitted their will to God's will. Those who in all things have failed to maintain a natural justice in their disposition, and have been actively disruptive of the inner principles of nature in a way that conflicts with the universal principle of well-being, will lapse completely from divine life, in accordance with their dedication to what lacks being; for they have opposed their will to God's will. It is this that separates them from God, for the principle of well-being, vivified by good actions and illumined by divine life, is not operative in their will.

55. The scales on which the disposition of each being, whether

angel or man, will be weighed at the last judgment is the principle
of nature, which shows clearly whether that angel or man inclines
towards well-being or its opposite. It is in accordance with this
inclination that each being participates or fails to participate in
divine life. For God will gather together into His presence all angels
and men according to their being and their eternal being. But He
will gather together in a special way according to their eternal well-
being only those who are holy, leaving to those who are not holy
eternal lack of well-being as the mixed fruit of their disposition.

56. In the mystery of the divine incarnation the distinction between the two natures, divine and human, in Christ does not imply
that He is divided into two persons. On the one hand, a fourth
person is not added to the Trinity, which would be the case if the
incarnate Christ was divided into two persons; while on the other
hand, since nothing can be coessential or cognate with the Divinity,
there must be a distinction between the divine and human natures
in Him. In other words, in the incarnation the two natures have
united to form a single person, not a single nature. Thus not only
does the hypostatic union formed by the coming together of the two
natures constitute a perfect unity, but also the different elements
which come together in the indivisible union retain their natural
character, free from all change and confusion.

57. With regard to Christ, we do not speak of a distinction of
persons, because the Trinity remained a Trinity after the incarnation of the Logos. A fourth person was not added to the Holy Trinity
as a result of the incarnation. We speak of a distinction of natures to
avoid asserting that the flesh is coessential in its nature with the
Logos.

58. He who does not distinguish the two natures in Christ has
no basis for affirming that the Logos became flesh without change.
He does not acknowledge that after the union that which assumed
and that which was assumed are preserved according to their nature
in the single person of the one Christ, our God and Saviour.

59. There is after the union a distinction in Christ between the
nature of His flesh and that of His divinity, for divinity and flesh
are never identical in their essence. Hence the union of the two
elements, divine and human, which have come together has generated not a single nature, but a single person. With regard to this
person, there is no distinction in Christ of any kind whatsoever, for

as a person the Logos is identical with His own flesh. Had there been such a distinction in Christ, He could not be one person in every way. Where the person of Christ is concerned, His oneness does not admit of any kind of distinction whatsoever, and in every way it is, and is affirmed to be, a unity for all eternity.

60. With the help of hope, faith perfects our love for God. By making us keep the commandments, a clear conscience gives substance to our love for our neighbour. For a clear conscience cannot be charged with the breaking of a commandment. Only those who seek true salvation believe in their hearts in these three things, faith, hope and love.

61. Nothing is swifter than believing, and nothing is easier than to confess orally the grace that comes from what has been believed. It is his belief that reveals the believer's living love for his Creator; it is his confession of the grace received that reveals his godly affection for his neighbour. Love and genuine affection – that is, faith and a clear conscience – are clearly the result of a hidden impulse of the heart; for the heart is fully able to generate without using external matter.

62. If a person's will is not directed towards what is good, it is inevitably directed towards evil; for it cannot be stationary with regard to both. Because it implies obduracy with regard to virtue Scripture describes the soul's sluggishness in pursuing what is good as 'stones'; while it describes as 'timber' the soul's readiness to commit evil (cf. Zech. 5 : 4). But sense perception allied with the activity of the intellect produces virtue with spiritual knowledge.

63. By 'dividing wall' (Eph. 2 : 14) Scripture means the natural law of the body, and by 'barrier' (ibid.) that attachment to the passions according to the law of the flesh which constitutes sin. For attachment to shameful passions is a barrier set up by the law of nature – of the passible aspect of nature – walling off soul from body, and preventing a person from practising the virtues in such a way that by means of the soul their principle passes into the flesh. Once their principle has passed into the flesh and has overthrown the law of nature – of the passible aspect of nature – it destroys the attachment to unnatural passions which that law imposes.

64. When through his guile the devil pillages the knowledge of God inherent in nature and arrogates it to himself, he is a thief, because he is attempting to transfer devotion from God to himself.

This he does by diverting the intellect from its contemplation of the spiritual essences of created things and by limiting its scope merely to their superficial visible aspects. Then, after perverting the soul's natural functions, he speciously impels it to practise what is contrary to nature: by means of what appears to be good he persuasively attaches its desire to what is evil, and by swearing falsely on the name of the Lord he leads the soul thus persuaded towards things other than those he has promised. He is a thief because he arrogates the spiritual knowledge of nature to himself; he is a perjurer because he persuades the soul to labour to no purpose for what is contrary to nature.

65. A thief is a man who in order to deceive his hearers pretends to reverence divine principles. Although he has not come to know the true quality of these principles through his actions, he traffics in glory merely by speaking about it, hoping that in this manner he will be thought righteous by his hearers and so capture their admiration. To put it simply, he whose way of life does not match his speech, and whose inner disposition is opposed to spiritual knowledge, is a thief whose appropriation of what is not his proves him to be evil. Scripture fittingly addresses these words to him: 'But to the wicked God says, "Why do you speak of my statutes and appropriate my covenant with your mouth?" ' (Ps. 50 : 16. LXX).

66. A man is also a thief when he conceals his soul's unseen evil behind a seemingly virtuous way of life, and disguises his inner disposition with an affected innocence. Just as one kind of thief filches his audience's mind by uttering words of wisdom, so this kind pilfers the senses of those who see him by his pretence of virtue. To him it will be said: 'Be ashamed of yourselves, all you who are dressed in clothes that do not belong to you' (cf. Zeph. 1 : 8), and: 'In that day the Lord will reveal their pretence' (Isa. 3 : 17. LXX). I seem to hear God saying these things to me daily in the hidden workshop of my heart, and feel that I am explicitly condemned on both counts.

67. A man is a perjurer – that is to say, he swears falsely on the name of the Lord – when he promises God that he will lead a life of virtue and instead pursues what is alien to his promise, in this way breaking, through neglect of the commandments, the vows of his profession of the religious life. To put it briefly, he who has freely chosen to live according to God and is not perfectly dead to this

present life is a liar and a perjurer, since he has sworn an oath before God – that is, he has promised Him to follow the spiritual path irreproachably – and he has not fulfilled his promise. For this reason he merits no praise at all. For although 'everyone that swears by Him shall be praised' (Ps. 63 : 11. LXX), this applies only to those who, having dedicated their life to God, fulfil the vows of their promise through truly performing works of righteousness.

68. He who simulates spiritual knowledge merely by the utterance of words filches the mind of those who hear him in order to boost his own reputation. Similarly, he who simulates virtue in his outward behaviour pilfers the sight of those who look at him, once more in order to promote his own self-glory. Both steal by means of deceit, the first perverting his audience's mind, the second the bodily sense of those who see him.

69. The person who fulfils the promises he has made merits praise because he has sworn an oath before God and has remained faithful to it; conversely, the person who breaks his promises will be impugned and dishonoured because he has sworn an oath before God and has been found false.

70. Not every man who comes into this world is necessarily enlightened by the Logos (cf. John 1 : 9), for many remain unenlightened and have no share in the light of knowledge. But every man who comes into the real world of the virtues by his own free will, and so through a voluntary birth, is unquestionably enlightened by the Logos, receiving an immutable state of virtue and an infallible understanding of true knowledge.

71. Not all persons and things designated in Holy Scripture by the same word are necessarily to be understood in exactly the same way. On the contrary, if we are to infer the meaning of the written text correctly, each thing mentioned must clearly be understood according to the significance that underlies its verbal form.

72. If always understood in the same way, none of the persons, places, times, or any of the other things mentioned in Scripture, whether animate or inanimate, sensible or intelligible, will yield either the literal or spiritual sense intended. Thus he who wishes to study the divine knowledge of Scripture without floundering must respect the differences of the recorded events or sayings, and interpret each in a different way, assigning to it the appropriate spiritual sense according to the context of place and time.

73. Everyone should be taught to live and govern himself according to his intelligence alone, and to have so little concern for his body that he is able to break, through strenuous effort, his soul's attachment to it, and so to free his soul from all images of material things. The senses, which at first rejected the intelligence and accepted the folly of sensual pleasure, like a sinuous snake, must be quelled by the intelligence. It was because man had rejected intelligence that the sentence of death was justly imposed on him in order to put an end to the devil's access to his soul.

74. The senses belong to a single family but are divided into five individual types. Through the apprehensive force particular to each individual type, the deluded soul is persuaded to desire the corresponding sensible objects instead of God. Hence the man of intelligence will choose to die voluntarily according to the flesh before the advent of that death which comes whether he likes it or not; and to this end he will completely sever his inner disposition from the senses.

75. When the senses have the intellect in their clutches, they propagate polytheism through each individual sense organ; because in their slavery to the passions they pay divine honours to the sensible objects corresponding to each organ.

76. When a man sticks to the mere letter of Scripture, his nature is governed by the senses alone, in this way proving his soul's attachment to the flesh. For if the letter is not understood in a spiritual way, its significance is restricted to the level of the senses, which do not allow its full meaning to pass over into the intellect. When the letter is appropriated by his senses alone, he receives it Judaic-wise merely in the literal sense, and so lives according to the flesh, spiritually dying each day the death of sin on account of his forceful senses; for he cannot put his body's pursuits to death by the Spirit in order to live the life of bliss in the Spirit. 'For if you live according to the flesh, you will die,' says St Paul, 'but if through the Spirit you put to death the body's pursuits, you will live' (Rom. 8 : 13).

77. Let us not light the divine lamp – that is, the illuminating principle of knowledge – through contemplation and the practice of the virtues, and then place it under the grain bin (cf. Matt. 5 : 15); for if we do we shall be condemned for confining the incomprehensible power of wisdom to the letter. On the contrary, let us put

it on a lampstand – the Holy Church – beaconing to all men the light of divine truth from the summit of contemplation.

78. He who like Job and the courageous martyrs bears the assaults of unsought-for trials and temptations with an unshakeable will is a powerful lamp; for by his bravery and patience he keeps the light of salvation burning, since he possesses the Lord as his strength and his song (cf. Ps. 118 : 14). And he who is familiar with the tricks of the devil and experienced in the close combat of the unseen warfare, is likewise illuminated by the light of spiritual knowledge and becomes another lamp, saying with St Paul, 'We are not ignorant of Satan's devices' (2 Cor. 2 : 11).

79. Through fear, devotion and spiritual knowledge the Holy Spirit purifies those blessed with the purity of the virtues. Through strength, counsel and understanding He illumines those worthy of light with the knowledge of the inner and quickening essences of created beings. Through radiant, simple and complete wisdom He grants perfection to those honoured with deification, leading them directly towards the Cause of created beings by every way that men can be so led. The perfect are known only by the divine qualities of goodness with which they recognize themselves in God and God in themselves, since there is no dividing wall between them. For nothing intervenes between wisdom and God. They will attain a state not subject to change or mutation, having entirely transcended all the intermediate states in which there is a danger of going astray with respect to spiritual knowledge. By these intermediate states is meant the being of the intelligible and sensible realities through which the human intellect is led on its journey to God, the Cause of all being.

80. Practical philosophy, or the practice of the virtues, is effectuated by fear, devotion and spiritual knowledge. Natural contemplation in the Spirit is achieved through strength, counsel and understanding. Mystical theology is granted only by divine wisdom.

81. A lamp cannot be kept burning without oil; nor can the light of spiritual gifts continue to shine unless one inwardly sustains it with actions and thoughts consonant with it. For every spiritual gift requires a corresponding inner quality in the recipient to feed it spiritually as though with oil, thus preserving its presence.

82. Without the olive tree there can be no genuine olive oil. Without a jar to keep it in, oil cannot be kept. Unless a lamp is fed

with oil, its light will go out. Similarly, without Holy Scripture, no intellection can be truly and divinely effective. Without an inward quality or disposition capable, like a jar, of embracing it, no divine intellection can be retained. Unless the light of spiritual knowledge present in God's gifts is fed with divine intellections, it will go out.

83. I think that the olive tree on the left side of the candlestick (cf. Zech. 4 : 3) signifies the Old Testament, in which the emphasis is mainly on practical philosophy; while that on the right signifies the New Testament, which teaches a new revelation and brings each believer to a state of contemplation. The first supplies the qualities of virtue, the second the principles of spiritual knowledge to those who meditate on what is divine. The first clears away the mist of visible things and raises the intellect to realities that are akin to it when it is purged of all material fantasies. The second purifies the intellect of its attachment to materiality, with resolute strength knocking out as though with a hammer the nails that rivet will and disposition to the body.

84. The Old Testament makes the body obedient to the intelligence and raises it towards the soul by means of the virtues, preventing the intellect from being dragged down towards the body. The New Testament fires the intellect with love and unites it to God. Thus the Old Testament makes the body one in its activity with the intellect; the New Testament makes the intellect one with God through the state of grace. So close is the likeness to God which the intellect acquires, that God, who is not known as He is by nature in Himself to anyone in any way at all, is known through it just as an archetype is known from an image.

85. Since the Old Testament is a symbol of the practice of the virtues, it brings the body's activity into harmony with that of the intellect. Since the New Testament confers contemplation and spiritual knowledge, it illumines with divine intellections and gifts of grace the intellect that cleaves to it mystically. The Old Testament supplies the man of spiritual knowledge with the qualities of virtue; the New Testament endows the man practising the virtues with the principles of true knowledge.

86. God may be called and actually is the Father by grace only of those whose will and disposition have been reborn in the Spirit through the practice of the virtues. By means of this birth they bear

in their soul and manifest in the virtues the imprint of God their Father. Through their way of life they make those who see them glorify God by reforming themselves, and so they provide an excellent pattern of virtue for others to imitate. For God is glorified not by mere words but by works of righteousness, which proclaim the majesty of God far more effectively than words.

87. Because it is concerned with the senses, the natural law is represented by the olive tree on the left (cf. Zech. 4 : 3): it supplies the qualities of virtue to the intelligence and makes spiritual knowledge express itself in action. Because it is concerned with the intellect, the spiritual law is represented by the olive tree on the right: it imbues sense-perception with the spiritual principles of created things and makes conduct purposive and intelligent.

88. He who embodies spiritual knowledge in his practice of the virtues and animates this practice with spiritual knowledge has found the perfect method of accomplishing the divine work. He in whom spiritual knowledge and ascetic practice are not united either makes the first an unsubstantial illusion or turns the second into a lifeless idol. For spiritual knowledge not put into practice does not differ in any way from illusion, lacking such practice to give it real substance; and practice uninformed by intelligence is like an idol, since it has no knowledge to animate it.

89. The mystery of our salvation informs our way of life with intelligence and makes intelligence the glory of our way of life. It turns our practice of the virtues into contemplation manifest in terms of action, and our contemplation into divinely initiated practice. To put it briefly, it makes virtue the manifestation of spiritual knowledge and spiritual knowledge the sustaining power of virtue. Through both virtue and spiritual knowledge it displays a single compact wisdom. In this way we may know that by grace both Testaments agree in all things with each other, in their combination consummating a mystery more single and undivided than soul and body in a human being.

90. Just as soul and body combine to produce a human being, so practice of the virtues and contemplation together constitute a unique spiritual wisdom, and the Old and New Testaments together form a single mystery. Goodness by nature belongs to God alone, from whom all things capable by nature of receiving light and goodness are enlightened and blessed with goodness by participation.

91. He who uses his intellect to apprehend the visible world contemplates the intelligible world. He imbues his sense-perception with the noetic realities that he contemplates, and informs his intellect with the inner essences of what he perceives with the senses. In various ways he transfers the structure of the noetic world to the world of the senses; and conversely he transfers the complex unity of the sensible world to the intellect. He apprehends the sensible world in the noetic world, since he has transferred into the intellect the inner essences of what can be perceived by the senses; and in the sensible world he perceives the noetic world, for he has adeptly harnessed his intellect with its archetypes to his sense-perception.

92. In the text, 'My head went down to the clefts of the mountains' (Jonah 2 : 6. LXX), the prophet called the first principle of unity the head, since it is the source of all virtue. The 'clefts of the mountains' are the counsels of evil spirits, by which our intellect is engulfed because of the fall. The lowest depths of the earth (cf. Jonah 2 : 7. LXX) are that inner state which has no perception whatsoever of divine knowledge or any impetus towards the life of virtue. The abyss (cf. Jonah 2 : 6. LXX) is the ignorance that overlays an evil disposition, like the deep waters covering the sea bed. Alternatively the abyss is the sea bed itself, signifying a firmly grounded evil disposition. The eternal bars (cf. Jonah 2 : 7. LXX) strengthening this abysmal state are impassioned attachments to material things.

93. The patient endurance of the saints exhausts the evil power that attacks them, since it makes them glory in sufferings undergone for the sake of truth. It teaches those too much concerned with a life in the flesh to deepen themselves through such sufferings instead of pursuing ease and comfort; and it makes the flesh's natural weakness in the endurance of suffering a foundation for overwhelming spiritual power. For the natural weakness of the saints is precisely such a foundation, since the Lord has made their weakness stronger than the proud devil.

94. The principle of grace has to pass through many trials in order to reach the human race – that is, the Church of the Gentiles – just as Jonah had to pass through many trials before he arrived at the great city of Nineveh. Only then does it persuade the ruling law of nature to rise from its throne – that is, to abandon its former evil

disposition due to its involvement with the senses; to remove its
robe – that is, to expunge the vanity of worldly glory from its conduct; to cover itself with sackcloth – that is, with mourning, and
with the difficult rough training in hardship such as befits a life lived
according to God; and to sit in ashes – symbolizing poverty of
spirit, in which everyone who is learning to live a devout life sits,
lashed by his conscience because of the sins he has committed (cf.
Jonah 3 : 1–9).

95. Observe, with reference to this passage from Jonah, how the
king represents the natural law. The throne is an impassioned disposition in alliance with the senses. The robe is the display of self-
esteem. Sackcloth is the grief of repentance. Ashes are humility.
Men are those who sin in relation to the intelligence; beasts those
who sin in relation to desire; cattle those who sin in relation to their
incensive power; and sheep those who sin in relation to the contemplation of visible things.

96. The passions of the flesh may be described as belonging to the
left hand, self-conceit as belonging to the right hand (cf. Jonah
4 : 11). Thus he who through the correct observance of virtue
makes himself oblivious to the passions of the flesh, and who because of his unfaltering spiritual knowledge is not infected by the
disease of self-conceit on account of his achievements, has become a
man who does not know his left hand or his right hand; for he is not
excited by the passions of the flesh, and he does not love transitory
glory. Hence it seems likely that by the right hand Scripture means
self-esteem on account of supposed achievements, and by the left
hand licentiousness in shameful passions. For the principle of virtue
does not know the sin of the flesh, which belongs to the left hand;
and the principle of knowledge does not know the soul's evil, which
belongs to the right hand.

97. Spiritual knowledge of virtue – true and actualized knowledge of the cause of virtue – naturally produces total ignorance of
the excess and deficiency which lie to the right and left of the norm
of virtue. Nothing in the intelligence can be contrary to the intelligence. Thus he who has come to apprehend the principle of virtue
will clearly have no way of knowing the state that is contrary to the
intelligence. One cannot examine two opposites simultaneously,
and know the one at the same time as the other.

98. There is no principle of unbelief in belief, or natural cause of

darkness in light, and the devil and Christ cannot manifest themselves jointly (cf. 2 Cor. 6 : 14–15). In the same way, nothing unintelligent can coexist with what is in accordance with the intelligence. If it is absolutely impossible for what is contrary to the intelligence to coexist with what is in accordance with it, he who has
come to apprehend the principle of virtue does not know the state
that is contrary to the intelligence in any way at all; for he knows
virtue only as it is, not as it is thought to be. That is why he has no
knowledge either of his right hand through excess, or of his left
hand through deficiency. For in both these what is contrary to the
intelligence is obviously present.

99. Unbelief means rejection of the commandments; belief is
acceptance of them. Darkness is ignorance of the good; light is
knowledge of it. Christ is the name given to the essence and sub-
sistence of the good; the devil is the depraved state that produces
all sins.

100. If the intelligence is a norm and measure of created beings,
what falls short of that norm and measure, or alternatively what goes
beyond it, is equivalent to unintelligence and so is contrary to the
intelligence. Both going beyond the norm and falling short of it induce a lapse from what truly exists. The first, by making the intellect
overstep its measure, produces the conviction that life's path is
uncertain and ill-defined, that it does not have God as its preconceived goal, and that there is something better than what is best; the
second, through slackness of the intellect, produces the conviction
that the preconceived goal is confined to the sensory world, and so
results in attention being given merely to the senses. Only he who
unites himself to the principle of virtue, and has concentrated the
whole power of his intellect in this principle, does not know and
experience these things; for he cannot be affected by anything that
goes beyond the intelligence or is contrary to it.

Fifth Century

1. Through the diligent practice of the virtues the natural intelligence is raised towards the intellect. Through contemplation the intellect leads towards wisdom the man who aspires to spiritual knowledge. Passion, which is contrary to the intelligence, induces the man who neglects the commandments to descend to the realm of the senses, and the result of this is the intellect's attachment to sensual pleasure.

2. Virtue is a stable and utterly dispassionate state of righteousness. Nothing stands opposed to it, for it bears the stamp of God, and there is nothing contrary to that. God is the cause of the virtues; and a living knowledge of God is realized when the person who has truly recognized God changes his inner state so that it conforms more closely to the Spirit.

3. If intelligence has determined the origin of each created being, no such being by nature either goes beyond itself or falls short of itself. Thus the norm for created things is their desire and knowledge of their Cause, and their measure is the active imitation of their Cause in so far as this is within their scope. For if created beings are carried in their desire beyond the proper norm and measure, this makes their life fruitless, since then they do not find their goal in God – and it is in God that the desire of all things finds its repose, receiving the enjoyment of Him as its self-subsistent consummation. When created beings in their desire fall short of the norm and measure, their life is again fruitless, since then they find their goal not in God but in the realm of the senses, in which there is a pleasurable but illusory enjoyment of the passions.

4. An intellect consecrated unconditionally to the Cause of created beings will be in a state of complete unknowing, since it will not contemplate any creative principle in God who, so far as all

causation is concerned, is in essence beyond such principles. When an intellect is drawn away from all created beings towards God, it does not observe their inner principles, but only contemplates God ineffably, being with Him by grace. For the intellect that reaches up to God in ecstasy relinquishes its knowledge of the inner principles of both corporeal and incorporeal things. For nothing sequent to God can be contemplated simultaneously with God.

5. Conceit is a truly accursed passion. It is a combination of two vices, pride and self-esteem. Pride denies the Cause of virtue and nature, while self-esteem adulterates nature and virtue itself. A proud man does nothing that accords with God's will, and a man full of self-esteem achieves nothing that accords with nature.

6. The mark of pride is to deny that God is the author of virtue and nature; the mark of self-esteem is to make divisions in nature and so to treat some things as worthless. Conceit is their natural offspring, being an evil state composed of a voluntary denial of God and ignorance of the equal dignity that things possess by nature.

7. Conceit is a mixture of pride and self-esteem. In its contempt for God it blasphemously maligns providence; while in its alienation from nature it treats everything belonging to nature in an unnatural way, and thus corrupts its beauty by misuse.

8. The spirit of scorching heat (cf. Jonah 4 : 8) signifies not only trials and temptations but also that abandonment by God which deprived the Jews of the gifts of grace. Affinity with the Spirit dissolves the soul's proclivity for the flesh, concentrates our longing on God and binds our will to Him.

9. When the intelligence is not dominated by the senses, the natural law persuades all men instinctively to embrace what is akin to them and of the same species, since nature itself teaches men to help those in need. In addition, the natural law persuades every man to wish for everybody else whatever he considers agreeable when done to him by others. This is what the Lord teaches when He says, 'Treat others as you want them to treat you' (Luke 6 : 31).

10. The work of the natural law is to bring into harmony all men's voluntary relationships with one another. Those whose nature is governed by the intelligence naturally share a single disposition. When men have the same disposition, their morality and living will obviously be of one kind. In such circumstances, the bond linking people together voluntarily will also be one and the

same, leading all men through their own volition towards the single principle of nature. When that principle is realized, the divisions now prevailing in nature because of man's self-love will totally vanish. The written law, which controls the unruly impulses of the foolish by fear of punishment, accustoms them by its teaching to think specifically about giving to each other what is equitable. In this way with the passing of time the rule of justice grows ever more firmly established within them, until it becomes part of their nature. It turns fear into a disposition which is gently and gradually strengthened by a conscious desire for the good, and habit into an inner state purified by a forgetfulness of past sins and giving birth within itself to a love for others.

11. The written law, by preventing wrongdoing through fear, accustoms one to do what is right. In time such custom produces a disposition filled with the love of righteousness, and this in turn produces a settled state of goodness, obliterating the memory of past sins.

12. The law of grace directly teaches those who are led by it to imitate God Himself. For – if it is permitted to speak in this way – despite the fact that because of sin we were His enemies, God loved us so much more than Himself that, although He is beyond every being, He entered without changing into our being, supra-essentially took on human nature, became man and, wishing to reveal Himself as a man among men, did not refuse to make His own the penalty we pay. And as in His providence He became man, so He deified us by grace, in this way teaching us not only to cleave to one another naturally and to love others spiritually as ourselves, but also, like God, to be more concerned for others than for ourselves, and as proof of our love for each other readily to choose, as virtue enjoins, to die for others. For, as Scripture tells us, there is no greater love than to lay down one's life for a friend (cf. John 15 : 13).

13. To recapitulate: the law of nature is a natural principle which takes control of the sense-realm in order to overcome its lack of intelligence; for lack of intelligence sunders what by nature belongs together. The written law is a natural principle which, when the lack of intelligence in the sense-realm has been overcome, acquires in addition the spiritual desire which maintains the reciprocity and interdependence of kindred beings. The law of grace is

a principle transcending nature whose purpose is our deification. It transforms nature without altering its fundamental character; and, in a manner which defies comprehension, reveals to human nature, as if in an image, the archetype that lies beyond being and nature and is the ground of eternal well-being.

14. To treat one's neighbour as oneself is to be concerned simply with his existence. This pertains to the natural law. To love one's neighbour as oneself is to care, in a way that accords with virtue, for his well-being. This is prescribed by the written law (cf. Lev. 19 : 18; Mark 12 : 33). To love one's neighbour more than oneself is a prerogative of the law of grace.

15. He who curbs the impulses towards bodily pleasure learns the laws of providence, which restrain the inflammatory matter of the passions. He who accepts the whips of bodily pain is taught the laws of judgment, which cleanse him from the defilement of his earlier life through unsought sufferings.

16. Scripture represents Jonah as grieving on account of the booth and the gourd – that is to say, on account of the flesh and the pleasure of the flesh – and it represents God as caring for Nineveh (cf. Jonah 4 : 1–11). From this it is clear that, compared with the things valued and prized by men, what is loved by God is better and more precious by far. For the things that men value lack being; they only seem to exist because of mistaken judgment, but have no principle of existence at all : there is only the fantasy, which cheats the intellect and through passion supplies non-existent things with empty form but no real substance.

17. An accurate knowledge of the utterances of the Spirit is revealed only to those who are worthy of the Spirit. When through diligent cultivation of the virtues they have swept the soot of the passions from their intellect, and have made it like a pure, resplendent mirror, they receive the knowledge of divine things which, as soon as it strikes them, is imprinted upon them and given form in them as a face is reflected in a mirror. Those whose life is smutted by the passions may possibly deduce knowledge of divine things by means of plausible guesswork; but they cannot grasp or express such knowledge with any accuracy.

18. A man whose intellect has been formed by the knowledge that comes by dint of the virtues through the divine Spirit is said to experience divine things; for he has acquired such knowledge not

by nature, thanks simply to his existence, but by grace, thanks to his participation in it. When a man has not received knowledge by grace, even though he calls a particular thing spiritual, he does not know its true character from experience. For mere learning does not produce a state of spiritual knowledge.

19. An intellect totally purified by the virtues is automatically initiated into their inner principles, and comes to express in its own character the spiritual knowledge which is divinely stamped with their impress. For in itself every intellect is formless and without any specific quality of expression: its form is acquired, being either that of the knowledge which arises from the virtues through the Spirit, or that of ignorance, which supervenes through the passions.

20. Everyone who has fallen away from divine love is ruled through sensual pleasure by the carnal law. With such a law, he cannot keep a single divine commandment, nor does he wish to: preferring a life of pleasure to a life ruled by virtue and lived in the Spirit of God, he embraces ignorance instead of knowledge.

21. A person who does not penetrate with his intellect towards the divine and spiritual beauty contained within the letter of the Law develops a propensity for pleasure – that is, an attachment to the world and a love of worldly things; for his knowledge derives merely from the literal expression of the Law.

22. The name Mephibosheth, meaning 'ignominy of mouth' (cf. 2 Sam. 4 : 4) signifies the intellect's preoccupation with thoughts devoted to the world and to bodily indulgence. When we do not penetrate with our intellect beyond the material form exhibited in the letter of the Law, such a world-loving disposition and such preoccupation with thoughts of sensual indulgence are bound to develop in accordance with the proclivity of our will. For our intellect will be preoccupied with whatever it is we gravitate towards.

23. Or again, 'ignominy of mouth' signifies that impulsion of the intellect which gives form to the passions and moulds beauty in a way that accords with sensual pleasure. For without the intellect's inventive power no passion can assume form. The name of Mephibosheth's brother Armoni, meaning 'anathema' (cf. 2 Sam. 21 : 8), signifies the gross, ugly and shapeless impulsion of the passions; while 'ignominy of mouth' signifies that impulsion of the intellect which gives form to the passion so that it can be perceived by the

senses, and which in the shape of mental images provides the passion with suitable matter to work on.

24. Anyone who believes that the sacrifices, feasts, sabbaths, and celebrations of the new moon specified in the Law have been instituted by God for the sake of physical licence and relaxation will fall completely into the power of the passions, and will be ignominiously polluted by the shameful thoughts they stimulate. He will be in the sway of the corruptible world and preoccupied with thoughts of bodily indulgence. Dominated by the matter and form of passion, he will be unable to value anything except what is subject to decay.

25. He who persuades himself that physical self-indulgence is commanded by God in the Law gleefully accepts gluttony as a gift from God. In this spirit he develops forms of behaviour which pollute the senses through misuse.

26. When the soul's contemplative faculty embraces self-indulgence as a divine command, it makes an unnatural use of the senses, not allowing them to express themselves at all in accordance with nature. In these circumstances the soul's contemplative faculty begets an implicit or else an active state of passion, and accepts gluttony as a divine prescription, thus developing forms of behaviour that defile the senses by misuse and destroy the natural principles and seeds in created beings.

27. Nobody can embrace the least natural principle or thought if he devotes himself merely to a literal observance of the Law, since symbols and nature are not identical. Because of the difference between symbols and the nature of created beings, a person who stops short at the symbols of the Law is incapable of a noetic vision of the nature of created beings and cannot encompass the inner essences implanted in them by their Creator.

28. He whose God is his belly and who prides himself on his ignominy as if it were something splendid (cf. Phil. 3 : 19) is merely cleaving to the shameful passions as if they were divine. Because of this he pursues only what is temporal, that is to say, matter and form and the perverted impulses of the five senses. When the senses combine with matter and form they produce passion, killing and effacing natural principles. For, in accordance with the principle of being, passion and nature in no way coexist with each other: the principle of nature is never naturally conjoined with passion, and passion is never coengendered with nature.

29. He who does not believe that the Scriptures are spiritual is unaware of his lack of spiritual knowledge, yet wastes away with hunger. Strictly speaking, however, hunger is a deprivation of blessings that we already know by experience and a total absence and dearth of the spiritual nourishment that sustains the soul. How, then, can one regard as hunger or loss one's complete destitution with regard to what one has never once known in any way at all?

30. The truly hungry are the faithful who have already acquired knowledge of the truth. So, too, is the soul of every man who has abandoned the grace of spiritual contemplation and become a slave to the literal and external forms of religion; for he does not nourish his intellect with the splendour of his intellections, but imbues his perception with impassioned fantasies derived from the material aspects of scriptural symbols.

31. Everyone who does not apply himself to the spiritual contemplation of Holy Scripture has, Judaic-wise, also rejected both the natural and the written law; and he is ignorant of the law of grace which confers deification on those who are obedient to it. He who understands the written law in a literal manner does not nourish his soul with the virtues. He who does not grasp the inner principles of created beings fails to feast his intellect on the manifold wisdom of God. And he who is ignorant of the great mystery of the new grace does not rejoice in the hope of future deification. Thus failure to contemplate the written law spiritually results in a dearth of the divine wisdom to be apprehended in the natural law; and this in its turn is followed by a complete ignorance of the deification given by grace according to the new mystery.

32. Every intellect endowed by the grace of Christ with discriminative and penetrating vision, always desires and seeks the face of the Lord. The face of the Lord is true contemplation and spiritual knowledge of divine things attained through virtue. When one seeks this contemplation and knowledge one learns the cause of one's destitution and dearth. For just as the face is the distinctive feature of each person, so spiritual knowledge is the special characteristic of what is divine. He who seeks such knowledge is said to seek the face of the Lord. But the person who has become carnal through bloody sacrifices performed in accordance with the letter of the Law possesses the ignorance which he desires; for he accepts commandments

only for the pleasure they give to the flesh and he confines his perception literally to the material sense of the written word.

33. In the case of the person who confines himself to a literal
observance of the Law, the matter which he engenders is the act of
sin that he commits, while the form that he devises in a materialistic
fashion is the intellect's assent to the sensual pleasures that attract
him to the act of sin. He who understands Scripture in a spiritual
way puts to death both the act of sin, which corresponds to matter,
and the assent to it, which corresponds to form; and he also puts to
death the misuse of the senses for the sake of pleasure. He does this
by means of thoughts that by nature pertain to higher levels of contemplation.

34. Once the external observance of the letter of the Law has
been superseded, together with the ignorance that goes with it, it is
then possible to put an end to the matter and form of which we have
been speaking, as well as to the five ways of misusing the five senses
with regard to matter and form – and by this I mean the impassioned
and unnatural association of the senses with sensible things subject
to time and change. The spiritual law, or intellect, destroys this
association by means of the higher principles and thoughts which are
found in natural contemplation. In this way the intellect, when it
has attained the heights of the law of spiritual contemplation,
destroys man's all-pervasive subjection, established through the
symbols of temporal things, to sense-perception and to the outward
form of things.

35. Without natural contemplation no one can appreciate the
disparity between the symbols through which the Law is expressed
and the divine realities which these symbols represent. Further, if
through such contemplation a man has not first discerned this disparity and, denying his sense-perception all access to the hidden
realm of divine and intelligible realities, does not long to penetrate
with his intellect into its beauty, he cannot be liberated completely
from the external diversity to be found in the symbols. So long as he
cleaves to the letter, his inner hunger for spiritual knowledge will
not be satisfied; for he has condemned himself like the wily serpent
to feed on the earth – that is, on the outward or literal form – of
Scripture (cf. Gen. 3 : 14), and does not, as a true disciple of
Christ, feed on heaven – that is, on the spirit and soul of Scripture,
in other words, on celestial and angelic bread. I mean that he does

not feed through Christ on the spiritual contemplation and knowledge of the Scriptures, which God gives unstintingly to those who love Him, in accordance with the text: 'He gave them the bread of heaven; man ate the food of angels' (Ps. 78 : 24–25. LXX).

36. Interpretation of the outward form of Scripture according to the norms of sense-perception must be superseded, for it clearly promotes the passions as well as proclivity towards what is temporal and transient. That is to say, we must destroy the impassioned activity of the senses with regard to sensible objects, as if destroying the children and grandchildren of Saul (cf. 2 Sam. 21 : 1–9); and we must do this by ascending to the heights of natural contemplation through a mystical interpretation of divine utterances, if in any way we desire to be filled with divine grace.

37. When the Law is understood only according to the letter, it is hostile to the truth, as the Jews were, and as is anyone else who possesses their mentality. For such a person limits the Law's power merely to the letter, and does not advance to natural contemplation, which reveals the spiritual knowledge hidden mystically in the letter; for this contemplation mediates between figurative representations of the truth and the truth itself, and leads its adepts away from the first and towards the second. On the contrary, he rejects natural contemplation altogether and so excludes himself from initiation into divine realities. Those who diligently aspire to a vision of these realities must therefore destroy the outward and evanescent interpretation of the Law, subject to time and change; and they must do this by means of natural contemplation, having ascended to the heights of spiritual knowledge.

38. A man totally obliterates the outward or literal sense of Scripture when through the practice of natural contemplation he destroys his soul's pleasure-provoked and body-indulging subjection – promoted by the written Law – to the restless and evanescent world of materiality. In this way he slays, as though it were Saul's children and grandchildren, his earth-bound understanding of the Law. At the same time, through this natural contemplation on the heights of spiritual knowledge, he openly confesses his error of previously interpreting the Law according to its outward form. For the text, 'to hang them before the Lord' (cf. 2 Sam. 21 : 9), may be understood to mean this: to bring into the light by means of spiritual knowledge his preoccupation with the letter of the Law

and the prejudice from which he suffers as a result. This is to show that, thanks to contemplation, the letter of the Law has been killed by spiritual knowledge.

39. 'The letter kills,' says Scripture, 'but the Spirit gives life' (2 Cor. 3 : 6). Consequently, the letter whose nature it is to kill must be killed by the life-giving Spirit. For what is material in the Law and what is divine – namely, the letter and the Spirit – cannot co-exist, nor can what destroys life be reconciled with that which by nature bestows life.

40. The Spirit bestows life, the letter destroys it. Thus the letter cannot function at the same time as the Spirit, just as what gives life cannot coexist with what destroys life.

41. Circumcision, in its mystical sense, is the complete cutting away of the intellect's impassioned attachment to all that comes into being in a contingent manner. Viewing things on the natural level, we recognize that the removal of an attribute naturally bestowed by God does not produce perfection. For nature does not bring about perfection when it is mutilated by human ingenuity, or when through over-subtlety men deprive it of something conferred on it by God at creation. Otherwise we would be attributing to human ingenuity more power to establish a perfect order of things than to God, and to an ingenious mutilation of nature the ability to make good shortcomings in God's creation. But if we understand circumcision figuratively, we learn that we are spiritually to circumcise the impassioned disposition of our soul. In this way our will, having freed the intellect from its impassioned subjection to the law that rules the birth of contingent things, is brought into harmony with nature.

42. Uncircumcision is natural. Everything that is natural is the work of divine creation and is excellent: 'And God saw everything that He had made, and, behold, it was very good' (Gen. 1 : 31). But the Law, by demanding on the grounds of uncleanness that the foreskin should be cut away by circumcision (cf. Gen. 17 : 10–14), presents God as amending His own work through human skill. This is a most blasphemous way of looking at things. He, then, who interprets the symbols whereby the Law is expressed in the light of knowledge attained through natural contemplation, knows that God does not set nature aright by means of human skill, but bids us circumcise the passible aspect of the soul so as to make it obedient to

the intelligence. This is indicated figuratively in terms of the body, and means that we are to excise the flaws from our will by means of spiritual knowledge acquired through the courageous practice of the virtues. The circumcising priest signifies spiritual knowledge, and the knife he uses is the courageous practice of the virtues, which cuts away the passions. When the Spirit triumphs over the letter, the tradition of the Law is abolished.

43. The sabbath (cf. Exod. 16 : 23; 20 : 10) signifies rest from the passions, and from the intellect's gravitation towards the nature of created beings. It signifies the total quiescence of the passions, a complete cessation of the intellect's gravitation towards created things, and its total entry into the divine. He who has attained this state – so far as God permits – by means of virtue and spiritual knowledge, must not ponder on any material thing at all for, like sticks (cf. Num. 15 : 32), such things excite the passions; and he must not call to mind any natural principle whatsoever. Otherwise, like the pagans, we will be affirming that God delights in the passions or is commensurate with nature. Perfect silence alone proclaims Him, and total and transcendent unknowing brings us into His presence.

44. A crown of goodness (cf. Ps. 65 : 11) is a pure faith, adorned with eloquent doctrine, and with spiritual principles and intellections, as if with precious stones, and set as it were on the head of the devout intellect. Or rather, a crown of goodness is the Logos of God Himself, who encircles the intellect as if it were a head, protecting it with manifold forms of providence and judgment – that is, with mastery of the passions that lie within our control and with patient endurance of those we suffer against our will; and who makes this same intellect more beautiful by enabling it to participate in the grace of deification.

45. In the preceding passage it is said that self-control is a work of God's providence, because it purifies the passions which lie within the control of the will. It is also said that patient endurance is a work of God's judgment, because it enables us to resist those trials we suffer against our will. Moreover, being a token of practical philosophy, such endurance brings those who have been enslaved in an Egypt of sin across to the realm of virtue.

46. God did not order the sabbath, the new moons and the feasts to be honoured because He wanted men to honour the days

themselves: this would have been tantamount to decreeing by the Law that men should worship creation rather than the Creator (cf. Rom. 1 : 25), and should regard the days as holy in themselves and therefore to be venerated. On the contrary, He indicated that He Himself was to be honoured symbolically through the days. For He is the sabbath, as the soul's repose after its exertions in the flesh, and as the cessation of its sufferings in the cause of righteousness. He is the Passover, as the liberator of those held in the bitter slavery of sin. He is the Pentecost, as the origin and consummation of all created beings, and as the principle through which all things by nature exist. Thus the Law destroys those who apprehend it in a literal or outward way, leading them to worship creation rather than the Creator, and to regard as holy in themselves things that were brought into existence for man's sake; for they remain ignorant of Him on whose account they were created.

47. The world is a finite place and possesses but limited stability. Time is circumscribed movement. It follows that the movement of living things within time is subject to change. When nature passes beyond place and time, actively and inwardly — that is, when it passes beyond those things which always accompany created being, namely, a limited state of stability and limited movement — it is united directly with providence, and finds in providence a principle which is by nature simple, stable, without limitation and thus completely without movement.

48. Since nature exists in the world in a temporal mode, its movement is subject to change because of the world's limited stability and its liability to alteration and corruption through the passing of time. When nature has come to exist in God through the essential unity of Him in whom it was created, it will possess an ever-moving stability and a stable and changeless form of movement generated eternally round that which is one, unique and always the same. It has been said that this state is a direct and permanent grounding in the first cause of created beings.[1]

49. The mystery of Pentecost is the direct union with providence of those things that are in its care. It is the union of nature with its principle, the Logos, under the guidance of providence; and in this union there is not the slightest trace of time or generation. Again,

[1] cf. Dionysios the Areopagite, *On the Celestial Hierarchy* vii, 2 (*P.G.* iii, 208B).

the Logos is our trumpet (cf. Lev. 23 : 24), summoning us with divine and hidden knowledge. He is our propitiation (cf. Lev. 25 : 9), since He expiates our offences in His own person by becoming like us, and divinizes our sinful nature by the gift of grace through the Spirit. He is our booth or tabernacle (cf. Lev. 23 : 42), since He is the realization of that immutability with which our inner being, conformed to God, is concentrated on the divine, and also the securing bond of our transformation into an immortal state.

50. If God rejoiced simply in bloody sacrifices, this would imply that He is governed by passion and wishes those who offer sacrifice to Him to value the passions; for the sincere worshipper gladly rejoices in the same things as does the God whom he worships. But the sacrifices of which Scripture speaks are rather the slaughter of the passions and the offering up of our natural powers. Of these powers, the ram typifies the intelligence (cf. Lev. 5 : 15), the bull the incensive power (cf. Exod. 29 : 36), and the goat represents desire (cf. Num. 15 : 27).

51. By spiritual sacrifices is meant not only the putting to death of the passions, slaughtered by 'the sword of the Spirit, which is the word of God' (Eph. 6 : 17), and the deliberate emptying out of all life in the flesh, as if it were blood; the term also signifies the offering up of the moral state we have gained through the practice of the virtues, together with all our natural powers, which we dedicate and offer to God as whole burnt sacrifices, to be consumed by the fire of grace in the Spirit, so that they are filled with divine power.

52. When a materialistic understanding of Scripture dominates the soul, it leads the soul to reject natural principles by misusing its natural powers; and so long as this understanding retains its hold it expels, pursues and destroys all such principles and thoughts. For it limits the Law to the flesh alone, and honours the shameful passions as divine. But natural thoughts, made fearless through the law of the Spirit, kill the passions at a stroke.

53. As soon as anyone practises the virtues with true intelligence, he acquires a spiritual understanding of Scripture. He worships God actively in the new way of the Spirit through the higher forms of contemplation, and not in the old way of the written code (cf. Rom. 7 : 6), which makes man interpret the Law in an outward and sensual manner and, Judaic-like, fosters the passions and encourages sin.

54. As soon as a person stops interpreting Scripture in an outward and sensual manner, his intellect reverts to its natural spiritual state: he accomplishes spiritually what the Jews performed in a purely external and physical manner, thereby provoking God's anger.

55. Every intellect caught up by God cuts off simultaneously both the energy of the passions and the uncouth jostle of thoughts. In addition to this it also puts an end to the licentious misuse of the senses. For the passions, brought triumphantly into subjection by the higher forms of contemplation, are destroyed by the sublime vision of nature.

56. The power of sin – or in other words, the will of the flesh – is destroyed by the grace of holy baptism, and by active obedience to God's commandments. Such obedience destroys the power of sin with the sword of the Spirit (cf. Eph. 6 : 17), that is, with the revelation of divine knowledge in the Spirit; for obedience secretly cries to the passion of sin as Samuel cried to Agag: 'As your sword has made women childless, so today shall your mother be childless among women' (1 Sam. 15 : 33).

57. Using the mellow thought of pleasure as if it were a sword, the passion of gluttony makes many virtues childless. By means of dissipation it kills the seeds of self-restraint; through greed it corrupts the equity of justice; with self-love it severs the natural bond of compassion. In short, the passion of gluttony destroys all virtue's offspring.

58. The passion of gluttony kills all the divine offspring of the virtues. But that passion itself is killed through the spiritual knowledge acquired by the grace of faith and by obedience to the divine commandments.

59. Our Lord is truly a light to the Gentiles (cf. Isa. 49 : 6; Luke 2 : 32): through true knowledge He opens the eyes of their mind, closed as they have been by the darkness of ignorance. Moreover, through His divine conduct He has made Himself a noble example of virtue to the faithful, becoming their model and pattern. Looking to Him as the author of our salvation, we attain the virtues by imitating Him in our own conduct, so far as this is possible for us.

60. Anyone who hates a man through envy, and maliciously slanders him because he is stronger in the struggle for virtue and richer in spiritual knowledge, is choked like Saul by an evil spirit

(cf. 1 Sam. 16 : 14): he cannot bear to see someone better than himself enjoying the glory that comes through virtue and spiritual knowledge. And he rages all the more because he cannot actually kill this good man (cf. 1 Sam. 18 : 10–11). In addition, he often bitterly banishes the beloved Jonathan from his presence (cf. 1 Sam. 19 : 4–5; 20 : 30–32) – that is, he suppresses the innate judgment of his conscience, which rebukes his unjust hatred and from a love of truth recounts the achievements of the man whom he hates.

61. Let us, too, beseech the noetic David to make our intellect, frenzied by material things, resonant with the lyre of spiritual contemplation and knowledge, and to drive out the evil spirit of material inconstancy that dominates the world of the senses (cf. 1 Sam. 16 : 23). In this way we may be able to understand the Law spiritually and find the divine principle hidden mystically within it, so that it becomes for us a lasting source of eternal life.

62. Every lover of salvation is totally committed either to the practice of the virtues or to the contemplative life. For without virtue and spiritual knowledge no one can attain salvation in any way whatsoever. For virtue controls the body's impulses, skilfully curbing with sound thoughts its gravitation towards unnatural conduct; while by means of contemplation one inwardly lays hold of what has been rightly conceived and intelligently assessed.

63. Since apprehension is intellective, and what is apprehended is intelligible, what is apprehended is, so to speak, the nourishment and substance of that which apprehends. Thus when God is apprehended by incorporeal beings – who are themselves intellects – and becomes intelligible to them to the degree to which they come into communion with Him, He illumines them from within, their intellects both apprehending Him and being nourished by Him.

64. The intelligible is one thing and the intellective is another, the first in some sense, as we have already indicated, nourishing the second. For what is apprehended – the intelligible – is superior and conceptually prior to that which apprehends, which is intellective. Beings that apprehend such superior intelligibles with the intellect are intellective. What is apprehended is intelligible, and it is this that nourishes the intellective – or, in other words, nourishes that which apprehends.

65. An effect enshrines, as far as possible, the image of its cause. All created things are effects, while what has brought them into

being is their cause. But there is no exact resemblance between cause and effect.

66. Although effects enshrine, so far as possible, the images of their causes, there is no exact resemblance between the two, since causes surpass and transcend effects with regard to their mode of origin. For what pertains to effects pre-exists superlatively and essentially in their causes.[1]

67. Effects comprise all created things in heaven and on earth, while the causes that have brought them into being are the three Persons of the Holy Trinity. It is therefore clear that there can be no exact resemblance between the two.

68. Our intellect possesses the power of apprehension through which it perceives intelligible realities; it also possesses the capacity for a union that transcends its nature and that unites it with what is beyond its natural scope. It is through this union that divine realities are apprehended, not by means of our own natural capacities, but by virtue of the fact that we entirely transcend ourselves and belong entirely to God. It is better to belong to God than to ourselves; for it is on those who belong to God that divine gifts are bestowed.

69. When the intellect wants to apprehend something, it descends from its own level to the level of intellection. For intellections are inferior to the subject that apprehends, since they are the means through which apprehension and understanding take place; and they disperse and divide the intellect's unity. The intellect is simple and integral, while intellections are multiple and dispersive: they are, so to speak, the forms of the intellect. For this reason intellective subjects – beings endowed with intellect – are inferior to intelligible realities that are the objects of apprehension. It is by virtue of its unity that the intellect reaches out to what is beyond its natural scope and attains the contemplation of God. This it does by transcending all that belongs to the sensible and intelligible worlds, and even its own activity; for only thus may it receive the ray of divine knowledge.

70. An intellective being that acts intellectively in accordance with its own principle naturally apprehends with its intellect. Moreover it will love what it apprehends and so in a passive manner, under the influence of the erotic impulse, it will be drawn out of

[1] From Dionysios the Areopagite (see appendix). §§ 68, 82, 83, 85, 86, 90 and 91 are also from Dionysios.

itself towards that which it loves; and this impulse will grow continually more urgent and intense. In this way it will not rest until it is entirely immersed in the total reality of what it loves, wholly and willingly encompassed by the wholeness of that reality, welcoming its saving embrace, and completely conformed to that which embraces it. So much will this be the case that it will now wish to be recognized not from itself but from what embraces it, like air made luminous by light or iron penetrated through and through by fire, or something else of this kind.

71. The relationship between the intellective faculty and intelligible realities, and between the sensory faculties and sensible realities, is in each case extremely close. Since man is constituted of soul and sentient body, he is limited and defined and he himself imposes limits and makes definitions by virtue of the natural and distinctive reciprocity that exists between himself and these two aspects of creation. As a compound of soul and body he is limited essentially by intelligible and sensible realities, while at the same time he himself defines these realities through his capacity to apprehend intellectually and to perceive with his senses. God, on the other hand, exists simply and without limitation beyond all created realities, whether comprehending or comprehended, for He has absolutely no relationship with anything at all.

72. Every forbidden sensual pleasure comes into being as a result of passion and through the perception of some sensible object. For sensual pleasure is nothing other than the form of sensation created in the sentient faculty by some sensible object, or else the mode of sensitive activity when this is set in motion by desire that is contrary to the intelligence. For when desire combines with the senses, it is changed into pleasure, itself contriving the form the pleasure takes. And when the senses are stimulated by desire, they produce pleasure, taking advantage of the sensible object. The saints recognize that the soul assumes an earthly form when, contrary to nature, it is impelled towards material things by means of the flesh; consequently they resolve to redirect their impulses in accordance with nature towards God by means of the soul, and to adapt their flesh to Him, adorning it as far as possible with images of the divine through the practice of the virtues.

73. The saints in their nobility pass through this present age of trials by acting unfailingly in accordance with nature. Once their

intellect has grasped the simple essences of created things, they unite their senses to it by means of the intelligence; then when the intellect has been completely liberated from all impulsion towards created things, and is at rest even from its own natural activity, they offer it to God. Wholly united with God in this way, they are totally immingled through the Spirit with the whole God, since they have put on the whole image of the heavenly (cf. 1 Cor. 15 : 49) – so far as human beings can do this – and have consecrated themselves to God, drawing the divine image to themselves, if it be permitted to speak thus, as much as being drawn by it.

74. We are told that God and man are exemplars of each other. Man's ability to deify himself through love for God's sake is correlative with God's becoming man through compassion for man's sake. And man's manifestation through the virtues of the God who is by nature invisible is correlative with the degree to which his intellect is seized by God and imbued with spiritual knowledge.

75. The person who has mortified the earthly aspects of himself (cf. Col. 3 : 5), thoroughly extinguishing the will of the flesh within him and repudiating the attachment to it which splits asunder the love we owe to God alone; who has disowned all the modalities of the flesh and the world for the sake of divine grace, so as to be able to say with Paul the apostle, 'What can separate us from the love of Christ?' (Rom. 8 : 35) – such a person has become, like Melchisedec, 'without father, without mother, without descent' (Heb. 7 : 3). For, because of the union with the Spirit that has taken place within him, he cannot now be dominated by flesh or by nature.

76. I do not think that the end of this present life is rightly called death. More accurately, it is deliverance from death, separation from corruption, liberation from slavery, cessation of turbulence, destruction of wars, dispelling of darkness, rest from suffering, calming of turmoil, eclipsing of shame, escape from passions and, to sum up, the termination of all evils. The saints who have achieved these things through voluntary mortification live as strangers and pilgrims in this life (cf. Heb. 11 : 13), fighting bravely against the world and the body and the assaults stemming from them. And, having stifled the deceit which both of these engender because of the close connexion existing between the senses and sensible objects, they keep the dignity of their soul unenslaved.

77. Nature itself gives no small token of the knowledge of provi-

dence planted naturally within us whenever it urges us instinctively towards God through prayer in times of sudden crisis, and makes us seek salvation from Him. For when we are suddenly overtaken by violent events, before thinking of anything else we involuntarily call upon God. It is as if providence itself, without any conscious thought on our part, were drawing us to itself, outstripping the speed of our noetic faculty and showing us that divine help is stronger than anything else. Nature would not lead us purposelessly to what does not naturally exist. It is clear to everyone that whatever is a natural consequence of something demonstrates its own authenticity with the force of truth.

78. Some things are good and others are bad, and these belong either to the present or to the future. A good which is expected in the future is called desire, and one which is possessed in the present is called pleasure. Conversely, an evil which is expected in the future is called fear, and one which is experienced in the present is called distress. Consequently, with regard to good things, whether really good or only thought to be so, pleasure and desire both exist and are to be observed; and the same may be said of distress and fear where evil things are concerned. Desire when fulfilled produces pleasure, and when frustrated results in distress.

79. It is said that distress is of its very nature evil. For although a man engaged in the practice of the virtues grieves over the evils that befall others, he is compassionate not primarily by deliberate choice but as a consequence of whatever misfortune it is that occurs. A contemplative, on the other hand, remains dispassionate in the face of such evils, since he has united himself with God and is detached from all that happens in this present life.

80. Since all the saints have truly grasped the divine and infallible Logos, they pass through this present age without printing their soul's footsteps on any of the delights which are to be found in it. For they have rightly made their intellect receptive to the loftiest principles concerning God accessible to man, the principles of goodness and love. They have learnt that God, moved by these principles, has endowed created things with being and granted them well-being as a gift of grace. Yet perhaps when referring to God, who alone is unmoved, we should speak not of movement but of will; for it is God's will that moves all things, brings all things into existence, sustains them, yet is never moved in any way whatsoever.

81. Since the soul is an intellective and intelligent substance, it both apprehends with its intellect and uses its intelligence. The intellect is its potentiality, the act of intellection its dynamic, and the intellectual concept or conceptual image its actualization. For the intellectual concept marks the completion of the act of intellection as regards both the intellective subject and the object intellectually apprehended: it intervenes between the two and determines their relation to each other. For when the soul apprehends, its act of intellection stops once the object of that act has been grasped: what has truly been apprehended once and for all no longer calls forth the potentiality of the soul to apprehend it. In this way the formation of an intellectual concept brings the act of intellection to an end.

82. Just as ignorance divides those who are deluded, so the presence of spiritual light draws together and unites those whom it enlightens. It makes them perfect and brings them back to what really exists; converting them from a multiplicity of opinions it unites their varied points of view – or, more accurately, their fantasies – into one simple, true and pure spiritual knowledge, and fills them with a single unifying light.

83. The beautiful is identical with the good, for all things seek the beautiful and good at every opportunity, and there is no being which does not participate in them. They extend to all that is, being what is truly admirable, sought for, desired, pleasing, chosen and loved. Observe how the divine force of love – the erotic power pre-existing in the good – has given birth to the same blessed force within us, through which we long for the beautiful and good in accordance with the words, 'I became a lover of her beauty' (Wisd. 8 : 2), and 'Love her and she will sustain you; fortify her and she will exalt you' (Prov. 4 : 6, 8).

84. Theologians call the divine sometimes an erotic force, sometimes love, sometimes that which is intensely longed for and loved.[1] Consequently, as an erotic force and as love, the divine itself is subject to movement; and as that which is intensely longed for and loved it moves towards itself everything that is receptive of this force and love. To express this more clearly: the divine itself is subject to movement since it produces an inward state of intense

---

[1] cf. Dionysios the Areopagite, *On the Divine Names* iv, 14 (*P.G.* iii, 712c).

longing and love in those receptive to them; and it moves others
since by nature it attracts the desire of those who are drawn towards it. In other words, it moves others and itself moves since it
thirsts to be thirsted for, longs to be longed for, and loves to be
loved.

85. The divine erotic force also produces ecstasy, compelling
those who love to belong not to themselves but to those whom they
love. This is shown by superior beings through their care of inferiors,
by those of equal dignity through their mutual union, and by
lower beings through their divine conversion towards those that are
highest in rank. It was in consequence of this that St Paul, possessed
as he was by this divine erotic force and partaking of its ecstatic
power, was inspired to say: 'I no longer live, but Christ lives in me'
(Gal. 2 : 20). He uttered these words as a true lover and, as he himself says, as one who has gone out from himself to God (cf. 2 Cor.
5 : 13), not living his own life but that of the beloved, because of
his fervent love for Him.

86. One must also in the name of truth be bold enough to affirm
that the Cause of all things, through the beauty, goodness and profusion of His intense love for everything, goes out of Himself in His
providential care for the whole of creation. By means of the supra-
essential power of ecstasy, and spell-bound as it were by goodness,
love and longing, He relinquishes His utter transcendence in order
to dwell in all things while yet remaining within Himself. Hence
those skilled in divine matters call Him a zealous and exemplary
lover, because of the intensity of His blessed longing for all things
and because He rouses others to imitate His own intense desire, revealing Himself as their exemplar; for in Him what is desirable is
worthy of emulation, and He deserves to be imitated by the beings
under His care.

87. God is said to be the originator and begetter of love and the
erotic force. For He externalized them from within Himself, that is,
He brought them forth into the world of created things. This is why
Scripture says that 'God is love' (1 John 4 : 16), and elsewhere that
He is 'sweetness and desire' (cf. Song of Songs 5 : 16. LXX), which
signifies the erotic force. For what is worthy of love and truly desirable is God Himself. Because loving desire is poured out from
Him, He Himself, as its begetter, is said to be in movement, while
because He is what is truly longed for, loved, desired and chosen,

He stirs into motion the things that turn towards Him, and which possess the power of desiring each in the degree appropriate to it.

88. You should understand that God stimulates and allures in order to bring about an erotic union in the Spirit; that is to say, He is the go-between in this union, the one who brings the parties together, in order that He may be desired and loved by His creatures. God stimulates in that He impels each being, in accordance with its own principle, to return to Him. Even though the word 'allurement' signifies something impure to the profane, here it stands for the mediation which effects the union with God.

89. The erotic impulsion of the Good, that pre-exists in the Good, is simple and self-moving; it proceeds from the Good, and returns again to the Good, since it is without end or beginning. This is why we always desire the divine and union with the divine. For loving union with God surpasses and excels all other unions.

90. We should regard the erotic force, whether divine, angelic, noetic, psychic or physical, as a unifying and commingling power. It impels superior beings to care for those below them, beings of equal dignity to act with reciprocity, and, finally, inferior beings to return to those that are greater and more excellent than they.

91. Spiritual knowledge unites knower and known, while ignorance is always a cause of change and self-division in the ignorant. Hence nothing, according to sacred Scripture, will shift him who truly believes from the ground of his true faith, in which resides the permanence of his immutable and unchanging identity. For he who has been united with the truth has the assurance that all is well with him, even though most people rebuke him for being out of his mind. For without their being aware he has moved from delusion to the truth of real faith; and he knows for sure that he is not deranged, as they say, but that through truth – simple and always immutably the same – he has been liberated from the fluctuating and fickle turmoil of the manifold forms of illusion.

92. The saints are full of goodness, compassion, kindliness and mercy. They manifest the same love for the whole human race. Because of this they hold fast throughout their lives to the highest of all blessings, humility, that conserves other blessings and destroys their opposites. Thus they become totally immune to vexing trials and temptations, whether those due to ourselves and subject to our

volition, or not from ourselves and beyond our control. They wither the attacks of the first type through self-control, and repel the assaults of the second type with patient endurance.

93. The perfect practice of virtue is produced by true faith and genuine fear of God. Unerring natural contemplation in the course of the spiritual ascent is produced by a sure hope and a sound understanding. Deification through assumption into the divine is produced by perfect love and an intellect voluntarily blinded, because of its transcendent state, to created things.

94. The function of practical philosophy is to purify the intellect of every impassioned fantasy. The function of natural contemplation is to initiate the intellect into the true knowledge that is found in created things and according to which they possess existence. The function of mystical theology is by grace to make the intellect like God and equal to Him – as far as this is possible – so that it becomes totally unaware, because of its transcendent state, of anything that is sequent to God.

95. Ether, or the fiery element, in the world of the senses corresponds in the world of the mind to understanding – a state that illumines and manifests the spiritual principles particular to each created being, revealing through these principles the Cause that is present in them all, and drawing out the soul's desire for the divine. Air in the world of the senses corresponds in the world of the mind to courage – a state that quickens, sustains and activates this innate life of the spirit, and invigorates the soul's ceaseless aspiration for the divine. Water in the world of the senses corresponds in the world of the mind to self-restraint – a state that produces a vitalizing fecundity in the spirit and generates an ever-resurgent erotic enchantment attracting the soul to the divine. Earth in the world of the senses corresponds in the world of the mind to justice – a state that begets all the inner principles of created things according to their kind, that in spirit shares out the gifts of life to each thing in an equitable way, and that is by its own free choice rooted and established immovably in beauty and goodness.

96. When the flesh flourishes and burgeons, the soul is afflicted and darkened by the passions, because the state of virtue and the illumination of spiritual knowledge withdraw. Conversely, when the soul is fortified and made resplendent with the divine beauty of the virtues and with the illumination of spiritual knowledge, the

outer man is weakened, because the flesh loses its natural vigour through the indwelling of the Logos.

97. Created man cannot become a son of God and god by grace through deification, unless he is first through his own free choice begotten in the Spirit by means of the self-loving and independent power dwelling naturally within him. The first man neglected this divinizing, divine and immaterial birth by choosing what is manifest and delectable to the senses in preference to the spiritual blessings that were as yet unrevealed. In this way he fittingly condemned himself to a bodily generation that is without choice, material and subject to death.

98. In his present state man acts either to satisfy the uncontrolled fantasies of passions deceitfully provoked for the sake of self-indulgence, or to perform work forced on him by some necessity, or in order to discover the natural laws of nature. In the beginning none of these things constrained man in this way, for he was above all things. That indeed is how it was right for the first man to be: not in the least distracted by anything below him, or around him, or over against him, and requiring only one thing for his perfection – an indomitable striving, backed by all the strength of his love, towards the God above him.

99. Nothing that had to be learnt interposed itself between God and the first man, impeding the free relationship that was to be sealed by love through his striving towards God. Being dispassionate by grace, he was not subject to the delusory fantasies of passions provoked by the desire for sensual pleasure. Being self-sufficient, he was free from needs forcing him to engage in some kind of work. Being wise, he possessed a spiritual knowledge that made him superior to the study of nature.

100. God, who created all nature with wisdom and secretly planted in each intelligent being knowledge of Himself as its first power, like a munificent Lord gave also to us men a natural desire and longing for Him, combining it in a natural way with the power of our intelligence. Using our intelligence, we struggle so as to learn with tranquillity and without going astray how to realize this natural desire. Impelled by it we are led to search out the truth, wisdom and order manifest harmoniously in all creation, aspiring through them to attain Him by whose grace we received the desire.

On the Lord's Prayer

A SHORT INTERPRETATION ADDRESSED TO A DEVOUT CHRISTIAN

I have, Sir, in receiving your inspiring letters, received you in your own person. Indeed, in spirit you are always present and cannot possibly be absent. But, following God's example, you have in your goodness also taken advantage of the opportunity God has given you to communicate with your servants. I have greatly admired your self-abasement, and have tempered my fear of you with affection, and from both have formed a love based on respect and goodwill. I have combined the two in case fear, stripped of affection, should turn into hatred, or affection, deprived of fear, should turn into over-familiarity. In this way, love becomes an inward law of tenderness, assimilating everything naturally akin to it, mastering hatred through goodwill, and over-familiarity through respect.

David the psalmist says, 'Fear of the Lord is pure, and endures for ever' (Ps. 19 : 9), because he knows that of all things fear is best able to preserve divine love. Such a fear is, he realizes, very different from the fear of being punished for crimes. This second type of fear is indeed ousted and destroyed by love, as John the Evangelist makes clear when he writes, 'Love casts out fear' (1 John 4 : 18). But the fear David is talking about is a natural expression of the law of true tenderness; and it is through this fear that the saints always keep intact the rule and practice of love, both for God and for each other.

Thus, as I have said, I too have tempered my fear of you, Sir, with affection and have maintained this law of love until now. Hitherto I have been held back from writing through respect, because I did not want to open the door to over-familiarity; but now I have been impelled to write through goodwill, lest my failure to do so should be construed as hatred. And so, as requested, I write, not what I think – for, as Scripture says, 'men's thoughts are pathetic' (Wisd. 9 : 14) – but what God wills and grants by grace so that good may come of it; for 'the Lord's counsel stands for ever,' says David, 'and the thoughts of His heart from generation to generation' (Ps. 33 : 11). Perhaps the counsel of God the Father to which David here refers is the unfathomable self-emptying of the only-begotten Son which He brought about for the deification of our nature, and by which He has set a limit to the ages; and perhaps the thoughts of His heart are the principles of providence and judgment by which He wisely orders our present and future life as if they were separate generations, assigning to each its appropriate mode of activity.

If the purpose of the divine counsel is the deification of our nature, and the aim of divine thoughts is to supply the prerequisites of our life, it follows that we should both know and carry into effect the power of the Lord's Prayer, and write about it in the proper way. And since you, Sir, in writing to me your servant have been inspired by God to mention this prayer in particular, it is necessarily the subject of my own words as well; hence I beseech the Lord, who has taught us this prayer, to open my intellect so that it may grasp the mysteries contained in it, and to give me words equal to the task of elucidating what I have understood. For hidden within a limited compass this prayer contains the whole purpose and aim of which we have just spoken; or, rather, it openly proclaims this purpose and aim to those whose intellects are strong enough to perceive them. The prayer includes petitions for everything that the divine Logos effected through His self-emptying in the incarnation, and it teaches us to strive for those blessings of which the true provider is God the Father alone through the natural mediation of the Son in the Holy Spirit. For the Lord Jesus is mediator between God and men, as the divine apostle says (cf. 1 Tim. 2 : 5), since He makes the unknown Father manifest to men through the flesh, and gives those who have been reconciled to Him access to the Father through the Holy Spirit (cf. Eph. 2 : 18). It was on their behalf and for their sake that without changing He became man, and is now the author and teacher of so many and such great new mysteries as yet beyond our understanding.

Of these mysteries that He has granted to men in His boundless generosity, seven are of more general significance; and it is these whose power, as I have said, lies hidden within the Lord's Prayer. These seven are theology, adoption as sons by grace, equality with the angels, participation in eternal life, the restoration of human nature when it is reconciled dispassionately with itself, the abolition of the law of sin, and the destruction of the tyranny that holds us in its power through the deceit of the evil one.

Let us examine the truth of what we have said. Theology is taught us by the incarnate Logos of God, since He reveals in Himself the Father and the Holy Spirit. For the whole of the Father and the whole of the Holy Spirit were present essentially and perfectly in the whole of the incarnate Son. They themselves did not become incarnate, but the Father approved and the Spirit co-operated when the Son Himself effected His incarnation. At the incarnation the Logos preserved His intellect and His life unimpaired: except by the Father and the Spirit He was not comprehended in essence by any other being whatsoever, but in His love for men was united hypostatically with the flesh.

The Logos bestows adoption on us when He grants us that birth and deification which, transcending nature, comes by grace from above through the Spirit. The guarding and preservation of this in God depends on the resolve of those thus born: on their sincere acceptance of the grace bestowed on them and, through the practice of the commandments, on their cultivation of the beauty given to them by grace. Moreover, by emptying themselves of the passions they lay hold of the divine to the same degree as that to which, deliberately emptying Himself of His own sublime glory, the Logos of God truly became man.

The Logos has made men equal to the angels. Not only did He 'make peace through the blood of His Cross . . . between things on earth and things in heaven' (Col. 1 : 20), and reduce to impotence the hostile powers that fill the intermediary region between heaven and earth, thereby making the festal assembly of earthly and heavenly powers a single gathering for His distribution of divine gifts, with humankind joining joyfully with the powers on high in unanimous praise of God's glory; but also, after fulfilling the divine purpose undertaken on our behalf, when He was taken up with the body which He had assumed, He united heaven and earth in Himself,

joined what is sensible with what is intelligible, and revealed creation as a single whole whose extremes are bound together through
virtue and through knowledge of their first Cause. He shows, I
think, through what He has accomplished mystically, that the Logos
unites what is separated and that alienation from the Logos divides
what is united. Let us learn, then, to strive after the Logos through
the practice of the virtues, so that we may be united not only with
the angels through virtue, but also with God in spiritual knowledge
through detachment from created things.

The Logos enables us to participate in divine life by making Himself our food, in a manner understood by Himself and by those who
have received from Him a noetic perception of this kind. It is by
tasting this food that they become truly aware that the Lord is full
of virtue (cf. Ps. 34 : 8). For He transmutes with divinity those who
eat it, bringing about their deification, since He is the bread of life
and of power in both name and reality.

He restores human nature to itself. First, He became man and
kept His will dispassionate and free from rebellion against nature, so
that it did not waver in the slightest from its own natural movement
even with regard to those who crucified Him; on the contrary, it
chose death for their sake instead of life, thereby demonstrating the
voluntary character of His passion, rooted as it is in His love for
humankind. Second, having nailed to the Cross the record of our
sins (cf. Col. 2 : 14), He abolished the enmity which led nature to
wage an implacable war against itself; and having summoned those
far off and those near at hand – that is, those under the Law and those
outside it – and having broken down the obstructive partition-wall –
that is, having explained the law of the commandments in His
teaching to both these categories of humankind – He formed the
two into one new man, making peace and reconciling us through
Himself to the Father and to one another (cf. Eph. 2 : 14–16): our
will is no longer opposed to the principle of nature, but we adhere
to it without deviating in either will or nature.

The Logos purifies human nature from the law of sin by not permitting His incarnation for our sake to be preceded by sensual
pleasure. For His conception took place miraculously without seed,
and His birth supranaturally without the loss of His Mother's virginity. That is to say, when God was born from His Mother, through
His birth He tightened the bonds of her virginity in a manner sur-

passing nature; and in those who are willing He frees the whole of human nature from the oppressive rule of the law which dominates it, in so far as they imitate His self-chosen death by mortifying the earthly aspects of themselves (cf. Col. 3 : 5). For the mystery of salvation belongs to those who choose it, not to those who are compelled by force.

The Logos destroys the tyranny of the evil one, who dominates us through deceit, by triumphantly using as a weapon against him the flesh defeated in Adam. In this way he shows that what was once captured and made subject to death now captures the captor: by a natural death it destroys the captor's life and becomes a poison to him, making him vomit up all those he was able to swallow because he had the power of death. But to humankind it becomes life, like leaven in the dough impelling the whole of nature to rise like dough in the resurrection of life (cf. 1 Cor. 5 : 6–7). It was to confer this life that the Logos who was God became man – a truly unheard of thing – and willingly accepted the death of the flesh.

The Lord's Prayer, as I have said, contains a petition for each of these things. First, it speaks of the Father, His name, and His kingdom. Second, it shows us that the person who prays is by grace the son of this Father. It asks that those in heaven and those on earth may be united in one will. It tells us to ask for our daily bread. It lays down that men should be reconciled with one another and unites our nature with itself when we forgive and are forgiven, for then it is not split asunder by differences of will and purpose. It teaches us to pray against entering into temptation, since this is the law of sin. And it exhorts us to ask for deliverance from the evil one. For the author and giver of divine blessings could not but be our teacher as well, providing the words of this prayer as precepts of life for those disciples who believe in Him and follow the way He taught in the flesh. Through these words He has revealed the hidden treasures of wisdom and knowledge (cf. Col. 2 : 3) that as pure form exist in Him; and in all who offer this prayer He kindles the desire to enjoy such treasures.

It is for this reason, I think, that Scripture calls this teaching 'prayer', since it contains petitions for the gifts that God gives to men by grace. Our divinely inspired fathers have explained prayer in a similar way, saying that prayer is petition for that which God naturally gives men in the manner appropriate to Him, while a vow, conversely, is a promise of what men who worship God sincerely resolve to offer Him. The fathers cite many Scriptural texts to illustrate this distinction such as, 'Make your vows to the Lord our God and perform them' (Ps. 76 : 11. LXX), and 'I will give Thee, O Lord, what I have vowed' (Jonah 2 : 10. LXX), which refer to vows. On the subject of prayer they quote such texts as 'Hannah prayed to the Lord, saying, O Lord of hosts, if Thou wilt indeed listen to Thy handmaid and give me a child' (cf. 1 Sam. 1 : 11),[1] and 'Hezekiah the king of Judah and the prophet Isaiah the son of Amoz prayed to the Lord' (cf. 2 Chr. 32 : 20), and 'Pray then like this: Our Father who art in heaven' (Matt. 6 : 9), as the Lord said to the disciples. Consequently, a vow is a decision to keep the commandments, confirmed by a promise on the part of the person making the vow; and a prayer is a petition by one who has kept the commandments that he may be transformed by the commandments he has kept. Or, rather, a vow is a contest of virtue that God welcomes most readily whenever it is offered to Him; and prayer is the prize of virtue that God gives joyfully when the contest is won.

Since, then, prayer is petition for the blessings given by the incarnate Logos, let us make Him our teacher in prayer. And when we have contemplated the sense of each phrase as carefully as possible, let us confidently set it forth; for the Logos Himself gives us, in the manner that is best for us, the capacity to understand what He says.

'Our Father who art in heaven, hallowed be Thy name; Thy kingdom come' (Matt. 6 : 9–10). It is appropriate that at the outset the Lord should teach those who pray to start with theology, and should initiate them into the mode of existence of Him who is by essence the creative Cause of all things. For these opening words of the prayer contain a revelation of the Father, of the name of the Father, and of the kingdom of the Father, so that from this beginning we may be taught to revere, invoke and worship the Trinity in unity. For the name of God the Father exists in substantial form as the only-begotten Son. Again, the kingdom of God the Father exists in substantial form as the Holy Spirit: what Matthew calls 'kingdom' in this context one of the other Evangelists has elsewhere called 'Holy Spirit', saying, 'May Thy Holy Spirit come and purify

---

[1] St Maximos quotes from memory. In fact the text of the Old Testament states that Hannah 'made a vow to the Lord, saying . . .'.

us.'[1] For the Father's name is not something which He has acquired, nor is the kingdom a dignity ascribed to Him: He does not have a beginning, so that at a certain moment He begins to be Father or King, but He is eternal and so is eternally Father and King. In no sense at all, therefore, has He either begun to exist or begun to exist as Father or King. And if He exists eternally, not only is He eternally Father and King but also the Son and the Holy Spirit coexist with Him eternally in substantial form, having their being from Him and by nature inhering in Him beyond any cause or principle: they are not sequent to Him, nor have they come into existence after Him in a contingent manner. The relationship of coinherence between the Persons embraces all three of them simultaneously, not permitting any of the three to be regarded as prior or sequent to the others.

At the outset of this prayer, then, we honour the coessential and supraessential Trinity as the creative cause of our coming into existence. Secondly, we are taught to proclaim the grace of our adoption, since we have been found worthy of addressing our Creator by nature as our Father by grace. Thus, venerating this title of our begetter by grace, we strive to stamp our Creator's qualities on our lives, sanctifying His name on earth, taking after Him as our Father, showing ourselves to be His children through our actions, and through all that we think or do glorifying the author of this adoption, who is by nature Son of the Father.

We hallow or sanctify the name of our heavenly Father by grace when we mortify our desire for material things and purify ourselves of corrupting passions. For sanctification is truly the complete mortification and cessation of desire in the senses. When we have achieved this we assuage the uncouth turbulence of our incensive power, for the desire that arouses it and persuades it to fight for its own pleasures has now been quelled by holiness. For anger, being by nature the protagonist of desire, stops of its own accord when once it sees that desire has been put to death.

It is thus fitting that, anger and desire repudiated, we should next

---

[1] cf. Luke 11 : 2, where most manuscripts read, as in Matthew 6 : 10, 'Thy kingdom come'. The rare variant cited here by St Maximos is also known to St Gregory of Nyssa: see his work *On the Lord's Prayer*, sermon 3 (*P.G.* xliv, 1157C), translated by H. Graef, *Ancient Christian Writers*, vol. xviii (Westminster, 1954), pp. 52-53.

invoke the rule of the kingdom of God the Father with the words
'Thy kingdom come' (Matt. 6 : 10), that is, 'May the Holy Spirit
come'; for, having put away these things, we are now made into a
temple for God through the Holy Spirit by the teaching and practice
of gentleness. 'For on whom shall I rest,' says Scripture, 'but on him
who is gentle and humble, and trembles at my words?' (cf. Isa.
66 : 2). It is clear from this that the kingdom of God the Father
belongs to the humble and the gentle. For 'blessed are the gentle,
for they will inherit the earth' (Matt. 5 : 5). It is not this physical
earth, which by nature occupies a middle place in the universe, that
God promises as an inheritance for those who love Him – not, at
least, if He is speaking truly when He says, 'In the resurrection they
neither marry nor are given in marriage, but are as the angels in
heaven' (Matt. 22 : 30), and 'Come, you whom my Father has
blessed, inherit the kingdom prepared for you from the foundation
of the world' (Matt. 25 : 34), and elsewhere again to someone else
who has striven with goodwill, 'Enter into the joy of your Lord'
(Matt. 25 : 21). And after the Lord St Paul also says, 'The trumpet
will sound and first the dead in Christ will rise up incorrupt; then
we who are alive and remain will be caught up with them in the
clouds to meet the Lord in the air; and so we shall be with the
Lord for ever' (cf. 1 Thess. 4 : 16–17).

Since these things have been promised to those who love the
Lord, what man prompted by intelligence and wishing to serve it
would ever say, from a literal reading of Scripture alone, that
heaven, and the kingdom prepared from the foundation of the world,
and the mystically hidden joy of the Lord, and the perpetual dwelling with the Lord enjoyed by the saints, are to be identified with
the earth? In this text (Matt. 5 : 5) I think that the word 'earth'
signifies the resolution and strength of the inner stability, immovably
rooted in goodness, that is possessed by gentle people. This state of
stability exists eternally with the Lord, contains unfailing joy, enables the gentle to attain the kingdom prepared from the beginning,
and has its station and dignity in heaven. It also permits the gentle to
inherit the principle of virtue, as if virtue were the earth that
occupies a middle place in the universe. For the gentle person holds
a middle position between honour and obloquy, and remains dispassionate, neither puffed up by the first nor cast down by the second.
For the intelligence is by nature superior to both praise and blame;

and so, when it has put away sensual desire, it is no longer troubled by either the one or the other, having anchored the whole power of the soul in divine and unassailable liberty. The Lord, wanting to impart this liberty to His disciples, says, 'Take my yoke upon you and learn from Me; for I am gentle and humble in heart; and you will find rest for your souls' (Matt. 11 : 29). He calls the rule of the divine kingdom 'rest' because it confers on those worthy of it a lordship free from all servitude.

If the indestructible power of the pure kingdom is given to the humble and the gentle, what man will be so lacking in love and so completely without appetite for divine blessings that he will not desire the greatest degree of humility and gentleness in order to take on the stamp of the divine kingdom, so far as this is possible for men, and to bear in himself by grace an exact spiritual likeness of Christ, who is by nature the truly great king? In this likeness, says St Paul, 'there is neither male nor female' (Gal. 3 : 28), that is, there is neither anger nor desire. Of these, the first tyrannically perverts judgment and makes the mind betray the law of nature; while the second scorns the one dispassionate cause and nature, that alone is truly desirable, in favour of what is inferior, giving preference to the flesh rather than to the spirit, and taking pleasure more in visible things than in the magnificence and glory of intelligible realities. In this way with the lubricity of sensual pleasure it seduces the intellect from the divine perception of spiritual realities that is proper to it.

It is our aim to make the intelligence stand alone, stripped through the virtues of its affection for the body; for this affection, even when totally dispassionate, is still natural. The spirit, completely triumphing over nature, has to persuade the intellect to desist from moral philosophy in order to commune with the supra-essential Logos through direct and undivided contemplation, in spite of the fact that moral philosophy helps the intellect to cut itself off from, and to go beyond, things pertaining to the flux of time. For when the intellect has become free from its attachment to sensible objects, it should not be burdened any longer with pre-occupations about morality as with a shaggy cloak.

Elijah clearly reveals this mystery in a typological manner through his actions (cf. 2 Kgs. 2 : 11–14). For when he was borne aloft he gave Elisha his cloak, that is, the mortification of the flesh which constitutes the chief glory of moral conduct. He did this so that Elisha should have the support of the Spirit in his battle against hostile powers and should triumph over the flux and instability of nature, typified by the Jordan; so that, in other words, he would not be immersed in the turbidity and slime of material attachment and thus prevented from crossing over into the holy land. Meanwhile, Elijah himself advanced freely towards God, unencumbered by attachment to any created thing. His desire being undivided and his will unmixed, he made his dwelling with Him who is simple by nature, carried there by the interdependent cardinal virtues, harnessed spiritually to one another like horses of fire.

Elijah knew that in the disciple of Christ there must be no imbalance of dispositions, for such diversity is proof of a lack of inward unity. Thus the passion of desire produces a diffusion of blood around the heart, and the incensive power when roused causes the blood to boil. He who already lives and moves and has his being in Christ (cf. Acts 17 : 28) has annulled in himself the production of what is imbalanced and disunited: as I have said, he does not bear within him, like male and female, the opposing dispositions of such passions. In this way, the intelligence is not enslaved by the passions and made subject to their fickleness. Naturally endowed with the holiness of the divine image, the intelligence urges the soul to conform itself by its own free choice to the divine likeness. In this way the soul is able to participate in the great kingdom that exists in a substantive manner in God the Father of all, and to become a translucent abode of the Holy Spirit, receiving – if it may be expressed in this way – the whole authority of the knowledge of the divine nature in so far as this is possible. Where this authority prevails, the production of what is inferior automatically comes to an end and only what is superior is generated; for the soul that through the grace of its calling resembles God keeps inviolate within itself the substance of the blessings bestowed upon it. In souls such as this Christ always desires to be born in a mystical way, becoming incarnate in those who attain salvation, and making the soul that gives birth to Him a Virgin Mother; for such a soul, to put it briefly, is not conditioned by categories like those of male and female that typify a nature subject to generation and corruption.

Let no one be shocked to hear me speak of the corruption that is inherent in generation. For when one has justly and dispassionately examined the nature of what comes into being and ceases to be, one will clearly see that generation begins with corruption and ends in corruption. Christ, and the Christ-like way of life and understanding, as I have said, are free of the passions characteristic of such generation. At least, this is the case if St Paul was speaking the truth when he said that in Christ Jesus 'there is neither male nor female' (Gal. 3 : 28), meaning by these terms the characteristics and passions of a nature subject to generation and corruption. For in Christ and the Christ-like way of life there is only a deiform understanding imbued with divine knowledge, and a single disposition of will and purpose that chooses only virtue.

Moreover, in Christ there is neither Greek nor Jew (cf. Gal. 3 : 28). By this is meant differing or, rather, contrary views about God. The Greek affirms a host of ruling principles and divides the one fundamental principle into opposing operations and powers, devising a polytheistic worship full of contradictions because of the multitude of objects to be venerated, and ridiculous because of its many modes of veneration. The Jew affirms a fundamental principle which, although one, is narrow, imperfect and almost non-existent, since it is devoid of immanent consciousness and life; and so he falls into an evil which is just as bad as that into which the Greek falls for the opposite reason, namely disbelief in the true God. For he limits the fundamental principle to a single Person, one that exists without Logos and Spirit, or that merely possesses Logos and Spirit as qualities; for he fails to realize what kind of God this would be if deprived of these two other Persons, or how He could be God if assigned them as accidents by participation, as is the case with created intelligent beings. Neither Greek nor Jew, then, has any place at all in Christ. In Him there is only the principle of true religion and the steadfast law of mystical theology, that rejects both the dilatation of the Divinity, as in Greek polytheism, and the contraction of the Divinity, as in Jewish monotheism. In this way the Divine is not full of internal contradictions, as it is with the Greeks, because of a natural plurality, nor is it regarded as passible, as it is by the Jews, because of being a single Person, deprived of Logos and Spirit, or only possessing Logos and Spirit as qualities, without itself being Intellect and Logos and Spirit.

Mystical theology teaches us, who through faith have been adopted by grace and brought to the knowledge of truth, to recognize

one nature and power of the Divinity, that is to say, one God contemplated in Father, Son and Holy Spirit. It teaches us to know
God as a single unoriginate Intellect, self-existent, the begetter of a
single, self-existent, unoriginate Logos, and the source of a single
everlasting life, self-existent as the Holy Spirit: a Trinity in Unity
and a Unity in Trinity. The Divinity is not one thing in another
thing: the Trinity is not in the Unity like an accident in a substance
or vice versa, for God is without qualities. The Divinity is not one
thing and another thing: the Unity does not differ from the Trinity
by distinction of nature; the nature is simple and single in both.
Nor in the Divinity is one thing dependent on or prior to another:
the Trinity is not distinguished from the Unity, or the Unity from
the Trinity, by inferiority of power; nor is the Unity distinguished
from the Trinity as something common and general abstracted in a
purely conceptual manner from the particulars in which it occurs:
it is a substantively self-subsistent essence and a truly self-consoli-
dating power. Nor in the Divinity has one thing come into being
through another: there is within it no such mediating relationship
as that of cause and effect, since it is altogether identical with itself
and free from relationships. Nor in the Divinity is one thing derived
from another: the Trinity does not derive from the Unity, since it is
ungenerated and self-manifested. On the contrary, the Unity and the
Trinity are both affirmed and conceived as truly one and the same,
the first denoting the principle of essence, the second the mode of
existence. The whole is the single Unity, not divided by the Persons; and the whole is also the single Trinity, the Persons of which
are not confused by the Unity. Thus polytheism is not introduced
by division of the Unity or disbelief in the true God by confusion of
the Persons.

When Christian doctrine avoids these errors it achieves a
genuine splendour. By Christian doctrine I mean the teaching of
Christ, the new proclamation of truth in which there is neither male
nor female, that is, the signs and passions of human nature when
subject to birth and decay; neither Greek nor Jew, that is, contrary
views of the Divinity; neither uncircumcision nor circumcision
(cf. Col. 3 : 11), that is, the different kinds of worship appropriate
to these views, the first divinizing nature because of the passions and
setting the creature against the Creator, and the second because of
its misuse of symbols of the Law vilifying visible creation and

slandering the Creator as the source of evil. Both constitute equally an insult to the Divine and lead equally to evil. Neither in Christian doctrine is there barbarian or Scythian, that is, the deliberate fragmentation of the single nature of human beings which has made them subject to the unnatural law of mutual slaughter; neither is there bond or free, that is, the fortuitous division of this same nature which leads to one person despising another although both are by nature of an equal dignity, and which encourages men to dominate others tyrannically, thus violating the divine image in man. 'But Christ is all and in all' (Col. 3 : 11), in spirit fashioning the unoriginate kingdom by means of that which lies beyond nature and law.

This kingdom is characterized, as we have shown, by humility and gentleness of heart. It is the combination of these two qualities that constitutes the perfection of the person created according to Christ. For every humble person is invariably gentle and every gentle person is invariably humble. A person is humble when he knows that his very being is on loan to him. He is gentle when he realizes how to use the powers given to him in a manner that accords with nature and, withdrawing their activity completely from the senses, places them at the service of the intelligence in order to produce the virtues. In this way his intellect moves incessantly towards God, while where his senses are concerned he is not in the least perturbed by any of the things that afflict the body, nor does he stamp his soul with any trace of distress, thereby disrupting his joy-creative state. For he does not regard what is painful in the senses as a privation of pleasure: he knows only one pleasure, the marriage of the soul with the Logos. To be deprived of this marriage is endless torment, extending by nature through all the ages. Thus when he has left the body and all that pertains to it, he is impelled towards union with the divine; for even if he were to be master of the whole world, he would still recognize only one real disaster: failure to attain by grace the deification for which he is hoping.

Let us, then, 'cleanse ourselves from all pollution of the flesh and spirit' (2 Cor. 7 : 1), so that when we have extinguished our sensual desire, which indecently wantons with the passions, we may hallow the divine name. And with our intelligence let us bind fast our anger, deranged and frenzied by sensual pleasure, so that we may receive the kingdom of God the Father, that comes to us through gentleness.

Having done all this, we may go on to the next phrase of the prayer, saying, 'Thy will be done on earth as it is in heaven' (Matt. 6 : 10). He who worships God mystically with the faculty of the intelligence alone, keeping it free from sensual desire and anger, fulfils the divine will on earth just as the orders of angels fulfil it in heaven. He has become in all things a co-worshipper and fellow-citizen with the angels, conforming to St Paul's statement, 'Our citizenship is in heaven' (Phil. 3 : 20). Among the angels desire does not sap the intellect's intensity through sensual pleasure, nor does anger make them rave and storm indecently at their fellow creatures: there is only the intelligence naturally leading intelligent beings towards the source of intelligence, the Logos Himself. God rejoices in intelligence alone and this is what He demands from us His servants. He reveals this when He says to David, 'What have I in heaven, and besides yourself what have I desired on earth?' (Ps. 73 : 25. LXX). Nothing is offered to God in heaven by the holy angels except intelligent worship; and it is this that God also demands from us when He teaches us to say in our prayers, 'Thy will be done on earth as it is in heaven' (Matt. 6 : 10).

Let our intelligence, then, be moved to seek God, let our desire be roused in longing for Him, and let our incensive power struggle to keep guard over our attachment to Him. Or, more precisely, let our whole intellect be directed towards God, tensed by our incensive power as if by some nerve, and fired with longing by our desire at its most ardent. For if we imitate the heavenly angels in this way, we will find ourselves always worshipping God, behaving on earth as the angels do in heaven. For, like that of the angels, our intellect will not be attracted in the least by anything less than God.

If we live in the way we have promised, we will receive, as daily and life-giving bread for the nourishment of our souls and the maintenance of the good state with which we have been blessed, the Logos Himself; for it was He who said, 'I am the bread that came down from heaven and gives life to the world' (cf. John 6 : 33–35). In proportion to our capacity the Logos will become everything for us who are nourished through virtue and wisdom; and in accordance with His own judgment He will be embodied differently in each recipient of salvation while we are still living in this age. This is indicated in the phrase of the prayer which says, 'Give us this day our daily bread' (Matt. 6 : 11).

I believe that the expression 'this day' refers to the present age. It is as if one should say, after a clearer understanding of the context of the prayer, 'Since we are in this present mortal life, give us this day our daily bread which Thou hast originally prepared for human nature so that it might become immortal (cf. Gen. 2 : 9); for in this way the food of the bread of life and knowledge will triumph over the death that comes through sin.' The transgression of the divine commandment prevented the first man from partaking of this bread (cf. Gen. 3 : 19). Indeed, had he taken his fill of this divine food, he would not have been made subject to death through sin.

He who prays to receive this daily bread, however, does not automatically receive it all as it is in itself: he receives it in accordance with his receptive capacity. For the Bread of Life in His love gives Himself to all who ask, but He does not give to all in the same way. He gives liberally to those who have done great things, and more sparingly to those who have achieved less. Thus He gives to each person in accordance with the receptive capacity of his or her intellect.

The Saviour Himself has led me to this interpretation of the phrase we are considering, because He commands His disciples explicitly not to take any thought at all for sensible food, saying, 'Do not worry about your life, what you will eat, or what you will drink, or about your body, what you will put on. For the heathen seek all these things. But seek first the kingdom of God and His righteousness, and all these things as well will be given to you' (Matt. 6 : 25, 32, 33). How then can it be that He teaches us to pray for what He commands us not to seek? Obviously He does not order us to do anything of the kind: we should ask in prayer only for things that we are commanded to seek. If the Saviour commanded us to seek only the kingdom of God and righteousness, then surely He intended those who desire divine gifts to ask for this kingdom in their prayers. In this way, by showing what petitions are blessed by His grace, He conjoins the intention of those who ask with the will of Him who bestows the grace.

If, however, we also take this clause to mean that we should pray for the daily bread that sustains our present life, let us be careful not to overstep the bounds of the prayer, presumptuously assuming that

we will live for many cycles of years and forgetting that we are
mortal and that our life passes by like a shadow; but free from
anxiety let us pray for bread sufficient for one day at a time, thus
showing that as Christian philosophers we make life a rehearsal for
death, in our purpose anticipating nature and, even before death
comes, cutting off the soul's anxiety about bodily things. In this way
the soul will not transfer its natural appetite to material things,
attaching itself to what is corruptible, and will not learn the greed
that deprives it of a rich possession of divine blessings.

Let us therefore shun the love of matter and our attachment to
matter with all the strength we have, as if washing dust from our
spiritual eyes; and let us be satisfied simply with what sustains our
present life, not with what pampers it. Let us pray to God for this,
as we have been taught, so that we may keep our souls unenslaved
and absolutely free from domination by any of the visible things
loved for the sake of the body. Let us show that we eat for the sake
of living, and not be guilty of living for the sake of eating. The first
is a sign of intelligence, the second proof of its absence. And let us
be exact in the way we observe this prayer, thereby showing through
our actions that we cleave fast to the one life lived in the spirit
alone, and that we use our present life to acquire this spiritual life.
We use it, that is to say, only in so far as we do not refuse to sustain
our body with bread and to keep it as far as possible in its natural
state of good health, our aim being not just to live but to live for
God. For we make the body, rendered intelligent by the virtues, a
messenger of the soul, and the soul, once it is firmly established in
the good, a herald of God; and on the natural plane we restrict our
prayer for this bread to one day only, not daring to extend our
petition for it to a second day because of Him who gave us the prayer.
When we have thus conformed ourselves to the sense of the prayer,
we can proceed in purity to the next petition, saying, 'And forgive
us our debts as we forgive our debtors' (Matt. 6 : 12).

According to the first interpretation proposed for the preceding
section of the prayer, the words 'this day' symbolize the present
age; and the person who prays in this age for the incorruptible bread
of wisdom, from which we were cut off by the original transgression,
delights in one thing only: the attainment of divine blessings. It is
God who by nature bestows these blessings, but it is the recipient's
free will that safeguards them. Similarly, such a person knows only

one pain: the failure to attain these blessings. It is the devil who prompts this failure, but it is the person himself who makes it an actuality, because of his weakness of will with regard to the divine, and because he does not hold fast to the precious gift for which he has prayed. But if someone is not in the least concerned with anything in the visible world, and consequently is not overcome by any bodily affliction, then such a person truly and dispassionately forgives those who sin against him; for no one can rob him of the good to which he aspires and which by nature is unassailable.

A person of this kind makes himself a pattern of virtue for God, if it may be put in this way; for by saying 'Forgive us our debts as we forgive our debtors', he exhorts God, who is beyond imitation, to come and imitate him; and he begs God to treat him as he himself has treated his neighbours. For he wishes to be forgiven by God as he himself has forgiven the debts of those who have sinned against him; hence, just as God dispassionately forgives His creatures, so such a person must himself remain dispassionate in the face of what happens to him and forgive those who offend him. He must not allow the memory of things that afflict him to be stamped on his intellect lest he inwardly sunders human nature by separating himself from some other man, although he is a man himself. When a man's will is in union with the principle of nature in this way, God and nature are naturally reconciled; but, failing such a union, our nature remains self-divided in its will and cannot receive God's gift of Himself.

This surely is why God wishes us first to be reconciled with one another. He Himself has no need to learn from us how to be reconciled with sinners and to waive the penalty for a multitude of atrocious crimes; but He wishes to purify us of our passions and show us that the measure of grace conferred on those who are forgiven corresponds to their inward state. It is evident that when man's will is in union with the principle of nature, he is not in a state of rebellion against God. Since the principle of nature is a law both natural and divine, and there is nothing in it contrary to the Logos, when a man's will functions in accordance with this principle it accords with God in all things. Such a condition of the will is an inner state actively characterized by the grace of what is good by nature and hence productive of virtue.

This, then, is the inner state of the man who prays for gnostic bread. After him comes the man who, constrained by nature, seeks ordinary bread, but sufficient for one day only. He will attain the same inner state as the first when he has forgiven his debtors their debts, as he knows that he is by nature mortal. Moreover, by accepting the uncertainty of the future and waiting each day for what is provided by nature, he anticipates nature, choosing to become dead to the world and to comply with the text, 'For Thy sake we are put to death all the day long; we are regarded as sheep for slaughtering' (Ps. 44 : 22; Rom. 8 : 36). He makes his peace with all in order to be free from all the depravities of this present age when he departs to eternal life, and to receive from the Judge and Saviour of the universe a just recompense ior what he has done in this life. Both these kinds of men, therefore, need to exhibit a pure disposition towards those who have offended them. This is true in general; but it has particular reference to the concluding words of the prayer: 'And lead us not into temptation, but deliver us from what is evil' (Matt. 6 : 13).

Scripture reveals in these words that he who has not completely forgiven those who stumble, and has not brought his heart to God free from grievance and illuminated with the light of reconciliation with his neighbour, will fail to attain the grace of the blessings he has prayed for. Indeed, he will justly be handed over to temptation and to evil, so that, having retracted his judgments of other people, he may learn to purify himself of his own sins. Scripture here means by temptation the law of sin, of which the first man was free when he was created. And by 'what is evil' it means the devil, who has mixed this law of sin with human nature, deceitfully persuading man to transfer his soul's desire from what is permitted to what is forbidden, and to turn aside to the transgression of the divine commandment. The result of this is the loss of the incorruptibility which had been given by grace.

Alternatively, by temptation Scripture means the soul's predilection for the passions of the flesh; and by 'what is evil' the actual way in which this impassioned proclivity is satisfied. The just Judge does not liberate a man from either of these if he has not forgiven his debtors their debts. So long as he prays merely in words for liberation, God allows him to be defiled by the law of sin; and so long as his will is stubborn and raw, He abandons him to the domination of evil; for he has chosen the shameful passions (cf. Rom.

1 : 26), of which the devil is the sower, in preference to nature, of which God is the creator. God leaves him free to incline, if he so wishes, towards the passions of the flesh, and actually to satisfy that inclination. Valuing the insubstantial passions more highly than nature, in his concern for these passions he has become ignorant of the principle of nature. Had he followed that principle, he would have known what constitutes the law of nature and what the tyranny of the passions – a tyranny brought about, not by nature, but by deliberate choice. He would then have accepted the law of nature that is maintained through activities which are natural; and he would have expelled the tyranny of the passions completely from his will. He would have obeyed nature with his intelligence, for nature in itself is pure and undefiled, faultless, free from hatred and alienation, and he would have made his will once more a companion to nature, totally stripped of everything not bestowed by the principle of nature. In this way he would have eradicated all hatred for and all alienation from what is by nature akin to him, so that when saying this prayer he would be heard and would receive from God a double rather than a single grace: forgiveness for offences already committed, and protection and deliverance from those which lie in the future. For he would not be allowed to enter into temptation and to fall into the power of evil for one simple reason: his readiness to forgive his neighbours their debts.

Thus – to go back a little and comment briefly on what has been said – if we really wish to be delivered from evil and not to enter into temptation, we should trust in God and forgive our debtors their debts. 'For if you do not forgive people their sins', says Scripture, 'your heavenly Father will not forgive you yours' (Matt. 6 : 15). We should do this not only to receive forgiveness for the offences we have committed, but also to defeat the law of sin – because then we would not be allowed to undergo the experience of being tempted by it – and to trample on the originator of this law, the evil serpent from whom we entreat God to deliver us. For Christ, who has overcome the world (cf. John 16 : 33), is our leader. He arms us with the laws of the commandments, and by enabling us to reject the passions He unites us in pure love with nature itself. Being the bread of life, of wisdom, spiritual knowledge and righteousness, He arouses in us an insatiable desire for Himself. If we fulfil His Father's will He makes us co-worshippers with the angels, when in our conduct we imitate them as we should and so conform to the heavenly state. Then He leads us up still further on the supreme ascent of divine truth to the Father of lights, and makes us share in the divine nature (cf. 2 Pet. 1 : 4) through participation by grace in the Holy Spirit. By virtue of this participation we are called children of God and, cleansed from all stain, in a manner beyond circumscription, we all encircle Him who is the author of this grace and by nature the Son of the Father. From Him, through Him and in Him we have and always will have our being, our movement and our life (cf. Acts 17 : 28).

When we pray, let our aim be this mystery of deification, which shows us what we were once like and what the self-emptying of the only-begotten Son through the flesh has now made us; which shows us, that is, the depths to which we were dragged down by the weight of sin, and the heights to which we have been raised by His compassionate hand. In this way we shall come to have greater love for Him who has prepared this salvation for us with such wisdom. Bringing the prayer to fulfilment through our actions, we shall manifestly proclaim God as our true Father by grace. We shall show that the evil one, who is always tyrannically attempting to gain control of our nature through the shameful passions, is not the father of our life, and that we are not unwittingly exchanging life for death. For both God and the devil naturally impart their qualities to those who approach either of them: God bestows eternal life on those who love Him, while the devil, operating through temptations that are subject to our volition, causes the death of his followers.

For according to Scripture there are two kinds of temptation, one pleasurable, the other painful. One is the result of deliberate choice; the other is unsought. The first kind generates sin. We have been commanded by the Lord's teaching to pray not to fall into this, for He says, 'Lead us not into temptation' (Matt. 6 : 13), and 'Watch and pray so that you do not enter into temptation' (Matt. 26 : 41). The other kind of temptation punishes sin, chastising a sin-loving disposition with sufferings that are unsought. To the person who endures this kind of temptation – which comes in the form of a trial – and who in particular is not riveted to evil, the words of the apostle James may be applied: 'My brethren, regard it as a great joy whenever you find yourselves beset by many trials; because the testing of your faith produces patient endurance; this endurance shapes the character; and the character thus shaped should be brought to fruition' (cf. Jas. 1 : 2–4; Rom. 5 : 4). The evil one works his malice both through the temptation that is subject to our volition and through the trial that comes unsought. Where the first is concerned, by sowing the soul with bodily pleasures and by exciting it in this manner, he contrives to divert its desire away from divine love. Where the trial is concerned, in his wish to destroy nature through pain, he cunningly tries to force the soul, enervated by its sufferings, to calumniate and abuse the Creator.

But, knowing the wiles of the evil one, let us pray for deliverance from the temptations subject to our volition, so that we do not deflect our desire from divine love; and let us bravely endure the trials that come unsought, since they visit us with God's consent and by enduring them we show that we have not put nature before the Creator of nature. May all of us who call upon the name of our Lord Jesus Christ be delivered from the present delights and the future afflictions of the evil one by participating in the reality of the blessings held in store and already revealed to us in Christ our Lord Himself, who alone with the Father and the Holy Spirit is praised by all creation. Amen.

ST THALASSIOS THE LIBYAN

Introductory Note

St Thalassios, priest and abbot at a monastery in Libya, was a personal friend of St Maximos the Confessor, whose largest work, *To Thalassios: On Various Questions relating to Holy Scripture*, consists of answers to difficulties raised by St Thalassios. The *Two Hundred Texts on Theology* by St Maximos are also dedicated to St Thalassios, and in addition five of St Maximos' letters are addressed to him.[1] Twice St Maximos describes himself as a disciple of St Thalassios.[2] Perhaps this is no more than an expression of courtesy towards someone older than himself, and it may have been St Thalassios who was in reality the disciple:[3] but it is not impossible that St Maximos was indeed decisively influenced by him.[4]

The four centuries here translated are the only known work of the Libyan abbot. They display at many points the influence of Evagrios, but lay greater emphasis upon the integral unity of body and soul. St Thalassios, like St Maximos, sees self-love as the source of all the vices, and the two agree in emphasizing the supreme importance of love.

In the church calendar St Thalassios is commemorated on 20 May.

For the present translation the Greek text in the *Philokalia* has been compared with that in Migne, *P.G.* xci, 1427–70, which is often more reliable.

---

[1] *Letters* 9, 26, 40–42.
[2] *Letter* 9 (*P.G.* xci, 449A); *Opuscula* (*P.G.* xci, 29D).
[3] This is the view of M. Viller, 'Aux sources de la spiritualité de S. Maxime', *Revue d'ascétique et de mystique* xi (1930), pp. 262–3.
[4] See M.-Th. Disdier, 'Le témoignage spirituel de Thalassius le Lybien', *Etudes byzantines* ii (1944), pp. 79–118.

On Love, Self-control and Life in accordance with the Intellect
WRITTEN FOR PAUL THE PRESBYTER

First Century

1. An all-embracing and intense longing for God binds those who experience it both to God and to one another.

2. An intellect that has acquired spiritual love does not have thoughts unworthy of this love about anyone.

3. He who conceals his hypocrisy beneath feigned love blesses with his mouth but curses inwardly.

4. He who has acquired love endures calmly and patiently the injuries and sufferings that his enemies inflict on him.

5. Love alone harmoniously joins all created things with God and with each other.

6. A person who does not tolerate suspicion or disparagement of others possesses true love.

7. He who does nothing to dispel love is precious in the sight of God and among men.

8. True words from a pure conscience betoken unfeigned love.

9. If you tell your brother how someone else denigrates him you conceal your own envy in the guise of goodwill.

10. Worldly virtues promote human glory, spiritual virtues the glory of God.

11. Love and self-control purify the soul, while pure prayer illumines the intellect.

12. A strong man is one who repels evil through the practice of the virtues and with spiritual knowledge.

13. He who has acquired dispassion and spiritual knowledge has been granted God's grace.

14. If you wish to overcome impassioned thoughts, acquire self-control and love for your neighbour.

15. Guard yourself from hatred and dissipation, and you will not be impeded at the time of prayer.

16. Perfume is not to be found in mud, nor the fragrance of love in the soul of a rancorous man.

17. Firmly control anger and desire, and you will speedily rid yourself of evil thoughts.

18. Inner work destroys self-esteem, and if you despise no one you will repel pride.

19. The signs of self-esteem are hypocrisy and falsehood; those of pride are presumption and jealousy.

20. The true ruler is he who rules over himself and has subjected soul and body to the intelligence.

21. The genuineness of a friend is shown at a time of trial, if he shares the distress you suffer.

22. Seal your senses with stillness and sit in judgment upon the thoughts that attack your heart.

23. Respond without rancour to thoughts of dejection, but oppose thoughts of self-indulgence with enmity.

24. Stillness, prayer, love and self-control are a four-horsed chariot bearing the intellect to heaven.

25. Waste your body with fasting and vigils, and you will repulse the lethal thoughts of pleasure.

26. As wax melts before fire, so does an impure thought before the fear of God.

27. The intelligent soul is greatly harmed when it dallies with an ignoble passion.

28. Patiently endure the distressing and painful things that befall you, for through them God in His providence is purifying you.

29. Now that you have renounced the world and material things, renounce evil thoughts as well.

30. The proper activity of the intellect is to be attentive at every moment to the words of God.

31. It is God's task to administer the world and the soul's task to guide the body.

32. With what hope will we meet Christ if we are still enslaved to the pleasures of the flesh?

33. Hardship and distress, whether of our own choosing or providential, destroy sensual pleasure.

34. The amassing of money fuels the passions, for it leads to increasing indulgence in all kinds of sensual pleasure.

35. The failure to secure sensual pleasure breeds dejection, while sensual pleasure itself is linked with all the passions.

36. How God treats you depends upon how you treat your body.

37. God's justice is a fair requital for what we have done through our bodies.

38. Virtue and spiritual knowledge lead to immortality, their absence is the mother of death.

39. Distress that accords with God's will puts an end to sensual pleasure, and the destruction of such pleasure is the soul's resurrection.

40. Dispassion is a state in which the soul does not yield to any evil impulse; and it can be realized only through Christ's mercy.

41. Christ is the saviour of both soul and body, and the person who follows in His footsteps is freed from evil.

42. If you wish to attain salvation, renounce sensual pleasure and learn self-control, love and how to pray with concentration.

43. The mark of dispassion is true discrimination; for one who has attained the state of dispassion does all things with discrimination and according to measure and rule.

44. Our Lord and God is Jesus Christ, and the intellect that follows Him will not remain in darkness (cf. John 12 : 46).

45. Concentrate your intellect, keep watch over your thoughts, and fight with any of them that are impassioned.

46. There are three ways through which thoughts arise in you: through the senses, through the memory, and through the body's temperament. Of these the most irksome are those that come through the memory.

47. The man to whom wisdom has been given knows the inward essences of immaterial things and what is the origin and consummation of the world.

48. Do not neglect the practice of the virtues and your intellect will be illumined; for it is written, 'I will open for you invisible secret treasures' (Isa. 45 : 3. LXX).

49. The man freed from his passions has been granted God's grace; and if he has been found worthy of spiritual knowledge he has received great mercy.

50. The intellect freed from the passions becomes like light, unceasingly illumined by the contemplation of created beings.

51. Holy knowledge is the light of the soul; bereft of it, 'the fool walks in darkness' (Eccles. 2 : 14).

52. The man who lives in darkness is a fool, and the murk of ignorance awaits him.

53. The lover of Jesus will be freed from evil; the disciples of Jesus will behold true knowledge.

54. The intellect freed from the passions forms conceptual images that are also passion-free, whether the body is asleep or awake.

55. The completely purified intellect is cramped by created beings and longs to go beyond them.

56. Blessed is he who has attained boundless infinity, transcending all that is transitory.

57. He who stands in awe of God searches for the divine principles that God has implanted in creation; the lover of truth finds them.

58. Rightly motivated, the intellect will find the truth; but motivated by passion it will miss the mark.

59. As God is unknowable in His essence, so is He infinite in His majesty.

60. God, whose essence is without origin or consummation, is also impenetrable in His wisdom.

61. The sublime providence of the Creator preserves everything that is.

62. In his mercy 'the Lord supports all who fall, and raises up all who are bowed down' (Ps. 145 : 14).

63. Christ in His justice rewards the living, the dead, and every single action.

64. If you wish to be in control of your soul and body, forestall the passions by rooting out their causes.

65. Yoke the powers of the soul to the virtues and they will be freed from the tyranny of the passions.

66. Curb the impulses of desire by means of self-control and those of anger with spiritual love.

67. Stillness and prayer are the greatest weapons of virtue, for they purify the intellect and confer on it spiritual insight.

68. Only spiritual conversation is beneficial; it is better to preserve stillness than to indulge in any other kind.

69. Of the five kinds of conversation choose the first three, be sparing of the fourth, and avoid the fifth.

70. The person who is unaffected by the things of this world loves stillness; and he who loves no human thing loves all men.

71. The conscience is a true teacher, and whoever listens to it will not stumble.

72. Only those who have reached the extremes of virtue or of evil are not judged by their consciences.

73. Total dispassion renders our conceptual images passion-free: perfect spiritual knowledge brings us into the presence of Him who is utterly beyond knowledge.

74. Failure to obtain pleasure induces a culpable kind of distress: he who scorns pleasure is free from distress.

75. In general, distress arises from the privation of pleasure, whether it be of a worldly kind or relate to God.

76. Kingship, goodness and wisdom belong to God; he who attains them dwells in heaven.

77. The person who in his actions shows that he prefers his body to his soul, and the world to God, is a pathetic creature.

78. He who does not envy the spiritually mature and is merciful to the wicked has attained an equal love for all.

79. The person who applies the laws of virtue to soul and body is truly fit to rule.

80. Spiritual commerce consists in being detached equally from the pleasures and the pains of this life for the sake of the blessings held in store.

81. Love and self-control strengthen the soul; pure prayer and contemplation, the intellect.

82. When you hear something to your benefit, do not condemn the speaker; for if you do you will nullify his helpful admonition.

83. A depraved mind thinks evil thoughts and regards as defects the achievements of a neighbour.

84. Do not trust a thought that would judge your neighbour: for it is the man who is a storehouse of evil that thinks evil thoughts (cf. Matt. 12 : 35).

85. A good heart produces good thoughts: its thoughts correspond to what it stores up in itself.

86. Keep watch over your thoughts and shun evil. Then your intellect will not be darkened but, on the contrary, will see.

87. Bear in mind the Jews and watch yourself carefully; for the Jews were blinded with jealousy and took Beelzebub for their Lord and God (cf. Matt. 12 : 24).

88. An evil suspicion darkens the mind (cf. Ecclus. 3 : 24) and diverts attention from the path to what lies beside it.

89. To each virtue there is an opposing vice; hence the wicked take vices for virtues.

90. If the intellect dallies with pleasure or dejection, it rapidly succumbs to the passion of listlessness.

91. A pure conscience rouses the soul, but an impure thought debases it.

92. When the passions are active they cast out self-esteem; when they are expelled, they reintroduce it.

93. If you want to be free of all the passions, practise self-control, love and prayer.

94. An intellect that gives itself over to God in prayer frees the soul's passible aspect from the passions.

95. God, who gave being to all that is, at the same time united all things together in His providence.

96. Being Master, He became a servant, and so revealed to the world the depths of His providence.

97. God the Logos, in becoming incarnate while remaining unchanged, was united through His flesh with the whole of creation.

98. There is a new wonder in heaven and on earth: God is on earth and man is in heaven.

99. He united men and angels so as to bestow deification on all creation.

100. The knowledge of the holy and coessential Trinity is the sanctification and deification of men and angels.

101. Forgiveness of sins is betokened by freedom from the passions; he who has not yet been granted freedom from the passions has not yet received forgiveness.

Second Century

1. If you want to be freed from all the vices simultaneously, renounce self-love, the mother of evils.

2. The soul's health consists in dispassion and spiritual knowledge; no slave to sensual pleasure can attain it.

3. Patient self-control and long-suffering love dry up the pleasures of soul and body.

4. Self-love – that is, friendship for the body – is the source of evil in the soul.

5. The intelligence by nature submits to the Logos and disciplines and subjugates the body.

6. It is an insult to the intelligence to be subject to what lacks intelligence and to concern itself with shameful desires.

7. For the deiform soul to abandon the Creator and worship the body is an act of depravity.

8. You were commanded to keep the body as a servant, not to be unnaturally enslaved to its pleasures.

9. Break the bonds of your friendship for the body and give it only what is absolutely necessary.

10. Enclose your senses in the citadel of stillness so that they do not involve the intellect in their desires.

11. The greatest weapons of someone striving to lead a life of inward stillness are self-control, love, prayer and spiritual reading.

12. The intellect will go on looking for sensual pleasure until you subjugate the flesh and devote yourself to contemplation.

13. Let us strive to fulfil the commandments so that we may be freed from the passions; and let us struggle to grasp divine doctrine so that we may be found worthy of spiritual knowledge.

14. The soul's immortality resides in dispassion and spiritual knowledge; no slave to sensual pleasure can attain it.

15. Subjugate your body, strip it of sensual pleasures, and free it from base servitude.

16. Created free and called to freedom (cf. Gal. 5 : 13), do not be enslaved by impure passions.

17. The demons bind the intellect to sensible things by means of desire and fear, distress and sensual pleasure.

18. Fear of the Lord conquers desire, and distress that accords with God's will repulses sensual pleasure.

19. Desire for wisdom scorns fear, and the delight of spiritual knowledge expels distress.

20. The Scriptures contain four things: commandments, doctrines, threats and promises.

21. Self-control and strenuous effort curb desire; stillness and intense longing for God wither it.

22. Do not goad your brother with obscure words; you would not put up with similar treatment at his hands.

23. Long-suffering and readiness to forgive curb anger; love and compassion wither it.

24. If you have been given spiritual knowledge, you have been given noetic light; should you dishonour that light, you will see darkness.

25. The keeping of God's commandments generates dispassion; the soul's dispassion preserves spiritual knowledge.

26. Contemplate sensible objects noetically and you will raise your sense-perception above the realm of such objects.

27. Woman symbolizes the soul engaged in ascetic practice; through union with it the intellect begets the virtues.

28. The study of divine principles teaches knowledge of God to the person who lives in truth, longing and reverence.

29. What light is to those who see and to what is seen, God is to intellective beings and to what is intelligible.

30. The sensible firmament symbolizes the firmament of faith in which all the saints shine like stars.

31. Jerusalem is the celestial knowledge of immaterial beings; within it the vision of peace can be contemplated.

32. Do not neglect the practice of the virtues; if you do, your spiritual knowledge will decrease, and when famine occurs you will go down into Egypt (cf. Gen. 41 : 57; 46 : 6).

33. Spiritual freedom is release from the passions; without Christ's mercy you cannot attain it.

34. The promised land is the kingdom of heaven whose ambassadors are dispassion and spiritual knowledge.

35. The Egypt of the spirit is the darkness of the passions; no one goes down to Egypt unless he is overtaken by famine.

36. If you make a habit of listening to spiritual teaching, your intellect will escape from impure thoughts.

37. God alone is good and wise by nature; but if you exert yourself your intellect also becomes good and wise through participation.

38. Control your stomach, sleep, anger and tongue, and you will not 'dash your foot against a stone' (Ps. 91 : 12).

39. Strive to love every man equally, and you will simultaneously expel all the passions.

40. The contemplation of sensible things is shared by the intellect and the senses; but the knowledge of intelligible realities pertains to the intellect alone.

41. The intellect cannot devote itself to intelligible realities unless you sunder its attachment to the senses and to sensible things.

42. The senses have a natural attachment to sensible things, and when distracted by them distract the intellect.

43. Devote your senses to the service of the intellect and give them no time to be diverted from it.

44. When the intellect gives its attention to sensible objects, withdraw your senses from them, bringing the objects into direct contact with the intellect.

45. A sign that the intellect is devoted to the contemplation of intelligible realities is its disdain for all that agitates the senses.

46. When the intellect is engaged in the contemplation of intelligible realities, its delight in them is such that it can hardly be dragged away.

47. When the intellect is rich in the knowledge of the One, the senses will be completely under control.

48. Prevent your intellect from pursuing sensible things, so that it does not reap the fruits of pleasure and pain which they produce.

49. When the intellect devotes itself continually to divine realities, the soul's passible aspect becomes a godlike weapon.

50. The intellect cannot be transformed by spiritual knowledge unless it first detaches itself from the soul's passible aspect by means of its own virtues.

51. The intellect becomes a stranger to the things of this world when its attachment to the senses has been completely sundered.

52. The proper function of the soul's intelligent aspect is devotion to the knowledge of God, while that of its passible aspect is the pursuit of self-control and love.

53. The intellect cannot dally with any sensible object unless it entertains at least some kind of passionate feeling for it.

54. The intellect is perfect when transformed by spiritual knowledge; the soul is perfect when permeated by the virtues.

55. The intellect's attachment to the senses enslaves it to bodily pleasure.

56. The intellect falls from the realm of spiritual knowledge when the soul's passible aspect abandons its own virtues.

57. Although we have received the power to become the children of God (cf. John 1 : 12), we do not actually attain this sonship unless we strip ourselves of the passions.

58. Let no one think that he has actually become a child of God if he has not yet acquired divine qualities.

59. We are sons of God or of Satan according to whether we conform to goodness or to evil.

60. A wise man is one who pays attention to himself and is quick to separate himself from all defilement.

61. An obdurate soul does not notice when it is whipped and so is unaware of its benefactor.

62. A soiled garment excludes one from the divine wedding feast and makes one a communicant of outer darkness (cf. Matt. 22 : 12–13).

63. He who fears God will pay careful attention to his soul and will free himself from communion with evil.

64. If you abandon God and are a slave to the passions you cannot reap God's mercy.

65. Even if we do not wish to believe Him, it was Jesus who said that no one can serve two masters (cf. Matt. 6 : 24).

66. A soul defiled by the passions becomes obdurate: it has to undergo knife and cautery before it recovers its faith.

67. Fearful afflictions await the hard of heart, for without great sufferings they cannot become pliable and responsive.

68. A wise man pays careful attention to himself, and by freely choosing to suffer escapes the suffering that comes unsought.

69. Concern for one's soul means hardship and humility, for through these God forgives us all our sins.

70. Just as desire and rage multiply our sins, so self-control and humility erase them.

71. Distress that accords with God's will shatters the heart; it is produced by the fear of punishment.

72. Such distress purifies the heart, expelling from it the defilements of sensual pleasure.

'73. Patient endurance is the soul's struggle for virtue; where there is struggle for virtue, self-indulgence is banished.

74. All sin is due to sensual pleasure, all forgiveness to hardship and distress.

75. If you are not willing to repent through freely choosing to suffer, unsought sufferings will providentially be imposed on you.

76. Christ is the Saviour of the whole world, and has conferred on men the gift of repentance so that they may be saved.

77. Repentance engenders the keeping of the commandments, and this in its turn purifies the soul.

78. The purification of the soul is release from the passions, and release from the passions gives birth to love.

79. A pure soul is one that loves God, and a pure intellect is one divorced from ignorance.

80. Struggle until death to fulfil the commandments: purified through them, you will enter into life.

81. Make the body serve the commandments, keeping it so far as possible free from sickness and sensual pleasure.

82. The flesh revolts when prayer, frugality and blessed stillness are neglected.

83. Blessed stillness gives birth to blessed children: self-control, love and pure prayer.

84. Spiritual reading and prayer purify the intellect, while love and self-control purify the soul's passible aspect.

85. Always keep the same measure of self-control; otherwise through irregularity you will go from one extreme to another.

86. If you lay down rules for yourself, do not disobey yourself; for he who cheats himself is self-deluded.

87. The soul filled with passion lies in noetic darkness, for in such a soul the sun of righteousness has set.

88. A son of God is a person who through wisdom, power and righteousness has become like God.

89. The soul's disease is an evil disposition, while its death is sin put into action.

90. Spiritual poverty is complete dispassion; when the intellect has reached this state it abandons all worldly things.

91. Preserve the harmony of the soul's virtues, and it will bring forth the fruit of righteousness.

92. The contemplation of noetic realities is said to be bodiless because it is completely free of matter and form.

93. Just as the four elements are a combination of matter and form, so the bodies that derive from them are likewise made up of matter and form.

94. When in His compassion for man the Logos became flesh, He changed neither what He was nor what He became.

95. Just as we speak of the one Christ as being 'from Godhead' and 'from manhood' and 'in Godhead' and 'in manhood', so we speak of Him as being 'from two natures' and 'in two natures'.

96. We confess that in Christ there is a single hypostasis, or subject, in two indivisibly united natures.

97. We glorify the one indivisible hypostasis of Christ and confess the union without confusion of the two natures.

98. We venerate the one essence of the Divinity in three Persons, or hypostases, and confess the coessential Trinity.

99. Particular to the three Persons are fatherhood, sonship and procession. Common to them are essence, nature, divinity and goodness.

Third Century

1. Think good thoughts about what is good by nature, and think well of every man.

2. On the day of judgment we shall be asked by God to answer for our words, acts and thoughts.

3. Whether we think, speak or act in a good or an evil manner depends upon whether we cleave inwardly to virtue or to vice.

4. An intellect dominated by the passions thinks base thoughts; words and actions bring these thoughts into the open.

5. An evil thought is preceded by passion. The passion is caused by the senses, but the misuse of the senses is clearly the fault of the intellect.

6. Shut out the senses, fight against prepossession and, with the commandments as your weapons, destroy the passions.

7. Inveterate wickedness requires long practice of the virtues; for an engrained habit is not easily uprooted.

8. The forceful practice of self-control and love, patience and stillness, will destroy the passions hidden within us.

9. Impel your intellect continually to prayer and you will destroy the evil thoughts that beset your heart.

10. Ascetic practice requires long and patient endurance: assiduous struggle will slowly root out self-indulgence.

11. You will not find the rigours of the ascetic life hard to bear if you do all things with measure and by rule.

12. Maintain a regular level of ascetic practice and do not break your rule unless forced to do so.

13. Just as love and self-control destroy evil thoughts, so contemplation and prayer destroy all self-exaltation.

14. Ascetic struggle – fasting, vigils, patience, forbearance – produces a clear conscience.

15. He who patiently endures unsought trials becomes humble, full of hope and spiritually mature.

16. Patient endurance is a continuous effort for the soul; it is born of suffering freely chosen and of trials that come unsought.

17. Perseverance in the face of adversity dissolves evil, while unremitting patience destroys it utterly.

18. The experience of suffering afflicts the senses; distress annuls sensual pleasure.

19. There are four prevalent passions which God in His wisdom sets one against the other.

20. Distress checks sensual pleasure; the fear of punishment withers desire.

21. The wise intellect tests the soul and trains the body with all kinds of ascetic practice.

22. Prove yourself a monk, not outwardly, but inwardly, by freeing yourself from the passions.

23. The first renunciation is that of material things, the second that of the passions, the third that of ignorance.

24. It is not difficult to get rid of material things if you so desire; but only with great effort will you be able to get rid of thoughts about them.

25. Control desire and you will dominate anger; for desire gives rise to anger.

26. We may have freed ourselves from impassioned thoughts; but have we yet been granted pure and immaterial prayer?

27. Great is the intellect that is freed from the passions, has separated itself from created beings, and lives in God.

28. The person advancing in the spiritual life studies three things: the commandments, doctrine, and faith in the Holy Trinity.

29. An intellect stripped of the passions has its attention focused on three things: passion-free conceptual images, the contemplation of created beings, and its own light.

30. The foulest passions are hidden within our souls; they are brought to light only when we scrutinize our actions.

31. Sometimes the intellect that has attained a partial dispassion will remain undisturbed; but this is because, in the absence of the things that provoke it, it is not put to the test.

32. As has been said,[1] our passions are roused through these

---

[1] cf. *Century* i, 46.

three things: the memory, the body's temperament, and the senses.

33. The intellect that has shut out the senses, and has achieved a balance in the body's temperament, has to fight only against its memories.

34. It is when self-control and spiritual love are missing that the passions are roused by the senses.

35. Moderate fasting, vigils and psalmody are natural means for achieving a balance in the body's temperament.

36. Three things upset the balance of the body's temperament: lack of restraint in our diet, a change in the weather, and the touch of the demonic powers.

37. Our memories can be stripped of passion through prayer, spiritual reading, self-control and love.

38. First shut out the senses through the practice of stillness and then fight against your memories by cultivating the virtues.

39. Mental evil resides in the misuse of conceptual images; active sin consists in the misuse of material things.

40. To misuse conceptual images and material things is to use them in a profane and improper manner.

41. Reprehensible passions chain the intellect, binding it to sensible objects.

42. The person who is not affected either by material things, or by his memories of them, has attained perfect dispassion.

43. A saint-like soul helps its neighbour and when ill-treated by him is patient, enduring what it suffers at his hands.

44. Malicious thoughts are a fully existent form of evil: if you do not get rid of them you will not become a disciple of spiritual knowledge.

45. The person who listens to Christ fills himself with light; and if he imitates Christ, he reclaims himself.

46. Rancour is the soul's leprosy. The soul contracts it as the result of disgrace or punishment, or because of suspicious thoughts.

47. The Lord blinds the intellect that is jealous and resentful of its neighbour's blessings.

48. The tongue of a back-biting soul is three-pronged: it injures the speaker, the listener and sometimes the person being maligned.

49. He who prays for those who offend him is without rancour; and the unstinting giver is set free from it.

50. Hatred for one's neighbour is the soul's death: the back-biting soul both suffers and inflicts such death.

51. Listlessness is an apathy of soul; and a soul becomes apathetic when sick with self-indulgence.

52. He who loves Jesus trains himself in suffering: perseverance in suffering dispels listlessness.

53. The soul is strengthened through ascetic suffering, and dispels listlessness by doing all things according to measure.

54. Control of the belly withers desire and keeps the intellect free from lecherous thoughts.

55. An intellect in control of itself is the temple of the Holy Spirit, but that of a glutton is like a nest of crows.

56. A surfeit of foods breeds desire; a deficiency sweetens even plain bread.

57. If you share secretly in the joy of someone you envy, you will be freed from your jealousy; and you will also be freed from your jealousy if you keep silent about the person you envy.

58. Shun whoever lives dissolutely, even if many hold him in high esteem.

59. Make a friend of the man who works hard and you will find protection.

60. The dissolute man is sold to many masters and lives his life in whatever way they lead him.

61. Such a man will treat you as a friend in the time of peace, but in the time of trial he will fight you as an enemy.

62. When his passions are quiescent, he will lay down his life for you; when they are roused, he will take it back again.

63. A dissolute soul is as full of impure passions as waste land is full of thistles.

64. A wise intellect restrains the soul, keeps the body in subjection, and makes the passions its servants.

65. Our actions disclose what goes on within us, just as its fruit makes known a tree otherwise unknown to us.

66. The hypocrite, like the false prophet, is betrayed by his words and actions.

67. An intellect that does not use its intelligence fails to chastise the soul, and so prevents it from acquiring love and self-control.

68. The cause of depraved thoughts is an evil disposition made up of pride and boastfulness.

69. Pride and boastfulness are characterized by hypocrisy, guile, trickery, pretence and, worst of all, falsity.

70. These characteristics are aided and abetted by envy, strife, anger, resentment and rancour.

71. Such is the state of those who live dissolutely, and such are the treasures hidden in my heart (cf. Matt. 12 : 35).

72. Hardship and humility save the soul and free it from all the passions.

73. A helpful word indicates an understanding mind; a good action reveals a saint-like soul.

74. An illumined intellect brings forth words of wisdom; a pure soul cultivates godlike thoughts.

75. The thoughts of a wise man are devoted to wisdom, and his words enlighten those who hear them.

76. A virtuous soul cultivates good thoughts; a soul full of evil breeds thoughts of depravity.

77. An impassioned soul produces evil thoughts: it is a fund of evil.

78. The virtues possess a fund of goodness from which the holy intellect brings forth blessings.

79. The intellect energized by divine love cultivates good thoughts about God; but when impelled by self-love it produces diabolic thoughts.

80. When the intellect is moved by love for its neighbour, it always thinks well of him; but when it is under diabolic influence it entertains evil thoughts about him.

81. The virtues generate good thoughts; the commandments lead us to the virtues; the practice of the virtues depends on our own will and resolution.

82. As virtue and evil come and go, they dispose the soul either to goodness or to malice, prompting in it the corresponding thoughts.

83. Evil begets evil thoughts; disobedience begets evil; the deceit of the senses gives rise to disobedience; and this deceit derives from the intellect's neglect of its own salvation.

84. In the case of those advancing on the spiritual way, their attitude to good and evil is easily changed; but in those who have achieved perfection it is hard to shift.

85. The soul's strength is its firm state of virtue; on reaching

such a state one may say with the invincible apostle Paul: 'What can separate us from the love of Christ?' (Rom. 8 : 35).

86. Self-love precedes all the passions, while last of all comes pride.

87. The three most common forms of desire have their origin in the passion of self-love.

88. These three forms are gluttony, self-esteem and avarice. All other impassioned thoughts follow in their wake, though they do not all follow each of them.

89. The thought of unchastity follows that of gluttony; of pride, that of self-esteem. The others all follow the three most common forms.

90. Thus thoughts of resentment, anger, rancour, envy, listlessness and the rest all follow these three most common forms.

A Prayer

91. Christ, Master of all, free us from all these destructive passions and the thoughts born of them.

92. For Thy sake we came into being, so that we might delight in the paradise which Thou hast planted and in which Thou hast placed us.

93. We brought our present disgrace upon ourselves, preferring destruction to the delights of blessedness.

94. We have paid for this, for we have exchanged eternal life for death.

95. O Master, as once Thou hast looked on us, look on us now; as Thou becamest man, save all of us.

96. For Thou camest to save us who were lost. Do not exclude us from the company of those who are being saved.

97. Raise up our souls and save our bodies, cleansing us from all impurity.

98. Break the fetters of the passions that constrain us, as once Thou hast broken the ranks of the impure demons.

99. Free us from their tyranny, so that we may worship Thee alone, the eternal light,

100. Having risen from the dead and dancing with the angels in the blessed, eternal and indissoluble dance. Amen.

Fourth Century

1. The person who has broken the bonds of his intellect's fawning friendship for the flesh has slain the body's evil acts through the life-giving Spirit.

2. Do not think that the intellect is free from its attachment to the flesh so long as it is still troubled by the activities that pertain to the flesh.

3. Just as the senses and sensible objects pertain to the flesh, so the intellect and intelligible realities pertain to the soul.

4. Withdraw your soul from the perception of sense objects, and the intellect will find itself in God and in the realm of intelligible realities.

5. Intelligible natures that can be grasped only by the intellect belong to the realm of divinity, while the senses and sense objects have been created for the service of the intellect.

6. Use the senses and sense objects as a means to spiritual contemplation but, on the contrary, do not use what provokes the desire of the flesh as food for the senses.

7. You have been commanded to mortify the acts of the body (cf. Col. 3 : 5), so that when the soul has been made dead to pleasure you may bring it back to life through your ascetic labours.

8. Be ruled by God and rule over your senses; and, being on a higher level, do not give authority to what is inferior to you.

9. God, who is eternal, limitless and infinite, has promised eternal, limitless and inexpressible blessings to those who obey him.

10. The intellect's role is to live in God and to meditate on Him, His providence and His awesome judgments.

11. You have the power to incline either upwards or downwards: choose what is superior and you will bring what is inferior into subjection.

12. Because they are the works of God, who is Himself good, the senses and sensible objects are good; but they cannot in any way be compared with the intellect and with intelligible realities.

13. The Lord has created intelligent and noetic beings with a capacity to receive the Spirit and to attain knowledge of Himself; He has brought into existence the senses and sense objects to serve such beings.

14. Just as it is absurd to subject a good master to a worthless servant, so it is absurd to subject the deiform intellect to the corruptible body.

15. An intellect that does not control the senses will fall into evil because of them: deceived by the pleasure of sense objects, it depraves itself.

16. While controlling your senses, control your memory as well; for when its prepossessions are roused through the senses they stir up the passions.

17. Keep your body under control, and pray constantly; in this way you will soon be free from the thoughts that arise from your prepossessions.

18. Devote yourself ceaselessly to the words of God: application to them destroys the passions.

19. Spiritual reading, vigils, prayer and psalmody prevent the intellect from being deluded by the passions.

20. Just as spring stimulates the growth of plants, so dispassion stimulates the intellect to attain a spiritual knowledge of created beings.

21. Keep the commandments, and you will find peace; love God, and you will attain spiritual knowledge.

22. You have been sentenced to eat the bread of spiritual knowledge with toil, struggle and the sweat of your face (cf. Gen. 3 : 19).

23. Negligence led our first forefather to transgress, and instead of enjoying paradise he was condemned to die (cf. Gen. 3 : 22).

24. You, too, should keep control of Eve; and you should watch out for the serpent, lest she is deceived by it and gives you the fruit of the tree (cf. Gen. 3 : 1–5).

25. As by nature the soul gives life to the body, so virtue and spiritual knowledge give life to the soul.

26. A conceited intellect is a waterless cloud (cf. Jude, verse 12) carried along by the winds of self-esteem and pride.

27. In controlling your self-esteem, beware of unchastity, so that you do not shun acclaim only to fall into dishonour.

28. Eschewing self-esteem, look to God, and beware lest you become presumptuous or unchaste.

29. A sign of self-esteem is an ostentatious manner; of pride, anger and scorn of others.

30. In cutting out gluttony, beware lest you seek the esteem of others, making a display of the pallor of your face.

31. To fast well is to enjoy simple food in small amounts and to shun other people's esteem.

32. After fasting until late in the day, do not eat your fill, lest in so doing you build up again what you have pulled down (cf. Gal. 2 : 18).

33. If you do not drink wine, do not glut yourself with water either; for if you do you will be providing yourself with the same fuel for unchastity.

34. Pride deprives us of God's help, making us over-reliant on ourselves and arrogant towards other people.

35. There are two remedies against pride; and if you do not avail yourself of them you will find yourself given a third, far more painful to bear.

36. Prayer with tears, and having no scorn for anyone, destroy pride; but so do chastisements inflicted against our will.

37. Chastisement through the trials imposed on us is a spiritual rod, teaching us humility when in our foolishness we think too much of ourselves.

38. The intellect's task is to reject any thought that secretly vilifies a fellow being.

39. Just as the gardener who does not weed his garden chokes his vegetables, so the intellect that does not purify its thoughts is wasting its efforts.

40. A wise man is one who accepts advice, especially that of a spiritual father counselling him in accordance with the will of God.

41. A man deadened by the passions is impervious to advice and will not accept any spiritual correction.

42. He who does not accept advice will never go by the straight path, but will always find himself among cliffs and gorges.

43. The truly monk-like intellect is one that has renounced the senses and cannot stand even the thought of sensual pleasure.

44. The truly physician-like intellect is one that first heals itself and then heals others of the diseases of which it has been cured.

45. Search after virtue and do not be deprived of it, lest you live sordidly and die a wretched death.

46. Our Lord Jesus has given light to all men, but those who do not trust in Him bring darkness upon themselves.

47. Do not think that the loss of virtue is a minor matter, for it was through such a loss that death came into the world.

48. Obedience to the commandments is the resurrection of the dead, for by nature life follows upon virtue.

49. When the intellect was deadened by the breaking of the commandment, the death of the body was a necessary consequence.

50. Just as Adam through transgressing became subject to death, so the Saviour through obedience put death to death.

51. Put evil to death so that you will not rise up dead and thus pass from a minor to a major death.

52. Because of Adam's transgression the Saviour became man, so that by nullifying the sentence passed on us He might resurrect all of us.

53. He who has put his passions to death and overcome ignorance goes from life to life.

54. Search the Scriptures and you will find the commandments; do what they say and you will be freed from your passions.

55. Obedience to a commandment purifies the soul, and purification of the soul leads to its participation in light.

56. The tree of life is the knowledge of God; when, being purified, you share in that knowledge you attain immortality.

57. The first step in the practice of the virtues is faith in Christ; its consummation, the love of Christ.

58. Jesus is the Christ, our Lord and our God, who grants us faith in Him so that we may live.

59. He manifested Himself to us in soul, body and divinity so that, as God, He could deliver soul and body from death.

60. Let us acquire faith so that we may attain love; for love gives birth to the illumination of spiritual knowledge.

61. The acquisition of faith leads successively to fear of God, restraint from sensual pleasure, the patient endurance of suffering, hope in God, dispassion and love.

62. Genuine love gives birth to the spiritual knowledge of the

created world. This is succeeded by the desire of all desires: the grace of theology.

63. When the intellect controls the passions it is doubtless out of fear that it does so, for it believes in God's threats and promises.

64. When you have been given faith, self-control is demanded from you; when self-control has become habitual, it gives birth to patient endurance, a disposition that gladly accepts suffering.

65. The sign of patient endurance is delight in suffering; and the intellect, trusting in this patient endurance, hopes to attain what is promised and to escape what is threatened.

66. The expectation of the blessings held in store links the intellect with what it expects. When it continually meditates on these blessings, it forgets the things of this world.

67. He who has tasted the things for which he hopes will spurn the things of this world: all his longing will be spent on what he hopes for.

68. It is God who has promised the blessings held in store; and the self-disciplined person who has faith in God longs for what is held in store as though it were present.

69. The sign that the intellect dwells among the blessings for which it hopes is its total oblivion to worldly things and the growth in its knowledge of what is held in store.

70. The dispassion taught by the God of truth is a noble quality; through it He fulfils the aspirations of the devout soul.

71. The blessings that lie in store for the inheritors of the promise are beyond eternity, before all ages, and transcend both intellect and thought.

72. Let us regulate our lives according to the rules of true faith, so that we do not deviate into the passions and thus fail to attain what we hope for.

73. Jesus is the Christ, one of the Holy Trinity. You are destined to be His heir.

74. If God has taught you a spiritual knowledge of created beings, you will not doubt the words of Scripture concerning the blessings held in store.

75. According to the degree to which the intellect is stripped of the passions, the Holy Spirit initiates the intellect into the mysteries of the age to be.

76. The more the intellect is purified, the more the soul is granted spiritual knowledge of divine principles.

77. He who has disciplined his body and dwells in a state of spiritual knowledge finds that through this knowledge he is purified still further.

78. The intellect that begins to pursue divine wisdom starts with faith; it then passes through the intermediate stages until it arrives once more at faith, though this time of the highest type.

79. Initially our search for wisdom is prompted by fear; but as we attain our goal we are led forward by love.

80. The intellect that begins its search for divine wisdom with simple faith will eventually attain a theology that transcends the intellect and that is characterized by unremitting faith of the highest type and the contemplation of the invisible.

81. The divine principles contemplated by the saints do not reveal God's essence, but the qualities that appertain to Him.

82. Of the principles that appertain to God, some are to be understood affirmatively and others negatively.

83. For example, being, divinity, goodness and whatever else we attribute to God in a positive manner, or cataphatically, are to be understood affirmatively. Unoriginateness, infinity, indefinableness and so on are to be understood in a negative manner, or apophatically.

84. Since the inmost divinity of the Holy Trinity is a single essence transcending intellect and thought, what has just been said, and other similar statements, refer to the qualities that appertain to the essence, and not to the essence itself.

85. Just as we speak of the single Godhead of the Holy Trinity, so we glorify the three Persons, or hypostases, of the one Godhead.

86. The affirmative and negative qualities mentioned above are to be understood as common to the holy and coessential Trinity, and not as indicating the individual characteristics of the three Persons. Most of these individual characteristics are to be understood affirmatively, although some are to be understood negatively.

87. The individual characteristics of the divine Persons are fatherhood, sonship, procession, and whatever else can be said of them individually.

88. A person may be defined as an essence with individual

characteristics. Thus each person possesses both what is common to the essence and what belongs individually to the person.

89. Of the qualities common to the Holy Trinity, those predicated of it negatively apply more aptly than those ascribed to it positively. But this is not the case with the individual characteristics. As we noted, some of these are expressed affirmatively and others negatively: 'begottenness' and 'unbegottenness' respectively are examples of both. Thus 'unbegottenness' differs from 'begottenness' only as regards its meaning, not as regards its aptness: the first term expresses the fact that the Father was not begotten and the second that the Son was begotten.

90. Verbs and nouns are used, as we said, to indicate the principles that in contemplation we apprehend as appertaining to the essence of the Holy Trinity, but do not refer to the essence itself. For the principles of the essence cannot be known by the intellect or expressed in words: they are known only to the Holy Trinity.

91. Just as the single essence of the Godhead is said to exist in three Persons, so the Holy Trinity is confessed to have one essence.

92. We regard the Father as unoriginate and as the source: as unoriginate because He is unbegotten, and as the source because He is the begetter of the Son and the sender forth of the Holy Spirit, both of whom are by essence from Him and in Him from all eternity.

93. Paradoxically, the One moves from itself into the Three and yet remains One, while the Three return to the One and yet remain Three.

94. Again, the Son and the Spirit are regarded as not unoriginate, and yet as from all eternity. They are not unoriginate because the Father is their origin and source; but They are eternal in that They coexist with the Father, the one begotten by Him and the other proceeding from Him from all eternity.

95. The single divinity of the Trinity is undivided and the three Persons of the one divinity are unconfused.

96. The individual characteristics of the Father are described as unoriginateness and unbegottenness; of the Son, as co-presence in the source and as being begotten by it; and of the Holy Spirit, as co-presence in the source and as proceeding from it. The origin of the Son and Holy Spirit is not to be regarded as temporal: how could it be? On the contrary, the term 'origin' indicates the source from

which Their existence is eternally derived, as light from the sun. For They originate from that source according to Their essence, although They are in no sense inferior or subsequent to it.

97. Each Person preserves His individual characteristics immutably and irremovably; and the common nature of Their essence, that is to say, Their divinity, is indivisible.

98. We confess Unity in Trinity and Trinity in Unity, divided but without division and united but with distinctions.

99. The Father is the sole origin of all things. He is the origin of the Son and the Spirit as Their begetter and source, coeternal, coinfinite, limitless, coessential and undivided. He is the origin of created things, as the one who produces, provides for, and judges them through the Son in the Holy Spirit. 'For all things are from Him and through Him, and have Him as their goal. To Him be glory throughout the ages. Amen' (Rom. 11 : 36).

100. Again, the Son and the Holy Spirit are said to be coeternal with the Father, but not co-unoriginate with Him. They are coeternal in that They coexist with the Father from eternity; but They are not co-unoriginate in that They are not without source: as has already been said, They are derived from Him as the light from the sun, even though They are not inferior or subsequent to Him. They are also said to be unoriginate in the sense that They do not have an origin in time. If this were not the case, They would be thought of as subject to time, whereas it is from Them that time itself derives. Thus They are unoriginate not with regard to Their source, but with regard to time. For They exist prior to, and transcend, all time and all the ages; and it is from Them that all time and all the ages are derived, together with everything that is in time and in the ages. This is because They are, as we said, coeternal with the Father: to Him, with Them, be glory and power through all the ages. Amen.

ST JOHN OF DAMASKOS

Introductory Note

On the Virtues and Vices, a concise and clear summary of standard ascetic teaching, is ascribed by St Nikodimos to St John of Damaskos (*c.* 675–*c.* 749), author of the celebrated doctrinal compendium *On the Orthodox Faith*, but it also appears among the works attributed to St Athanasios of Alexandria (*c.* 296–373)[1] and St Ephrem the Syrian (*c.* 306–373).[2] Probably it is not by any of these three, and its date and provenance remain hard to determine. For his analysis of temptation the author is clearly indebted to St Mark the Ascetic (? early fifth century) – whom, indeed, he cites by name in another connection – and probably also to St John Klimakos (? seventh century). He adopts Evagrios' teaching on the three aspects of the soul and the eight evil thoughts, and his remarks on self-love suggest an acquaintance with the writings of St Maximos. It has been argued that the beginning and the end of the treatise, on the virtues of the soul and the body, are of Syrian origin – which would account for the ascription to Ephrem – and are possibly taken from John the Solitary (*c.* 500).[3] St Nikodimos praises the treatise as 'a touchstone, discriminating with exactness between the tried and tested gold of the virtues and the copper alloy of the vices'.

[1] *P.G.* xxviii, 1396–408.
[2] *Opera*, vol. iii (Rome, 1746), pp. 425–35.
[3] I. Hausherr, *Jean le Solitaire: Dialogue sur l'âme et les passions des hommes* (*Orientalia Christiana Analecta* 120: Rome, 1939), p. 13.

On the Virtues and the Vices

Man is a twofold being comprising soul and body, and has two orders of senses and two corresponding orders of virtues. The soul has five senses and the body five. The senses of the soul, which are also called the faculties, are intellect, reason, opinion, fantasy and sense-perception. The senses of the body are sight, smell, hearing, taste and touch. The virtues which belong to these senses are twofold and so, too, are the vices. Everyone should know how many virtues there are of the soul and how many of the body, and what kind of passions belong to the soul and what kind to the body. The virtues which we ascribe to the soul are primarily the four cardinal virtues: courage, moral judgment, self-restraint and justice. These give birth to the other virtues of the soul: faith, hope, love, prayer, humility, gentleness, long-suffering, forbearance, kindness, freedom from anger, knowledge of God, cheerfulness, simplicity, calmness, sincerity, freedom from vanity, freedom from pride, absence of envy, honesty, freedom from avarice, compassion, mercifulness, generosity, fearlessness, freedom from dejection, deep compunction, modesty, reverence, desire for the blessings held in store, longing for the kingdom of God, and aspiration for divine sonship.

Besides these there are the bodily virtues or, rather, the tools or instruments of virtue. When used with understanding, in accordance with God's will, and without the least hypocrisy or desire to win men's esteem, they make it possible to advance in humility and dispassion. They are self-control, fasting, hunger, thirst, staying awake, keeping all-night vigils, constant kneeling, not washing, the wearing of a single garment, eating dry food, eating slowly, drinking nothing but water, sleeping on the ground, poverty, total shedding of possessions, austerity, disregard of personal appearance, unselfishness, solitude, preserving stillness, not going out, enduring scarcity, being self-supporting, silence, working with your own hands, and every kind of hardship and physical asceticism, with other similar practices. When the body is strong and disturbed by carnal passions, they are all indispensable and extremely beneficial. When the body is weak, however, and with the help of God has overcome these passions, such practices are not as vital as holy humility and thanksgiving, which suffices for everything.

Something should also be said about the vices or the passions of the soul and the body. The passions of the soul are forgetfulness, laziness and ignorance. When the soul's eye, the intellect, has been darkened by these three, the soul is dominated by all the other passions. These are impiety, false teaching or every kind of heresy, blasphemy, wrath, anger, bitterness, irritability, inhumanity, rancour, back-biting, censoriousness, senseless dejection, fear, cowardice, quarrelsomeness, jealousy, envy, self-esteem, pride, hypocrisy, falsehood, unbelief, greed, love of material things, attachment to worldly concerns, listlessness, faint-heartedness, ingratitude, grumbling, vanity, conceit, pomposity, boastfulness, love of power, love of popularity, deceit, shamelessness, insensibility, flattery, treachery, pretence, indecision, assent to sins arising from the soul's passible aspect and dwelling on them continuously, wandering thoughts, self-love, the mother of vices, avarice, the root of all evil (cf. 1 Tim. 6 : 10) and, finally, malice and guile.

The passions of the body are gluttony, greed, over-indulgence, drunkenness, eating in secret, general softness of living, unchastity, adultery, licentiousness, uncleanness, incest, pederasty, bestiality, impure desires and every passion which is foul and unnatural, theft, sacrilege, robbery, murder, every kind of physical luxury and gratification of the whims of the flesh (especially when the body is in good health), consulting oracles, casting spells, watching for omens and portents, self-adornment, ostentation, foolish display, use of cosmetics, painting the face, wasting time, day-dreaming, trickery, impassioned misuse of the pleasures of this world, and a life of bodily ease, which by coarsening the intellect makes it cloddish and brute-like and never lets it raise itself towards God and the practice of the virtues.

The roots or primary causes of all these passions are love of sensual pleasure, love of praise and love of material wealth. Every evil has its origin in these. As Mark, wisest of the ascetics, says, a man cannot commit a single sin unless the three powerful giants, forgetfulness, laziness and ignorance, first overpower him and enslave him.[1] And these giants are the offspring of sensual pleasure, luxury, love of men's esteem, and distraction. The primary cause and vile mother of them all is self-love, which is a senseless love of one's body and an impassioned attachment to it. A dispersed and dissipated intellect given to frivolous talk and foul language produces many vices and sins. Laughter and loose, immodest speech also lead to sin.

Moreover, impassioned love of sensual pleasure takes a great variety of forms; for when the soul slackens its vigilance and is no longer strengthened by the fear of God, when it ceases to apply itself in its love for Christ to the practice of the virtues, the pleasures which deceive it are many. For countless pleasures surge to and fro attracting the eyes of the soul: pleasures of the body, of material things, of over-indulgence, of praise, laziness, anger, of power, avarice and greed. These pleasures have a glittering and attractive appearance which, though deceptive, readily seduces those who do not have any great love for virtue and are not willing to endure hardship for its sake. Every attachment to material things produces pleasure and delight in the man subject to such attachment, thus showing how useless and harmful is the soul's desiring aspect when governed by passion. For when the man subject to this aspect of the soul is deprived of what he is wanting he is overcome by wrath, anger, resentment and rancour. And if through such senseless attachment some small habit gains the upper hand, the man to whom this happens is imperceptibly and irremediably held fast by the pleasure hidden in the attachment until he breaks free of it.

As we have said already, sensual concupiscent pleasure takes a great many forms. It finds satisfaction not only in unchastity and other bodily indulgences but also in every other passion. For self-restraint does not consist only in abstaining from unchastity and sexual pleasure; it also means renouncing all the other forms of indulgence too. Hence a man addicted to material wealth, avarice or greed is also licentious and dissolute. For just as the sensual man loves the pleasures of the body, so the avaricious man lusts for the pleasures of material possessions. Indeed, the latter is the more dissolute in that the force driving him is by nature less compelling. For

[1] See St Mark the Ascetic, *Letter to Nicolas the Solitary* (*The Philokalia*, vol. i, pp. 158–60).

in all fairness a charioteer can be called unskilled, not when he fails to control a difficult and unmanageable horse, but only if he cannot control a much less spirited animal. It is quite obvious that a desire for material things is altogether abnormal and contrary to nature, and that it derives its power not from nature but from a deliberate sinful choice; he who has yielded freely to such desire therefore sins inexcusably. So we must realize that the love of pleasure is not limited merely to the over-indulgence and pampering of the body, but includes every craving and attachment of the soul, whatever the form or object of the desire.

In order to make it easier to recognize the passions in terms of the tripartite division of the soul we will classify them briefly. The soul has three aspects: the intelligent, the incensive and the desiring aspect. The sins of the intelligent aspect are unbelief, heresy, folly, blasphemy, ingratitude and assent to sins originating in the soul's passible aspect. These vices are cured through unwavering faith in God and in true, undeviating and orthodox teachings, through the continual study of the inspired utterances of the Spirit, through pure and ceaseless prayer, and through the offering of thanks to God. The sins of the incensive aspect are heartlessness, hatred, lack of compassion, rancour, envy, murder and dwelling constantly on such things. They are cured by deep sympathy for one's fellow men, love, gentleness, brotherly affection, compassion, forbearance and kindness. The sins of the desiring aspect are gluttony, greed, drunkenness, unchastity, adultery, uncleanliness, licentiousness, love of material things, and the desire for empty glory, gold, wealth and the pleasures of the flesh. These are cured through fasting, self-control, hardship, a total shedding of possessions and their distribution to the poor, desire for the imperishable blessings held in store, longing for the kingdom of God, and aspiration for divine sonship.

You should also learn to distinguish the impassioned thoughts that promote every sin. The thoughts that encompass all evil are eight in number: those of gluttony, unchastity, avarice, anger, dejection, listlessness, self-esteem and pride. It does not lie within our power to decide whether or not these eight thoughts are going to arise and disturb us. But to dwell on them or not to dwell on them, to excite the passions or not to excite them, does lie within our power. In this connection, we should distinguish between seven different terms: provocation, coupling, wrestling, passion, assent (which comes very close to performance), actualization and captivity. Provocation is simply a suggestion coming from the enemy, like 'do this' or 'do that', such as our Lord Himself experienced when He heard the words 'Command that these stones become bread' (Matt. 4 : 3). As we have already said, it is not within our power to prevent provocations. Coupling is the acceptance of the thought suggested by the enemy. It means dwelling on the thought and choosing deliberately to dally with it in a pleasurable manner. Passion is the state resulting from coupling with the thought provoked by the enemy; it means letting the imagination brood on the thought continually. Wrestling is the resistance offered to the impassioned thought. It may result either in our destroying the passion in the thought – that is to say, the impassioned thought – or in our assenting to it. As St Paul says, 'The flesh desires in a way that opposes the Spirit, the Spirit in a way that opposes the flesh: the one is contrary to the other' (Gal. 5 : 17). Captivity is the forcible and compulsive abduction of the heart already dominated by prepossession and long habit. Assent is giving approval to the passion inherent in the thought. Actualization is putting the impassioned thought into effect once it has received our assent. If we can confront the first of these things, the provocation, in a dispassionate way, or firmly rebut it at the outset, we thereby cut off at once everything that comes after.

These eight passions should be destroyed as follows: gluttony by self-control; unchastity by desire for God and longing for the blessings held in store; avarice by compassion for the poor; anger by goodwill and love for all men; worldly dejection by spiritual joy; listlessness by patience, perseverance and offering thanks to God; self-esteem by doing good in secret and by praying constantly with a contrite heart; and pride by not judging or despising anyone in the manner of the boastful Pharisee (cf. Luke 18 : 11–12), and by considering oneself the least of all men. When the intellect has been freed in this way from the passions we have described and been raised up to God, it will henceforth live the life of blessedness, receiving the pledge of the Holy Spirit (cf. 2 Cor. 1 : 22). And when it departs this life, dispassionate and full of true knowledge, it will stand before the light of the Holy Trinity and with the divine angels will shine in glory through all eternity.

The soul, as we have already explained, has three aspects or powers: the intelligent, the incensive and the desiring. When the incensive power is imbued with love and deep sympathy for one's fellow men, and desire with purity and self-restraint, the intelligence is illuminated. But when dislike of one's fellow men dominates the incensive power, and desire is dissolute, the intelligence is in darkness. The intelligence is healthy, restrained and enlightened when it has the passions under control, perceives the inner essences of God's creatures spiritually, and is raised up towards the Blessed and Holy Trinity. The incensive power functions in accordance with nature when it loves all men and does not bear a grievance or harbour malice against anybody. Desire likewise conforms with nature when through humility, self-control and a total shedding of possessions, it kills the passions – that is, the pleasures of the flesh, and the appetite for material wealth and transient glory – and turns to the love that is divine and immortal. For desire is drawn towards three things: the pleasure of the flesh, vain self-glory, and the acquisition of material wealth. As a result of this senseless appetite it scorns God and His commandments, and forgets His generosity; it turns like a savage beast against its neighbour; it plunges the intelligence into darkness and prevents it from looking towards the truth. He who has acquired a spiritual understanding of this truth will share, even here on earth, in the kingdom of heaven and will live a blessed life in expectation of the blessedness that awaits those who love God. May we too be worthy of that blessedness through the grace of our Lord Jesus Christ. Amen.

Virtue, however, can only be attained by unremitting effort. This means that we struggle all our life to pay close practical attention to such things as acts of compassion, self-control, prayer, love and the other general virtues. A person may practise these virtues to a greater or lesser degree. He may from time to time perform acts of compassion; if he does so only infrequently we cannot legitimately call him compassionate, especially if what he does is not done in a good manner and in a way that conforms with God's will. For the good is not good if it is not rightly done. It is really good only if it is not done with the purpose of receiving some reward: as, for instance, the search for popularity or glory may be rewarded by fame, or by excessive gain, or by something else that is wrong. God is not interested in what happens to turn out to be good or in what appears to be good. He is interested in the purpose for which a thing is done. As the holy fathers say, when the intellect forgets the purpose of a religious observance, the outward practice of virtue loses its value. For whatever is done indiscriminately and without purpose is not only of no benefit – even though good in itself – but actually does harm. Conversely, what appears to be evil is really good if it is done for a godly purpose and accords with God's will. The action of a man who goes into a brothel to rescue a prostitute from destruction is a case in point.

Hence it is clear that someone who occasionally shows compassion is not compassionate, and someone who occasionally practises self-control is not self-controlled. A compassionate and self-controlled man is someone who fully, persistently, and with unfailing discrimination strives all his life for total virtue; for discrimination is greater than any other virtue, and is the queen and crown of all the virtues. The same is true of the vices: we call a man a fornicator, a drunkard or a liar not on account of a single lapse, but only when he keeps on falling into the sin in question and makes no attempt to correct himself.

There is something else which you must know if you really want to attain virtue and avoid sin. Just as the soul is incomparably better than the body and in many major respects altogether more excellent and precious, so the virtues of the soul are infinitely superior to the virtues of the body. This is especially true of those virtues which imitate God and bear His name. Conversely, the vices of the soul are much worse than the passions of the body, both in the actions they produce and in the punishments they incur. I do not know why, but most people overlook this fact. They treat drunkenness, unchastity, adultery, theft and all such vices with great concern, avoiding them or punishing them as something whose very appearance is loathsome to most men. But the passions of the soul are much worse and much more serious then bodily passions. For they degrade men to the level of demons and lead them, insensible as they are, to the eternal punishment reserved for all who obstinately cling to such vices. These passions of the soul are envy, rancour, malice, insensitivity, avarice – which according to the apostle is the root of all evil (cf. 1 Tim. 6 : 10) – and all vices of a similar nature.

We have arranged our homily clearly and concisely, explaining each point in a simple manner, as far as our lack of knowledge permits, so that anyone can easily distinguish the various categories of the virtues and the passions, and acquire a detailed understanding of their nature. We have set forth each category with all its forms and varieties so that, as far as possible, we all become aware of every kind of virtue or vice. In this way we may strive wholeheartedly to acquire the virtues – particularly the virtues of the soul, for through these we draw close to God – and resolutely avoid the vices. Truly blessed is the man who seeks virtue and pursues it and inquires diligently into its nature, since it is through virtue that he approaches God and enters into spiritual communion with Him. For it is above all by moral judgment, courage, wisdom, true knowledge and in-alienable wealth that we are led through the practice of the virtues to spiritual contemplation. Virtue (*areti*) is so called because it is something we choose (*to aireisthai*). We choose it and will it in the sense that we do good by deliberate choice and of our own free will, not unintentionally and under compulsion. Moral judgment (*phronisis*) is so called because it conveys (*to pherein*) to the intellect whatever is profitable.

As a golden seal to this plain homily, we will add a brief account of the way in which what is most precious of all that God has created – the noetic and intelligent creature, man – has been made, alone among created beings, in God's image and likeness (cf. Gen. 1 : 26). First, every man is said to be made in the image of God as regards the dignity of his intellect and soul – as regards, that is to say, the quality in man that cannot be scrutinized or observed, is immortal and endowed with free will, and in virtue of which he rules, begets and constructs. Second, every man is said to be made in the likeness of God as regards his possession of the principle of virtue and as regards his imitation of God through virtuous and god-like actions. Such actions consist in having deep sympathy for one's fellow men, in mercy, pity and love towards one's fellow servant, and in showing heartfelt concern and compassion. 'Be merciful,' says Christ our God, 'as your heavenly Father is also merciful' (cf. Luke 6 : 36). Every man possesses that which is according to the image of God, 'for the gifts of God are irrevocable' (cf. Rom. 11 : 29). But only a few – those who are virtuous and holy, and have imitated the goodness of God to the limit of human powers – possess that which is according to the likeness of God. May we too be found worthy of His sublime compassion, having conformed ourselves to Him through good actions and become imitators of all who have ever been faithful servants of Christ. For mercy is His and to Him are due all glory, honour and worship, together with His unoriginate Father and His all-holy, blessed and life-creating Spirit, now and always and through all the ages. Amen.

ABBA PHILIMON

Introductory Note

The *Discourse* that follows, unlike most of the material in the *Philokalia*, is narrative in form; doubtless it was included by the editors because of the long and important passages on inward meditation and on watchfulness. Apart from what is recorded in the present text, nothing is known about Abba Philimon. The *Discourse*, while stating that he lived in Egypt and was a priest, provides no clear indication of his date. Certainly he was earlier than the twelfth century, since the *Discourse* is mentioned by St Peter of Damaskos. Egypt seems in Philimon's day to be still part of the Roman Empire, which suggests that he lived in the sixth century, or at the latest in the early seventh just before the Arab conquest.[1] The Jesus Prayer is cited by Philimon in what has come to be regarded as its standard form, 'Lord Jesus Christ, Son of God, have mercy upon me': the *Discourse* seems to be the earliest source to cite explicitly this precise formula.

[1] Hieromonk [now Archbishop] Basile Krivochéine, 'Date du texte traditionnel de la "Prière de Jésus" ', *Messager de l'Exarchat du Patriarche russe en Europe occidentale* 7–8 (1951), pp. 55–59; I. Hausherr, *The Name of Jesus*, trans. by C. Cummings (*Cistercian Studies Series* 44: Kalamazoo, 1978), pp. 270–7.

A Discourse on Abba Philimon

It is said that Abba Philimon, the anchorite, lived for a long time enclosed in a certain cave not far from the Lavra of the Romans. There he engaged in the life of ascetic struggle, always asking himself the question which, it is reported, the great Arsenios[1] used to put to himself: 'Philimon, why did you come here?' He used to plait ropes and make baskets, giving them to the steward of the Lavra in exchange for a small ration of bread. He ate only bread and salt, and even that not every day. In this way he took no thought for the flesh (cf. Rom. 13 : 14) but, initiated into ineffable mysteries through the pursuit of contemplation, he was enveloped by divine light and established in a state of joyfulness. When he went to church on Saturdays and Sundays he walked alone in deep thought, allowing no one to approach him lest his concentration should be interrupted. In church he stood in a corner, keeping his face turned to the ground and shedding streams of tears. For, like the holy fathers, and especially like his great model Arsenios, he was always full of contrition and kept the thought of death continually in his mind.

When a heresy arose in Alexandria and the surrounding area, Philimon left his cave and went to the Lavra near that of Nikanor. There he was welcomed by the blessed Paulinos, who gave him his own retreat and enabled him to follow a life of complete stillness. For a whole year Paulinos allowed absolutely no one to approach him, and he himself disturbed him only when he had to give him bread.

On the feast of the holy resurrection of Christ, Philimon and Paulinos were talking when the subject of the eremitical state came

1 See *Apophthegmata*, alphabetical collection, Arsenios 40: trans. Sister Benedicta Ward, *The Sayings of the Desert Fathers*, p. 15.

up. Philimon knew that Paulinos, too, aspired to this state; and with this in mind he implanted in him teachings taken from Scripture and the fathers that emphasized, as Moses had done, how impossible it is to conform to God without complete stillness; how stillness gives birth to ascetic effort, ascetic effort to tears, tears to awe, awe to humility, humility to foresight, foresight to love; and how love restores the soul to health and makes it dispassionate, so that one then knows that one is not far from God.

He used to say to Paulinos: 'You must purify your intellect completely through stillness and engage it ceaselessly in spiritual work. For just as the eye is attentive to sensible things and is fascinated by what it sees, so the purified intellect is attentive to intelligible realities and becomes so rapt by spiritual contemplation that it is hard to tear it away. And the more the intellect is stripped of the passions and purified through stillness, the greater the spiritual knowledge it is found worthy to receive. The intellect is perfect when it transcends knowledge of created things and is united with God: having then attained a royal dignity it no longer allows itself to be pauperized or aroused by lower desires, even if offered all the kingdoms of the world. If, therefore, you want to acquire all these virtues, be detached from every man, flee the world and sedulously follow the path of the saints. Dress shabbily, behave simply, speak unaffectedly, do not be haughty in the way you walk, live in poverty and let yourself be despised by everyone. Above all, guard the intellect and be watchful, patiently enduring indigence and hardship, and keeping intact and undisturbed the spiritual blessings that you have been granted. Pay strict attention to yourself, not allowing any sensual pleasure to infiltrate. For the soul's passions are allayed by stillness; but when they are stimulated and aroused they grow more savage and force us into greater sin; and they become hard to cure, like the body's wounds when they are scratched and chafed. Even an idle word can make the intellect forget God, the demons enforcing this with the compliance of the senses.

'Great struggle and awe are needed to guard the soul. You have to divorce yourself from the whole world and sunder your soul's affection for the body. You have to become citiless, homeless, possessionless, free from avarice, from worldly concerns and society, humble, compassionate, good, gentle, still, ready to receive in your heart the stamp of divine knowledge. You cannot write on wax unless you have first expunged the letters written on it. Basil the Great teaches us these things.[1]

'The saints were people of this kind. They were totally severed from the ways of the world, and by keeping the vision of heaven unsullied in themselves they made its light shine by observing the divine laws. And having mortified their earthly aspects (cf. Col. 3 : 5) through self-control and through awe and love for God, they were radiant with holy words and actions. For through unceasing prayer and the study of the divine Scriptures the soul's noetic eyes are opened, and they see the King of the celestial powers, and great joy and fierce longing burn intensely in the soul; and as the flesh, too, is taken up by the Spirit, man becomes wholly spiritual. These are the things which those who in solitude practise blessed stillness and the strictest way of life, and who have separated themselves from all human solace, confess openly to the Lord in heaven alone.'

When the good brother heard this, his soul was wounded by divine longing; and he and Abba Philimon went to live in Sketis where the greatest of the holy fathers had pursued the path of sanctity. They settled in the Lavra of St John the Small, and asked the steward of the Lavra to see to their needs, as they wished to lead a life of stillness. And by the grace of God they lived in complete stillness, unfailingly attending church on Saturdays and Sundays but on other days of the week staying in their cells, praying and fulfilling their rule.

The rule of the holy Elder was as follows. During the night he quietly chanted the entire Psalter and the Biblical canticles, and recited part of the Gospels. Then he sat down and intently repeated 'Lord have mercy' for as long as he could. After that he slept, rising towards dawn to chant the First Hour. Then he again sat down, facing eastward, and alternately chanted psalms and recited by heart sections of the Epistles and Gospels. He spent the whole day in this manner, chanting and praying unceasingly, and being nourished by the contemplation of heavenly things. His intellect was often lifted up to contemplation, and he did not know if he was still on earth.

His brother, seeing him devoted so unremittingly to this rule and completely transformed by divine thoughts, said to him: 'Why, father, do you exhaust yourself so much at your age, disciplining your

---

[1] *Letter* ii, 2 (*P.G.* xxxii, 325B), trans. R. J. Deferrari, Loeb Classical Library, vol. i (London, 1950), p. 11.

body and bringing it into subjection?' (cf. 1 Cor. 9 : 27). And he replied: 'Believe me, my son, God has placed such love for my rule in my soul that I lack the strength to satisfy the longing within me. Yet longing for God and hope of the blessings held in store triumph over bodily weakness.' Thus at all times, even when he was eating, he raised his intellect up to the heavens on the wings of his longing.

Once a certain brother who lived with him asked him: 'What is the mystery of contemplation?' Realizing that he was intent on learning, the Elder replied: 'I tell you, my son, that when one's intellect is completely pure, God reveals to him the visions that are granted to the ministering powers and angelic hosts.' The same brother also asked: 'Why, father, do you find more joy in the psalms than in any other part of divine Scripture? And why, when quietly chanting them, do you say the words as though you were speaking with someone?' And Abba Philimon replied: 'My son, God has impressed the power of the psalms on my poor soul as He did on the soul of the prophet David. I cannot be separated from the sweetness of the visions about which they speak: they embrace all Scripture.' He confessed these things with great humility, after being much pressed, and then only for the benefit of the questioner.

A brother named John came from the coast to Father Philimon and, clasping his feet, said to him: 'What shall I do to be saved? For my intellect vacillates to and fro and strays after all the wrong things.' After a pause, the father replied: 'This is one of the outer passions and it stays with you because you still have not acquired a perfect longing for God. The warmth of this longing and of the knowledge of God has not yet come to you.' The brother said to him: 'What shall I do, father?' Abba Philimon replied: 'Meditate inwardly for a while, deep in your heart; for this can cleanse your intellect of these things.' The brother, not understanding what was said, asked the Elder: 'What is inward meditation, father?' The Elder replied: 'Keep watch in your heart; and with watchfulness say in your mind with awe and trembling: " Lord Jesus Christ, have mercy upon me." For this is the advice which the blessed Diadochos gave to beginners.'[1]

The brother departed; and with the help of God and the Elder's prayers he found stillness and for a while was filled with sweetness

[1] St Diadochos of Photiki, *On Spiritual Knowledge*, §§ 59, 61 (*The Philokalia*, vol. i, pp. 270–1).

by this meditation. But then it suddenly left him and he could not practise it or pray watchfully. So he went again to the Elder and told him what had happened. And the Elder said to him: 'You have had a brief taste of stillness and inner work, and have experienced the sweetness that comes from them. This is what you should always be doing in your heart: whether eating or drinking, in company or outside your cell, or on a journey, repeat that prayer with a watchful mind and an undeflected intellect; also chant, and meditate on prayers and psalms. Even when carrying out needful tasks, do not let your intellect be idle but keep it meditating inwardly and praying. For in this way you can grasp the depths of divine Scripture and the power hidden in it, and give unceasing work to the intellect, thus fulfilling the apostolic command: "Pray without ceasing" (1 Thess. 5 : 17). Pay strict attention to your heart and watch over it, so that it does not give admittance to thoughts that are evil or in any way vain and useless. Without interruption, whether asleep or awake, eating, drinking, or in company, let your heart inwardly and mentally at times be meditating on the psalms, at other times be repeating the prayer, "Lord Jesus Christ, Son of God, have mercy upon me." And when you chant, make sure that your mouth is not saying one thing while your mind is thinking about another.'

Again the brother said: 'In my sleep I see many vain fantasies.' And the Elder said to him: 'Don't be sluggish or neglectful. Before going to sleep, say many prayers in your heart, fight against evil thoughts and don't be deluded by the devil's demands; then God will receive you into His presence. If you possibly can, sleep only after reciting the psalms and after inward meditation. Don't be caught off your guard, letting your mind admit strange thoughts; but lie down meditating on the thought of your prayer, so that when you sleep it may be conjoined with you and when you awake it may commune with you (cf. Prov. 6 : 22). Also, recite the holy Creed of the Orthodox faith before you fall asleep. For true belief in God is the source and guard of all blessings.'

On another occasion the brother asked Abba Philemon: 'In your love, father, explain to me the work in which your intellect is engaged. Then I too may be saved.' And the Elder said: 'Why are you curious about these things?' The brother got up and, clasping and kissing the saint's feet, he begged for an answer. After a long time, the Elder said: 'You cannot yet grasp it: for only a person estab-

lished in righteousness can give to each of the senses the work proper
to it. And you have to be completely purged of vain worldly thoughts
before you are found worthy of this gift. So if you want such things,
practise the inward meditation with a pure heart. For if you pray
ceaselessly and meditate on the Scriptures, your soul's noetic eyes
are opened, and there is great joy in the soul and a certain keen and
ineffable longing, even the flesh being kindled by the Spirit, so that
the whole man becomes spiritual. Whether it is at night or during
the day that God grants you the gift of praying with a pure intellect,
undistractedly, put aside your own rule, and reach towards God
with all your strength, cleaving to Him. And He will illumine your
heart about the spiritual work which you should undertake.' And
he added: 'A certain elder once came to me and, on my asking him
about the state of his intellect, he said: "For two years I entreated
God in my whole heart, unremittingly asking Him to imprint in my
heart continuously and undistractedly the prayer which He Himself
gave to His disciples; and seeing my struggle and patient endurance,
the munificent Lord granted me this request." '

Abba Philimon also said this: 'Thoughts about vain things are
sicknesses of an idle and sluggish soul. We must, then, as Scripture
enjoins, guard our intellect diligently (cf. Prov. 4 : 23), chanting
undistractedly and with understanding, and praying with a pure
intellect. God wants us to show our zeal for Him first by our outward asceticism, and then by our love and unceasing prayer; and
He provides the path of salvation. The only path leading to heaven is
that of complete stillness, the avoidance of all evil, the acquisition
of blessings, perfect love towards God and communion with Him in
holiness and righteousness. If a man has attained these things he will
soon ascend to the divine realm. Yet the person who aspires to this
realm must first mortify his earthly aspects (cf. Col. 3 : 5). For
when our soul rejoices in the contemplation of true goodness, it
does not return to any of the passions energized by sensual or bodily
pleasure; on the contrary, it turns away from all such pleasure
and receives the manifestation of God with a pure and undefiled
mind.

'It is only after we have guarded ourselves rigorously, endured
bodily suffering and purified the soul, that God comes to dwell in
our hearts, making it possible for us to fulfil His commandments
without going astray. He Himself will then teach us how to hold

fast to His laws, sending forth His own energies, like rays of the sun, through the grace of the Spirit implanted in us. By way of trials and sufferings we must purify the divine image in us in accordance with which we possess intelligence and are able to receive understanding and the likeness to God; for it is by reforging our senses in the furnace of our trials that we free them from all defilement and assume our royal dignity. God created human nature a partaker of every divine blessing, able to contemplate spiritually the angelic choirs, the splendour of the dominions, the spiritual powers, principalities and authorities, the unapproachable light, and the refulgent glory. Should you achieve some virtue, do not regard yourself as superior to your brother, thinking that you have succeeded whereas he has been negligent; for this is the beginning of pride. Be extremely careful not to do anything simply in order to gain the esteem or goodwill of others. When you are struggling with some passion, do not flinch or become apathetic if the battle continues; but rise up and cast yourself before God, repeating with all your heart the prophet's words, "O Lord, judge those who injure me (Ps. 35 : 1. LXX); for I cannot defeat them." And He, seeing your humility, will quickly send you His help. And when you are walking along the road with someone, do not indulge in idle talk, but keep your intellect employed in the spiritual work in which it was previously engaged, so that this work becomes habitual to it and makes it forget worldly pleasures, anchoring it in the harbour of dispassion.'

When he had taught the brother these and many other things, Abba Philimon let him go. But after a short time the brother came back to him and began questioning him, saying: 'What must I do, father? During my night rule sleep weighs me down and does not allow me to pray with inner watchfulness, or to keep vigil beyond the regular period. And when I sing psalms, I want to take up manual work.' Abba Philimon said: 'When you are able to pray with inner watchfulness, do not engage in manual work. But if you are weighed down by listlessness, move about a little, so as to rid yourself of it, and take up manual work.'

The brother again asked him: 'Father, are you not yourself weighed down by sleep while practising your rule?' He replied: 'Hardly ever. But if sleep does sometimes lay hold on me a little, I move about and recite from the Gospel of John, from the beginning, turning the mind's eyes towards God; and sleepiness at once disappears. I do the same with regard to evil thoughts: when such a thought comes, I encounter it like fire with tears, and it disappears. You cannot as yet defend yourself in this manner; but always meditate inwardly and say the daily prayers laid down by the holy fathers. By this I mean, try to recite the Third, Sixth, and Ninth Hours, Vespers and the night services. And, so far as you can, do nothing simply to gain the esteem or goodwill of others, and never bear ill will towards your brother, lest you separate yourself from God. Strive to keep your mind undistracted, always being attentive to your inner thoughts. When you are in church, and are going to partake of the divine mysteries of Christ, do not go out until you have attained complete peace. Stand in one place, and do not leave it until the dismissal. Think that you are standing in heaven, and that in the company of the holy angels you are meeting God and receiving Him in your heart. Prepare yourself with great awe and trembling, lest you mingle with the holy powers unworthily.' Arming the brother with these counsels and commending him to the Lord and to the Spirit of His grace (cf. Acts 20 : 32), Abba Philimon let him go.

The brother who lived with the Abba also related the following: 'Once, as I sat near him, I asked him whether he had been tempted by the wiles of the demons while dwelling in the desert. And he replied: "Forgive me, brother; but if God should let the temptations to which I have been subjected by the devil come to you, I do not think you would be able to bear their venom. I am in my seventieth year, or older. Enduring a great number of trials while dwelling in extreme stillness in solitary places, I was much tempted and suffered greatly. But nothing is to be gained by speaking of such bitter things to people who as yet have no experience of stillness. When tempted, I always did this: I put all my hope in God, for it was to Him that I made my vows of renunciation. And He at once delivered me from all my distress. Because of this, brother, I no longer take thought for myself. I know that He takes thought for me, and so I bear more lightly the trials that come upon me. The only thing I offer from myself is unceasing prayer. I know that the more the suffering, the greater the reward for him who endures it. It is a means to reconciliation with the righteous Judge.

' "Aware of this, brother, do not grow slack. Recognize that you are fighting in the thick of the battle and that many others, too, are fighting for us against God's enemy. How could we dare to fight against so fearful an enemy of mankind unless the strong right arm of the Divine Logos upheld us, protecting and sheltering us? How could human nature withstand his ploys? 'Who', says Job, 'can strip off his outer garment? And who can penetrate the fold of his breastplate? Burning torches pour from his mouth, he hurls forth blazing coals. Out of his nostrils come smoke of burning soot, with the fire of charcoal. His breath is charcoal, a flame comes from his mouth, power lodges in his neck. Destruction runs before him. His heart is hard as stone, it stands like an unyielding anvil. He makes the deep boil like a cauldron; he regards the sea as a pot of ointment, and the nether deep as a captive. He sees every high thing; and he is king of all that is in the waters' (Job 41 : 13, 19–22, 24, 31–32, 34. LXX). This passage describes the monstrous tyrant against whom we fight. Yet those who lawfully engage in the solitary life soon defeat him: they do not possess anything that is his; they have renounced the world and are resolute in virtue; and they have God fighting for them. Who has turned to the Lord with awe and has not been transformed in his nature? Who has illumined himself with the light of divine laws and actions, and has not made his soul radiant with divine intellections and thoughts? His soul is not idle, for God prompts his intellect to long insatiably for light. Strongly energized in this way, the soul is not allowed by the spirit to grow flabby with the passions; but like a king who, full of fire and fury against his enemies, strikes them mercilessly and never retreats, it emerges triumphant, lifting its hands to heaven through the practice of the virtues and the prayer of the intellect." '

The same brother also spoke as follows about the Elder: 'In addition to his other virtues, Abba Philimon possessed this characteristic: he would never listen to idle talk. If someone inadvertently said something which was of no benefit to the soul, he did not respond at all. When I went away on some duty, he did not ask: "Why are you going away?"; nor, when I returned, did he ask: "Where are you coming from?" Or "What have you been doing?" Once, indeed, I had to go to Alexandria by ship; and from there I went to Constantinople on a church matter. I said goodbye to the brethren at Alexandria, but told Abba Philimon nothing about my journey. After spending quite a time in Constantinople, I returned to him in Sketis. When he saw me, he was filled with joy and, after greeting

me, he said a prayer. Then he sat down and, without asking me anything at all, continued his contemplation.

'On one occasion, wanting to test him, for days I did not give him
any bread to eat. And he did not ask for any, or say anything. After
this I bowed low to him and said: "Tell me, father, were you distressed that I did not bring you your food, as I usually do?" And he
replied: "Forgive me, brother, even if for twenty days you did not
bring me any bread, I would not ask you for it: so long as my soul
can last out, so can my body." To such a degree was he absorbed in
the contemplation of true goodness.'

'He also used to say: "Since I came to Sketis, I have not allowed
my thought to go beyond my cell; nor have I permitted my mind to
dwell on anything except the fear of God and the judgment of the
age to be; for I have meditated only on the sentence which threatens
sinners, on the eternal fire and the outer darkness, on the state of the
souls of sinners and of the righteous, and on the blessings laid up for
the righteous, each receiving 'his own payment for his own labour'
(1 Cor. 3 : 8): one for his growing load of suffering, another for
his acts of compassion and for his unfeigned love, another for his
total shedding of possessions and renunciation of the whole world,
another for his humility and consummate stillness, another for his
extreme obedience, another for his voluntary exile. Pondering
these things, I constrain all other thoughts; and I can no longer be
with people or concern my intellect with them, lest I be cut off
from more divine meditations."

'He also spoke of a certain solitary who had attained dispassion
and used to receive bread from the hand of an angel; but he grew
negligent and so was deprived of this honour. For when the soul
slackens the intellect's concentration, darkness comes over it.
Where God does not illumine, everything is confused, as in darkness; and the soul is unable to look only at God and tremble at His
words. "I am a God close at hand, says the Lord, not a distant God.
Can a man hide himself in secret, and I not see him? Do I not fill
heaven and earth? says the Lord" (Jer. 23 : 23–24. LXX). He also recalled many others who had similar experiences, among them
Solomon. For Solomon, he said, had received such wisdom and been
so glorified by men that he was like the morning-star and illumined
all with the splendour of his wisdom; yet for the sake of a little
sensual pleasure he lost that glory (cf. 1 Kings 11 : 1–11). Negligence

is to be dreaded. We must pray unceasingly lest some thought comes and separates us from God, distracting our intellect from Him. For the pure heart, being completely receptive to the Holy Spirit, mirrors God in His entirety.

'When I heard these things', said the brother, 'and saw his actions, I realized that all fleshly passions were inoperative in him. His desire was always fixed on higher things, so that he was continually transformed by the divine Spirit, sighing with "cries that cannot be uttered" (Rom. 8 : 26), concentrating himself within himself, assessing himself, and struggling to prevent anything from clouding his mind's purity and from defiling him imperceptibly.

'Seeing all this and spurred to emulate his achievements, I was continually prompted to question him. "How, like you, can I acquire a pure intellect?" I asked. And he replied: "You have to struggle. The heart has to strive and to suffer. Things worth striving and suffering for do not come to us if we sleep or are indolent. Even earth's blessings do not come to us without effort on our part. If you want to develop spiritually you must above all renounce your own will; you must acquire a heart that is sorrowful and must rid yourself of all possessions, giving attention not to the sins of others but to your own sins, weeping over them day and night; and you must not be emotionally attached to anyone. For a soul harrowed by what it has done and pricked to the heart by the memory of past sins, is dead to the world and the world to it; that is to say, all passions of the flesh become inoperative, and man becomes inoperative in relation to them. For he who renounces the world, ranging himself with Christ and devoting himself to stillness, loves God; he guards the divine image in himself and enriches his likeness to God, receiving from Him the help of the Spirit and becoming an abode of God and not of demons; and he acts righteously in God's sight. A soul purified from the world and free from the defilements of the flesh, 'having no spot or wrinkle' (Eph. 5 : 27), will win the crown of righteousness and shine with the beauty of virtue.

' "But if when you set out on the path of renunciation there is no sorrow in your heart, no spiritual tears or remembrance of endless punishment, no true stillness or persistent prayer, no psalmody and meditation on the divine Scriptures; if none of these things has become habitual in you, so that whether you like it or not they are forced on you by the unremitting perseverance of the intellect; and if awe of God does not grow in your mind, then you are still attached to the world and your intellect cannot be pure when you pray. True devoutness and awe of God purify the soul from the passions, render the intellect free, lead it to natural contemplation, and make it apt for theology. This it experiences in the form of bliss, that provides those who share in it with a foretaste of the bliss held in store and keeps the soul in a state of tranquillity.

' "Let us, then, do all we can to cultivate the virtues, for in this way we may attain true devoutness, that mental purity whose fruit is natural and theological contemplation. As a great theologian puts it, it is by practising the virtues that we ascend to contemplation.[1] Hence, if we neglect such practice we will be destitute of all wisdom. For even if we reach the height of virtue, ascetic effort is still needed in order to curb the disorderly impulses of the body and to keep a watch on our thoughts. Only thus may Christ to some small extent dwell in us. As we develop in righteousness, so we develop in spiritual courage; and when the intellect has been perfected, it unites wholly with God and is illumined by divine light, and the most hidden mysteries are revealed to it. Then it truly learns where wisdom and power lie, and that understanding which comprehends everything, and 'length of days and life, and the light of the eyes and peace' (Baruch 3 : 14). While it is still fighting against the passions it cannot as yet enjoy these things. For virtues and vices blind the intellect: vices prevent it from seeing the virtues, and virtues prevent it from seeing vices. But once the battle is over and it is found worthy of spiritual gifts, then it becomes wholly luminous, powerfully energized by grace and rooted in the contemplation of spiritual realities. A person in whom this happens is not attached to the things of this world but has passed from death to life.

' "The person pursuing the spiritual life and drawing close to God must, therefore, have a chaste heart and a pure tongue so that his words, in their purity, are fit for praising God. A soul that cleaves to God continuously communes with Him.

' "Thus, brethren, let our desire be to attain the summit of the virtues, and not to remain earth-bound and attached to the passions. For the person engaged in spiritual struggle who has drawn close to God, who partakes of the holy light and is wounded by his longing

---

[1] A quotation from St Gregory of Nazianzos: *Oration* 4, 133 (*P.G.* xxxv, 649B).

for it, delights in the Lord with an inconceivable spiritual joy. It is as the psalm says: 'Delight in the Lord, and may He grant you the petitions of your heart . . . May He reveal your righteousness like the light, and your judgment like the noonday' (cf. Ps. 37 : 4, 6. LXX). For what longing of the soul is as unbearably strong as that which God promotes in it when it is purged of every vice and sincerely declares: 'I am wounded by love' (Song of Songs 5 : 8. LXX)? The radiance of divine beauty is wholly inexpressible: words cannot describe it, nor the ear grasp it. To compare the true light to the rays of the morning star or the brightness of the moon or the light of the sun is to fail totally to do justice to its glory and is as inadequate as comparing a pitch-black moonless night to the clearest of noons. This is what St Basil, the great teacher, learnt from experience and subsequently taught us." '[1]

The brother who lived with Abba Philimon related these and many other things. But equally wonderful, and a great proof of his humility, is the fact that, although Abba Philimon had long been a presbyter and both his conduct and knowledge were of a celestial order, he held back from fulfilling his priestly functions to such an extent that in his many years of spiritual struggles he hardly ever consented to approach the altar; and in spite of the strictness of his life, he never partook of the divine mysteries if he had been talking with other people, even though he had not said anything worldly and he had spoken only to help those who questioned him. When he was going to partake of the divine mysteries, he supplicated God with prayers, chanting, and confession of sins. During the service, he was full of fear when the priest intoned the words, 'Holy things to the holy.' For he used to say that the whole church was then filled with holy angels, and that the King of the celestial powers Himself was invisibly celebrating, transformed in our hearts into body and blood. It was on account of this that he said that we should dare to partake of the immaculate mysteries of Christ only when in a chaste and pure state, as it were outside the flesh and free from all hesitation and doubt; in this way we would participate in the illumination that comes from them. Many of the holy fathers saw angels watching over them, and so they maintained silence, not entering into conversation with anyone.

---

[1] *Longer Rules* ii, 1 (909c), trans. W. K. L. Clarke, *The Ascetic Works of Saint Basil* (London, 1925), p. 154.

The brother also said that when Abba Philimon had to sell his handiwork, he pretended to be a fool, in case speaking and answering questions might lead him into some lie, or oath, or chatter, or some other kind of sin. Whenever anyone bought anything he simply paid what he thought fit. The Abba, this truly wise man, made small baskets, and accepted gratefully whatever was given, saying absolutely nothing.

ST THEOGNOSTOS

Introductory Note

St Nikodimos, while expressing reservations about the date of the text that follows, is inclined to ascribe it to Theognostos of Alexandria (third century). This, however, cannot be the case, since the author quotes St John of Damaskos (§ 73), and so is not earlier than the second half of the eighth century; perhaps he lived in the fourteenth.[1] The chief originality of the work lies in its comments on priesthood and Eucharist. Theognostos was himself a priest (§ 72), and seems to envisage a daily celebration of the Divine Liturgy (§ 14). The long passage (§ 26) from St John of Karpathos is probably a later insertion, and not part of Theognostos' own text.

[1] See J. Gouillard, 'L'acrostiche spirituel de Théognoste (XIVe s. ?)', *Echos d'Orient* xxxix (1940), pp. 126–37.

On the Practice of the Virtues, Contemplation and the Priesthood

1. When you are completely detached from all earthly things and when, your conscience clear, you are at any moment ready in heart to leave this present life and to dwell with the Lord, then you may recognize that you have acquired true virtue. If you want to be known to God, do all that you can to remain unknown to men.

2. Watch out for any unnecessary demands coming from the body and ignore them, lest they should lead you to relax your efforts before you have attained dispassion. Regard as loss, not the privation of sensual pleasure, but the failure to attain higher things as a result of having indulged in such pleasure.

3. Consciously look on yourself as an ant or a worm, so that you can become a man formed by God. If you fail to do the first, the second cannot happen. The lower you descend, the higher you ascend; and when, like the psalmist, you regard yourself as nothing before the Lord (cf. Ps. 39 : 5), then imperceptibly you will grow great. And when you begin to realize that you have nothing and know nothing, then you will become rich in the Lord through practice of the virtues and spiritual knowledge.

4. 'Break the arm of the sinful and evil man' (Ps. 10 : 15), by which I mean the sensual pleasure and evil from which all vice arises. Break it through self-control and the innocence born of humility, so that when your actions are assessed and judged, no sin will be found in you, however rigorous the search. For our sins are eradicated once we come to hate what causes them and to do battle against it, repairing earlier defeat with final victory.

5. Nothing is better than pure prayer. From it, as from a spring,

come the virtues: understanding and gentleness, love and self-control, and the support and encouragement that God grants in response to tears. The beauty of pure prayer is made manifest when our mind dwells in the realm of intelligible realities alone and our longing to attain what is divine is endless. Then the intellect, tracking its Master through the contemplation of created beings, and ardently thirsting to find and see Him who cannot be seen, or else contemplating the darkness that is His secret place (cf. Ps. 18 : 11), in awe withdraws again into itself, for the moment satisfied and encouraged by the vision revealed to it for its own benefit; but it is full of hope that it will reach the object of its desire when, set free from appearances and the shadow-like fantasies seen indistinctly, as in a mirror, it is granted a pure unceasing vision 'face to face' (cf. 1 Cor. 13 : 12).

6. Do not try to embark on the higher forms of contemplation before you have achieved complete dispassion, and do not pursue what lies as yet beyond your reach. If your wish is to become a theologian and a contemplative, ascend by the path of ascetic practice and through self-purification acquire what is pure. Do not pursue theology beyond the limits of your present state of development: it is wrong for us who are still drinking the milk of the virtues to attempt to soar to the heights of theology, and if we do so we will flounder like fledglings, however great the longing roused within us by the honey of spiritual knowledge. But, once purified by self-restraint and tears, we will be lifted up from the earth like Elijah or Habakkuk (cf. 2 Kgs. 2 : 11; Bel and Dr., verses 36–39), anticipating the moment when we will be caught up into the clouds (cf. 1 Thess. 4 : 17); and transported beyond the world of the senses by undistracted prayer, pure and contemplative, we may then in our search for God touch the fringe of theology.

7. If you wish to be granted a mental vision of the divine you must first embrace a peaceful and quiet way of life, and devote your efforts to acquiring a knowledge of both yourself and God. If you do this and achieve a pure state untroubled by any passion, there is nothing to prevent your intellect from perceiving, as it were in a light breeze (cf. 1 Kgs. 19 : 12. LXX), Him who is invisible to all; and He will bring you good tidings of salvation through a yet clearer knowledge of Himself.

8. Just as lightning presages thunder, so divine forgiveness is

followed by the calming of the passions. This in its turn is accompanied by a foretaste of the blessedness held in store for us. There is no divine mercy or hope of dispassion for the soul that loves this world more than its Creator, and is attached to visible things and clings wholly to the pleasures and enjoyments of the flesh.

9. Do not attempt to discover with the intellect what or where God is: since He transcends everything He is beyond being and independent of place. But contemplate – so far as this is possible – only God the Logos. Though circumscribed, He is radiant with the divine nature; though descried in a particular place, He is yet present everywhere because of the infinite nature of His Godhead. The greater your purification, the more you will be granted His illumination.

10. If you ardently long for true knowledge and unequivocal assurance of salvation, first study how to break the soul's impassioned links with the body; then, stripped of all attachment to material things, descend to the depths of humility, and there you will find the precious pearl of your salvation hidden in the shell of divine knowledge. This will be your pledge of the radiance of God's kingdom.

11. He who has achieved inward self-renunciation and has subjected his flesh to the spirit no longer needs to submit himself to other men. Such a person obeys God's word and law like a grateful servant. But we who are still engaged in the war between body and soul must be subject to someone else; we must have a commander and helmsman who will skilfully arm and guide us, lest we should be destroyed by our spiritual enemies or submerged beneath our passions because of our inexperience.

12. If you are untroubled by any passion; if your heart yearns more and more for God; if you do not fear death but regard it as a dream and even long for your release – then you have attained the pledge of your salvation and, rejoicing with inexpressible joy, you carry the kingdom of heaven within you.

13. If you have been found worthy of divine and venerable priesthood, you have committed yourself sacrificially to die to the passions and to sensual pleasure. Only then dare you approach the awesome, living sacrifice; otherwise you will be consumed by the divine fire like dry tinder. If the seraphim did not dare to touch the divine coal without tongs (cf. Isa. 6 : 6), how can you do so unless you have attained dispassion? You must through dispassion have a

consecrated tongue, purified lips, and a chaste soul and body; and your very hands, as ministers of the fiery, supraessential sacrifice, must be more burnished than any gold.

14. To grasp the full import of my words, remember that you look daily on the salvation of God which, when he saw it but once, so terrified and amazed Symeon the Elder that he prayed for his deliverance (cf. Luke 2 : 29). If you have not been assured by the Holy Spirit that you are equal to the angels and so an acceptable intermediary between God and man, do not presumptuously dare to celebrate the awesome and most holy mysteries, which even angels venerate and from whose purity many of the saints themselves have in reverent fear drawn back. Otherwise, like Zan, you will be destroyed because of your pretence to holiness.

15. 'Watch yourself attentively', it is said (cf. Exod. 23 : 21. LXX). Always offer the sacrifice first of all on behalf of your own sins: then if, because of your weakness, some defilement exists in you already or now enters into you, it will be consumed by the divine fire. In this way, as a chosen vessel, serviceable, pure and worthy of such a sacrifice, you will have power to change wooden or clay vessels into silver or gold, provided that you have intimate communion with God and He hears your prayers. For where God hears and responds there is nothing to hinder a change from one thing to another.

16. Ponder deeply on the angelic honour of which you have been found worthy and, whatever the rank to which you have been called, strive through virtue and purity to keep yourself unsullied. For you know from what height Lucifer fell on account of his pride. Do not dream up great ideas about yourself and suffer the same fate. Regard yourself as dust and ashes (cf. Gen. 18 : 27), or as refuse, or as some cur-like creature; and lament continuously, for it is only on account of God's inexpressible compassion and kindness that you are permitted to handle the holy things at the celebration of the dread mysteries, and so are called to communion and kinship with Him.

17. A priest should be pure from all passions, especially unchastity and rancour, and should keep his imagination passion-free. Otherwise he will be rejected with loathing, as if he were some foul leper who touches the body of a king.

18. When your tears have washed you whiter than snow and your conscience is spotless in its purity, and when the angel-like white-

ness of your outer garments reveals your soul's inner beauty – then, and only then, you may in holiness touch holy things. Make sure that you do not rely only on human traditions in celebrating the divine mysteries, but let God's grace inwardly and invisibly fill you with the knowledge of higher things.

19. If you aspire to incorruptibility and immortality, pursue with faith and reverence whatever is life-giving and does not perish; long to depart from this world as one made perfect through faith. If you still fear death, you have not yet been intermingled with Christ through love, although you have been found worthy to sacrifice Him with your own hands and have been filled with His flesh. For, were you linked to Him in love, you would make haste to join Him, no longer concerned about this life or the flesh.

20. You who sacrifice God's flesh and share in it through holy communion should also be united to Him by dying the death that He died (cf. Rom. 6 : 5). As St Paul says (cf. Gal. 2 : 20), you should live, not for yourself, but for Him who was crucified and died on your behalf. If, dominated by passion, you live for the flesh and the world, prepare yourself for deathless punishment through death unless you resign of your own accord from your priesthood before you die. But many unworthy priests have been snatched away by sudden death and sent to the halls of judgment.

21. There was once a monk-priest who had a reputation for piety and was held in honour by many on account of his outward behaviour, though within he was licentious and defiled. One day he was celebrating the Divine Liturgy and, on reaching the cherubic hymn, he had bent his head as usual before the holy table and was reading the prayer, 'No one is worthy . . .', when he suddenly died, his soul having left him in that position.

22. Nothing is more important than true intelligence and spiritual knowledge, for they produce both fear of God and longing for Him. Fear of God purifies us through awe and self-abasement. Longing for Him brings us to perfection through discrimination and inward illumination, raising our intellect to the heights of contemplation. Without fear we cannot acquire intense love for the divine, and so cannot spread our wings and find our resting-place in the realm of our aspiration.

23. Be persuaded by me, you who ardently and in all seriousness long for salvation: make haste, search persistently, ask ceaselessly,

knock patiently, and continue until you reach your goal. Establish a basis of firm faith and humility. You will have achieved what you want not simply when your sins are forgiven but when, fearlessly and joyously separated from the flesh, you are no longer excited or scared by the eruption of any passion.

24. Ask with many tears to be given the full assurance of salvation, but – if you are humble – do not ask to be given it long before your death, in case you grow negligent and indifferent. Ask that you may obtain it when you are close to your departure – but make your request in all seriousness, lest out of presumption you should delude yourself into believing that you possess such assurance only to find, when the time comes, that you have failed to attain it. Where will you go then, unhappy man, deprived of the foretaste and unquestionable assurance of salvation given by the Spirit?

25. If you aspire to the dispassion that deifies, find it first of all through obedience and humility, lest by travelling along some other path you end up in trouble. The person who has attained dispassion is not sometimes disturbed by the passions and at other times calm and at rest, but enjoys dispassion continually and, even when the passions are still present within him, he remains unaffected by the things that provoke them. Above all he is not affected by the images which the passions generate.

26. When the soul leaves the body, the enemy advances to attack it, fiercely reviling it and accusing it of its sins in a harsh and terrifying manner. The devout soul, however, even though in the past it has often been wounded by sin, is not frightened by the enemy's attacks and threats. Strengthened by the Lord, winged by joy, filled with courage by the holy angels that guide it, and encircled and protected by the light of faith, it answers the enemy with great boldness: 'Fugitive from heaven, wicked slave, what have I to do with you? You have no authority over me; Christ the Son of God has authority over me and over all things. Against Him have I sinned, before Him shall I stand on trial, having His Precious Cross as a sure pledge of His saving love towards me. Flee from me, destroyer! You have nothing to do with the servants of Christ.' When the soul says all this fearlessly, the devil turns his back, howling aloud and unable to withstand the name of Christ. Then the soul swoops down on the devil from above, attacking him like a hawk attacking a crow. After this it is brought rejoicing by the holy

angels to the place appointed for it in accordance with its inward state.[1]

27. The longing for transient things will not drag you earthwards if you keep your mind on the things of heaven; but when you are shackled by an attachment to earthly things you are like an eagle caught in a trap by its claw and prevented from flying. Regard all you possess as trash in the hope of better things. Shake off even your body when the time comes, and follow the angel of God that takes you from it.

28. Just as a coin that does not bear the image of the king cannot be placed in the royal treasuries with the other currency, so without true spiritual knowledge and dispassion you cannot receive a foretaste of divine blessedness and depart with courage and confidence from this world to take your place among the elect in the next. By spiritual knowledge, I do not mean wisdom, but that unerring apperception of God and of divine realities through which the devout, no longer dragged down by the passions, are raised to a divine state by the grace of the Spirit.

29. Even though you have successfully practised all the virtues, do not assume that you have attained dispassion and can dwell in the world without anxiety; for your soul may still bear within it the imprint of the passions, and so you will have difficulties when you die. But, guided always by fear, keep careful watch over your mutable and ever-changing nature and shun the causes of passion. For changeless dispassion in its highest form is found only in those who have attained perfect love, have been lifted above sensory things through unceasing contemplation, and have transcended the body through humility. The flame of the passions no longer touches them: it has been cut off by the voice of the Lord (cf. Ps. 29 : 7), since the nature of such people has already been transmuted into incorruptibility.

30. Do not try to attain dispassion prematurely and you will not suffer what Adam suffered when he ate too soon from the tree of spiritual knowledge (cf. Gen. 3 : 6). But patiently labour on, with constant entreaty and self-control in all things; and if by means of self-reproach and the utmost humility you keep the ground you have won, you will then in good time receive the grace of dispassion. The

[1] This passage is almost entirely identical with St John of Karpathos, *Texts for the Monks in India*, § 25 (*The Philokalia*, vol. i, pp. 303–4).

harbour of rest is reached only after many storms and struggles; and God is not being unjust to those walking on the true path if He keeps the gate of dispassion closed until the right moment comes.

31. Slothful and inexperienced as you are, you too should 'go to the ant' (Prov. 6 : 6): imitate its simplicity and insignificance, and know that God, self-sufficient and superabundant, has no need of our virtues. On the contrary, He richly bestows His gifts on us and through His grace saves those who are consciously grateful, though in His compassion He also accepts whatever work we are able to do. If, then, you labour as one in debt to God for blessings already received, you do well and God's mercy is close to you. But if you think that God is in your debt because of the good things you imagine you have done, you are quite deluded. For how can the bestower of gifts be the debtor? Work like a hired servant and, advancing step by step, you will by God's mercy attain what you seek.

32. Shall I show you another path to salvation – or, rather, to dispassion? Through your entreaties constrain the Creator not to let you fail in your purpose. Constantly bring before Him as intercessors all the angelic powers, all the saints, and especially the most pure Mother of God. Do not ask for dispassion, for you are unworthy of such a gift; but ask persistently for salvation and with it you will receive dispassion as well. The one is like silver, the other like pure gold. In particular, let inward meditation on God be your hand-maid, and turn your whole attention to the secret mysteries concerning Him: for the principles of these mysteries will deify you, and God delights in them and is won over by them.

33. Strive to receive a sure, unequivocal pledge of salvation in your heart, so that at the time of your death you will not be distraught and unexpectedly terrified. You have received such a pledge when your heart no longer reproaches you for your failings and your conscience stops chiding you because of your fits of anger; when through God's grace your bestial passions have been tamed; when you weep tears of solace and your intellect prays undistracted and with purity; and when you await death, which most people dread and run away from, calmly and with a ready heart.

34. The words of eternal life which, according to the chief of the apostles (cf. John 6 : 68), God the Logos possesses, are the inner essences of all the things created by Him. Thus the person who, because of his purity, has been initiated into the mystery of these

inner essences has already acquired eternal life, a pledge of the Spirit and confident expectation of salvation. He who values the flesh more than the soul and is attached to worldly things is not worthy of such gifts.

35. An intelligent person is not merely someone who has the power of speech, for this is common to all men. On the contrary, he is someone who seeks for God with his intelligence. But he will never find the essence of Him who transcends all being, for this is beyond the scope of all created nature. But in much the same way as a builder is to be seen in his work, so the sovereign artificer is to be found and as it were perceived in the creative wisdom inherent in living things, and in His providential care, governance, unification, guidance and conservation of them.

36. You cannot achieve a condition of total poverty without dispassion, or dispassion without love, or love without the fear of God and pure prayer, or fear of God and pure prayer without faith and detachment; for it is when winged by faith and detachment that the intellect discards all base concern and soars upwards in search of its Lord.

37. Let chastity be as dear to you as the pupil of your eye, and then you will become a temple of God and His cherished dwelling place. For without self-restraint you cannot live with God. Chastity and self-restraint are born of a longing for God combined with detachment and renunciation of the world; and they are conserved by humility, self-control, unbroken prayer, spiritual contemplation, freedom from anger and intense weeping. Without dispassion, however, you cannot achieve the beauty of discrimination.

38. Let no one deceive you, brother: without holiness, as the apostle says, no one can see God (cf. Heb. 12 : 14). For the Lord, who is more than holy and beyond all purity, will not appear to an impure person. Just as he who loves father or mother, daughter or son (cf. Matt. 10 : 37) more than the Lord is unworthy of Him, so is he who loves anything transient and material. Even more unworthy is the person who chooses foul and fetid sin in preference to love for the Lord; for God rejects whoever does not repudiate all filthiness: 'Corruption does not inherit incorruption' (1 Cor. 15 : 50).

39. You will not be worthy of divine love unless you possess spiritual knowledge, or of spiritual knowledge unless you possess faith. I do not mean faith of a theoretical kind, but that which we

acquire as a result of practising the virtues. You will achieve true compunction only when through self-control and vigil, prayer and humility, you have withered the propensity to sensual pleasure congenital to the flesh and have been crucified with Christ (cf. Gal. 2 : 19–20), no longer living the life of the passions but living and walking in the Spirit, filled with the hope of heavenly glory.

40. Cry out to God, ' "I know that Thou favourest me, because my enemy does not exult over me" (Ps. 41 : 11); he will not domineer over me and plague me to the very end through the passions. But Thou wilt snatch me from his hands before I die and, granting me life in the Spirit according to Thy will, through a holy death Thou wilt bring me, saved, before Thy judgment seat. There, through Thy mercy, I shall receive the pledge of salvation and the assurance that is beyond all doubting. Thus I shall not be troubled and unprepared at the time of my departure from the world, nor shall I find the ordeal unbearable, more harsh and baleful than a death sentence or torture.'

41. Faith and hope are not merely casual or theoretical matters. Faith requires a steadfast soul, while hope needs a firm will and an honest heart. How without grace can one readily believe in things unseen? How can a man have hope concerning the hidden things held in store unless through his own integrity he has gained some experience of the Lord's gifts? These gifts of grace are a gage of the blessings held in store, which they manifest as present realities. Faith and hope, then, require both virtue on our part and God's inspiration and help. Unless both are present we labour in vain.

42. The offspring of true virtue is either spiritual knowledge or dispassion or both together. If we fail to acquire them then we labour in vain, and our apparent virtue is not genuine; for if it were it would have produced fruit as well as leaves. In reality, however, it does not enjoy God's blessing but is false, a matter of self-satisfaction, or else something feigned in order to gain the esteem of others or from some other motive not in accordance with God's will. But if we correct our motive, we shall undoubtedly receive the grace of God that bestows both spiritual knowledge and dispassion at the time and in the measure appropriate.

43. Discern the wiles of the enemy with the light of grace and, throwing yourself before God with tears, confess your weakness,

counting yourself nothing, even though the deceiver tries to persuade you to think otherwise. Do not even ask for spiritual gifts unless they contribute to your salvation and help you to remain humble. Seek the knowledge that does not make you conceited, but leads you to the knowledge of God. Pray to be released from the tyranny of the passions before you die, and to depart this life in a state of dispassion or – more humbly – of compassion for the sins of others.

44. Just as it is impossible to fly without wings, so we cannot attain the blessings for which we hope without already in this life receiving an assurance that is beyond doubt. Because of their extreme humility, or through the grace of the Holy Spirit, such assurance is given to those who have been reconciled with God, and who possess a dispassion that is less or more perfect in proportion to the degree of their reconciliation and purification. Those who depart from the body before receiving this assurance die while still in the winter of the passions, or else on the sabbath (cf. Matt. 24 : 20) – refraining, that is to say, from the work of the virtues – and they are subject to trial and judgment, being culpable at the time of retribution.

45. Since salvation comes to you as a free gift, give thanks to God your saviour. If you wish to present Him with gifts, gratefully offer from your widowed soul two tiny coins, humility and love, and God will accept these in the treasury of His salvation more gladly than the host of virtues deposited there by others (cf. Mark 12 : 41–43). Dead through the passions, pray like Lazarus to be brought to life again, sending to God these two sisters to intercede with Him (cf. John 11 : 20–44); and you will surely attain your goal.

46. The practice of the virtues does not by itself bring you to the dispassion that enables you to pray undistracted and in purity: spiritual contemplation must also in its turn confer on your intellect illuminative knowledge and the understanding of created beings. Thus winged and enlightened, the intellect is totally rapt by the love of true prayer and raised up to the cognate light of the incorporeal orders; thence, in so far as this is possible, it is borne towards the ultimate light, the triple sun of the Trinity supremely divine.

47. We will not be punished or condemned in the age to be because we have sinned, since we were given a mutable and unstable nature. But we will be punished if, after sinning, we did not repent

and turn from our evil ways to the Lord; for we have been given the power to repent, as well as the time in which to do so. Only through repentance shall we receive God's mercy, and not its opposite, His passionate anger. Not that God is angry with us: He is angry with evil. Indeed, the divine is beyond passion and vengefulness, though we speak of it as reflecting, like a mirror, our actions and dispositions, giving to each of us whatever we deserve.

48. When you fall from a higher state, do not become panic-stricken, but through remorse, grief, rigorous self-reproach and, above all, through copious tears shed in a contrite spirit, correct yourself and return quickly to your former condition. Rising up again after your fall, you will enter the joyous valley of salvation, taking care so far as is possible not to anger your Judge again, so as not to need atoning tears and sorrow in the future. But if you show no such repentance in this present life, you will certainly be punished in the age to be.

49. Let us return to the subject of the priesthood. As an angelic order it requires of us an angelic purification, and a degree of discretion and self-restraint greater than in our previous life. What is defiled can in some measure become pure; it is far worse for the pure to become defiled. If we mix darkness with light, foul odours with sweet, we shall inherit calamity and destruction because of our sacrilege, like Ananias and Sapphira (cf. Acts 5 : 1–10).

50. If, lost and useless though you are, you decide after superficial purification to enter the heavenly, angelic order of the priesthood and to become a chosen vessel, suitable for the Lord's use, as St Paul says (cf. 2 Tim. 2 : 21; Acts 9 : 15), then you should keep unsullied the office of which you have been found worthy, guarding the divine gift as you would the pupil of your eye. Otherwise, fulfilling your role in a perfunctory manner, you will be cast down from the heights into the abyss and find it hard to climb out again.

51. Wisely bear in mind that, if God acquits, no one can condemn (cf. Rom. 8 : 33–34). If you have been called to enter into the supramundane grace of the priesthood, do not worry about your past life, even if to some extent it has been soiled: for it has been purified once more by God and through your own self-correction. But afterwards be diligent and watchful, so as not to eclipse the grace. Then if someone stupidly casts aspersions on your priesthood be-

cause of your past, he will hear a voice from heaven saying, 'What God has cleansed, do not call unclean' (Acts 10 : 15).

52. The office of the priesthood is light and its yoke easy (cf. Matt. 11 : 30) so long as it is discharged as it should be, and so long as the grace of the Holy Spirit is not put up for sale. When what is beyond price is bartered in the name of human expedience and for perishable gifts, and when the call is not from above, the burden is heavy indeed; for it is borne by someone unworthy, whose powers it exceeds. The yoke is then extremely harsh, chafing the neck of him who carries it and sapping his strength; and unless it is taken from him, it will exhaust and destroy him utterly.

53. When you boldly take up the yoke of the priesthood, you should mend your ways and expound the truth rightly, thus working out your salvation with fear and trembling; 'for our God is a consuming fire' (Heb. 12 : 29). If you are as gold and silver and you touch this fire, have no fear of being burnt, just as the three children in Babylon had no fear (cf. Dan. 3 : 17). But if you are like grass or reeds or some other easily combustible material as a result of your earthly thoughts, then tremble lest you should be reduced to ashes in the heavenly fire – unless like Lot (cf. Gen. 19 : 17, 29) you escape God's wrath by quitting the priesthood. Yet it may be that some of the lighter faults that result from weaknesses are consumed by this divine fire during the celebration of the Liturgy, while you yourself remain unburned and unharmed in the fire, like the fragile bush in the desert (cf. Exod. 3 : 2).

54. If like someone with gonorrhoea you lack the strength to break with your impassioned state because it has become chronic, how can you dare, wretched as you are, to touch what even to angels is untouchable? Either shudder with awe and renounce the sacred ministry, in this way propitiating God; or else, obdurate and incorrigible, expect to fall into the hands of the living God and to experience His wrath. God will not spare you out of compassion, but will punish you mercilessly for daring to come to the royal wedding feast with both soul and garment defiled, unworthy even of entry, much less of joining in the celebration (cf. Matt. 22 : 12).

55. I myself have known a priest who dared to celebrate the divine mysteries unworthily, having succumbed to the passion of unchastity. First he fell victim to a dreadful, incurable disease and was near death. Then, after unavailingly doing everything he could

to rid himself of this disease – in fact it got even worse – he began to realize that he was dying because he had celebrated the mysteries unworthily. Straight away he took a vow to desist from celebrating, and recovered at once, so that not even a trace of his illness remained.

56. The priestly dignity, like the priestly vestments, is full of splendour, but only so long as it is illumined from within by purity of soul. Once it has been disgraced through lack of attentiveness, and no notice is taken of the protests of the conscience, then the light becomes darkness, the harbinger of eternal darkness and eternal fire. Our only recourse in such a case is to leave this precipitous path, and to take the road that leads safely, by way of virtue and humility, to the kingdom of God.

57. Salvation is attained through simplicity and virtue, not through the glories of the priesthood, which demands of us an angelic way of life. Either, then, you should become dispassionate like the angels, in thought and purpose superior to the world and the flesh, climbing the ladder to heaven in this way; or else, aware of your weakness, you should in fear avoid the high rank of the priesthood, terrified of the great fall should you prove unworthy of it. Choose the form of life followed by the laity, for it brings one no less close to God than priesthood. Moreover, should you fall while pursuing it, through God's mercy and grace you will easily rise again by repenting.

58. 'Flesh and blood cannot inherit the kingdom of God' (1 Cor. 15 : 50). How is it, then, that you who partake of God's flesh and blood, do not become one body with Him and commingle with Him through His blood? Although the kingdom of heaven is within you, are you still besieged by the passions of your own flesh and blood? I fear that the Spirit of God will not remain within you in your non-spiritual state, and that on the day of judgment you will be sentenced with the utmost severity: the priesthood will be taken from you because of your unworthiness of such grace, and you will be sent to eternal punishment.

59. If there is no fear of God before your eyes, you will think it a trivial matter to officiate unworthily, for you will be deceived by your own self-love into imagining that God will be charitable to you. Long ago Dathan and Abiram imagined the same thing until the earth opened beneath them and swallowed them up (cf. Num. 16 : 25–33). Standing with genuine awe and fear before Him who is

to be feared, recognize how grave a matter it is to officiate, and either engage in the priesthood worthily and purely – as it were like an angel – or wisely keep away from the dread ministry. Otherwise, slighting your office, and using specious arguments against your conscience when it rebukes you, you will say in your agony as you are condemned on the day that all things are judged and set aright: 'The fear that I feared has come upon me, and what I dreaded has visited me' (Job 3 : 25).

60. Watchfully and sedulously you should offer, with contrition and tears, the world-saving and holy sacrifice first of all in propitiation for your own sins. Who after your death will offer it on your behalf with such concern? Anticipate wisely, therefore: bury yourself and commemorate yourself in advance. Offer the holy gifts to God on the holy table as the means of your salvation, making present the voluntary death He suffered in His love for man.

61. Inexpressible is the soul's delight when in full assurance of salvation it leaves the body, stripping it off as though it were a garment. Because it is now attaining what it hopes for, it puts off the body painlessly, going in peace to meet the radiant and joyful angel that comes down for it, and travelling with him unimpeded through the air, totally unharmed by the evil spirits. Rising with joy, courage and thanksgiving, it comes in adoration before the Creator, and is allotted its place among those akin to it and equal to it in virtue, until the universal resurrection.

62. I shall tell you something strange, but do not be surprised by it. Should you fail to attain dispassion because of the predispositions dominating you, but at the time of your death be in the depths of humility, you will be exalted above the clouds no less than the man who is dispassionate. For even if the treasure of those who are dispassionate consists of every virtue, the precious stone of humility is more valuable than them all: it brings about not only propitiation with the Creator, but also entry with the elect into the bridal chamber of His kingdom.

63. Having received from God a propitiation for your offences, glorify Him who is long-suffering and forgiving, and make every effort to avoid deliberate sin. For though your sins may be forgiven daily until your death, it would be foolish of you to sin glibly with full knowledge of what you are doing. None the less, if you drive off the dog of despair with the stone of hopefulness and supplicate

boldly and insistently, your many sins will be forgiven you. Then, in the age to be, as a debtor you too will love the God who is beyond all goodness and yet has compassion for you.

64. When, energized by divine grace, you find yourself full of tears in prayer before God, lie on the ground stretched out in the form of a cross, beat the earth with your brow and ask for deliverance from this life as a release from corruption and a liberation from trials and temptations. But ask that this may be granted, not as you wish, but as and when God wills. For your part, you should long for your departure now, hoping that, if you come before God with tears and in the depths of humility, you will stand firm and confident in the fire of your desire and your prayer; but you should also be ready for your death to be delayed for the time being, should God foresee something better for you. Pursue your goal forcefully, dedicating your whole life to God, in all your actions, words and intentions seeking by all possible means not to fall away from Him.

65. While still in the flesh, do not try to plumb the inner depths of intelligible realities even if the noetic power of your soul is drawn towards them by its purity. For unless the bodiless part of man, now mingled with breath and blood, is released from the grossness of materiality and enters the realm of the intelligible realities, it cannot grasp these realities properly. You should therefore prepare yourself to issue from this material world as though from some dark second maternal womb, and to enter that immaterial and radiant realm, joyfully glorifying our Benefactor who carries us through death towards the fulfilment of our hopes. Be watchful at all times because of the ungodly demons that surround us, always plotting to disgrace us and craftily watching for our heel (cf. Gen. 3 : 15), that is, for the end of our life, in order to trip us up. Until your death, therefore, go in fear and trembling because of the uncertainty of what is to come; for, endowed as you are with free will, you have been created with a mutable and fluctuating nature.

66. The enemy attacks us with fierce and terrible temptations when he perceives that our soul aspires to scale great heights of virtue. This we learn from the words of the Lord's Prayer and from our own attempts to ascend beyond the material duality of our flesh and sensory things. The hater of mankind tries us with such malice that we despair even of life. Of course, in his futility, he does not

realize that he confers many blessings on us, testing our endurance and weaving for us more splendid garlands.

67. No struggle is greater than the struggle for self-restraint and virginity. He who honours celibacy is admired even by the angels and is crowned just as athletes are. If, bound to flesh and blood, he strives to imitate through chastity the immaterial nature of the angels, terrible is the battle he has to fight; and if he is successful, so great is his achievement that it appears virtually impossible and beyond our nature. Indeed, it would be impossible if God did not help us from above, supporting the weakness of our nature, mending what is rotten, and somehow raising us from the ground through divine love and through hope for the gifts held in store for us.

68. Flesh flabby from over-drinking and over-sleeping is a great obstacle to self-restraint. True self-restraint is unaffected even by the fantasies that arise during sleep. If the intellect pursues these fantasies, this indicates that it still bears deep within itself the sickness of the passions. But if through grace it is found worthy to commune with God outside the body during sleep, it remains unaffected by these fantasies and serves as a vigilant guardian of soul and body, both of which are at peace. The intellect is then like a sheep-dog that keeps watch against the cunning wolves, not letting them ravage the flock.

69. Once more, I shall tell you something strange at which you are not to be startled. A mystery is accomplished secretly between the soul and God in the higher reaches of perfect purity, love and faith. When a man is completely reconciled to God he is united with Him through unceasing prayer and contemplation. Such was Elijah's state when he closed the heavens, causing a drought (cf. 1 Kgs. 17 : 1), and burnt the sacrifice with fire from heaven (cf. 1 Kgs. 18 : 36–38). In such a state Moses divided the sea (cf. Exod. 14 : 21) and defeated Amalek by stretching out his arms (cf. Exod. 17 : 11–13). In such a state Jonah was saved from the whale and from the deep (cf. Jonah 2 : 1–10). For the person found worthy of this mystery compels our most compassionate God to do whatever he wants. Even when still in the flesh, he has passed beyond the limits of corruption and mortality, and he awaits death as if it were an everyday sleep that pleasurably brings him to the fulfilment of his hopes.

70. Be full of reverence for our Lord's sufferings, for the

self-emptying of the divine Logos for our sake and, above all, for the sacrifice of the divine, life-creating body and blood and their inter-fusion with us. For we have been found worthy not only to partici-pate in them but also to officiate at the sacrifice. Humble yourself like a sheep for the slaughter, truly regarding all men as your superiors, and strive not to wound the conscience of any man, especially without reason. Do not dare to touch the holy gifts un-purified, lest you should be burnt like grass by the divine fire and destroyed like melting wax.

71. If you celebrate the divine, revered and awesome mysteries in the proper manner, with absolutely nothing on your conscience, you may hope for salvation; for the benefit you derive from this will be greater than that which derives from any work or from contem-plation. But if you cannot celebrate as you should, you will yourself realize that it is better to acknowledge your weakness and to with-draw from the priesthood than to fulfil your priestly ministry im-perfectly and impurely, appearing exalted in the eyes of many but being in reality a corpse to be wept over because of your unworthi-ness.

72. As the sun excels the stars so do the worship, propitiation and invocation of the priest excel all psalmody and prayer. For we priests sacrifice, set forth and offer in intercession the Only-Begotten Himself who in His freely-given compassion was slain on behalf of sinners. And, provided that our consciences are not pol-luted, we receive thereby not only remission of sins, but all the things for which we pray and which are for our benefit. What is united to the Divinity burns the brushwood of sin like coal and illumines the hearts of those who approach in faith. Similarly, the divine and precious blood cleanses and purifies more than any hyssop every stain and defilement in those who dare to receive it with all the purity and holiness of which they are capable.

73. As one of the saints[1] has said, it is not the ascended body of God the Logos that comes down from heaven and is sacrificed; it is the bread and wine themselves that are changed into the body and blood of Christ through the rites celebrated with faith, fear, longing and reverence by those found worthy of the holy priesthood. And this interchange takes place through the action and presence of the

[1] St John of Damaskos, *On the Orthodox Faith* iv, 13 (*P.G.* xcv, 1144–5; ed. Kotter, p. 194).

Holy Spirit. The bread and wine do not become a body other than that of our Lord, but are changed into His body, being then a source of immortality and no longer perishable. What therefore must be the purity and holiness required of the priest who touches the divine body? And what boldness must he not have as mediator between God and man, having as co-intercessors the most holy Mother of God, all the heavenly, angelic powers, and the saints from every age? Since he has an angelic, or even archangelic, office, in my view he needs to be like the angels and archangels.

74. You should note, Pisinios, that the holy gifts awaiting consecration lie on the altar after the Creed uncovered because there has to be a kind of voiceless supplication to God on behalf of those offering them. Seeing them uncovered, He does not overlook or despise this supplication; for He keeps in mind His voluntary self-emptying for us sinners, His ineffable self-abasement and His compassionate death. He did not ransom and save us through His passion because we deserved it but, blessed and forbearing as He is, He had mercy on us and restored us in spite of our offences.

75. Even though, through the practice of pure prayer that immaterially unites the immaterial intellect with God, you receive the pledge of the Spirit and see as in a mirror the blessedness that awaits you after this present life, and even though you fully and consciously experience the kingdom of heaven within you, do not allow yourself to be released from the flesh without foreknowledge of your death. Pray persistently for this knowledge and be in good hope of receiving it when you are close to death, if this is for your profit. Prepare yourself constantly for death, casting aside all fear, so that, traversing the air and escaping the evil spirits, you may boldly enter the vaults of heaven. Ranked with the angelic orders and numbered among all the righteous and elect, you will then behold the Divinity, in so far as this is possible. You will perceive, that is to say, the blessings that come from Him, as well as the Logos of God shedding His light through the regions above the heavens, adored in His unsullied flesh, together with the Father and the Spirit, in a single act of worship by all the host of heaven and all the saints. Amen.

GLOSSARY

AGE (αἰών – aeon): the ensemble of cosmic duration. It includes the angelic orders, and is an attribute of God as the principle and consummation of all the centuries created by Him. The term is used more particularly in two ways:

(i) Frequently a distinction is made between the 'present age' and the 'age to come' or the 'new age'. The first corresponds to our present sense of time, the second to time as it exists in God, that is, to eternity understood, not as endless time, but as the simultaneous presence of all time. Our present sense of time, according to which we experience time as sundered from God, is the consequence of the loss of vision and spiritual perception occasioned by the fall and is on this account more or less illusory. In reality time is not and never can be sundered from God, the 'present age' from the 'age to come'. Because of this the 'age to come' and its realities must be thought of, not as non-existent or as coming into existence in the future, but as actualities that by grace we can experience here and now. To indicate this, the Greek phrase for these realities (τὰ μέλλοντα – ta mellonta) is often translated as 'the blessings held in store'.

(ii) Certain texts, especially in St Maximos the Confessor, also use the term aeon in a connected but more specific way, to denote a level intermediate between eternity in the full sense (ἀϊδιότης – aïdiotis) and time as known to us in our present experience (χρόνος – chronos). Where this is the case we normally employ the rendering 'aeon' instead of 'age'. There are thus three levels:

(a) eternity, the totum simul or simultaneous presence of all time and reality as known to God, who alone has neither origin nor end, and who therefore is alone eternal in the full sense;

(b) the aeon, the totum simul as known to the angels, and also to human persons who possess experience of the 'age to come':

although having no end, these angelic or human beings, since they are created, are not self-originating and therefore are not eternal in the sense that God is eternal;

(c) time, that is, temporal succession as known to us in the 'present age'.

APPETITIVE ASPECT OF THE SOUL, or the soul's desiring power (τὸ ἐπιθυμητικόν – to epithymitikon): one of the three aspects or powers of the soul according to the tripartite division formulated by Plato (see his Republic, Book iv, 434D–441C) and on the whole accepted by the Greek Christian Fathers. The other two are, first, the intelligent aspect or power (τὸ λογιστικόν – to logistikon: see Intelligent); and, second, the incensive aspect or power (τὸ θυμικόν – to thymikon), which often manifests itself as wrath or anger, but which can be more generally defined as the force provoking vehement feelings. The three aspects or powers can be used positively, that is, in accordance with nature and as created by God, or negatively, that is, in a way contrary to nature and leading to sin (q.v.). For instance, the incensive power can be used positively to repel demonic attacks or to intensify desire for God; but it can also, when not controlled, lead to self-indulgent, disruptive thought and action.

The appetitive and incensive aspects, in particular the former, are sometimes termed the soul's passible aspect (τὸ παθητικόν – to pathitikon), that is to say, the aspect which is more especially vulnerable to pathos or passion (q.v.), and which, when not transformed by positive spiritual influences, is susceptive to the influence of negative and self-destructive forces. The intelligent aspect, although also susceptible to passion, is not normally regarded as part of the soul's passible aspect.

ASSENT (συγκατάθεσις – synkatathesis): see Temptation.

ATTENTIVENESS (προσοχή – prosochi): see Watchfulness.

COMPUNCTION (κατάνυξις – katanyxis): in our version sometimes also translated 'deep penitence'. The state of one who is 'pricked to the heart', becoming conscious both of his own sinfulness and of the forgiveness extended to him by God; a mingled feeling of sorrow, tenderness and joy, springing from sincere repentance (q.v.).

CONCEPTUAL IMAGE (νόημα – noïma): see Thought.

CONTEMPLATION (θεωρία – theoria): the perception or vision of the intellect (q.v.) through which one attains spiritual knowledge (q.v.). It may be contrasted with the practice of the virtues (πρακτική – *praktiki*) which designates the more external aspect of the ascetic life – purification and the keeping of the command- ments – but which is an indispensable prerequisite of contempla- tion. Depending on the level of personal spiritual growth, contemplation has two main stages: it may be either of the inner essences or principles (q.v.) of created beings or, at a higher stage, of God Himself.

COUPLING (συνδυασμός – *syndyasmos*): *see* Temptation.

DELUSION (πλάνη – *plani*): *see* Illusion.

DESIRE, Desiring power of the soul: *see* Appetitive aspect of the soul.

DISCRIMINATION (διάκρισις – *diakrisis*): a spiritual gift per- mitting one to discriminate between the types of thought that enter into one's mind, to assess them accurately ánd to treat them accordingly. Through this gift one gains 'discernment of spirits' – that is, the ability to distinguish between the thoughts or visions inspired by God and the suggestions or fantasies coming from the devil. It is a kind of eye or lantern of the soul by which man finds his way along the spiritual path without falling into extremes; thus it includes the idea of discretion.

DISPASSION (ἀπάθεια – *apatheia*): among the writers of the texts here translated, some regard passion (q.v.) as evil and the conse- quence of sin (q.v.), and for them dispassion signifies passionless- ness, the uprooting of the passions; others, such as St Isaiah the Solitary, regard the passions as fundamentally good, and for them dispassion signifies a state in which the passions are exercised in accordance with their original purity and so without committing sin in act or thought. Dispassion is a state of reintegration and spiritual freedom; when translating the term into Latin, Cassian rendered it 'purity of heart'. Such a state may imply impartiality and detachment, but not indifference, for if a dispassionate man does not suffer on his own account, he suffers for his fellow creatures. It consists, not in ceasing to feel the attacks of the demons, but in no 'longer yielding to them. It is positive, not negative: Evagrios links it closely with the quality of love (*agapi*) and Diadochos speaks of the 'fire of dispassion' (§ 17: in our translation, vol. i, p. 258). Dispassion is among the gifts of God.

ECSTASY (ἔκστασις – *ekstasis*): a 'going out' from oneself and from all created things towards God, under the influence of *eros* or intense longing (q.v.). A man does not attain ecstasy by his own efforts, but is drawn out of himself by the power of God's love. Ecstasy implies a passing beyond all the conceptual thinking of the discursive reason (q.v.). It may sometimes be marked by a state of trance, or by a loss of normal consciousness; but such psycho-physical accompaniments are in no way essential. Occasionally the term *ekstasis* is used in a bad sense, to mean infatuation, loss of self-control, or madness.

FAITH (πίστις – *pistis*): not only an individual or theoretical belief in the dogmatic truths of Christianity, but an all-embracing rela-tionship, an attitude of love and total trust in God. As such it involves a transformation of man's entire life. Faith is a gift from God, the means whereby we are taken up into the whole thean-thropic activity of God in Christ and of man in Christ through which man attains salvation.

FALLEN NATURE (παλαιὸς ἄνθρωπος – *palaios anthropos*): literally, the 'old man'. *See* Flesh, sense (ii).

FANTASY (φαντασία – *fantasia*): denoting the image-producing faculty of the psyche, this is one of the most important words in the hesychast vocabulary. As one begins to advance along the spiritual path one begins to 'perceive' images of things which have no direct point of reference in the external world, and which emerge inexplicably from within oneself. This experience is a sign that one's consciousness is beginning to deepen: outer sensations and ordinary thoughts have to some extent been quietened, and the impulses, fears, hopes, passions hidden in the subconscious region are beginning to break through to the surface. One of the goals of the spiritual life is indeed the attainment of a spiritual knowledge (q.v.) which transcends both the ordinary level of consciousness and the subconscious; and it is true that images, especially when the recipient is in an advanced spiritual state, may well be projections on the plane of the imagination of celestial archetypes, and that in this case they can be used cre-atively, to form the images of sacred art and iconography. But more often than not they will simply derive from a middle or lower sphere, and will have nothing spiritual or creative about them. Hence they correspond to the world of fantasy and not to the world of the imagination in the proper sense. It is on this account that the hesychastic masters on the whole take a negative attitude towards them. They emphasize the grave dangers involved in this kind of experience, especially as the very production of these images may be the consequence of demonic or diabolic activity; and they admonish those still in the early stages and not yet possessing spiritual discrimination (q.v.) not to be enticed and led captive by these illusory appearances, whose tumult may well overwhelm the mind. Their advice is to pay no attention to them, but to continue with prayer and invocation, dispelling them with the name of Jesus Christ.

FLESH (σάρξ – sarx): has various senses: (i) the human in contrast to the divine, as in the sentence, 'The Logos became flesh' (John 1 : 14); (ii) fallen and sinful human nature in contrast to human nature as originally created and dwelling in communion with God; man when separated from God and in rebellion against Him; (iii) the body in contrast to the soul. The second meaning is probably the most frequent. If the word is being employed in this sense, it is important to distinguish 'flesh' from 'body' (σῶμα – soma). When St Paul lists the 'works of the flesh' in Gal. 5 : 19–21, he mentions such things as 'seditions', 'heresy' and 'envy', which have no special connection with the body. In sense (ii) of the word, 'flesh' denotes the *whole* soul–body structure in so far as a man is fallen; likewise 'spirit' denotes the *whole* soul–body structure in so far as a man is redeemed. The soul as well as the body can become fleshly or 'carnal', just as the body as well as the soul can become spiritual. Asceticism involves a war against the flesh – in sense (ii) of the word – but not against the body as such.

GUARD OF THE HEART, OF THE INTELLECT (φυλακὴ καρδίας, νοῦ – phylaki kardias, nou): see Watchfulness.

HEART (καρδία – kardia): not simply the physical organ but the spiritual centre of man's being, man as made in the image of God, his deepest and truest self, or the inner shrine, to be entered only through sacrifice and death, in which the mystery of the union between the divine and the human is consummated. ' "I called with my whole heart", says the psalmist – that is, with body, soul and spirit' (John Klimakos, *The Ladder of Divine Ascent*, Step 28, translated by Archimandrite Lazarus [London, 1959], pp. 257–8).

'Heart' has thus an all-embracing significance: 'prayer of the heart' means prayer not just of the emotions and affections, but of the whole person, including the body.

ILLUSION (πλάνη – plani): in our version sometimes also translated 'delusion'. Literally, wandering astray, deflection from the right path; hence error, beguilement, the acceptance of a mirage mistaken for truth. Cf. the literal sense of sin (q.v.) as 'missing the mark'.

INCENSIVE POWER or aspect of the soul (θυμός – thymos; τὸ θυμικόν – to thymikon): see Appetitive aspect of the soul.

INNER ESSENCES OR PRINCIPLES (λόγοι – logoi): see Logos.

INTELLECT (νοῦς – nous): the highest faculty in man, through which – provided it is purified – he knows God or the inner essences or principles (q.v.) of created things by means of direct apprehension or spiritual perception. Unlike the dianoia or reason (q.v.), from which it must be carefully distinguished, the intellect does not function by formulating abstract concepts and then arguing on this basis to a conclusion reached through deductive reasoning, but it understands divine truth by means of immediate experience, intuition or 'simple cognition' (the term used by St Isaac the Syrian). The intellect dwells in the 'depths of the soul'; it constitutes the innermost aspect of the heart (St Diadochos, §§ 79, 88: in our translation, vol. i, pp. 280, 287). The intellect is the organ of contemplation (q.v.), the 'eye of the heart' (Makarian Homilies).

INTELLECTION (νόησις – noīsis): not an abstract concept or a visual image, but the act or function of the intellect (q.v.) whereby it apprehends spiritual realities in a direct manner.

INTELLIGENT (λογικός – logikos): the Greek term logikos is so closely connected with Logos (q.v.), and therefore with the divine Intellect, that to render it simply as 'logical' and hence descriptive of the reason (q.v.) is clearly inadequate. Rather it pertains to the intellect (q.v.) and qualifies the possessor of spiritual knowledge (q.v.). Hence when found in conjunction with 'soul' (logiki psychi), logikos is translated as 'deiform' or as 'endowed with intelligence'. Intelligence itself (τὸ λογικόν – to logikon; τὸ λογιστικόν – to logistikon; ὁ λογισμός – ho logismos) is the ruling aspect of the intellect (q.v.) or its operative faculty.

INTENSE LONGING (ἔρως – eros): the word eros, when used in these texts, retains much of the significance it has in Platonic thought. It denotes that intense aspiration and longing which impel man towards union with God, and at the same time something of the force which links the divine and the human. As unitive love *par excellence*, it is not distinct from *agapi*, but may be contrasted with *agapi* in that it expresses a greater degree of intensity and ecstasy (q.v.).

INTIMATE COMMUNION (παρρησία – *parrisia*): literally, 'frankness', 'freedom of speech'; hence freedom of approach to God, such as Adam possessed before the fall and the saints have regained by grace; a sense of confidence and loving trust in God's mercy.

JESUS PRAYER (᾽Ιησοῦ εὐχή – *Iisou evchi*): the invocation of the name of Jesus, most commonly in the words, 'Lord Jesus Christ, Son of God, have mercy on me', although there are a number of variant forms. Not merely a 'technique' or a 'Christian mantra', but a prayer addressed to the Person of Jesus Christ, expressing our living faith (q.v.) in Him as Son of God and Saviour.

LOGOS (Λόγος – *Logos*): the Second Person of the Holy Trinity, or the Intellect, Wisdom and Providence of God in whom and through whom all things are created. As the unitary cosmic principle, the Logos contains in Himself the multiple *logoi* (inner principles or inner essences, thoughts of God) in accordance with which all things come into existence at the times and places, and in the forms, appointed for them, each single thing thereby containing in itself the principle of its own development. It is these *logoi*, contained principially in the Logos and manifest in the forms of the created universe, that constitute the first or lower stage of contemplation (q.v.).

MIND: *see* Reason.

NOETIC (νοητός – *noïtos*): that which belongs to or is characteristic of the intellect (q.v.). *See also* Intellection.

PASSION (πάθος – *pathos*): in Greek, the word signifies literally that which happens to a person or thing, an experience undergone passively; hence an appetite or impulse such as anger, desire or jealousy, that violently dominates the soul. Many Greek Fathers regard the passions as something intrinsically evil, a 'disease' of the soul: thus St John Klimakos affirms that God is not the creator of the passions and that they are 'unnatural', alien to man's true self (*The Ladder of Divine Ascent*, Step 26, translated by Archimandrite Lazarus [*op. cit.*], p. 211). Other Greek Fathers, however, look on the passions as impulses originally placed in man by God, and so fundamentally good, although at present distorted by sin (cf. St Isaiah the Solitary, § 1 : in our translation, vol. i, p. 22). On this second view, then, the passions are to be educated, not eradicated; to be transfigured, not suppressed; to be used positively, not negatively (*see* Dispassion).

PRACTICE OF THE VIRTUES (πρακτική – *praktiki*): *see* Contemplation.

PREPOSSESSION (πρόληψις – *prolipsis*): *see* Temptation.

PROVOCATION (προσβολή – *prosvoli*): *see* Temptation.

REASON, mind (διάνοια – *dianoia*): the discursive, conceptualizing and logical faculty in man, the function of which is to draw conclusions or formulate concepts deriving from data provided either by revelation or spiritual knowledge (q.v.) or by sense-observation. The knowledge of the reason is consequently of a lower order than spiritual knowledge (q.v.) and does not imply any direct apprehension or perception of the inner essences or principles (q.v.) of created beings, still less of divine truth itself. Indeed, such apprehension or perception, which is the function of the intellect (q.v.), is beyond the scope of the reason.

REBUTTAL (ἀντιλογία – *antilogia*; ἀντίρρησις – *antirrisis*): the repulsing of a demon or demonic thought at the moment of provocation (q.v.); or, in a more general sense, the bridling of evil thoughts.

REMEMBRANCE OF GOD (μνήμη Θεοῦ – *mnimi Theou*): not just calling God to mind, but the state of recollectedness or concentration in which attention is centred on God. As such it is the opposite of the state of self-indulgence and insensitivity.

REPENTANCE (μετάνοια – *metanoia*): the Greek signifies primarily a 'change of mind' or 'change of intellect': not only sorrow, contrition or regret, but more positively and fundamentally the conversion or turning of our whole life towards God.

SENSUAL PLEASURE (ἡδονή – *hidoni*): according to the context the Greek term signifies either sensual pleasure (the most frequent meaning) or spiritual pleasure or delight.

SIN (ἁμαρτία – *hamartia*): the primary meaning of the Greek word is 'failure' or, more specifically, 'failure to hit the mark' and so a 'missing of the mark', a 'going astray' or, ultimately, 'failure to achieve the purpose for which one is created'. It is closely related, therefore, to illusion (q.v.). The translation 'sin' should be read with these connotations in mind.

SORROW (λύπη – lypi): often with the sense of 'godly sorrow' – the sorrow which nourishes the soul with the hope engendered by repentance (q.v.).

SPIRITUAL KNOWLEDGE (γνῶσις – gnosis): the knowledge of the intellect (q.v.) as distinct from that of the reason (q.v.). As such it is knowledge inspired by God, and so linked with contemplation (q.v.) and immediate spiritual perception.

STILLNESS (ἡσυχία – hesychia): from which are derived the words hesychasm and hesychast, used to denote the whole spiritual tradition represented in the Philokalia as well as the person who pursues the spiritual path it delineates (see Introduction, vol. i, pp. 14–16): a state of inner tranquillity or mental quietude and concentration which arises in conjunction with, and is deepened by, the practice of pure prayer and the guarding of heart (q.v.) and intellect (q.v.). Not simply silence, but an attitude of listening to God and of openness towards Him.

TEMPERAMENT (κρᾶσις – krasis): primarily the well-balanced blending of elements, humours or qualities in animal bodies, but sometimes extended to denote the whole soul–body structure of man. In this sense it is the opposite to a state of psychic or physical disequilibrium.

TEMPTATION (πειρασμός – peirasmos): also translated in our version as 'trial' or 'test'. The word indicates, according to context: (i) a test or trial sent to man by God, so as to aid his progress on the spiritual way; (ii) a suggestion from the devil, enticing man into sin.

Using the word in sense (ii), the Greek Fathers employ a series of technical terms to describe the process of temptation. (See in particular Mark the Ascetic, On the Spiritual Law, §§ 138–41, in vol. i of our translation, pp. 119–20; John Klimakos, Ladder, Step 15, translated by Archimandrite Lazarus [op. cit.], pp. 157–8; Maximos, On Love, i, §§ 83–84, in vol. ii of our translation, pp. 62–63; John of Damaskos, On the Virtues and Vices, also in vol. ii of our translation, pp. 337–8.) The basic distinction made by these Fathers is between the demonic provocation and man's *assent*: the first lies outside man's control, while for the second he is morally responsible. In detail, the chief terms employed are as follows:

(i) *Provocation* (προσβολή – *prosvoli*): the initial incitement to evil. Mark the Ascetic defines this as an 'image-free stimulation in the heart'; so long as the provocation is not accompanied by images, it does not involve man in any guilt. Such provocations, originating as they do from the devil, assail man from the outside independently of his free will, and so he is not morally responsible for them. His liability to these provocations is not a consequence of the fall: even in paradise, Mark maintains, Adam was assailed by the devil's provocations. Man cannot prevent provocations from assailing him; what does lie in his power, however, is to maintain constant watchfulness (q.v.) and so to reject each provocation as soon as it emerges into his consciousness – that is to say, at its first appearance as a thought in his mind or intellect (μονολόγιστος ἔμφασις – *monologistos emphasis*). If he does reject the provocation, the sequence is cut off and the process of temptation is terminated.

(ii) *Momentary disturbance* (παραρριπισμός – *pararripismos*) of the intellect, occurring 'without any movement or working of bodily passion' (see Mark, *Letter to Nicolas the Solitary*: in our translation, vol. i, p. 153). This seems to be more than the 'first appearance' of a provocation described in stage (i) above; for, at a certain point of spiritual growth in this life, it is possible to be totally released from such 'momentary disturbance', whereas no one can expect to be altogether free from demonic provocations.

(iii) *Communion* (ὁμιλία – *homilia*); *coupling* (συνδυασμός – *syndyasmos*). Without as yet entirely assenting to the demonic provocation, a man may begin to 'entertain' it, to converse or parley with it, turning it over in his mind pleasurably, yet still hesitating whether or not to act upon it. At this stage, which is indicated by the terms 'communion' or 'coupling', the provocation is no longer 'image-free' but has become a *logismos* or thought (q.v.); and man is morally responsible for having allowed this to happen.

(iv) *Assent* (συγκατάθεσις – *synkatathesis*). This signifies a step beyond mere 'communion' or 'coupling'. No longer merely 'playing' with the evil suggestion, a man now resolves to act upon it. There is now no doubt as to his moral culpability: even if circumstances prevent him from sinning outwardly, he is judged by God according to the intention in his heart.

(v) *Prepossession* (πρόληψις – *prolipsis*): defined by Mark as 'the involuntary presence of former sins in the memory'. This state of 'prepossession' or prejudice results from repeated acts of sin which predispose a man to yield to particular temptations. In principle he retains his free choice and can reject demonic provocations; but in practice the force of habit makes it more and more difficult for him to resist.

(vi) *Passion* (q.v.). If a man does not fight strenuously against a prepossession, it will develop into an evil passion.

THEOLOGY (θεολογία – *theologia*): denotes in these texts far more than the learning about God and religious doctrine acquired through academic study. It signifies active and conscious participation in or perception of the realities of the divine world – in other words, the realization of spiritual knowledge (q.v.). To be a theologian in the full sense, therefore, presupposes the attainment of the state of stillness (q.v.) and dispassion (q.v.), itself the concomitant of pure and undistracted prayer, and so requires gifts bestowed on but extremely few persons.

THOUGHT (λογισμός – *logismos*; νόημα – *noïma*): (i) frequently signifies not thought in the ordinary sense, but thought provoked by the demons, and therefore often qualified in translation by the adjective 'evil' or 'demonic'; it can also signify divinely-inspired thought; (ii) a 'conceptual image', intermediate between fantasy (q.v.) and an abstract concept; this sense of *noïma* is frequent in the texts of St Maximos, where the rendering 'conceptual image' is normally adopted.

WATCHFULNESS (νῆψις – *nipsis*): literally, the opposite to a state of drunken stupor; hence spiritual sobriety, alertness, vigilance. It signifies an attitude of attentiveness (προσοχή – *prosochi*), whereby one keeps watch over one's inward thoughts and fantasies (q.v.), maintaining guard over the heart and intellect (φυλακὴ καρδίας/νοῦ – *phylaki kardias/nou*; τήρησις καρδίας/νοῦ – *tirisis kardias/nou*). In Hesychios, *On Watchfulness and Holiness*, §§ 1–6 (in our translation, vol. i, pp. 162–3), watchfulness is given a very broad definition, being used to indicate the whole range of the practice of the virtues. It is closely linked with purity of heart and stillness (q.v.) The Greek title of the *Philokalia* is 'The

Philokalia of the Niptic Fathers', i.e. of the fathers who practised and inculcated the virtue of watchfulness. This shows how
central is the role assigned by St Nikodimos to this state.

WRATH, wrathfulness: *see* Appetitive aspect of the soul.

APPENDIX

The *Various Texts* attributed to St Maximos the Confessor

As indicated in the introductory note (pp. 49–50), the five centuries of *Various Texts on Theology, the Divine Econony, and Virtue and Vice* are only in part by St Maximos. In detail the source of these texts is as follows:

M: from the works of Maximos (often the wording has been adapted by the compiler).

S: from the *scholia* on *To Thalassios: On Various Questions*.

MS: partly from Maximos, partly from the *scholia*.

D: from St Dionysios the Areopagite.

FIRST CENTURY

1–25	?M	77–8	S
26–42	M	79–83	M
43	?M	84	S
44–7	M	85	MS
48	MS	86–8	M
49–53	M	89	S
54	S	90–1	M
55–61	M	92–3	S
62	MS	94	M
63–4	S	95	S
65–70	M	96	M
71	S	97	MS
72–4	M	98	S
75	S	99–100	M
76	M		

SECOND CENTURY

1	M	59	S
2–3	S	60	M
4–10	M	61	S
11	MS	62–3	M
12–13	S	64	S
14–18	M	65	MS
19–21	S	66–7	M
22–3	M	68–9	S
24	S	70–2	MS
25	MS	73	M
26	S	74–5	S
27	MS	76	M
28–9	S	77	S
30–4	M	78–9	M
35–7	S	80	S
38	M	81–4	M
39–41	S	85	MS
42	M	86	S
43–4	S	87	MS
45–8	M	88–9	S
49	S	90	M
50–3	M	91	S
54–5	MS	92	MS
56	M	93–9	M
57	S	100	S
58	M		

THIRD CENTURY

1	MS	13	S
2	M	14	M
3	S	15	S
4	MS	16–17	M
5–6	S	18	S
7	M	19	MS
8	S	20	M
9–12	M	21	MS

THIRD CENTURY (cont.)

22	M	61–2	S
23	S	63	M
24	MS	64–8	S
25	M	69–71	M
26–7	S	72–4	S
28–31	M	75–6	M
32–3	S	77	S
34	M	78	M
35–7	S	79	S
38	MS	80–7	M
39–40	M	88–9	S
41	S	90	M
42	M	91	S
43	MS	92	M
44–50	S	93	S
51	M	94–5	M
52	S	96	S
53–4	M	97	M
55	?	98–9	S
56–7	S	100	M
58–60	M		

FOURTH CENTURY

1	S	23	MS
2	M	24	S
3	S	25	M
4	MS	26	S
5	S	27–9	M
6–8	M	30	S
9	S	31–3	M
10	M	34	S
11–12	S	35	M
13	M	36	S
14	S	37	M
15–21	M	38	S
22	S	39–40	M

FOURTH CENTURY (cont.)

41	S	71–4	M
42–4	M	75	S
45	MS	76–8	M
46	S	79	MS
47	M	80	S
48	MS	81–4	M
49–52	M	85–8	S
53–5	S	89	M
56	M	90	MS
57–8	S	91–2	S
59	M	93	MS
60	S	94	M
61	M	95	S
62	S	96	MS
63–7	M	97–8	M
68	S	99	S
69	M	100	M
70	S		

FIFTH CENTURY

1–2	S	25	S
3–4	MS	26–7	MS
5	M	28	M
6	S	29	MS
7	M	30	M
8	S	31–2	MS
9	M	33	S
10	MS	34	M
11	S	35	MS
12–13	M	36–7	M
14–15	S	38	MS
16–17	M	39	M
18–19	S	40	S
20–1	M	41	M
22–3	MS	42	S
24	M	43	MS

FIFTH CENTURY (cont.)

44	M	59–65	M
45	S	66	D
46	MS	67	M
47–9	M	68	D
50	S	69–81	M
51	M	82–3	D
52	MS	84	M
53	M	85–6	D
54	S	87–9	M
55	MS	90–1	D
56–7	M	92–100	M
58	S		

INDEX

[Major entries are given in bold type]

PERSONS AND SOURCES

Alonios, Abba (?4th–5th cent.), 34n.
Apophthegmata, 34n., 37n., 344n.
Arsenios, Abba (early 5th cent.), 37, 344
Athanasios of Alexandria, St (c. 296–373), 333

Basil the Great, St (c. 330–79), 346, 356

Cassian, St John (c. 360–435), 381
Chrysostom, St John (c. 347–407), 28

Diadochos of Photiki, St (c. 400–c. 486), 347, 381, 384
Dionysios the Areopagite, St (c. 500), 49, 50, 64, 83, 272n., 276n., 280n., 391

Elpidios the Presbyter (7th cent.), 52
Ephrem the Syrian, St (c. 306–373), 333
Evagrios the Solitary (345/6–399), 13, 26n., 27n., 29n., 49, 306, 333, 381

Gregory of Nyssa, St (c. 330–c. 395), 178, 291n.
Gregory the Theologian (of Nazianzos), St (329–89), 18, 50, 64, 70, 355n.

Hesychios of Vatos, St (?8th–9th cent.), 389

Isaac the Syrian (of Nineveh), St (7th cent.), 384

Isaiah the Solitary, St (? d. 89/91), 381, 386

John, contemporary of Philimon, 347
John Cassian: *see* Cassian
John Chrysostom: *see* Chrysostom
John of Damaskos, St (c. 675–c. 749), 333, 358, 376n., 387
John of Karpathos, St (? 7th cent.), 358, 365n.
John Klimakos: *see* Klimakos
John Philoponos (6th cent.), 69n.
John the Solitary (c. 500), 333
Josephus (c. 37–c. 100), 71

Klimakos, St John (7th cent.), 333, 383, 385, 387

Makarian Homilies (? late 4th cent.), 384
Makarios of Corinth, St (1731–1805), 50
Mark the Ascetic, St (? early 5th cent.), 19n., 24n., 333, 335, 336n., 387, 388, 389
Maximos the Confessor, St (c. 580–662), 13, 27n., 48–51, 306, 333, 379, 387, 391

Neilos the Ascetic, St (d. c. 430), 29n.
Nikodimos of the Holy Mountain, St (1749–1809), 9, 50, 333, 358, 390

Origen (c. 185–c. 254), 49

SUBJECTS

by the Logos, 361; known from
creation, 180, 189; not known
rationally but by faith, 115–16, 146;
not known by man's natural power,
110, 120; natural desire for, 284;
not outside but within us, 146, 175;
direct experience of, 242.

Transcendence of God, 114–15,
124; has no opposite, 87; alone has
substantive or absolute existence,
87–8, 115, 164; beyond being and
existence, 87, 114, 137, 165, 215,
263; beyond potentiality, 114; simplicity of, 101, 132, 137, 138, 165;
has no accidents or qualities, 165,
295–6; category of relationship not
applicable to, 115, 277, 296.

God is not an intellect, 138; God
as Intellect, 142, 164–5, 196, 384,
385; Intellect, Logos and Spirit,
189, 295–6; plurality and unity in,
222, 295.

God as fire, 371; as impassible,
295, 370; unmoved, 279; yet subject to motion, 280–1; goes out
from Himself in ecstasy, 281; as
centre of circle, 138; as Creator,
100–1; and created being, 114; and
time, 70, 115, 123–4, 332; 'eyes'
of God, 220; face of God, 267.
See Energy, Essence, Father, Light,
Spirit, Trinity, Wrath
Golden calf, 177
Gospel: and the Law, 124, 133–4,
144, 150. See New Testament
Grace: and nature, 181, 192, 196,
212, 228, 238–9, 263–4, 265; and
natural law, 258, 262–4, 267;
necessity of, 19, 30, 31, 41, 72,
76, 212, 214, 368, 375; salvation
by grace alone, 127, 366, 369, 377;
grace as a free gift, 228; grace and
free will, 27–8, 216, 217–18, 287,
300, 301, 368; and eternal being,
86; and dispassion, 155, 284, 308,
309, 365; and incorruption, 302;
deification by grace, 87, 142, 160,
178, 181–2, 218, 263, 267, 271,
284, 287, 297; grace as the pledge
of the Spirit, 110; gifts of grace from

the Spirit, 15, 145, 186–7; not to
be sought as an end in themselves,
369; to be shared, 119, 133; grace
of theology, 329; loss of grace, 184,
211, 213. See Abandonment, Law
Greed: see Gluttony
Greek philosophy, 155, 163; polytheism, 295. See Philosophy
Guard of heart, intellect: see Heart,
Intellect, Watchfulness

Habakkuk, 360
Habit, influence of, 27, 39, 40, 46,
95, 203, 263, 319, 336, 371
Haran, 143
Harvest, symbolical meaning of, 121–3
Healing, gift of, 217, 238
Heart, 383–4; and the intellect, 384;
the two identified, 109; distinguished, 211; hidden workshop of,
252; judgment seat of, 29; dwelling-
place of God, 109, 158; of good
thoughts, 312; of evil thoughts, 20;
of evil spirits, 181, 323; does not
need external matter, 251; circumcision of the heart, 123; guarding
of the heart, 36, 308, 347, 348,
389; and stillness, 387; meditation
in the heart, 347; prayer of the
heart, 348, 384; pure heart, 27, 33,
109, 157–8; equivalent to dispassion, 381; and watchfulness, 389
Heaven, 25, 160–1, 287. See Firmament
Hell, 25, 139, 353, 372; Christ's
descent into, 143
Herdsman: signifies practice of virtues,
74
Hermits, 17. See Hesychasm
Herod, 128–9, 182
Hesychasm, 16–17, 85, 387. See
Stillness
Hezekiah, 204, 208, 210, 214
High priest, 132, 142, 145
Holy communion, 351, 356, 372. See
Liturgy
Holy of holies, 132, 142, 145, 172
Hope, 21, 53, 65, 99, 170, 201–3,
283, 320, 328, 368, 373
Horeb, 156

Promises to God, 207, 253, 290

Providence, 58, 68, 72, 73, 81, 99, 102, 139, 141, 212, 271, 272, 278–9, 286, 308, 310, 312, 367, 385; and judgment, 61, 64, 82, 88, 141, 218, 264, 271, 286; symbolized by the number ten, 130

Provocation, of demons, things or evil thoughts, 16, 89, 337–8, 387–8. *See* Temptation

Psalm 23, interpreted, 81–3

Psalmody, psalter, 20, 57, 106, 321, 326, 347, 348

Purity, perfect, 375. *See* Dispassion, Heart, Intellect, Prayer

Ram: typifies intelligence, 273

Rancour, 19, 85, 97–8, 103–5, 321, 323

Ravishment: *see* Ecstasy

Reason, 386; distinguished from intellect, 41, 334, 384; from intelligence, 223; God not known rationally, 115; doctrines of Trinity and incarnation transcend reason, 146, 167; faith superior to reason, 116, 190

Rebuttal, 338, 386

Red Sea, 124

Relationship, category of, not applicable to God, 115, 128

Relatives, 14–15, 24, 66

Remembrance of God, 34, 200, 201, 386

Renunciation, three forms of, 320; vows of, 351

Repentance, 27, 259, 354, 369–70, 386

Resentment: *see* Rancour

Resurrection: of Christ, 126–7, 144, 145, 241; of God within us, 202; of the will through virtue, 241; of life, 289; of the soul, 309; mystical, 125–6; of the body or the dead, 25, 60, 110, 236, 292, 328, 373. *See* Incorruption

Revelation, 239

Riches, love of: *see* Avarice

Roman empire, 163

Rule, need to maintain a regular, 319; monastic rule, 23

Sabbath: observed spiritually, 80; preparation for, 118, 126; symbolical meaning, 121–5, 152–3, 271–2, 369; sabbath rest of God, 123, 125, 126, 138

Sacraments: *see* Baptism, Liturgy

Sacrifice, animal, 147, 196–7, 273; of praise, 134

Saints, intercession of, 366, 377

Salvation: three stages, 141; and faith, 239; by grace, 127, 366, 369; how attained, 372; and the incarnation, 49

Samaritan, the Good, 110

Samuel, 150, 230, 274

Saul, 93, 149–50, 230–1, 269, 274

Scripture: meditation on, 348–9; recitation of, 346–7, 350; contains four things, 314; interpretation of, 193; literal and spiritual sense, 134–5, 142, 147–8, 151, 155–6, 189, 205–6, 207, 253–4, 267–9, 273–4. *See* Symbols

Second coming of Christ, 135, 141, 144. *See* Judgment

Self-control (*enkrateia*), 16, 18–19, 59, 63, 68, 102, 204, 271, 283, 310, 314, 329, 359, 367, 368; and the fear of God, 53; and love, 89, 307, 308, 311, 313, 316, 317, 321; opposite of self-love, 84; leads to dispassion, 35; but distinguished from it, 27

Self-esteem (*kenodoxia*), 57, 62, 66, 68, 83, 92–3, 95, 105, 188, 226–7, 229, 262, 308, 312, 326–7; one of the three chief passions, 26, 75, 92, 324; and avarice, 96; and unchastity, 128–9; symbolized by Absalom, 225. *See* Praise, Pride

Self-examination, daily, 36

Self-indulgence: *see* Pleasure

Self-love (*philavtia*), 333, 372; as attachment to the body, 35, 66, 75, 84, 92, 175, 313, 336; source of all evil, 27, 34, 84, 171–2, 306, 313, 323; mother of all passions and vices, 66, 75, 92, 324, 335, 336; causes fragmentation of human nature, 173, 263, 274; purified self-love, 171, 174, 284

Self-restraint (*sophrosyni*), 18–19, 57, 68, 76, 274, 283, 336, 367, 375

Senses: the five, 130, 254, 334; in animals and in man, 40; two orders, of body and soul, 334; two forms of sense-perception, 118; its inadequacy, 41, 156; senses not evil, 67, 325; yet linked with the power of sin, 176; misused at the fall, 44–5, 239, 243, 254.

Senses connected with pleasure and pain, 176, 231–7, 243; linked to the passions, 60, 77, 261, 266, 269, 277, 319, 321; but distinguished from them, 177, 201; senses misused by soul or intellect, 266, 268, 319; conflict between senses and intellect, 235; devil enters intellect through senses, 176, 201, 204.

Senses controlled by intellect or intelligence, 33, 39, 176, 182, 194–5, 235, 254, 258, 274, 278, 315–16; detachment from senses and sensible objects, 135, 176, 184, 225, 234, 297, 314, 325; senses to be shut or stilled, 148, 204, 215, 308, 319; can be sanctified, 116, 145, 176; reforged, 350; transmuted into intellect and incorrupt, 223; sensible and intelligible realms united, 287–8. *See* Images

Seven: symbolizes time, 130; seventh day of creation, 124–6

Sexual appetites, 67–8, 71, 83, 93, 108, 168. *See* Desire

Shepherd: signifies gnostic, 75

Sick, care of, 22

Silence, 21, 31, 120, 352, 356–7; silence beyond intellection, 131; proclaims God, 271; and stillness, 387

Sin, 15, 386–7; misuse of what is good, 97; not part of human nature, 167; and death, 254, 299; and sensual pleasure, 15, 234; dominion of, 246; law of, 237, 288, 302, 303; as death of the soul, 244; and the law of the flesh, 251; habitual and impulsive, 95; active, 70, 321;

of body and intellect, 76; dying to sin, 240–1; cannot penetrate to spiritual realm, 176; five things that cut us off from, 79; becoming sinless in Christ, 159

Six, signifies practice of the virtues, 223; sixth day of creation, 124–6

Slander, 59, 111, 274

Sleep, 20, 206, 350; sense-perception during, 118, 310; fantasies and demonic attacks during, 77, 79, 375; pure images during, 63; prayer during, 348; sleeping on the ground, 25, 42, 45, 227, 334

Sobriety (*nipsis*): see Watchfulness

Solitude, 22. See Hesychasm

Solomon, 353

Son of God: see Christ, Logos

Sonship, grace of (*uiothesia*), 129, 287, 291, 316, 318, 334, 337

Sorrow, 387

Soul: contrasted with body, 39, 43–4, 53–4, 174–5, 176, 194, 254, 277, 308, 334, 340, 361; the two in harmony, 163; both created by God, 94; soul contrasted with flesh, 91, 134, 237, 277, 283–4; but may become flesh, 383; soul and intelligence, 88, 308; and intellect, 311, 312, 334, 335, 337, 384; and spirit, 228, 352.

Senses of the soul, 334; natural powers, 273; three powers or aspects, 16, 18, 38, 60, 61–2, 66–7, 105, 177, 178, 193, 202–3, 207–8, 259, 298, 333, 337, 339, 380; different classification of three powers, 88; passible aspect of, 73, 82, 89, 91, 99, 107, 153, 312, 315, 316, 335, 380; passions of, 15–16, 59, 61, 334–5, 340; impurity of, 89; death of, 244, 318, 322; virtues of, 316, 334, 340; as wax or clay, 116.

All souls essentially equal, 116; soul as *logiki* or deiform, 18, 116, 313, 384; and the divine image, 116, 148, 294, 341; true home in spiritual realities, 176; immortality of, 88, 313; inmost shrine of, 29; as God's dwelling, 116, 176; birth